The Routledge Concise History of Canadian Literature

York St John
Library and Information Services
7 Day Loan

Please see self service receipt for return date.

1 2 MAY 2023

WITHDRAWN

Fines are payable for late return

The Routledge Concise History of Canadian Literature introduces the fiction, poetry and drama of Canada in its historical, political and cultural contexts.

In this clear and structured volume, Richard Lane outlines:

- the history of Canadian literature from colonial times to the present
- key texts for Canadian First Peoples and the literature of Québec
- the impact of English and the Canadian immigrant experience
- critical themes such as landscape, identity, orality, war and postmodernism
- contemporary debates on the canon, feminism, postcoloniality, queer theory and cultural identities
- the range of canonical and lesser-known authors from Catharine Parr Traill and Susanna Moodie to Robert Service and Margaret Atwood, Douglas

Written in an engaging and accessible style and offering a glossary, maps and further reading, this book introduces readers to Canadian Literature for students working in the field of Canadian Literature.

Richard J. Lane is Professor of English at Vancouver Island University, Canada. His main fields of interest include postcolonial literature, Canadian Literature and British Literature. His previous publications include *Fifty Key Literary Theorists* (Routledge, 2006), *Reading Walter Benjamin* (2005), *Contemporary British Fiction* (2003), *Beckett and Philosophy* (2002), and *Jean Baudrillard* (Routledge Critical Thinkers series, 2000, second ed. 2009).

D0278351

Routledge Concise Histories of Literature series

The Routledge Concise Histories series offers students and academics alike an interesting and accessible route into the literature of a specific period, genre, place or topic. The books situate the literature within its broader historical, cultural and political context, introducing the key events, movements and theories necessary for a fuller understanding of the writing. They engage readers in the debates of the period, genre or region adding a more exciting and challenging element to the reading.

Accessible and engaging, offering suggestions for further reading, explanatory text boxes, bullet pointed chapter summaries and a glossary of key terms, the Routledge Concise Histories are the ideal starting point for the study of literature.

Available:

The Routledge Concise History of Southeast Asian Writing in English
By Rajeev S. Patke and Philip Holden

The Routledge Concise History of Nineteenth-Century Literature
By Josephine Guy and Ian Small

The Routledge Concise History of Science Fiction
By Mark Bould and Sherryl Vint

Forthcoming:
The Routledge Concise History of Twentieth-Century British Literature
By Ashley Dawson

The Routledge Concise History of Canadian Literature

Richard J. Lane

YORK ST. JOHN
LIBRARY & INFORMATION
SERVICES

Routledge
Taylor & Francis Group

LONDON AND NEW YORK

First edition published 2011
by Routledge
2 Park Square, Milton Park, Abingdon, Oxon OX14 4RN

Simultaneously published in the USA and Canada
by Routledge
711 Third Avenue, New York, NY 10017

Routledge is an imprint of the Taylor & Francis Group, an informa business

© 2011 Richard J. Lane

The right of Richard J. Lane to be identified as author of this work has been
asserted by him in accordance with sections 77 and 78 of the Copyright,
Designs and Patents Act 1988.

All rights reserved. No part of this book may be reprinted or reproduced or
utilised in any form or by any electronic, mechanical, or other means, now
known or hereafter invented, including photocopying and recording, or in
any information storage or retrieval system, without permission in writing
from the publishers.

British Library Cataloguing in Publication Data
A catalogue record for this book is available from the British Library

Library of Congress Cataloging in Publication Data
Lane, Richard J., 1966-
The Routledge concise history of Canadian literature / Richard J. Lane.
p. cm. – (Routledge concise histories of literature)
Includes bibliographical references and index.
1. Canadian literature – History and criticism. 2. French-Canadian
literature – History and criticism. I. Title.
PR9184.6.L36 2011
810.9'3271 – dc22
2011001375

ISBN 13: 978-0-415-47045-2 (hbk)
ISBN 13: 978-0-415-47046-9 (pbk)
ISBN 13: 978-0-203-82958-5 (ebk)

Typeset in Times by Taylor & Francis Books

MIX
Paper from
responsible sources
FSC
www.fsc.org   FSC® C004839

Printed and bound in Great Britain by
CPI Antony Rowe, Chippenham, Wiltshire

For Sarah

Contents

Preface

This is a *concise* history of Canadian literature in English and in English translation, meaning that many authors have necessarily been left out due to space restrictions. I have attempted to give a sketch of some of the main authors, movements and literary trends in Canada, as well as foregrounding some of the shifts in literary critical understanding that have led to a re-assessment of issues such as gender and race, or literary production under colonialism. Longer, more comprehensive Canadian literary histories are listed at the end of this book in the Guide to further reading, in the section called Literary histories and encyclopaedias. The purpose of this book is to (hopefully) serve as an accessible introduction to the topic, with chapters that can stand alone (therefore there is some necessary overlap between chapters). Where possible, I have quoted critics who have offered significant new readings of Canadian literature – for example, some of the new ideas concerning Canadian modernism. Sources are deliberately made visible throughout the text, and I encourage students to read the primary texts and to turn to some of the excellent thought-provoking criticism listed in the bibliographies to gain a deeper appreciation and understanding of the literature covered. More difficult literary critical terms are defined in the glossary at the end of the text. Errors herein contained are all mine, and I hope that critical corrections might work their way into a future edition of this book.

Acknowledgements

I am grateful for all of the expert guidance and support I have received from Polly Dodson and Emma Nugent at Routledge. Many academics have helped and inspired me during my exploration of Canadian literature, including John Thieme (University of East Anglia) and Deborah Madsen (University of Geneva). At The University of British Columbia (UBC) I had the pleasure of studying as a Canada Commonwealth Scholar with Bill New, Laurie Ricou, and Sherrill Grace; more recently, with Miguel Mota I co-directed the 2009 UBC/Green College Malcolm Lowry International Symposium. A special thanks goes to Mark Vessey, Principal of Green College, UBC, for providing me with a temporary research base and a truly interdisciplinary intellectual environment among highly committed students and faculty. My visiting research fellowship at Chawton House Library, UK (2009), provided space to investigate the works of Frances Brooke. Virtually all of the bibliographical labyrinths that I encountered were made accessible by UBC reference librarian emeritus Joseph Jones. Carmen Concilio, at The University of Turin, provided me with a venue to discuss Canadian literature in depth, and it was a pleasure working with her on an edited collection of essays called *Image Technologies in Canadian Literature: Narrative, Film, and Photography* (2009). At The University of Debrecen, Hungary, valuable discussions were had with Zoltan Abádi Nagy, Tamás Bényei and Nóra Séllei; the *Canada in the European Mind* conference, at The University of Debrecen in 2002, greatly facilitated my early studies in this area. A decade spent reviewing Canadian literature criticism for The English Association's *The Year's Work in English Studies* (Oxford University Press, 10 volumes, 80 to 89), provided invaluable background reading and a unique chance to get a global overview of critical trends. The publications in which I first aired some of my ideas concerning Canadian literature are listed in the Works cited. In some cases I draw directly upon these critical works, especially my book on Bertrand William Sinclair, and my essays on Margaret Atwood, Pauline Johnson, Eden Robinson, postmodernism, and Canadian theatre. At Vancouver Island University,

Canada, my research assistants working on this project were: Belinda Levasseur, Melaina Haas, Holly H. Knox, Philip Laven, Iris Koker, and Emily Garrett. I also received considerable assistance from the staff and subject librarians of the Vancouver Island University Library, who continue to offer exceptional guidance to local scholars. Finally, this book could not have been written without the ongoing support of my wife, Sarah.

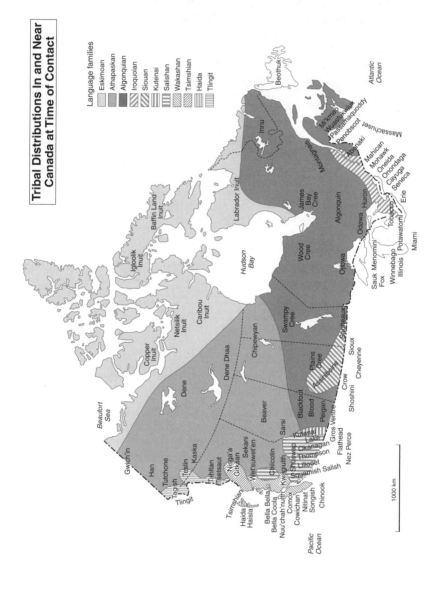

Map 1 Tribal distributions in Canada at time of contact

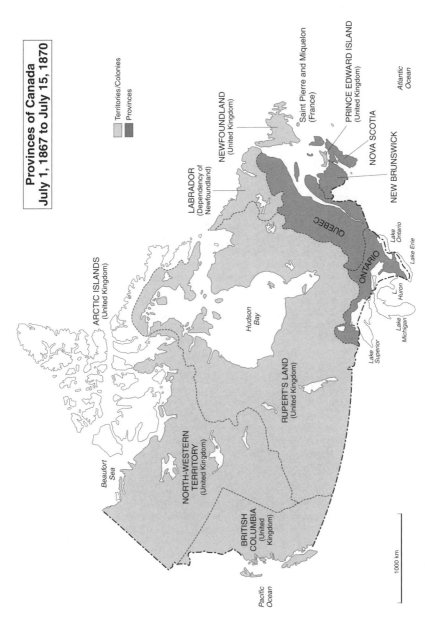

Map 2 Provinces of Canada, July 1, 1867 to July 15, 1870

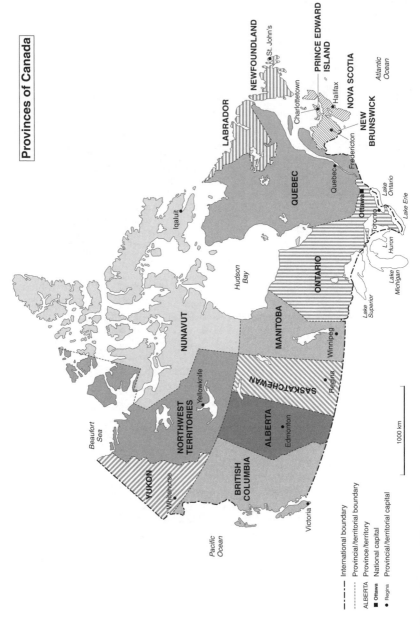

Map 3 Political map of Canada

International boundary
Provincial/territorial boundary
ALBERTA Province/territory
■ Ottawa National capital
● Regina Provincial/territorial capital

1000 km

Pacific
Ocean

Beaufort
Sea

YUKON
Whitehorse

NORTHWEST
TERRITORIES
Yellowknife

NUNAVUT

Iqaluit

BRITISH
COLUMBIA

Victoria

ALBERTA
Edmonton

SASKATCHEWAN
Regina

MANITOBA
Winnipeg

Hudson
Bay

LABRADOR

NEWFOUNDLAND
St. John's

QUEBEC

Quebec

ONTARIO

Ottawa

Toronto

Lake
Superior

Lake
Michigan

Lake
Huron

Lake
Erie

Lake
Ontario

Charlottetown

PRINCE EDWARD
ISLAND

Halifax

NOVA SCOTIA

Fredericton

NEW
BRUNSWICK

Atlantic
Ocean

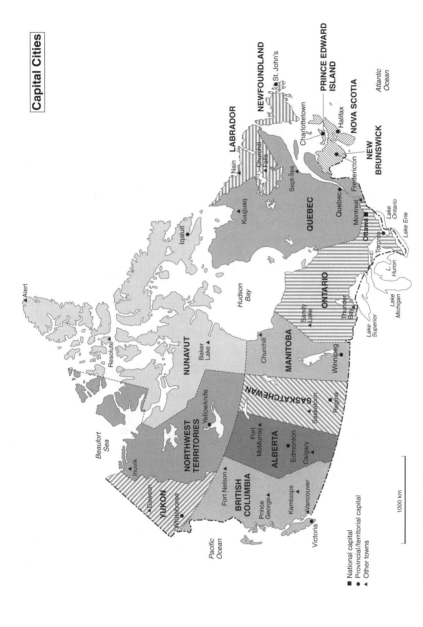

Map 4 Geographical map of Canada

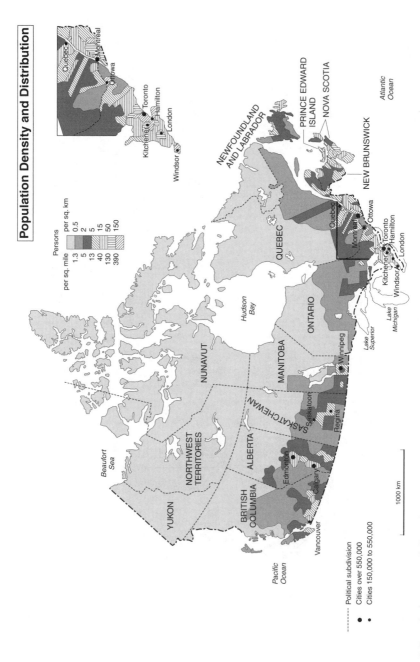

Population Density and Distribution

Persons
per sq. mile	per sq. km
1.3	0.5
5	2
13	5
40	15
130	50
390	150

Québec
Montréal
Ottawa
Toronto
Hamilton
London
Kitchener
Windsor

-------- Political subdivision
● Cities over 550,000
● Cities 150,000 to 550,000

1000 km

Map 5 Population map of Canada

Beaufort
Sea

YUKON

NORTHWEST
TERRITORIES

NUNAVUT

BRITISH
COLUMBIA

ALBERTA

SASKATCHEWAN

MANITOBA

Pacific
Ocean

Vancouver

Calgary

Edmonton

Saskatoon

Regina

Winnipeg

Hudson
Bay

QUEBEC

ONTARIO

NEWFOUNDLAND
AND LABRADOR

Lake
Superior

Lake
Michigan

Québec

Montreal

Ottawa

Toronto
Hamilton
London
Kitchener
Windsor

PRINCE EDWARD
ISLAND

NOVA SCOTIA

NEW BRUNSWICK

Atlantic
Ocean

1 Introduction

First Peoples and the colonial narratives of Canadian literature

Overview

Paradoxically, Canadian literature begins before written texts existed: with the oral stories of Canada's First Peoples. These narratives exist today in spoken and written form, with competing accounts from different indigenous groups, and from other cultural perspectives (anthropological transcripts, for example). Colonial allegories and narratives of adventure and conquest eventually overlayered and re-interpreted indigenous stories; re-naming became a key process in the colonial claiming of cultural and economic space. Written literature, based upon European models such as the Bible and what we now simply call "the canon", took priority, and indigenous stories were often perceived as ethnographical data, best preserved before indigenous peoples died out or were assimilated (the "vanishing Indian" myth or fantasy). But while Canada was partly formed through European and North American political battles and land-grabs, indigenous cultures continued to survive and grow with their own notions of belonging and place. After Confederation, while the story of the unified nation state continued, marginalized and oppositional voices were increasingly heard: such as those in the regions, or the Quebecois who demanded autonomy and freedom. Increasingly strong ethnic and minority groups re-shaped Canada, and the old colonial notion of uniformity or homogeneity gave way to modern ideas of heterogeneity or diversity. New narratives emerged among ethnically diverse groups, re-claiming and re-writing the stories of Canada.

First Peoples and founding narratives

Pondering "pivotal moments" in indigenous history, Mohawk writer Brian Maracle (b. 1947) rejects locating his native identity in key Canadian events as they involve "our interactions with so-called 'white people'" (2). In other words, from an indigenous perspective, "They were not about *us*. Most of them involve things that happened to *us*. They have helped determine where and how we live but they have not determined how we think or what we believe" (2). Maracle prefers to go back to the moment of creation as the key indigenous founding event, which he narrates in his "First Words": "With a few quick movements, the glowing being reached down, scooped up a handful of clay from the riverbank, and shaped it into the doll-like form of a man. The being then laid the doll-like figure on the riverbank next to the woman and gently blew into its mouth. Instantly, the clay doll was transformed into a human being" (3). For many indigenous people, history starts with creation stories. The "handful of clay" in "First Words" is indicative of a close relationship between indigenous peoples and the land, a relationship that is honoured from the very beginning of existence:

> [The stories] ... emphasize and confirm the peoples' fundamental attachment to the land. The Gitksan of northern British Columbia maintain that the Upper Skeena River valley is their garden of Eden; several groups, such as the Salish Thompson River people and the Ojibwa, believe that their first ancestors were born of the earth; the Athapaskan Beaver hold that humans crawled through a hollow log in order to reach earth, an obvious birth analogy; the Iroquoians (including the Huron), that the mother of mankind, Aataentsic, fell through a hole in the sky and landed on a tortoise with earth piled on its back. On another plane, the Tsimshian have legends in which migration is a theme.
>
> (Dickason, 4)

Such creation stories, including those that concern migration, share an important feature: they are autonomous, fully descriptive, coherent cultural and spiritual narratives. In other words, they do not need some other perspective to validate them. Such stories, on the whole, tell us that Canada's First Peoples have occupied the land since time immemorial.

Other founding narratives tell the story of a vast migration approximately 15,000 years ago, whereby retreating ice and a lowered sea level created a land bridge between Siberia and Alaska. The word "bridge" may be misleading: the land was up to 2,000 kilometres across, offering a challenging but nonetheless liveable environment, with land and sea food sources hunted and gathered by the *Homo sapiens* who made their way across into North America, and then east and south throughout the entire land mass, with groups settling along the way. This migration took place over thousands of years, with complex cultures and language groups developing in the process. Archaeological evidence for these migratory routes and settlements include the delicately produced fluted stone arrow heads used in hunting, although other technologies were also developed for the hunting, gathering and preserving of food, such as the bow and arrow (introduced by Paleo-Eskimos), collecting and grinding tools, the existence of the latter leading some scholars to note that the largely Eurocentric myth of the *nomadic* native is incorrect: "[T]he mobile lifestyle in pursuit of different food resources cannot be assumed to have been universal at any period; and even when it was practised, it followed a seasonal pattern within a known area. The vision of early humans as aimless wanderers in search of food does not equate with the evidence at hand; in fact, the contrary is strongly indicated, that they have always lived in communities that were as stable as food resources permitted" (Dickason, 16).

At contact, then, diverse and self-sufficient First Peoples existed in the land that would eventually become known as Canada. There were twelve main indigenous language groups or families, with up to seventy different languages spoken. The two largest population densities occurred in the culturally rich Pacific Northwest and in southern Ontario (using modern terms for these places), although a country-wide trading network also existed. The Iroquois (in the East) forged a confederacy in the sixteenth century known as the Great League of Peace. Such peace treaties were an important factor in the ongoing maintenance of political and social stability, and while warfare existed, indigenous societies were largely concerned with a holistic, respectful relationship with their natural and spiritual environments (the two are in some ways indistinguishable from an indigenous perspective).

Overall population densities have been estimated as somewhere between 500,000 and two million First Peoples (depending upon methodological approaches to this question), with a high level of cultural and religious sophistication, embedded and shared in an oral and at times highly ritualized culture. Yet all of these ways of describing Canada's First Peoples represent what would be an inconvenient truth for the masters of "discovery" and conquest who would eventually arrive from Europe, beginning with the Norse in 1000 CE. This truth essentially reveals that the land was already occupied. Centuries of re-description of indigenous peoples would follow contact, casting them as less-civilized nomads who did not have a claim (or only had a weak claim) to place. Ironically, it is now thought that indigenous peoples actually helped the first non-native visitors to North America survive in harsh conditions; as Currie argues, "The discourse of 'discovery' now belongs to a colonial version of history to which there are alternatives" (7).

Negotiating contact

Scholarly and cultural efforts have enabled a more complex understanding of contact, with an important shift in understanding whereby Canada's First Peoples are now understood to have taken an active part in negotiating and constructing the terms and conditions of contact. Thus the Norse, having encountered on Baffin Island and the North Atlantic coast early indigenous peoples known as Dorset and Beothuk, were soon involved in positive trading relationships. The Norse named these people Skraelings (small or little people), probably the first case of Europeans taking control of the naming of indigenous ethnic groups. The Norse failed to endure in Canada, having made four expeditions to their settlement at L'Anse aux Meadows in Newfoundland; scholars debate whether this was supposed to be a permanent or temporary settlement, but either way the Skraelings' battle skills meant it was not a viable location. Yet it was not land that would be of primary interest for the next wave of European visitors: it was the rich cod fisheries that attracted fishermen from England and Spain. While it was Christopher Columbus who had "discovered" America (he initially thought he had arrived at Asia) with his landing at the Bahamas in October 1492, it was the Genoese Giovanni Caboto (1461–99), representing the English Crown as John Cabot, who claimed Newfoundland for King Henry VII during his expedition of 1497. A more extensive expedition the following year, with considerable exploration of the East coast, provided data on the teeming Bank Fisheries. The Portuguese visited the region in 1500 and 1501 under the leadership of Gaspar Corte Real (d. 1501?); they claimed the region as *Terra Corterealis*, taking slaves in the process. The person who discovered New York harbour, Giovanni da Verrazzano (1486?–1528), also gave the name Acadia to the Maritimes, annexing the region for King Francis I. Yet it was a French explorer, Jacques Cartier (1491–1557), who would have the greatest impact upon the early colonial contact period, with three voyages in 1534, 1535–36, and 1541–42.

Naming culture: colonial interpretation, or, power-knowledge narratives

Names are of great importance: when the spoken stories of Canada's First Peoples, handed on from generation to generation, are called "oral literature" then one cultural tradition – that of "orature" – is being interpreted and measured by a different cultural tradition.

Oral stories, in other words, belong to an alternative expressive paradigm, one which is situational and community based. Such stories don't so much change as develop in different ways, for different environments, or for the cares and concerns of the speaker and the community in which he or she is embedded. Many of the subtle nuances of a story being shared come about during its delivery: bodily gesture, vocal shifts, and group responses, such as laughter or surprise, all contribute to the performative nature of story-telling

Orature is the transmission of cultural and religious knowledge through spoken stories, rather than through writing or print; the *Oxford English Dictionary* notes that it occurs in societies where speech "is the primary medium of communication", or, in what Walter Ong calls "primary oral cultures" (1). Oral transmission is an event: it is something that takes place, or is performed, in the moment, in a particular context (time and place), with a specific audience; such an event is unique, even though the story may be repeated with variations and a new context, by another speaker. The word "orature" is often used to avoid the contradictions embedded in the more common phrase "oral literature", where "literature" implies a written-down text (which, in "orature", does not exist).

and therefore the meaning that emerges for a particular story-teller and audience. While Canada's First Peoples have been passing on their stories for generations, non-indigenous peoples have, since contact, been involved in collecting, preserving, interpreting, distorting and at times attempting to disrupt and destroy these stories; the engagement with Aboriginal story-telling and stories, in other words, has often been agonistic (based on conflict or at the least competition), and at times problematic.

Nuu-Chah-Nulth artist and poet Ron Hamilton (b. 1948) contextualizes this agonistic relationship in a poem called "Telling" in which he says "We long for a new reading of history", one where:

> Warriors would drop their rifles.
> Constructed residential schools
> Could be deconstructed.
> Dying languages would find
> Our throats once more.
> The Indian Act would be unwritten.

(169)

The poem ends with a comment on ownership: "Such a story would remain our own / ... Gentle and honest and telling, / Before all eyes" (169). In the residential schools, indigenous stories were not allowed, and in fact even the act of indigenous naming was overwritten with a European name system.

In *My Name Is Seepeetza*, her autobiographical account of her time spent at a residential school, Interior Salish author Shirley Sterling (b. 1948) narrates this frightening moment of re-naming:

The Indian Act (1876) is the regulatory legislation that defines Canada's First Peoples and their cultural existence from a colonial perspective, restrictively mapping-out their land, and encouraging assimilation into White Canada. The initial act was subject to many modifications, such as the banning of potlatches (a gift-giving ceremony) and spirit dances in section 3 of the Indian Act of 1880, strengthened in the Indian Act of 1927. An internal political system, based on the European model, was introduced to Canada's First Peoples, instituting elected chiefs and a "band" system, which, from an indigenous perspective, is largely meaningless. Land and money is set aside by the government for the provision of Canada's First Peoples, but always controlled by the Department of Indian Affairs. For many activists, the Indian Act, which is still in force, remains one of the main obstacles to progress in cultural and societal recovery. In July 2010, Shawn A-in-chut Atleo, the National Chief of the Assembly of First Nations and Chancellor of Vancouver Island University, called for the Indian Act to be repealed within two to five years.

... Sister Maura asked me what my name was. I said, my name is Seepeetza. Then she got really mad like I did something terrible. She said never to say that word again. She told me if I had a sister to go and ask what my name was. I went to the intermediate rec and found Dorothy lying on a bench reading comics. I asked her what my name was. She said it was Martha Stone. I said it over and over. Then I ran back and told Sister Maura. After that she gave me a number, which was 43. She got some of the older girls to teach us how to embroider. Then we had to chain stitch our numbers on all our school clothes.

(18–19)

In this passage there are a number of subtleties: Seepeetza's new western name is told to her by her sister, who has already been integrated into the residential school's ideological system; but then the name change is even further transformed: by turning it into a number. Using a non-indigenous craft – embroidery – Seepeetza has to label herself with that number. The idea behind this re-naming/numbering system is to remove any last vestiges of indigeneity before starting again with a "blank slate" on which a white Canadian sensibility can be inscribed. The end result of this process was a double consciousness, one reflected by the compound name that Tomson Highway's (b. 1951) semi-autobiographical protagonist creates for himself in *Kiss of the Fur Queen* (1998): "Champion-Jeremiah – he was willing to concede that much of a name-change for now" (58). Reclaiming oral culture is of great importance to counter colonial processes of re-naming, something Sterling further addresses in her exploration of matriarchy in *Quaslametko and Yetko* (1995) and *The Grandmother Stories* (1997).

Cultural re-naming and the Indian Act

Re-naming was clearly a powerful colonial tool designed to challenge the cultural and political autonomy of Canada's First Peoples. If oral stories are a cultural storehouse, and naming has immense cultural significance, then the impact of the residential school system is clear, even before other aspects of the experience are taken into account. Re-naming during the colonial period did not stop at individuals: it included the re-naming of indigenous places and nations. As Dickason notes:

Labels such as "Cree", "Huron", "Beaver", "Haida" were imposed by Europeans and do not represent how the people termed themselves, at least aboriginally. In some cases a single label, such as "Cree", "Abenaki", or "Odawa", included a number of distinct groups, more or less closely related by language. These three all belong to the Algonkian language group. [...] While many of the Europeanized labels have come to be accepted by the Aboriginal peoples, some have not; for instance, the tundra-dwellers of the Arctic objected to "Eskimo" on the grounds that it was pejorative as it had come to be popularly believed that it came from an Ojibwa term that translated as "eaters of raw meat", despite the opinion of linguists that it actually derived from a Montagnais term meaning "she nets a snowshoe". The tundra-dwellers won their point, and their term for themselves, "Inuit" ("the people", "Inuk" in the singular), has been officially accepted.

(xiv)

Indigenous places would also be claimed and re-named by European explorers and settlers, for example, the Haida archipelago in British Columbia was named, by Captain George Dixon in 1778, "The Queen Charlotte Islands" (the name of his boat, after the wife of King George III). In 2009, the islands were claimed back by Aboriginal peoples and re-named "Haida Gwaii".

Indigenous oral stories preserve and transmit a dynamic, living culture, yet colonial acts of re-naming and cultural attack were in many cases quite profound. Such efficacy derives from the fact that in 1880 the Indian Act codified in law the suppression of Aboriginal rituals and rights known as the "Potlatch" (a gift-giving process, including the awarding of meaningful names and titles) and the "Tamanawas" (a spirit dance); this Act would not be countermanded in Canada until 1951. As Mathias and Yabsley argue, the suppression of Aboriginal land rights can be seen, but "less obvious is the extent to which federal law in particular reached into Indian communities in an effort to suffocate the most forceful elements of traditional Indian political life and cultural identity. The Indian Act was repeatedly used to destroy traditional institutions of Indian government and to abolish those cultural practices that defined Indian identity" (36). By striking at the heart of these "forceful elements", then, the Canadian government was directly recognizing the efficacy of Aboriginal story-telling and performance, trying, over an extended period, to suppress such story-based power.

First stories – textualization

In a history of Canadian *literature*, the earliest narratives covered are usually the oral stories of Canada's First Peoples; however, the "literature" paradigm often refers to written or transcribed versions of those stories, that have subsequently been printed. Yet it is clear that to transcribe a story is to represent it in a *different* form, no matter how close to the original that transcription is, or claims to be. The earliest such transcriptions in Canada occur with the *Jesuit Relations*, a set of reports from 1610, sent from Quebec to the Society of Jesus in Paris. The reports are a comprehensive, extensive collection of documents covering all aspects of missionary life in Canada, including ethnographic texts on Canada's First Peoples, with emphasis on Algonquin speakers and Iroquoians: "Among the ethnographic data reported by the Jesuits are numerous materials relevant to verbal art, including descriptions of the situations where and when performances might occur and of some performance components, representations of what might be said or sung in those situations (mostly translated into French, but occasionally in attempted depictions of Native tongues), and summaries of Native belief systems" (Clements, 55). The textualization of oral stories in the *Jesuit Relations* is largely descriptive and interpretive, but Clements makes two important observations about this material: first, that the earliest of these accounts record encounters with people who had a pre-contact mindset, and second, given the importance of the performative quality of oral stories – that is, the mode of delivery, context, setting and audience response – the description of these aspects are as historically crucial as transcribed "content".

Another mode of textualization can be observed with Henry Rowe Schoolcraft (1793–1864) who published *Algic Researches* in 1839, based upon his time spent with the Ojibwa, whom he had first encountered in 1820 when he was working as an explorer and geologist. In 1822 Schoolcraft was made Indian Agent to the Ojibwa, a post he held for two decades. One of the differences between the *Jesuit Relations* and the *Algic Researches* is the ethnographic approach of the latter: Schoolcraft learnt the Ojibwa language, and collected their actual stories (rather than just *describing* them in a European language). He also edited, interpreted, and translated the stories following a westernized notion of literary aesthetics.

Aboriginal stories, in ethnographic field work, are perceived as data: information to be collected about other peoples. In Canada, the myth of the "vanishing Indian" gave impetus to such ethnographic collecting, since this colonial myth argued that within a few generations Aboriginal peoples would become extinct. The race was on to preserve as much about them as possible, for storage in archives and museums. The Nova Scotian philologist Silas Rand (1810–89) compiled translation tools – a Micmac grammar book in 1875, and a Micmac dictionary in 1888 – while working as a missionary in the Micmac communities of New Brunswick and Nova Scotia. Apart from his Micmac translation of the Bible, he published *A Short Statement of Facts Relating to the History, Manners, Customs, Language, and Literature of the Micmac Tribe of Indians* (1850), and *Legends of the Micmacs* (1894). But it was the German anthropologist Franz Boas (1858–1942) who approached the collection and preservation of stories on a vast scale – and in an academic fashion – influencing generations of subsequent ethnographers. Boas, who studied at the universities of Heidelberg, Bonn, and Kiel, was initially interested in geography and physics, writing a dissertation on the colour of water, but a trip to Baffin Island in 1883 led to a newfound intense interest in the Inuit and an intellectual shift into anthropological research. The romantic vision of the early anthropologist involves the westerner heading out into the wilderness to study "natives": in Boas's case, it was a visit of a group of Bella Coola Nuxalk First Nation to Berlin that inspired him to visit the Pacific Northwest in 1886. Eventually becoming Professor of Anthropology at Columbia University, Boas published extensively on Aboriginal cultures, languages, and oral stories; key selected works being *The Central Eskimo* (1888), *The Mythology of the*

Bella Coola Indians (1898), and *The Kwakiutl of Vancouver Island* (1909), among many others.

European colonial historical narratives of conquest and warfare: "settlement" and trade to 1650

The explorer Jacques Cartier first sailed from France in search of the fabled Northwest Passage on a voyage that encompassed what we would call today Newfoundland, Labrador, Prince Edward Island and New Brunswick. In the summer of 1534, on the shores of the Gaspé Peninsula, Cartier and his men erected a thirty-foot cross adorned with the French shield of arms. The symbolic value of this act cannot be underestimated: the two strongest colonial forces, and narratives, in Canada would be those of economics and Christianity. In his second voyage, Cartier named the St. Lawrence river, travelling up it to find the geographically imposing Iroquois settlement of Stadacona, which would eventually become Quebec City; travelling further up river in small boats, Cartier encountered the Iroquois village of Hochelaga that stood at the base of a mountain re-named by Cartier Mount Royal, eventually becoming the city of Montreal. Cartier's garrisons at Stadacona, and Charlesbourg Royal, were a failure: in their first winter at Stadacona, all of Cartier's men would have died from scurvy (caused by a lack of vitamin C) if the local First Peoples had not shown them how to combat this disease with indigenous plants. It is significant, as historians have pointed out, that none of Canada's original colonial settlers passed on among themselves this crucial indigenous knowledge, which could have saved many European lives. Sporadic attempts at exploration and colonization following Cartier came to very little until France had resolved its internal political and religious differences, under the leadership of the Catholic King Henri IV.

Establishment of a permanent colonial presence in Canada came under the dynamic leadership of Samuel de Champlain (1567?–1635) who sailed to the St. Lawrence in 1608, discovering that Stadacona had also been abandoned; it was here that he founded Quebec, a successful *habitation* composed of a fortress and a warehouse for the fur trade. The fur trade, while important, had remained fairly static since the 1570s when new demand arose from Europe with the depletion and disruption of their own animal stocks (Dickinson and Young, 17). Economic success depended upon negotiated access to indigenous hunting and trading networks, mainly brokered by the Montagnais at Tadoussac, and the Algonquins and Hurons in the Great Lakes region. This meant that regardless of the European demand for fur, indigenous peoples controlled the supply, catering to their own levels of need in the exchange of goods. What brought this situation to an end? The fact is that the fur trade was inherently unstable, with variable prices, uncontrollable supply chains, cultural disruption through Christian missionary work driven most aggressively by the Jesuits, and most potent of all, the onset of virulent diseases such as smallpox and influenza to which First Peoples had no immunity; by 1650, the decline in indigenous populations had become so severe that Europeans now dominated the region (Dickinson and Young, 19–20). New France, as it was known, had survived all of this turmoil, initially under the management of the (largely unprofitable) Company of the Hundred Associates, formed in 1627 by Cardinal de Richelieu; the Company worked in parallel with the Catholic missionaries, but immigration and settlement remained low until with the collapse of the indigenous population new workers and settlers were needed to keep New France and its trade networks functioning.

Multiple theatres of war: Canada and European empires

The early colonial history of Canada was fundamentally affected by global rivalry and warfare between European Empires: for over one hundred years, the power of New France and the British, who had an exponentially increasing presence in Canada, depended upon fights that largely took place elsewhere. When the European powers fought their battles in North America, the outcome was usually inconsequential or considered a downright failure. One example that occurred during Queen Anne's War, or the War of Spanish Succession (1700–13), was the failed British sea expedition to take Quebec, under the command of Sir Hovenden Walker (d. 1728). Later, during King George's War (1744–48) the French improved their military power base in New France with construction of a series of fortresses, none so impressive as Louisbourg on Cape Breton Island, which not only appeared to offer a safe harbour for ships of the realm, but also had a symbolic presence, leading to the Acadians' sense of security and unwillingness to take the oath of allegiance to the English Crown (Roberts, 112). Attacked in 1745 by Governor Shirley of Massachusetts with 4,000 men and four Royal Navy battleships, one hundred transports landed the troops for a combined land and sea siege, ending with the surrender by Duchambon and the expulsion of 5,000 men to France.

The British exchanged Louisbourg for Madras in the Treaty of Aix-la-Chapelle (1748), and they focused on consolidating their presence in Canada by founding of the city of Halifax at Chebucto harbour, in Nova Scotia. Caught between their allegiance (and at times military assistance) to France, and the enforced attempts at allegiance to the British Crown, 5,000 Acadians would eventually be brutally expelled by the British from their own lands in 1755. The following year saw the outbreak of the Seven Years War, although historians note that in reality it was peace that had never truly broken out in North America. The great fortress of Louisbourg fell to the British again in 1758, under the leadership of General Amherst and James Wolfe, but this time the entire fortress and its surrounding battlements were completely destroyed by the British.

Wolfe went on to fight General Montcalm (Louis Joseph de Montcalm-Gozon, Marquis de Montcalm [1712–59]) at Quebec, who was defending the city with troops in the garrison and ranged along the shore of the Montmorenci River. Wolfe, surprisingly, chose to end his extensive and relatively ineffective plan of attack (which included blockading the city) and instead took twenty-four men up a small pathway on the side of the Mountain of Quebec to spearhead the movement of his troops on to the Plains of Abraham, and thereby on to a successful battle (in which both Wolfe and Montcalm lost their lives). The British had won Quebec, a significant and highly symbolic victory, this time reinforced by the peace settlement known as The Treaty of Paris (1763). A more astounding settlement could not be imagined: France in effect handed over virtually all of New France to the British, excepting some fishing rights and, further south, the territory of Louisiana. Historians have called this treaty "potentially a complete disruption of Canadian history" (Finlay and Sprague, 74), with the British initially trying to impose a Protestant way of life and British legal and political structures upon New France. The assimilationist project did not succeed, however, even if half of the nobility had returned to France. As Finlay and Sprague note, "The Quebec Act of 1774 confirmed the legal basis of the seigneurial system, abolished religious tests that discouraged Roman Catholicism, endorsed the tithe and other clerical privileges, maintained political absolutism as the appropriate system of government, and restored the pre-war boundaries of Quebec" (77).

"American" theatres of war

What we would now call the American theatres of war during this period also had an unexpected outcome: a strengthened and more politically coherent Canada. This did not seem to be a possibility when, under the yoke of heavy colonial taxes, the Thirteen Colonies began to resist their burdens. At the Boston Tea Party in 1773, Americans boarded trade vessels from England and threw cheap tea imports into the sea in protest at unfair price differentials; such events presaged deeper unrest and a war of independence that broke out in 1775, lasting until 1783. The Quebec Act of 1774, while not aimed at the Thirteen Colonies, was perceived as a threat and a model of colonial control to be strongly resisted, such resistance encoded in the Bill of Rights at Philadelphia that same year.

Up to 45,000 Loyalists who were forced out of the Thirteen Colonies moved North (others had returned to Britain) into Nova Scotia, the newly created New Brunswick, and Quebec; 3,500 were Black Loyalists, and 2,000 were Iroquois, which would have later implications in the War of 1812. Most of the Loyalists were Protestant, and this would have a profound influence on the social and religious structure of Canadian society, although it was not until the institution of the Canada Act in 1791 that a Protestant and British constitutional parliamentary model would be imposed upon the country. The second wave of American unrest culminated in the War of 1812, which Pierre Berton called a war that Canada "*did not lose,* by successfully repulsing the armies that tried to invade and conquer British North America" (19). As he goes on, "The War was fought almost entirely in Upper Canada, whose settlers, most of them Americans, did not invite the war, did not care about the issues, and did not want to fight" (19).

Colonial modes of power: the emerging nation after 1812

What did the strengthened, emerging nation after the 1812 war offer Canada's First Peoples? The temporary alliance with Tecumseh and others had helped the British more than the Iroquois. Early European traders had brought some economic prosperity, relying on the knowledge and skill of Native trappers, but they had also brought diseases to which there was no natural immunity among indigenous peoples; perhaps more profoundly in the long term, Europeans also brought Christianity and a missionary zeal for conversion. Dickason cautions that just because there was a change in hunting and trading systems after contact, historians should not conflate such change with the loss of indigenous identity: "Just as Europeans benefited from Amerindian technology (toggling harpoons for whaling, moccasins for footwear, maize as a food crop), so did Amerindians from that of Europeans. In both cases, adaptations were selective and within established cultural patterns" (85).

An important colonial narrative would become that of the decline of indigenous peoples, the "vanishing Indian" theory whereupon the "less civilized" races would eventually disappear. Recent historians and critics have shown how this colonial narrative is inaccurate, although that is not to say that indigenous peoples were not subject to massive cultural assault, in terms of land use, belief systems, social structures, and individual subjectivity. Model villages of Christianized First Peoples were initially experimented with, some being "successful" from a colonial (that is, assimilationist) perspective, others being little more than open prison or military camps. Native land was exchanged for reserves, and treaties were negotiated to extinguish Native land title (although this was a piecemeal affair, one still unresolved today).

As the new nation grew after the War of 1812, so did the need for unencumbered land: treaties were a way of appearing to make a fair exchange for that land, although in reality, they were often convenient ways of ensuring future success for colonial settlers. From an indigenous perspective, treaties are not considered static, closed agreements: they are ongoing, in need of continual re-assessment and renewal. From the perspective of the settlers, treaties were legally binding and complete. But there were other methods of reducing the power and autonomy of indigenous peoples, namely the introduction of the residential school system, whereby children were sent to boarding schools and subject to a form of cultural indoctrination, and in some cases physical and sexual abuse.

Starting with three schools in 1883, the residential school system would run until 1996; an apology for this system, given to Canada's First Peoples, was delivered by Prime Minister Stephen Harper in 2008. Canada's First Peoples, in summary, were useful to the colonizers when it came to trade and assistance in warfare, but overall, they were also considered a barrier to the settling and "civilizing" of the nation. How, then, did this diverse new nation, made up of First Peoples, and Catholic and Protestant colonists, under the control of the British since the Treaty of Paris, turn into the successful and peaceful country now known simply as "Canada"? The answer involves a process of growing autonomy and complexity, in land settlement, political responsibility, and nationality.

Religious and national differences between upper and lower Canada

Clearly the Treaty of Paris created more problems than it solved: the Quebec Act of 1774 had not ameliorated tensions between Protestants and Catholics, and the Loyalists soon expressed their desire for political representation under an English system of governance. The Constitutional Act of 1791 was supposed to resolve these issues, dividing Quebec into Upper and Lower Canada, with English law for Upper Canada, English Criminal law and French Civic law for Lower Canada. While Lower Canada received an elected assembly (as did Upper Canada), it also lost land to the Church of England in the form of clergy reserves of one-seventh of all non-seigneurial land. French-speaking peoples were allowed to maintain their language and their religion, as well as the seigneurial system, but the division of power between the colonial Governor and largely British-appointed elites called the Legislative Council, versus the elected House of Assembly, would soon lead to "deepening social and ethnic conflict in Lower Canada" (Dickinson and Young, 59–60). In both new provinces the tension between unelected and elected officials would boil to crisis point, with the aim of the people being "Responsible Government" – that is to say, democratically elected representatives who were not subject to the arbitrary decisions of the Crown's officials.

In New Brunswick, the Assembly wanted the right to set taxes and control revenue, including their own remuneration, but in this they were repeatedly blocked by the Upper House until a stalemate meant that the legislature ground to a halt between 1796 and 1799. In 1814, the Assembly of Lower Canada impeached two justices, Chief Justice Sewell and Judge Monk of Montreal, demanding their suspension from office; the Executive refused this demand, once again blocking the will of the people. These, and many other grievances, were examined by a Canada Committee that reported in 1828: the Assemblies were given, among other things, power over the collection and distribution of duties, and unelected officials were weeded out. French Canadians were to have proper representation, but this did not become a reality. In fact the Legislative Assembly of Lower Canada issued its Ninety-Two Resolutions in 1834, which detailed the stark contrast between English and French preferment by the Crown, the former extensively favoured over the latter. Upper Canada issued its Seventh Report on Grievances, which was similarly critical, advocating elected, not elite, officials. Canada appeared to be heading, not in the direction of unity, but rather towards fragmentation and social unrest.

Louis-Joseph Papineau and the Patriotes

French Canadian interests were clearly not being served by the British colonial system. In 1827, the Speaker of the Assembly, Patriote leader Louis-Joseph Papineau (1786–1871), was denied his rightful place in the House by the Governor General. As Dickinson and Young note: "The term Parti patriote, first used in 1827 to designate the Parti canadien, became common after 1832 – a year that saw the arrest of leading reformers, various riots, and a cholera epidemic. The Patriotes approved a tricolour flag of green, white, and red ... and under Papineau's leadership attracted broad support" (161). The land agent Robert Gourlay, whose list of thirty-one questions distributed in Upper Canada focused people's grievances to the point in which they started to gather threateningly, was swiftly dealt with: an act was passed which forbade such gatherings, and Gourlay was arrested and eventually tried for sedition, upon which he was expelled from Upper Canada.

Papineau could not be dealt with in such a scurrilous manner; he was a respected seignior who had served in the War of 1812; called to the bar in 1811, he spent most of his life in politics, being elected to the Assembly to represent Montreal West in 1814, elected Speaker of the Assembly in 1815. The Patriotes cut across all classes and utilized multiple political strategies, from journalism to active revolutionary activity, gathering momentum as they increasingly fomented rebellion. Riots were violently put down, such as that which occurred in 1832 in Montreal's West Ward, eventually leading to the Patriote leaders regrouping in the Richelieu Valley and Two Mountains areas. The Patriotes were not ultimately successful on the ground, but their ideological programme would not be totally quashed, as was the rebellion itself.

William Lyon Mackenzie and radical reforming zeal

In Upper Canada, rebellion occurred under the leadership of William Lyon Mackenzie (1795–1861), founder in 1824 of the political journal *The Advocate*. Mackenzie used his journal to attack the "family compact" or governing elites, until they manufactured the destruction of his printing press, the ensuing case for damages making Mackenzie a hero. Expelled five times from the Assembly for his radical reforming zeal, he became instead mayor of Toronto (in 1835). Dissolving the House in 1836, the new Governor, Sir Francis Bond Head, engaged in the unusual activity of electioneering; Mackenzie issued a "Declaration of the Reformers" and used the absence of the British regular troops (who were in Lower Canada) to lead an insurrection, establishing his "Provisional Government" on Navy Island on the Niagara River. Five hundred of Mackenzie's troops marched on the government along Yonge Street but they were easily defeated by the militia who also burnt the rebels' temporary headquarters – Montgomery's Tavern – to the ground. A similar uprising led by Charles Dunscombe was also defeated. Mackenzie was arrested, ironically, by the US authorities for breach of their neutrality laws.

The Durham Report and Canadian Confederation

The Durham Report (1839), commissioned by the British government following the uprisings in Upper and Lower Canada, sowed the seeds of future Canadian confederation. The report advocated Responsible Government, the abolition of life-long appointed elites, legislative union between Upper and Lower Canada, and a whole host of measures to encourage increased equitable settlement, such as the abolition of the Crown and Clergy Reserves, and the construction of an intercolonial railway. All of these measures would complement one another in the facilitation of the rapid growth of Canada. The building of the railways, starting in the 1850s, would have a profound psychological effect on the nation, connecting the vast distances between settlements, as well as opening up new territory for expansion and trade. In fact squabbles over how the railroad was to be funded led to debates in the Maritimes concerning union: the Canadian provinces got on this bandwagon at the conference in Charlottetown held on the first of September 1864, whereupon a wider, all-encompassing union was considered, bolstered by the Seventy-Two Resolutions of the Quebec Conference that followed two weeks later.

The push for Confederation, with a bicameral parliamentary system, was not widely welcome back in the provinces; the West was enthusiastic, but the Eastern provinces resisted. Eventually New Brunswick, which had resisted most strongly, was manoeuvred into joining Nova Scotia and Canada in a visit to London whereupon the Quebec Resolutions were drafted and submitted to Parliament. The British North America Act followed with Royal Assent on 29 March 1867. Canada was also guaranteed a loan of three million dollars for the building of its intercolonial railway (which would be completed in 1876 with a total of 21 million dollars borrowed to cover construction costs).

The newly formed Dominion of Canada offered the advantages of federal and provincial control over local matters, but a unified allegiance to the Crown. As the Act came into being on the first of July, this was known as Dominion Day, called since 1982 "Canada Day", in a postcolonial gesture of re-naming, reflecting Canada's autonomy. Upper and Lower Canada became respectively Ontario and Quebec, with the newly formed provinces and Prince Edward Island all joining the confederation by 1905. In 1999, the territory of Nunavut was formed, becoming the most recent addition to Canada. Under the Trudeau government, and going against the wishes of Quebec, Canada's Constitution Act came into force in 1982. Canada was finally free to uphold its own laws, and protect its own Charter of Rights and Freedoms.

Countering colonial notions of "progress": Aboriginal literary resistances

Nineteenth-century colonial notions of "progress" and "civilization" demanded that Aboriginal peoples should shift away from oral cultures and move towards a written culture, whether in English or French. The colonial understanding was that spoken cultures were more "primitive" than cultures that were embedded in written documents. Religion also played a significant role in this ideology of progress and achievement: indigenous belief systems were regarded as "barbaric" in contrast to the religion that was encoded in the Christian Bible. Such a narrative of progress is now considered to be false: the demand for a written culture means that Aboriginal literature developed side-by-side with the survival of Aboriginal orature, creating a rich narrative fabric that is in complex and creative dialogue. It is also one that eventually undertook its own critique of colonial history and society.

George Copway and early indigenous writers in English

Turning to some of the earliest indigenous writers in English, the role of organized Christianity is considerable. Ojibway author George Copway (1818–63) became a Wesleyan Methodist Missionary and later converted to Roman Catholicism shortly before his death; he was one of a group of Ojibway who formed the first indigenous "literary coterie", the others being Peter Jones, George Henry, Peter Jacobs, John Sunday, Allen Salt, and Henry Steinhauer (Petrone, 35). His prolific output includes the first Canadian Aboriginal book published in English: *The life, history, and travels of Kah-ge-ga-gah-bowh (George Copway)* (1847), as well as *The life, letters, and speeches of Kah-ge-ga-gah-bowh* (1850), *The traditional history and characteristic sketches of the Ojibway nation* (1850); *Recollections of a forest life* (1851); *Indian life and Indian history* (1858); *The Ojibway Conquest* (1860); and *Running Sketches* (1861). Categorizing Aboriginal stories, Copway labelled them "the Amusing, the Historical, and the Moral" (Petrone, 12); it is important to recognize that such classifications are also interpretations, and that subsequent attempts to fit orature into English or French narrative concepts invariably distort and re-code the original stories.

Copway's notion of indigenous peoples gaining their salvation through Christianity was tempered by his understanding of the damage done by colonialism, especially through the loss of land; early Ojibway missionaries would thus direct energy into attempts to repair some of the damage done to their people, either through their writing or through the political act of visiting England to petition for rights at the highest level, as did Peter Jones (1802–56) when he visited Queen Victoria during his visit of 1837–38. Critic Penny van Toorn makes the important observation that far from turning away from orature, these first Aboriginal writers in English moved "back and forth between oral and literary institutions *within* European culture, as well as *between* European and Native cultures" (29). Adopting a highly performative mode gained from knowledge of oral culture, the new Aboriginal writers produced a diverse range of hybrid texts: "Whether in theatrical performances, sermons, or political negotiations, oratorical skills became more, rather than less, important at the interface between Aboriginal and European cultures" (Ibid., 29).

Performing ethnicity: Pauline Johnson (Tekahionwake)

Mohawk poet Pauline Johnson (Tekahionwake) (1861–1913) utilized the interface or liminal space between Aboriginal and European cultures for her poetry performances whereby she would appear in indigenous and European costume during the same evening (see Chapter 3); subsequently her publications have a hybrid status, her first book, *The White Wampum* (1895), being a collection of texts for performance. Johnson was also involved in the textualization of indigenous cultures, her *Legends of Vancouver* (1911) being a transcription of stories told to her by the Salish Chief Capilano. Johnson differs from the Ojibway "literary coterie" not just in gender, but also in her role as a mediator between indigenous and non-indigenous cultures.

The native performer in the nineteenth century, outside of missionary circles, was utterly stereotyped, nowhere more so than in Buffalo Bill's Wild West Show, which consisted of "re-enactments" of historical battles between "cowboys and Indians", in effect providing entertainment that also fueled the western fantasy of the "red Indian"; it was crucial, for Pauline Johnson's promoters, to keep her separate from this world, as well as that of the more respectable and conservative realm of the missionaries, so that she remained in the liminal space between Aboriginal and "high" European art: in other words, she was indeterminately positioned in her "role as mediator between elite and popular cultures, especially in bringing Natives, commonly reduced to burlesque figures, into arenas of high culture performance, such as drawing-rooms and theatres" (Strong-Boag and Gerson, 112).

Buffalo Bill's Wild West Show began in 1882, in North Platte, Nebraska, as an outdoor extravaganza of "cowboys" performing stunts and showcasing their skills to a delighted Fourth of July (Independence Day) audience. Born in Iowa in 1846, William F. (Buffalo Bill) Cody worked as a cowboy and driver on a wagon train, got involved in the gold rush, hunted buffalo, worked for the Pony Express, and served in the Civil War, and was the real-life model for Ned Buntline's (Edward Zane Carroll Judson, 1823–86) character Buffalo Bill, and a series of action-packed "dime novels" based around his exploits. Buntline wrote "The Scouts of the Prairie" in which Buffalo Bill performed in 1872, but it was not until he conceived of a larger-scale show, involving authentic cattle ranchers and, eventually, American Natives, that his performances took off. The "Wild West Show" was performed in Canada, in 1885, and in England, in 1887, in front of Queen Victoria. Real Native peoples from historical battles and events joined the Wild West Show, including Sitting Bull, Black Elk, and Gabriel Dumont. Daniel Francis argues that "Prior to the Hollywood movie, no other entertainment medium was as popular a purveyor of the Indian image as the Wild West Show" (93).

"The Two Sisters": the textualized short story as a mediating device

Johnson's mediating role can be examined in relation to one of the textualized stories that she published called "The Two Sisters", set in Vancouver at a time when "there were no twin peaks like sentinels guarding the outposts of this sunset coast" (13). This is a time of "Indian" (Johnson's word) domination of the land and law, when a "great Tyee" or chief had two daughters who reached puberty at the same time: this moment must be celebrated with an immense potlatch, arranged during a time of war. The potlatch brings peace to the region, and the "Sagalie Tyee" celebrates by making the chief's daughters immortal: "In the cup of His hands He lifted the chief's two daughters and set them for ever in a high place, for they had borne two offspring – Peace and Brotherhood – each of which is now a great Tyee ruling this land" (15). Johnson has textualized an indigenous story concerning belief narratives and the beneficial role of the potlatch; additionally, her version of the story also includes the framing narrative of the situation in which the chief is initially surprised to learn that the "Two Sisters" are called "throughout the British Empire" (12) "The Lions": "He seemed so surprised at the name that I mentioned the reason it had been applied to them, asking him if he had seen the Landseer Lions in Trafalgar Square [in London, England]. Yes, he remembered those splendid sculptures, and his quick eye saw the resemblance instantly" (12).

At this point in the story there are two distinct visions of landscape: that of Aboriginal orature and the potlatch, and that of a nineteenth-century English artist Sir Edwin Henry Landseer (1802–73) and his Lions in London's Trafalgar Square. Johnson *does* mediate between these two visions, but problematically, she appears to resolve the two opposing perspectives by making it clear that one belongs in the present ("The Lions"), and one in the past ("The Two Sisters" or "The Chief's Daughters", which she calls "legend"). In other words, the Landseer Lions remain dominant in the geo-political sense of being transposed to British Columbia, naming two mountain peaks (we now know what they *used* to be called), and the indigenous "legend" has the slightly quaint air of a Victorian museum-piece. But there is a more subversive side to this mediation: during the period in which the potlatch was made illegal, Johnson's story advocates the potlatch as a peace-making process, and furthermore, the Canadian name for these mountain peaks is shown to belong to the *myth-making* history of the British Empire. In other words, the act of naming geological features has in both ethnic cases cultural significance, and Johnson is allowing the reader to weigh-up the relative merits of this significance.

Johnson's performances were immensely popular, and her published works were eagerly awaited by the reading public; her first poetry collections were *The White Wampum* (1895) and *Canadian Born* (1903); she collected and re-presented these poems in *Flint and Feather* (1912) and key stories in *Legends of Vancouver* (1911); her children's stories were collected and published posthumously as *The Shagganappi* (1913), and further stories and prose articles were published as *The Moccasin Maker* (1913). Johnson's hybridity was both her strength and her weakness (see Strong-Boag and Gerson for one of the most comprehensive accounts of Johnson's achievements); however, as Francis notes, over time the mediating function served non-Native interests in Canada: "This need to satisfy the demands of a White audience stultified Pauline Johnson's development as a writer and limited her effectiveness as a spokesperson for Native people" (120). What Francis recognizes is the power of the audience – of the market – to command aesthetic and political obedience.

Johnson's writing was often subtly subversive and at times oppositional in its force, but shortly after her death, literary audiences in Canada would be highly controlled and manipulated by the government as part of its attempt to win the hearts and minds of the nation to support the British in the First World War. If Johnson's persona is criticized for its constructed nature, then a constructed audience needs to be recognized as the next phase in the literary history of Canada, one that took virtually no account of the needs of Canada's First Peoples. It is no coincidence that the most popular "Indians" during the decades following Johnson's death were in fact imposters: a British man called George Stansfield ("Archie") Belaney (1888–1938) posing as "Grey Owl", and a Black American called Sylvester Clark Long (1890–1932) posing as Chief Buffalo Child Long Lance. Both men served in the Canadian Expeditionary Force during World War One, and both did considerably better for themselves in life using their fake identities, especially Long who suffered in the US from racial prejudice.

The trope of incarceration: Aboriginal protest writing in the twentieth century

While the period that follows the death of Johnson up to the 1960s and 1970s is one of great transformation in Aboriginal writing in English (see Chapter 7), two socio-political factors that contributed to this transformation need to be kept in mind: first, there is evidence that many of the people who had power within the residential school system were attempting to efface indigeneity, replacing native values with those of White culture, and second, out of this cultural genocide would emerge a new native politics and a strong desire to repair and rebuild the expanding (*not* dying or disappearing) indigenous communities of Canada. Another way of sketching this period, therefore, is to turn to the trope of incarceration, and resistances to this trope (based on actual experiences). Deena Rymhs notes that for many critics and historians, not only does the residential school system prefigure and create the conditions for the prison system, but the trope of incarceration that subsequently emerges functioned across Native society as disrupted and constrained by Whites: "Just as schools and adoptive families have been experienced as prisons, even home, the reserve, in its physical segregation, curtailing of indigenous territory, and concentration of economic poverty, has been compared to a prison" (5).

Writing from the prison, however it is conceived, is fundamentally protest writing, and indigenous authors and critics have noted how "much First Nations literature proceeds from a tradition of protest writing that seeks to address, among other things, the historical criminalization of indigenous people and the use of institutions such as prisons to wear away at their cultural identity" (Rymhs, 7). Carceral systems and tropes are predicated upon the notion of "aboriginal sin" (Peltier in Rymhs, 85) which can purportedly be transformed by the state or its representatives (religious or secular) in the processes of incarceration. The reality of this situation for indigenous peoples is that the colonial processes of incarceration created damage *and resistance to that damage* often expressed through journalism and literary texts. As Taiaiake Alfred writes: "The lesson of the past is that indigenous people have less to fear by moving away from colonialism than by remaining bound by it" (33).

Conclusion

- Textualization is a way of preserving – but also interpreting and potentially misrepresenting – orature, which is a living, developing mode of spoken narrative expression.
- Early examples of textualization can teach us about the colonial presence in Canada, and it can be reclaimed by First Peoples to help in the recovery of indigenous cultural knowledge and ways of being.
- Canada's First Peoples survived the impact of colonialism and are in the process of recovering and rebuilding artistic and social forms; orature, as a vehicle for cultural and belief-systems, is as important today as written literature.
- The narratives of conquest and settlement, as well as political modes of being, form an important part of the colonial era; these narratives have since been critiqued and have at times been replaced by alternative stories concerning colonialism.
- Canada's ethnic diversity and difference is one of its great strengths; a historical overview reveals how competing notions of the state, alongside allegiances to other dominant forces, such as the Catholic Church in Quebec, shape people's understanding of ethnicity and belonging.

2 Literatures of landscape and encounter
Canadian Romanticism and pastoral writing

Overview

The emergence of strong literary movements that articulated Canada's peoples engaging in the simple tasks of the everyday world also marks the beginnings of the New World recoding of European literary forms. The Mouvement Littéraire Du Québec, founded in 1860 by the poet Octave Crémazie (1827–70), fostered a nationalistic French and French-Canadian aesthetic up until Confederation. The growing desire for confederation meant that in the Anglophone world a more self-reflexive nationalistic writing was also seen in its popular and literary presses. The desire for autonomy (that is, breaking free from British control) was not just political, but also cultural and aesthetic. While intertextual resonances between the Confederation Poets and their Romantic precursors can be heard, the New World environment also called for aesthetic adaptation and modification. Differences of gender and race also begin to be articulated, particularly in the writings of Isabella Valancy Crawford and Pauline Johnson (also known by her indigenous name which was Tekahionwake).

Beginnings of a Canadian canon: Edward Hartley Dewart's *Selections from Canadian Poets* (1864)

Canadian literary expression was perceived in the nineteenth century as the creative result of the writer's encounter with Nature and God (Dewart, xi); as Edward Hartley Dewart (1828–1903) wrote in a now famous "Introductory Essay" to his 1864 anthology *Selections from Canadian Poets*: "Poetry is the medium by which the emotions of beauty, joy, admiration, reverence, harmony, or tenderness kindled in the poet-soul, in communion with Nature and God, is conveyed to the souls of others" (Ibid., xi). Born in Ireland, Dewart emigrated to Canada with his family in 1834, moving to Dummer Township in Upper Canada (Ontario). Educated at the Normal School in Toronto, Dewart's first career was that of probationer and then Minister in the Wesleyan Methodist Church, where he was a prominent advocate for temperance (abstaining from all alcohol); in 1869 he became the president of the Dominion Alliance Ontario branch, and editor of the *Christian Guardian* newspaper (est. 1829; merged with *The New Outlook* in 1925), based in

Toronto. As editor of this widely read and influential publication, as well as being an essayist and a poet, Dewart was in a position to shape cultural tastes, especially with the publication of his anthology in 1864. Apart from his increasingly polemical editorials, key publications were *Songs of Life: A Collection of Poems* (1869) and *Essays for the Times: Studies of Eminent Men and Important Living Questions* (1898). While Dewart is best known today for his statement that "A national literature is an essential element in the formation of national character" (Ibid., ix), a complex interplay between European and New World modes of writing also contributed in this era to a new literary hybridity. And yet there was a sense in nineteenth-century Canada that a home-grown literature was not really valued, poetic output being met by the general populace with "coldness and indifference" (Dewart, x), unless the text in question took a straightforward descriptive or realist approach (Bentley 2004, 173).

Dewart's "Introductory Essay" – a key text in the formation of an early Canadian canon – undertakes a rhetorical battle with those who would denigrate poetry. The argument is ethical *and* religious, since as Dewart suggests: "The Poet's work is a lofty and sacred work" (xiii). More specifically, this is a Christian notion of poetry, whereby the utilitarian objection that poetic language is "indefinite" can be turned back upon itself, in the sense that "the subjects with which" poetry "converses" are themselves already "indefinite":

> Beauty, truth, the human soul, the works of God, the mystery of life, – are not themes whose significance can be easily compressed into rigid and superficial forms of speech. Let it not therefore be supposed, that because poetry is not fruitful in direct and palpable results, that its influence is small or its mission unimportant. It soothes human sorrow. It ministers to human happiness. It fires the soul with noble and holy purpose. It expands and quickens. It refines the taste. It opens to us the treasures of the universe, and brings us into closer sympathy with all that is beautiful, and grand, and true. It sheds a new charm around common objects; because it unveils their spiritual relations, and higher and deeper typical meanings. And it educates the mind to a quicker perception of the harmony, grandeur, and truth disclosed in the works of the Creator.
>
> (xiii)

This idealistic and ethical conception of the poet's work is also deeply Eurocentric (steeped in European values). Yet it would be wrong to think that Dewart – a deep thinker and advocate for Canada's cultural production – does not understand the colonial contexts of his views. As he says a bit later on in his essay: "Our colonial position, whatever may be its political advantages, is not favorable to the growth of an indigenous literature" (xiv). What does he mean by this? He argues that because Canada's immigrants are still emotionally attached to their original homelands, Canadian literary production does not, and cannot, lay a claim to their affections. This is partly due to an idealization of that which is now distant and old (the original overseas homeland and its literature), leading to a lack of interest and attraction in that which is new, familiar and "near" (xv). Also, Dewart suggests that it is easier for people to subscribe to the critical consensus, whereby the established mainly European canon is what has attracted most praise, so must therefore be most praiseworthy. This in turn leads to another famous statement from Dewart, that "if a Milton or a Shakspere [sic], was to arise among us, it is far from certain that his merit would be recognized" (xv). Dewart also says that religious intolerance plays a part in suppressing appreciation of a genuinely Canadian literature, and that the idiosyncrasies of the book trade in the nineteenth century, which made it cheaper to buy imported British or American books, also cause problems. However, it is as damaging, he suggests, to puff up and promote every mediocre poet just because he or she is Canadian.

What Dewart concludes his essay with is some specific Canadian canon building of his own. And rather than dwelling on the disadvantages of being a writer in nineteenth-century Canada, he ends with the advantages or compensations:

> If we are deprived of many of the advantages of older countries, we have ample compensation in more unshackled freedom of thought, and broader spheres of action. Though poor in historic interest, our past is not altogether devoid of events capable of poetic treatment. But if Memory cannot draw rich materials for poetry from treasures consecrated to fame, Hope unfolds the loftier inspiration of a future bright with promise. If we cannot point to a past rich with historic names, we have the inspiring spectacle of a great country, in her youthful might, girding herself for a race for an honourable place among the nations of the world. In our grand and gloomy forests – in our brilliant skies and varied seasons – in our magnificent lakes and rivers – in our hoary mountains and fruitful valleys, external Nature unveils her majestic forms to exalt and inspire the truly poetic soul; while human nature – especially human nature in its relation to the spiritual and the divine – still presents an exhaustless mine of richest ore, worthy of the most exalted genius, and of the deepest human and spiritual knowledge.
>
> (xix)

Dewart does not just celebrate Canada's natural scenery, he uses the metaphor of primary resource extraction – here, mining – to suggest that Canadian literary production should "mine" what is best in the non-human *and* human worlds.

Dewart's underlying metaphor is not as "indigenous" at this stage as he appears to think, because he regards the Canadian landscape via the largely European concept of the sublime – a concept that had been theorized in the eighteenth century by Burke and Kant, feeding into the European Romanticism of the nineteenth century (see Glossary, and Lane, 2007).

Nature, in other words, is not just "out there" to be used, it is conceived via European notions of value. Closer examination of Dewart's emerging canon of Canadian authors reveals that this issue – of applying European concepts and notions of aesthetics to Canada – is part of the dynamic hybridity of nineteenth-century Canadian literature.

Dewart places most firmly at the foreground of the newly emerging Canadian literature (in order of preference), poets Charles Sangster (1822–93) and Alexander McLachlan (1817–96), devoting a paragraph of his essay to them; one paragraph is awarded the rest of his list, again in Dewart's order of preference: Charles Heavysege (1816–76); Pamelia Sarah Vining (1826–97); Jennie E. Haight (1836–1916); Isidore G. Ascher (1835–1914); Rosanna Leprohon (1829–79); George William Chapman (1850–1917); Susanna Moodie (1803–85); John F. McDonnell (1838–68); and Helen M. Johnson (1834–63). This is very much a "pre-Confederation" list of poets, many of whom would be swept aside by later anthology editors, or remembered for their prose writings, not their poetry (see Gerson, 1997).

Charles Sangster, Alexander McLachlan, and Charles Heavysege

Born in Kingston, Upper Canada (Ontario), Sangster trained in all aspects of editing and journalism while working for the *Amherstburg Courier*, the *British Whig* and the Kingston *Daily News*. He published two important volumes of poetry – *The St. Lawrence and the Saguenay and Other Poems* (1856) and *Hesperus and Other Poems and Lyrics* (1860) – as well as an undated chapbook called *Our Norland*. Nature and patriotism are two key components of Sangster's verse, or, as Dewart puts it, he works with "Canadian themes" (xvii). For example, Sangster draws upon key Canadian historical figures which he fuses with lush nature imagery and rich mythology. In "The St. Lawrence and the Saguenay" the picturesque (graphic or vivid style) dominates, transforming the riverscape into a paradisiacal place where "crystal streams through endless landscapes flow, / And o'er the clustering Isles the softest breezes blow". Latham notes that "As the voyage nears the poet's source of inspiration (symbolized by the river's divine origin), he questions whether art can compete with the splendour of God's work, humbly musing that the expressive calm of silence in the northern wilderness is a Godlike eloquence" (1035). Sangster's ultimate answer to this question is the trinity of art, nature and love: "As love excites us to perceive the earth as heavenly, God inspires us to share that vision with others" (Ibid.).

Alexander McLachlan, born in Strathclyde, Scotland, was a more prolific poet than Sangster, publishing six books of poetry, including his longest, unfinished poem *The Emigrant* (1861). Known as the "Burns of Canada", McLachlan's poems utilize "the rhyme schemes and rhythmic patterns of established tradition" of Burns (Waterston, 25), and are a strategic mixture of political and social criticism, alongside British patriotism. Daniel Coleman (2006) compares and contrasts "the anti-aristocratic, anti-English feeling typical among decidedly *British* North Americans" (88) in McLachlan's poem *Young Canada; or, Jack's as Good's His Master* with that of his poem *Britannia*. In *Young Canada*, Canada is celebrated as a place "Where no one moils and strains and toils / That snobs might thrive the faster", whereas in *Britannia*, Britain is "Thou birthplace of the brave and free, / Thou ruler of the land and sea." How can we make sense of this contradiction? Coleman suggests that the differences here articulated "are consistent with the larger project of Scots throughout the empire to placate their English rivals with expressions of homage and loyalty that operated as a kind of flux between the categories of Britishness and Englishness, not just to fuse themselves into empire's central alloy but also to recompose the character of that alloy according to their own values" (90). It can be seen at the wider level of poetic reflection – of nature, of character in the New World, of the relationships between New and Old Worlds – nineteenth-century Canadian literature was a strategic mode of writing for multiple, more ethnically complex audiences than contemporary readers might now perceive, *and* for multiple market places.

The third person in Dewart's canonizing list, Charles Heavysege (born in Liverpool, England), reveals the extent to which nineteenth-century Canadian literature was dependent upon European literary modes and models. Writing long poems such as *Jephthah's Daughter* (1865) and the closet dramas *Saul* (1857; rev. 1859) and *Count Filippo* (1860), Heavysege's settings are anything but Canadian, with the Bible, Milton and Shakespeare being primary influences. While critics have largely written off Heavysege in the context of Canadian literary history – as Lorne Pierce writes, for example, "There is nothing Canadian about Heavysege's work; the effect of his poetry on subsequent Canadian literature has been nil" (64) – the fact that he received acclaim and international recognition is in itself significant for the period. Also, while it is true that there is nothing distinctively Canadian in Heavysege's main body of work, the fact that for his technical proficiency or workmanship he could claim a place in the world of letters from a Canadian base laid some of the groundwork for later authors.

Two other names in Dewart's pre-Confederation list of authors are of significance in relation to the question of a Canadian "setting": Rosanna Leprohon and Susanna Moodie (see Chapter 3 for their prose writing). Leprohon's serialized novel "The Manor House of De Villerai", which appeared in the Montreal *Family Herald* from 1859 to 1860, not only has a New France setting, but depicts events from the French Canadian point-of-view (Mary Jane Edwards). Dewart published five of her poems in his anthology, including *Winter in Canada*: "What! dare to rail at our snow storms – O why / Not view them with poet's or artist's eye" (quoted in Dewart, 160). Leprohon suggests that if the visitor stays in Canada long enough not only will she "rail at our winters then no more", but "New health and fresh life through your veins shall glow, / Spite of piercing winds, spite of ice and snow" (quoted in Dewart, 160). *Winter in Canada* is in dialogue with those English visitors who "shrink from the thought of wintering" in Canada, because their frame of reference or comparison, according to Leprohon, is the extreme weather of Siberia! Leprohon reminds these folk that it is cold and bare in England, as well as Canada, in wintertime, yet in the latter there are also blue skies, a bright sun, and a gleaming, glittering snowscape. While not using such complex imagery as is found in the twentieth-century Canadian poet Margaret Avison's "Snow" ("The astonished cinders quake / With rhizomes"), Leprohon's dialogue utilizes competent iambic pentameter to reveal the *advantages* and beauty of the Canadian winter landscape.

Susanna Moodie, whose best-known book, *Roughing it in the Bush* (1852), is a mixture of autobiographical narrative and poetry, also engages in conversation with the potential immigrant in her poem *O Can You Leave Your Native Land?* Here, the future bride of a "woodsman" is asked if she can cope with the hardships ahead, going into exile from her "mother's home and cheerful hearth". As with *Roughing it in the Bush*, this poem makes it clear that the construction of Canada is one that is gendered; not just the demands of nature, and a harsh climate, but also the demands of the labouring man that the female immigrant will potentially be in relationship with: "Can these dear hands, unused to toil / The woodsman's wants supply"; the European home, by comparison, will appear "An Eden, whose delicious bloom / Will make the wild more drear-".

The Confederation Poets

The British North America Act of 1867, which united the provinces of Ontario, Quebec, New Brunswick and Nova Scotia as The Confederated Dominion of Canada, was a foundational event in the formation of a national literary identity. Given the name "The Confederation Poets", six men would come to dominate the literary scene: Charles G.D. Roberts (1860–1943); Bliss Carmen (1861–1929); Archibald Lampman (1861–99); Frederick George Scott (1861–1944); Duncan Campbell Scott (1862–1947); and William Wilfred Campbell (1858–1918). While other names have since been added to this list, such as Isabella Valancy Crawford (1850–87) and Pauline Johnson (Tekahionwake) (1861–1913), the core identity of the group remains in their self-identified male-dominated quest to transcend all other poets and poetry in Canada. In the case of the Confederation Poets, their family resemblance (a number of shared attributes and traits that override the differences of individual members) was created by: a concern for technical excellence or "workmanship"; admiration of the major English Romantics (such as Keats and Wordsworth) and Victorian poets and critics (such as Matthew Arnold); a concern for Nature, especially as a "therapeutic" force; and Christian and other related transformative modes of spirituality or supernaturalism (see Bentley 2004). The question of English literary influence – here the Romantics – arises at a point in which Canadian identity is formed via a sense of independence: of spirit, if not in the political sphere. The Canada First group, which was formed after Confederation, advocated Canadian autonomy within the framework of the British Empire. They wanted to know in which direction Canada was moving (towards true independence or simply expressing a different form of integration within the Empire?), and even what it meant to be Canadian in the first place. The diversity of the movement was a strength, as each member could express the need for national unity in a way that spoke to different parts of the nation: George T. Denison (1839–1925) argued for a militaristic society, one which should prove itself through war with the USA; Robert Grant Haliburton (1831–1901) contended that Canadians were ethnically more pure and hardy compared to their Southern neighbours; Charles Mair (1838–1927) advocated a poetic discourse of Canadian "manifest destiny"; William Foster (1840–88), in response to the Red River Rebellion in 1870, used highly emotive language to stir up a response against Riel (Farrell, 17; Gagan, 38). Things went wrong for Canada First when they tried to directly intervene in Canadian politics: they thought that politics should serve their idea of a transcendent nation. Yet, as the *Canadian Monthly* put it in 1877, "the Canada First movement did manage to successfully infuse a national spirit into the policy of our statesmen and people" whereby "The working of the national spirit manifests itself in both parties" (quoted in Altfest, 61).

A "national spirit" is sensed in the early work of the Confederation Poets, but this is tempered by their intertextual relationship with the European Romantics. One important fact, as with the reception to Heavysege, is that the Confederation Poets received international recognition and acclaim. Suddenly, there was a real sense that recognizably good literature could be produced from Canada – written by Canadians – as Archibald Lampman wrote in response to his reading of Charles G.D. Roberts's *Orion, and Other Poems* (1880):

> ... I had been under the depressing conviction that we were situated hopelessly on the outskirts of civilization, where no art and literature could be, and that it was useless to expect that anything great could be done by any of our companions, still more useless to expect that we could do it ourselves. I sat up all night reading and re-reading *Orion* in a state of the wildest excitement and when I went to bed I could not sleep. It seemed to me a wonderful thing that such work could be done by a Canadian, by a young man, one of ourselves. It was like a voice from some new paradise of art calling us to be up and doing.
>
> (Quoted in Ware, 116)

Orion, and Other Poems has been called "the most famous unread book in Canadian literature" (Early, 8), although this might simply be in part because Roberts's most widely read poem, *The Tantramar Revisited*, was published in a later collection. In fact his poem was first published in the third issue of *The Week* as *Westmoreland Revisited*, and reprinted with a change of title in the collection of poems *In Divers Tones* (1886). Even Lampman, for all his gushing praise, was critical of Roberts's *Orion*; later on in his review, he refers to Roberts's "deficiencies", suggesting that "he lacks tenderness, variety, elasticity, and that he never approaches the nobler attitudes of feeling" (quoted in Early, 9). Nonetheless, it is important to note that *Orion, and Other Poems*, while youthful work, contains poetry of considerable achievement, and that it functioned for some critics as a powerful collection that rose above the vagaries of literary-critical disputes. As Malcolm Ross suggests: "Lampman's note on *Orion* makes the right entry to the work of the whole Confederation group. Unquestionably, Lampman here reflects the peculiar national spirit of the immediate post-Confederation period" (viii).

Roberts drew upon a number of conventional poetic modes in "The Tantramar Revisited" to create a hybrid voice, one that is further "enabled" by his "combination of the international and the local, the classical and the Canadian" (Bentley 2004, 62). "Tantramar" is a Canadian idyll, in the style of the neo-classical idyll, that is to say a "short poem describing a picturesque rustic scene or incident" (Gray, 102). Descriptions of nature and memory combine, as with Wordsworth's "Lines Written a Few Miles Above Tintern Abbey" (1798), to form an elegiac description of the coast of New Brunswick. As James Cappon notes: "There is no direct picture of life in the poem, not a single human figure, but the landscape is powerfully painted in large, distant, softened traits, the true colour of elegiac reminiscence" (32). The poem opens with the passing of time: "Summers and summers have come, and gone with the flight of the swallow." The poet has returned to a scene that he now begins to sketch for the reader. It is a timeless scene, one which has *endured* through all the changes of life: "Only in these green hills, aslant to the sea, no change!" The opening echoes Wordsworth's "Tintern Abbey", where the poet is looking down upon an expansive vision: "These hedge-rows, hardly hedge-rows, little lines / Of sportive wood run wild: these pastoral farms, / Green to the very door" (Wordsworth). Similarly, the view in "Tantramar" is vast, made clear by the repetition throughout the poem of the phrase "miles on miles": "Miles on miles beyond the tawny bay is Minudie. / There are the low blue hills; villages gleam at their feet." This vastness and apparent accompanying superhuman perception soon triggers the realization that what is being described could not possibly be seen by the human eye from such a vantage point; instead, fine details are being drawn from memory: "Well I remember the piles of blocks and ropes, and the net-reels / Wound with the beaded nets, dripping and dark from the sea!" Roberts's local knowledge of the Tantramar marshes in New Brunswick enables the fine details of this memory or *close-up* (to think about the poem here through notions and technologies of visual perspective), and we can also see that Roberts has cleverly combined temporal and spatial co-ordinates.

This is not just description of an external world: it is also a psychological landscape, one where if there is change it is in the perceiving poet. Here the links with Wordsworth and the English Romantics can be sketched: in "Tintern Abbey" the development occurs in the speaker and his sister, while nature has undergone no significant change during five long years. As in Wordsworth, Roberts's "province is that border-land wherein Nature and the heart of Man act and react upon each other" (Ware, 132). The self-reflective poetic mood is melancholy, and it is this mood that is projected onto the landscape, such as the "Golden afternoon" which is "lonesome" or the driftnet which is "Myriad-meshed" and "uploomed sombrely over the land". The poet decides to maintain his distance, even though he remembers "the old-time stir" which "stung me with rapture": "Yet will I stay my steps ... / [...] / Lest on too close sight I miss the darling illusion, / Spy at their task ... " The rapture of past experiences can be remembered, but not re-attained through direct contact with the present community of the Tantramar marshes. The poet remains a spy (to develop a possible resonance in the phrase "Spy at their task"), alienated from the landscape and the marsh community that once was his home. Has the poet now understood the origins of the "darling illusion" – the attempt at recovering the past? Ware argues that "By understanding that he had half-created the Tantramar's former sanctity, by accepting responsibility for his changing perceptions of nature, he is able to internalize, and so gain some control over, the forces of 'chance and change'" (143).

Rather than being wholly reliant on Romanticism, Roberts re-codes Romanticism from a Canadian perspective, testing the possibilities of Romanticism in exploring the variety of perceptual responses to this situation/ scene; the melancholy vision is inspired by a *Canadian* landscape and community, and a sense of lost contact with that place and its peoples. In other words, Romanticism is simply one of the poetic tools deployed to create a more complex aesthetic of time and place. Even those authors who explicitly rejected Confederation – such as the unofficial French Canadian poet laureate Louis Fréchette (1839–1908) – utilized Romanticism. In Fréchette's case, it is the Romanticism of the French author Victor Hugo (1802–85) upon which he draws most significantly; *La voix d'un exilé* (1867–68), Fréchette's anti-Confederation critique in verse form, was published in Quebec (1867–68) and Chicago (1868 and 1869), but he is most famous for his prize-winning collection of poems *Les fleurs boréales* (1879), his plays *Papineau* (1880) and *Le retour de l'exilé* (1880), and his long historical poem *La légende d'un peuple* (1887). In the poem *Le Niagara* from *Les fleurs boréales*, the sublime is encountered in the majesty of a wave that appears to be moving slowly among calm waters but which suddenly collapses into a never-ending abyss: "Dans l'abîme sans fond le fleuve immense croule." Intriguingly, the sublime mountain landscape does emerge, from the great Niagara Falls themselves: "D'eau verte se transforme en monts d'écume blanche, / Farouches, éperdus, bondissant, mugissant ... " In this sublime waterscape and rising mountainscape, fragile life can survive the immense powers that destroy all else. Fréchette's sublime is translated into other modes: the epic, writing the history of the French Canadian nation, and narratives of resistance to Anglophone rule; as with a later British Canadian author, Malcolm Lowry (1909–57), Fréchette would be accused of plagiarism, but contemporary notions of intertextuality and bricolage (building texts from other sampled sources) suggest that Fréchette, like Roberts, is instead occupying and re-coding European modes of aesthetic perception.

The Confederation Poets and the Canadian landscape

One of the most frequently made comparisons with Roberts's *Tantramar* is that of Bliss Carmen's poem *Low Tide on Grand Pré* (1886), set in the Minas Basin in Nova Scotia. Like *Tantramar*, *Low Tide* is a return poem, one with an air of melancholy, projected onto the landscape: "The sun goes down, and over all / These barren reaches by the tide / Such unelusive glories fall." The speaker is viewing the mudflats in a sombre mood, using a sombre tone, apparent in the word "barren" and the image of a "fall" of glories; Ware notes the echo of Wordsworth in "glories": "The glory and the freshness of a dream" which is from Wordsworth's "Intimations of Immortality" ode (149). In Canada, the strikingly "unelusive" glories are extensive yet still ephemeral or impermanent. The poet appears to want to maintain the glories in a dream-like state, while Nature will nonetheless impose its rhythms (and by implication, its seasons). These rhythms are apparent at the level of content and form, such as the iambic tetrameter which is in itself suggestive of waves breaking upon the shore (McGillivray, 20). Ware regards this opening as establishing two temporal orders: "the epiphanic and the linear. The problem of integrating these two orders is central to Carmen's poetry and to the return poem" (149). While Nature is more powerful than the human poetic vision (the dream will be overtaken by the reality of the tide), *Low Tide* is the natural world as projected through the poet's aesthetic; thus the pleasing paradox expressed by Coleridge's command: "to make the external internal, the internal external, to make nature thought, and thought nature" (quoted in Ware, 152). Only mystical vision and insight can succeed here, although it is preceded in stanzas two and three by a feeling of loss, of a loved one, the "one beloved face" which is "So long from home and Acadie". The central stanzas of the poem recount time spent with the absent one, as the pace of the poem slows, going beyond time to a mystical moment: "There down along the elms at dusk / We lifted dripping blade to drift, / [...] And that we took into our hands / Spirit of life or subtler thing – / Breathed on us there, and loosed the bands / Of death ... "

The imagery in *Low Tide on Grand Pré* is that of transcendence and mysticism, an epiphanic moment not just of insight, but of illumination: "Spirit of life or subtler thing –". The deceleration in these stanzas is also a transmutation as water is turned into "running gold" and time itself is both moment and eternity. Is this an erotic moment, or is it a moment that transcends entirely the sensual body? The imagery is certainly erotic: the "musk" and the taking "into our hands" of that which is "breathed" on the two lovers; yet "breath" is also a Biblical word meaning "Spirit"; the "Spirit of life" can be read as the Holy Spirit, and it is the crucified and risen Christ who "loosed the bands / Of death" from humanity. While Carmen did have a Christian upbringing (as did most of the Confederation Poets), Carmen's Transcendentalism is, at this stage in his writing career, balanced by sensualism; his spiritual and mystical beliefs would eventually turn into pantheism (all material existence is sacred), with a concomitant recognition that sexuality can be regarded as a powerful component of the mystical experience; Carmen's pantheism was one of the driving forces behind his successful *Songs from Vagabondia* (1894), written with Richard Hovey.

Returning to the end of "Low Tide", the mystical moment passes as night falls, and the tide "comes drifting home"; the melancholy poet now grieves the flood which "is bursting home".

Inhabited nature

Contemporary readers of *The Tantramar Revisited* and *Low Tide on Grand Pré* might observe the *absence* of people; they are of course there, since both poems are about memory, loss, perception and insight (or vision): precisely in the minds and hearts of the poets who are observing and interpreting these landscapes. *Traces* of other people are also present: such as the fishermen in *Tantramar* or the lovers in *Low Tide*. Yet, regardless of such traces, these are landscapes that feel strangely devoid of human beings. During the Confederation years, the Dominion of Canada was growing at a rapid pace, extending to the prairies in 1870, with British Columbia joining the Confederation in 1871, and Prince Edward Island in 1873. Yet Canada had nowhere near the number of immigrants required to rapidly develop the country, and in fact between 1867 and 1896 almost two million Canadians left for opportunities in the USA and elsewhere (Bothwell, 218). While the infrastructure for expansion and development was being put into place, there were deep divisions within society that had the potential to work against such expansion: "The divisions were racial, between Natives, or half-Natives like the Métis, and the majority whites; linguistic, again between Natives and whites, but also between English and French; religious, between Catholic and Protestant, and among the various Protestant sects; geographical, pitting region against region; and finally constitutional, between the layers of government in Canada's federal system, meaning the dominion against the provinces" (Ibid.). In the poetry of Isabella Valancy Crawford and Pauline Johnson (Tekahionwake), these divisions are explored, and in some tentative and partial ways temporarily bridged.

Transcendentalism is a belief in a higher spiritual world which can be intuited through artistic and other modes of being, such as an extended experience of Nature, rather than needing to engage in organized religion (the church and its associated belief systems and activities); its chief practitioners in nineteenth-century USA were Ralph Waldo Emerson (1803–82) and Henry David Thoreau (1817–62). Transcendentalism is an important source of inspiration for the Confederation Poets in Canada.

Crawford's most enduring poem, *Malcolm's Katie: A Love Story* (1884), uses a conventional romance mode to articulate concerns of gender and race. Crawford, who was born in Dublin, Ireland, emigrated to Canada in 1858, and spent much of her childhood in Ontario, beginning in Paisley in Bruce County, where her father had a medical practice. Family life involved home-schooling to a high standard – reading Horace and Dante, studying in Latin, English and French – in an environment which was typical pioneering land, not just the newly cleared farms but also the activity and industry of the sawmills and the peace and wilderness of the lakes and forests that Crawford loved to explore. In other words, this was a *working* landscape, one of prac-tical struggle, endurance, and sometimes financial reward. Crawford's father, who had become the township treasurer, was forced to leave Paisley after financial improprieties were discovered; the family moved to Lakefield, where Crawford got to know Catherine Parr Traill, and then to Peterborough in 1869; a final move to Toronto took place in 1876, a year after her father's death. Early poems and stories by Crawford appeared in Toronto in *The Mail* from 1873, and in the *Evening Telegram* from 1879. Her volume of poetry, *Old Spookses' Pass, Malcolm's Katie and Other Poems* (1884), was financed by Crawford, and sold few copies. Early prose appeared in the American Leslie's *Illustrated Newspaper*, beginning with *Wrecked; or, The Rosclerras of Mistree* (1872–73), followed by a novel called *Winona; or, The Foster Sisters* in *The Favorite* (published in Montreal, 1873).

Malcolm's Katie, a long poem in blank verse with a narrative structure and a romance plot, combines Crawford's strengths in writing poetry and racy prose. The protagonist, Katie, is being romantically pursued by two potential lovers: Alfred (the villain) and Max (the eventual winner of her love); the story is complicated by the fact that Katie is still under the guardianship of her father, and from a patriarchal perspective, he controls his daughter's sexuality and the appointment of her future husband. Critics have noted how the surface romance at times obscures the deeper importance of this poem: "[O]n its surface … [*Malcolm's Katie* is] a very competently run and managed morality play of the kind that was beginning to appeal increasingly to would-be sophisticated middle and upper-middle class Victorian readers" (Rudzik, 55). Digging a bit deeper "into the very fabric of this domestic quasi-tragedy working through to a pastoral resolution" one finds "a great deal of imagery that is highly theatrical and highly charged, psychologically and aesthetically" (Ibid.). Katie may be embedded in a deeply patriarchal society, but using a double discourse, she articulates not only gender concerns, but also those of race, such as her depiction of the *Indian Summer* and the indigenous north and south spirit winds, an intertextual reference to Longfellow's *The Song of Hiawatha* (Sugars and Moss, 341):

The South Wind laid his moccasins aside,
Broke his gay calumet of flow'rs, and cast
His useless wampum, beaded with cool dews,

Far from him, northward: his long, ruddy spear
Flung sunward, whence it came, and his soft locks
Of warm, fine haze grew silver as the birch.
His wigwam of green leaves began to shake ...

The "Native" terminology here is drawn from Longfellow's "Vocabulary" appended to his "Indian Edda" (see Bentley 1987, xliv); however, Crawford also weaves together the imagery of an indigenous landscape with that of the pioneer. In other words, land is being cleared in *Malcolm's Katie*, but it is land already embedded and imaged in another prior culture, thus troubling the notion of "virgin" territory.

Much of the development of Canada is presented by Crawford as a discursive, speculative dream: not just expressed by Max, and other pioneers, who want to own some land of their own, but also in a wider sense, as the collective dream of nation-building itself:

Then came smooth-coated men, with eager eyes,
And talk'd of steamers on the cliff-bound lakes;
And iron tracks across the prairie lands;
And mills to crush the quartz of wealthy hills;
And mills to saw the great, wide-arm'd trees;
And mills to grind the singing stream of grain;
And with such busy clamour mingled still
The throbbing music of the bold, bright Axe –
The steel tongue of the Present, and the wail
Of falling forests – voices of the Past.

While the synaesthesia creates the impression of industry achieved – especially with the repetition of the word "mills" suggestive of a production-line rhythm – Crawford also cleverly frames the entire vision as boosterism, the projection through words or mere "talk" of what might be. This boosterism was essential in not just driving infrastructural expansion, but attracting immigrants to Canada in the first place (a more gentle version of boosterism is found in Oliver Goldsmith's (1794–1861) *The Rising Village* (1825, modified version 1834): " ... thus the village each successive year / Presents new prospects, and extends its sphere."). What *Malcolm's Katie* suggests is that the sexual economy of patriarchy is equally important in the expansion of Canada: it is Katie that the protagonist Max dreams of as he thinks of his promised land, not just as his future mate with her "yellow hair" but equally important, "her household ways". Katie is also suspicious of male words, as Bentley observes: "she quickly emerges as a sceptical critic of her lover's 'words' who, despite her scepticism, is prepared to play constructively with his analogies [concerning women], relating them to her own experiences as a woman and turning them, like Crawford herself, with the male-generated myths and metaphors of her culture, to her own creative and self-expressive purposes" (1987, xix). This sceptical playfulness is part of the framing device questioning male language: "O words!" exclaims Katie in the first part of the poem, "only words!", as she re-codes and re-figures Max's idealistic and romantic notion of her identity – an identity that is closely entwined with the future of nation-building.

Crawford's use of indigenous imagery, however problematic, represents an alternative mythos with which she reveals the fact that the Canadian landscape is *already* peopled and creatively imagined. Other indigenous characters in the poem are the "half-breed lad" (line 165), and Alfred's fantasized or maliciously imagined wife for Max: "An Indian woman, comelier than her kind" with "lake-like eyes of mystic Indian brown" (lines 105 and 107). These stereotypically portrayed characters are, at least, a presence in the emerging literary landscape, yet it would take another female poet to overtly assert indigenous rights and their ancestors' presence since time immemorial, which gave them a claim to land title – as Emily Pauline Johnson (Tekahionwake) wrote in *A Cry from an Indian Wife*: "By right, by birth we Indians own these lands, / Though starved, crushed, plundered, lies our nation low … " It is no coincidence that the threat to Katie in Crawford's poem is perceived to be a Native wife, while in Johnson's poem it is the Native wife who asserts her rights, since, as Strong-Boag and Gerson note: "First Nations women were key figures in this [colonialist] negative portrayal [of indigenous peoples], and efforts to control female sexuality, especially that of Aboriginals, stood near the heart of imperial dominion in Canada. The cultural and physical reproduction of Native societies was systematically undermined by persistent portrayals of women as inadequate and degenerate wives and mothers" (21).

Johnson (Tekahionwake) – as her doubled name indicates – was born to mixed parents: her mother was British, her father was a Mohawk chief. Thus she crossed a boundary that colonial and Eurocentric culture was doing its best to maintain:

> … the 1869 provision of the Canadian Indian Act … denied status to Native women marrying White men, in much the same way in which their British counterparts lost their nationality on wedding a foreigner. In the United States, in contrast, Indian women, regardless of husbands, retained tribal membership. […] In Canada, however, women whose Indian inheritance came from mothers were largely lost to tribal communities until the 1985 reform of the Indian Act. In contrast, women of European origin were cast as moral superiors, essential harbingers of imperial civilization. A clear distinction between the two types of women, the wild and the civilized, was critical in justifying the defeat of Natives and the triumph of Europeans. By confounding this boundary Pauline Johnson called into question the logic of the imperial project.
>
> (Strong-Boag and Gerson, 21)

Johnson grew up in Chiefswood, Ontario, on the Six Nations Reserve, where her father Henry Martin Johnson (Onwanonsyshon) had built a colonial mansion (which is now a Canadian historic site of national importance). Chiefswood was a house where many cultures intersected. Johnson's great-grandfather, Jacob Tekahionwake, had served with the Six Nations Loyalists in the American Revolution and had returned to Canada to live on the reserve set aside for them; it was from her great-grandfather that Johnson would take her indigenous name, and through knowledge of this hereditary line, especially hearing the stories of her grandfather John Smoke Johnson, a veteran of the War of 1812, her understanding of Mohawk history and culture. Johnson's mother, Emily S. Howells, brought her English culture to bear upon the children's upbringing; while she upheld indigenous values, she also instilled a love of European literature and music, knowledge of which Johnson later called a "mixed blessing" (Strong-Boag and Gerson 21). Johnson began writing while she was still at college, where she developed her talent for poetry, eventually publishing (sometimes anonymously) in magazines such as *Gems of Poetry*, *The Week*, the *Musical Journal*, and *Saturday Night*. But it was performing her poetry that caught the attention of the Canadian public and the critics, and one event established her reputation: the "Evening with Canadian Authors" which author Frank Yeigh (1861–1935) had organized for the Young Men's Liberal Club, Toronto, for 16 January 1892. Johnson followed the far more famous authors William Wilfred Campbell, William Douw Lighthall, Agnes Maule Machar, and Duncan Campbell Scott; as the unknown contributor to the event, it is ironic that Johnson's performance of her poem "A Cry from an Indian Wife" should have received the only encore of the evening, especially as this poem is essentially critical of the history of the cultural elite who were in attendance: "Curse to the fate that brought them from the East / To be our chiefs – / […] / Still their new rule and council is well meant. / They but forget we Indians owned the land / From ocean to ocean; that they stand / Upon a soil that centuries agone / Was our sole kingdom … " Perhaps the most striking line said in this poem, by the Métis wife of the soldier off to fight, is "Still their new rule and council is well meant": it jars now with postcolonial sentiment, yet it may have been an ameliorating statement for Johnson's White audience, enabling them to treat the poem as having historical interest, not immediacy. In other words, the fact that the speaker in this poem asserts that all colonization has brought indigenous peoples is "but war and graves" can be bracketed, or turned into a part of the aesthetic event, or, regarded as belonging to the recent history of the Northwest Rebellion of 1885.

Frank Yeigh helped Johnson capitalize upon this performance, by organizing a series of speaking engagements subsequent to her well-received evening; Johnson would not only cross the country for the next fifteen years, but she would also perform in America and England, her celebrity status and powerful writing fueling public interest. Yet this is only part of Johnson's story, since it was in November 1892 that she modified her performance by appearing on

The Northwest Rebellion of 1885 had its roots in the dissatisfaction of the sale of Rupert's Land by the Hudson's Bay Company to the Canadian government in 1869; at the settlement of Red River, Métis and other local peoples attempted to negotiate better terms and conditions under the leadership of Métis Louis Riel (1844–85), who executed one of his opponents – a Canadian called Thomas Scott – before escaping to the US. Riel was invited to return to Canada in 1884, to negotiate with the government concerning settlement over the loss of Métis land along the North Saskatchewan River; Riel eventually led a rebellion which culminated in a battle at Batoche, where he had his headquarters. Sentenced to death in 1885 by the victorious government, Riel became a symbol of French Canadian "minority rights unjustly trampled by an unfeeling majority" (Bothwell, 229) and indeed historians of Quebec see the execution of Riel as one in a string of "linguistic and ethnic crises" that "made clear Quebec's vulnerability in the federation" (Dickinson and Young, 249). Riel is an important figure in the history of indigenous resistance to colonial rule.

stage in indigenous dress for the "Indian" readings, changing back into a dinner gown for her White poems. Her costume was hybrid in form, consisting of a mixture of different indigenous costumes, including a buckskin dress, leggings, and moccasins, a hunting knife and Huron scalp, a woolen cloak, rabbit pelt shawl and a bear claw necklace acquired from Ernest Thompson Seton. For her contemporary audiences, this costume appeared authentic, genuinely "Indian"; in reality, it was derived from a drawing of a native character called Minnehaha from Longfellow's *Hiawatha*. So Johnson's double persona was given illustration, and then clothed, via stereotypical White notions of indigeneity, even though some of the costume's components were authentic. As Strong-Boag and Gerson perceptively suggest: "Whatever Johnson thought of the complexities of her personal situation as a Mixed-race woman, she knew how to play to settler audiences' expectations of stage Indians by adorning herself with an eclectic combination of tokens of nature that connote the noble savage, and Indigenous cultural artefacts that suggest the primitive warrior" (111).

Conclusion

- Edward Hartley Dewart's anthology *Selections from Canadian Poets* was an important text for Canadian canon formation; Dewart's essay on Canadian literature also raises some important questions concerning people and place, aesthetics and idealism, and the need for an educated audience.
- The Confederation Poets and the Canada First movement share a sense of national pride and spirit, expressed in poetry and prose.

Gaining an international readership, the Confederation Poets both drew upon and modified European Romantic and Victorian writing conventions, within a specifically Canadian landscape, seen especially in two of the most famous poems of the period, G.D. Roberts's *The Tantramar Revisited* and Bliss Carmen's *Low Tide on Grand Pré*.

- The role of gender and race in the Confederation period is seen in the writings of Isabella Valancy Crawford and Pauline Johnson (Tekahionwake). Johnson's poetry readings or performances, whereby she drew upon her indigenous and White backgrounds, continue to inform critics concerning hybrid ethnic identities.

3   A new nation

Prose fiction and the rise of the Canadian novel during the eighteenth and nineteenth centuries

Overview

The Canadian novel develops a New World sensibility that is constituted by a double discourse – often looking through the lens of the Old World, yet at the same time seeing, and articulating, something new. While European genres, modes and aesthetic conventions are utilized by the early Canadian novelists, they are also experimented with, and in diverse ways are subverted by new narrational and rhetorical devices. Examples include the re-working of the eighteenth-century concept of "sensibility" in the first Canadian novel – Frances Brooke's *The History of Emily Montague* (1769) – and the development of a Canadian gothic in numerous early texts. There is also a historical dimension that occurs early on in the rise of the Canadian novel, one which is an abreaction (or cathartic emotional release) to the shocking conclusion to the Seven Years' War, which was the transfer of French Canada to the British. French strategy during the war had been superb, with psychological operations designed not just for military success, but to scare off British colonists (Simms, 388). Native and French peoples worked in co-operation, with the former becoming "so militarily sophisticated that they could take on larger formations of militia, and even regulars, and defeat them" (Simms, 388–89). Four key early Canadian novels, which are historically situated in the extended period of conflict between England and France, are: Brooke's *The History of Emily Montague*; Major John Richardson's *Wacousta* (1832); Rosanna Leprohon's *Antoinette De Mirecourt; or, Secret Marrying and Secret Sorrowing* (1864); and William Kirby's *Le Chien d'Or (The Golden Dog): A Legend of Québec* (1877). Each of these novels comment, indirectly or directly, on the impact of the transfer of power and possessions to the British, or the battles and intrigues that led to this political outcome.

Double discourse and New World sensibility

As noted in Chapter 1, the transfer of French Canada to the British was part of a larger negotiated settlement between European nation states. In England, the public had clamoured for what would now be called the "ethnic cleansing" of New France: the forced removal of all of the French-speaking inhabitants, as had happened with the deportation of the Acadian population in 1755. This did not occur since, from a diplomatic viewpoint, such a harsh penalty would simply have sustained, if not encouraged, future hostilities: "British statesmen were prepared to show restraint in the peace negotiations with France, and resist pressure from a public sphere whose appetite had been whetted by the victories of 1759. The *Monitor*, the *Evening Post* and many pamphleteers expected the complete ejection of the French from Canada at the very least. In contrast, the government was even prepared to be flexible on the future of Canada; they did not think in terms of total annexation. To do so seemed to them a recipe for perpetual war" (Simms, 459). Politically, the Seven Years' War had extended European hegemony not just as a top-down form of power, but as a far more sophisticated power network that interconnected Old and New worlds. Simms makes the point that "whether they liked it or not, the Indian tribes had become an integral part of the European state system" (432). As effective military actors on the ground, there needed to be more than a stereotypical knowledge of indigenous peoples; thus they were under intense scrutiny, if not surveillance, as part of the power-knowledge networks of French and English Canada.

The first Canadian novel models the discursive surveillance reports on Canada which was perceived as an economic, social and political space in need of a cultural shift to impose British hegemony. Born 24 January 1724, in Claypoole, Lincolnshire, Frances Moore, as she was then called, grew up mainly in Peterborough, where her family moved after the death of her father. Coming into her inheritance of £1,000, Frances moved a few years later to London (in 1748), where she rapidly became part of the literary and theatrical scene, also following in the family tradition by marrying a clergyman, the Reverend John Brooke, in 1756. Before she had married, Brooke had been busy writing poetry, drama and journalism. She had written a play called *Virginia*, and she edited and wrote much of a weekly periodical called *The Old Maid*, published in 1755 and 1756, modelled partly upon Eliza Haywood's (c.1693–1756) *Female Spectator*. Brooke edited *The Old Maid* under a pseudonym, "Mary Singleton, Spinster". As Lorraine McMullen suggests: "In Mary Singleton, Mrs. Brooke had taken on the role of a single woman of independent mind, and very early, in the second issue, while asserting her right to speak on any topic, as she saw fit, established her mandate to speak for and of her own sex" (17). From the beginnings of her literary success, Brooke wrote with a strong feminist voice, however framed and fragmented by the multiple perspectives of the periodical format. For example, she favoured romantic choice over arranged marriages, or love rather than expediency, and she often wrote about the importance of education, for young women (Ibid.). Brooke knew the leading thinkers and artists of the day, including Samuel Johnson (1709–84), David Garrick (1717–79), the actors James Quin (1693–1766) and Margaret "Peg" Woffington (1714?–60), as well as some of novelist Samuel Richardson's (1689–1761) circle, in particular

Thomas Edwards (1699–1757) and John Duncombe (1729–86). Brooke would later become friends with novelist Frances Burney (1752–1840). Brooke's journey to the novel form took place via her translation of one of the most popular French epistolary novels of sensibility, Madame Riccoboni's (1714–92) *Letters from Juliette Catesby, to her friend, Lady Henrietta Campley* (1760); this provided Brooke with the model for her own highly successful epistolary novel, *The History of Lady Julia Mandeville*, published in 1763. During this period, Brooke's husband John had been away working, without pay, as a chaplain in America with the British army. From 1757 until his official appointment as the Quebec garrison chaplain in 1761, John's ministry to the Gospel took precedence in his life. Even with a newly acquired salary, the Brookes waited until the settlement of the Treaty of Paris in 1763, when Canada was formally ceded to Britain, before Frances travelled to Canada to be once more with her husband. She would live there for five years, with one visit back to England in this period, and it is during this time that she wrote *The History of Emily Montague*. Upon her return to England, Brooke had twenty highly productive years, with two more translations, a tragedy, two comic operas, and two novels to her name. Her comic opera *Rosina* (1783) was immensely popular, as were her translations. Her last novel, *The History of Charles Mandeville*, was published in 1790, one year after her death.

Starting with letter 72 in *The History of Emily Montague* (1995), Frances Brooke's character Sir William Fermor notes that "The French, in the first settling this colony, seem to have had an eye only to the conquest of ours: their whole system of policy seems to have been military, not commercial; or only so far commercial as was necessary to supply the wants, and by so doing gain the friendship, of the savages, in order to make use of them against us" (letter 72, 141). This accusation against the French could just as easily be applied to the British, since for them the colonies were "a source of wealth, raw materials and manpower to support Britain's European interests" (Simms, 449). For Sir William Fermor, this militarization of the entire colony extends to the ways in which the land is used: "The lands are held on military tenure: every peasant is a soldier, every seigneur an officer, and both serve without pay whenever called upon" (1995, letter 72, 141). Sir William compares the "peasants" with indigenous peoples, saying that "they love war, and hate labor; are brave, hardy, alert in the field, but lazy and inactive at home; in which they resemble the savages, whose manners they seem strongly to have imbibed" (Ibid., letter 72, 141). Behind this bleak assessment lies the notion that the British rule should implement a more efficient economic system, as well as the acknowledgement that the British might have won the war, but they had not yet won the peace.

Sir William is not the only character in the novel who criticizes the French; as early as letter five, the male character of feeling or sensibility – Ed Rivers – performs a critique of the Roman Catholic nunneries: "I cannot help being fir'd [sic] with a degree of zeal against an institution equally incompatible with public good, and private happiness; an institution which cruelly devotes beauty and innocence to slavery, regret, and wretchedness; to a more irksome imprisonment than the severest laws inflict on the worst of criminals" (Ibid., letter 5, 19). Yet *The History of Emily Montague* does not simply provide the stereotypical English view of the French colonies and indigenous peoples; Brooke's choice of the epistolary form – the novel is written as a series of letters – is crucial, because it provides multiple narrational perspectives that exceed and at times transgress solely Eurocentric perspectives. Surveillance, in other words, is shown in this novel to be partial and faulty. Even the "burden" placed on characters who are reporting back to England is intolerable, as Ed Rivers writes: "[Y]ou really, Lucy, ask me such a million of questions, 'tis impossible to know which to answer first; the country, the convents, the balls, the ladies, the beaux – 'tis a history, not a letter, you demand, and it will take twelvemonth to satisfy your curiosity" (Ibid., letter 2, 9). To comprehend the power-knowledge surveillance and reporting in this novel requires the reader to situate Sir William Fermor and Ed Rivers in the discourse of "sensibility" as articulated most powerfully by the novel's coquette figure, Arabella Fermor, daughter of Sir William. In recognizing this articulation, Brooke's novel can be re-read more theoretically via a Kristevan understanding of "sensibility" and the abject.

Strategic sensibility in eighteenth-century female writing

The deployment of an "interregnum" in patriarchal power that Brooke employs, creating an extended period of female power in *The History of Emily Montague*, is also related to the dynamic space of the abject within the novel, and furthermore, we can see that the novel is in itself abjected within the history of Canadian literature. The abject, Kristeva suggests, is that which must be expulsed to maintain subjectivity, but it is also that which in the act of expulsion helps to – ambiguously – constitute subjectivity. A useful definition of abjection can be found in Kristeva's *Powers of Horror*, where she argues that "We may call it a border; abjection is above all ambiguity. Because, while releasing a hold, it does not radically cut off the subject from what threatens it – on the contrary, abjection acknowledges it to be in perpetual danger. But also because abjection itself is a composite of judgment and affect of condemnation and yearning, of signs and drives" (9–10).

Critics have noted that in the eighteenth century, "unlike 'mere' sentimentality, sensibility was the union of judgment with a conscious openness to feelings" (Backscheider and Cotton, xxiii). This nuanced definition goes beyond the stereotypical notion of sensibility as being merely a heightened sensitivity or state of feeling which leads to a moral aesthetic devoid of political action; rather, sensibility, from a feminist and psychoanalytical perspective, shares the space of abjection, precisely as Kristeva defines it as "a composite of judgment and affect" (Kristeva, 10). MacCarthy, in *The Female Pen*, is scornful of sensibility because she argues that it does not allow for a realistic political analysis. This appears reasonable at one level, but then it becomes troubling, because it

implies that there is a real world that eighteenth-century female novelists fail
to portray accurately from their perspective of sensibility. The opposite is the
case: the creation of an abject discourse – one which disturbs, unsettles, is an
interregnum in male power – is already a political manoeuvre.

Sensibility, in *The History of Emily Montague*, is also that which escapes
from the economy of mimetic desire (which means desiring what other people
desire); as the character Ed Rivers writes – bearing in mind that in a gender
reversal this male character is feminized by his own expressions of "sensibility":
"What a charm ... is there in sensibility! 'Tis the magnet which attracts all to
itself: virtue may command esteem, understanding and talents admiration,
beauty a transient desire, but 'tis sensibility alone which can inspire love"
(1769, XII, 83). Rivers rejects mimetic desire as being a kind of living death;
he calls it "insensibility" (Ibid., XII, 84), something that raises a human being
just a little above his or her "natural vegetative state" (Ibid., XII, 83).
"Insensibility" may appear to relate to others – via the mechanism of mimetic
desire – but in reality it is shallow and selfish mirroring behaviour; thus as
Rivers says of Melmouth: "He admires Emily [Montague] because he has
seen her admired by all the world ... " (Ibid., XVII, 106). The concept of
sensibility being re-coded is in fact a "New World sensibility", one which is at
odds with the apparent endorsement of British cultural and political superiority in the novel. *The History of Emily Montague* is thus written with a
double discourse, whereby the New World sensibility subtly critiques and
undermines Old World Superiority. In this way, *The History of Emily Montague* is in no way a "dead end" within the history of Canadian literature as
W.J. Keith asserts, because its double discourse is not only feminist, but also
deeply subversive of Old World, colonialist values. Undoubtedly there is an
Old World framework with which the novel opens and closes, suggesting that
Canada is an Edenic, "unreal interlude" or liminal space. But, acknowledging
the double discourse at work in the novel, this "unreal interlude" becomes
very real indeed – and the reality of Canadian difference is what the European
sensibility ultimately recoils from. Here the sublime is not a Eurocentric
projection, but a Eurocentric *analogy*, for that recoil or inability of the Old
World sensibility encountering the Canadian abject.

Who then controls, within the novel, the creation of this New World sensibility?
Feminist critics have noted the importance of the coquette in this domain,
as well as the gender reversal that occurs with the eighteenth-century "man
of feeling" or sensibility, such as the character of Ed Rivers. Rogers notes
that "Sentiment in *Emily Montague* appears sometimes as an excessive regard
for emotional susceptibility, but also as a simple respect for subtle but
important feelings – a respect which was particularly valuable to women
because in the real world their feelings were habitually overruled in favour
of order or family convenience" (161). The coquette controls – or at the
least comments on and attempts to sway – this "respect" via the interregnum
of male power, brought about by the period of courtship. As critics
have noted, the coquette "extends" or tries "to extend the time of her

The coquette is a term from the eighteenth and nineteenth centuries, meaning a flirtatious, sexually provocative woman who nonetheless retains her chastity; the coquette is often a woman of great wit and linguistic skill, who transgresses gender boundaries, occupying a liminal space which is one that is neither totally confined to domesticity nor completely open to the world of action and politics. The coquette has become a character type of great interest to feminist critics because she cannot be entirely pinned down by the patriarchal sexual politics of the day, yet she also works subversively with, rather than entirely against, oppressive social and political structures.

power and postpone or avoid her subjection" to patriarchy (Spencer, quoted in Sellwood, 68).

The double image: the coquette and resemblance

The coquette in *The History of Emily Montague* is called Arabella Fermor, and she comments on the interregnum in male power in letter 31: "I congratulate you, my dear; you will at least have six months longer your own mistress; which, in my opinion, when one is not violently in love, is a consideration worth attending to." Arabella's advice to Emily Montague is straightforward: create the boundaries of the interregnum: "Send him [her fiancé] up to his regiment at Montreal with the Melmoths, stay the winter with me, flirt with somebody else to try the strength of your passion ... " (1995, 156–57; 157). Of course Brooke does not endorse the values of the coquette, rather, she frames – or brackets – the coquette's focalization via the literary device of the "double image" which McMullen calls "an adroit manipulation of opposing yet complementary women characters, which provides the author with the opportunity both to endorse and to question the values of her age" (quoted in Sellwood, 66). The coquette creates a space in the novel which Brooke as a public literary persona is distanced from, just as her pseudonymous voice as "Mary Singleton" gave her a prior distancing in her journal publication *The Old Maid*. Yet it would be a mistake to regard this distance – and the double image – as a straightforward alternative subjectivity, because within the strictures of a patriarchal society, these positions are also abject: in-between, neither inside nor outside of patriarchy.

This abjected subjectivity can be examined more closely, using the example of "resemblance". In a number of uncanny comments, various characters in the novel note the importance of resemblance, especially in matters of love. For example, Emily Montague suggests that her old rival, Madame Des Roches, resembles her lover Ed Rivers: " ... do you know I think she has some resemblance of you? There is something in her smile, which gives me an idea of you" (1769, CXXV, 53). Bizarrely, Emily already resembles Ed, as he theorizes later in the novel. Emily herself comments, indirectly, on her resemblance to Ed, by saying that if she could not be herself, she would be the woman who already resembles him: " ... the delight of loving you appears to me so superior to all other pleasures, that, of all human beings, if I was not Emily Montague, I would be Madame Des Roches" (Ibid., CXXV, 55). Critics have noted and worked with the notion of resemblance in the novel of sensibility, but in *The History of Emily Montague*, it is even more intense. Arch notes that "This insistence on resemblance is a deep and disturbing aspect of the novel, edging insidiously toward the 'resemblance' of incest at numerous points" (474). Arch also theorizes the epistolary novel as being " ... the means to bridge ... difference, to open up the soul to its mirror image ... " (476). Characters are, or become, uncanny doubles of one another. Doubles are commonly thought of as harbingers of death, and revealers of one's core narcissism. The doubles in this novel are also incestuously bound to one another, occupying ambiguous gender roles and positions. Incestuous characters "stand on a fragile threshold" (84), as Kristeva says; they are "stranded on account of an impossible demarcation" (85). These abjected, incestuous doubles are stranded at the edge of Empire – yet are also at the "centre" or "home" of Empire, from which the uncanny emerges. The desire for similitude is a narcissistic and political projection on the Other – in this case the French Canadian, whose land was a spoil of war for the British. Kristeva, writing about the most famous of incestuous characters, Oedipus, notes that with the shift to *Oedipus at Colonus*, and the concomitant contextual shift into "democracy", "A bridge has been built toward another logic of abjection" (88). Thus, she argues that "it is no longer defilement to be excluded ritually as the Other facet of the sacred ... but *transgression* due to a *misreading* of the law" (88). This other logic of abjection is actually the one that is at work with the incestuous doubles in *The History of Emily Montague*; the "misreading" of the law is also projected via the double discourse: first, the suspension or interregnum of the law of the Father is a "misreading" of the patriarchal notion of the courtship period, a notion parodied with the character of Melmoth, who is clearly in love with himself, which is in itself an ironic charge, since true love in this novel involves one's double; for Melmoth, even a relationship with one's double would feel like a crowd. The second "misreading" of the law, however, is more complex – and it involves subverting the colonialist discourse of Sir William Fermor, who we have seen sends back to England reports on the Canadian economy, culture, and political situation. Such reports are undercut by the New World sensibility within the novel. For example, Sir William Fermor's report on the Jesuits has been preceded by the imaginative fantasies of the New World sensibility. Sir William starts his letter in the following way: "It is very true, my Lord, that the Jesuit missionaries still continue in the Indian villages in Canada; and I am also afraid it is no less true, that they use every art to instil into those people an aversion to the English; at least I have been told this by the Indians themselves, who seem equally surprised and piqued that we do not send missionaries among them" (1769, CL, 104 (Bk III)).

The "re-structuring" of power in French and British Canada

The "misreading" of the law of colonialism occurs in the Edenic dream or fantasy that Arabella has: "In short, we should have been continually endeavouring, following the luxuriancy of female imagination, to render more charming the sweet abodes of love and friendship; while our heroes, changing their swords into plough-shares, and engaged in more substantial, more profitable labors, were clearing land, raising cattle and corn, and doing every thing becoming good farmers ... " (1769, CXLIX, 102 (Bk III)). The citation of the most well-known phrase from Isaiah 2:4 in this passage – "changing their swords into plough-shares" – carries with it the intertextual weight of the entire verse, completed by "nation shall not lift up sword against nation, neither shall they learn war any more" (King James Version). In other words, the Realpolitik of Sir William Fermor's agonistic reports on Canada are countered not merely by an idealistic sensibility, but one which carries the ethical weight of Biblical law. Furthermore, this citation of Isaiah deepens the reader's conception of the "Edenic" imagery of the New World, since Brooke is, in effect, and within the context of the time, misreading the law of colonial rule by interposing a law with greater authority. The double discourse of *The History of Emily Montague* thus creates an uncomfortable tension between the "master" discourse and that which is abjected. Arabella's greater or even transcendent moral authority must be expulsed, banished, since her coquettish discourse, to use Kristeva's terms, " ... lies outside, beyond the set, and does not seem to agree to ... [the] rules of the game. And yet, from its place of banishment, the abject does not cease challenging its master" (2). Kristeva sees the abject as accompanying "re-structurings" (17) of moral authority, even more so the "collapse" (17) of such authority. In *The History of Emily Montague*, such a re-structuring, as noted, occurs with the shift in power from the French to the British with the settlement of the Seven Years' War, and the analogous shift from Catholicism to Protestant rule; there is also the desire for a linguistic shift, as the British attempt to impose a cultural hegemony. But the "re-structuring" is also apparent in the gender shifts of the novel, especially expressed via the biting, funny comments made throughout by Arabella Fermor, who writes, contra the conduct books of the day, of how she stage-manages her affairs, and enjoys directing her desires. For example, when she recounts walking with her future husband: "I remember one day in summer we were walking tête à tête in the road to Cape Rouge, when he wanted me to strike into a very beautiful thicket: 'Positively, Rivers,' said I, 'I will not venture with you into that wood.' 'Are you afraid of *me*, Bell?' 'No, but extremely of myself'" (1769, L, 222 (Vol I)). As with the uncanny doubling in the novel, where, as Ellen Pollack notes, "the narrative of incest and its prohibition" generates "a discursive matrix within which 'truths' about culture, gender, and desire are produced" (5), so the re-structuring of gender in the abjected spaces of *The History of Emily Montague* creates a domain in which identity is constantly de-stabilized and re-configured.

New world aesthetics: Major John Richardson's *Wacousta* (1832)

Major John Richardson's account of garrison life in Canada during the Seven Years' War uses the literary modes of the gothic and the picturesque to create a complex and uncanny portrait of colonial rule and misrule. Richardson, who was born in Queenston, Upper Canada (Ontario), joined the 41st Regiment of the British army in 1812, at the age of fifteen; he fought with General Brock, and was eventually taken prisoner by the American forces, and was released in 1814, whereupon he travelled to England. The earliest work attributed to Richardson is *Tecumseh; or, The Warrior of The West* (1828); he also published *Ecarté; or, The Salons of Paris* (1829), and *Franscati's; or, Scenes in Paris* (1830), before writing his best-selling *Wacousta; or, The Prophecy* (1832), and its sequel, *The Canadian Brothers; or, The Prophecy Fulfilled* (1840).

Opening with a geographical description of Canada, the second chapter of *Wacousta* bursts into life with a gothic intensity as a stranger mysteriously penetrates the supposedly protected garrison of Detroit. Military discipline being circumvented so easily suggests an otherworldly power at work: " ... the appearance of a stranger within its walls at the still hour of midnight could not fail to be regarded as an extraordinary event" (27). More disturbing still is the impact this stranger has on the most senior military man – the Governor – who issues from his inner sanctum in a state of shock: "His countenance was pale; and his features, violently agitated, betrayed a source of alarm which those who were familiar with his unusual haughtiness of manner were ill able to comprehend" (27–28). Stirred like a hornet's nest, the responding frenzied activity within the garrison is described via self-reflective narrative comments concerning artistic representation, as "picturesque": "this picturesque moment" (29) and "The scene, though circumscribed in limit, was picturesque in effect, and might have been happily illustrated by the pencil of the painter" (40). Casting his eye in more detail on the characters present, the narrator again calls the scene picturesque: " ... a blazing torch, reflecting with picturesque yet gloomy effect the bright bayonets and equipment of the soldiers and the anxious countenances of the women and invalids" (41). Linking the breakdown of military order and technologies of surveillance with comments on the aesthetic qualities of the scene may appear bizarre, yet this also foregrounds the self-awareness throughout the novel, that Canada's recent history is conducive to literary and artistic representation. *Wacousta*, then, suggests that a reconsideration of Canadian topics and landscapes worthy of artistic representation needs to be undertaken; folding such aesthetic self-awareness into the novel itself confirms that the picturesque is a "pause of our judgment" (Raimond and Watson, 214), and that furthermore, a new notion of aesthetics should follow. That is not to say that the picturesque scenes of military pro-wess and violence are devoid of the emotion of novels of sensibility: the opposite is the case, since *Wacousta* explores "sensibility" with the figure of "the man of feeling".

The "man of feeling" and psychological space

Often represented by the single tear coursing silently down his face, the "man of feeling" occupies a liminal gender space: his masculinity is intertwined with the heightened *receptivity* of his sensibility. In *Wacousta*, the character of Charles de Haldimar "even shed tears" (45), while with Halloway – the doomed soldier – we are told that "a tear was distinctly seen by many coursing down his manly cheek" (46). Halloway, who is shot for disobeying orders, has generated feelings in other men, visible in "the large tears coursing each other over the furrowed cheeks of some of our oldest soldiers" (214). Such men symbolically occupy the positions of the typical female protagonist of the early novel, and thus there is a shift or transposition in gender performance and roles, but while the military men enforcing Britain's colonial claims are feminized, indigenous people are made abject. As Clara de Haldimar says to her cousin Madeline: "I feel that I could not so far overcome my disgust as to sit at the table with them [indigenous peoples] ... since the war, I have witnessed and heard so much of their horrible deeds, that I shall never be able to endure the sight of an Indian face again" (299).

Critics have long noted the portrayal of complex psychological states in *Wacousta*, with Hurley suggesting that the many borders in Richardson's novel represent not just topographical but also "mental" spaces (29), and Moss arguing that the frontier in *Wacousta* is "a state of mind" (quoted in Hurley, 29). Justin Edwards notes that Wacousta's masterminding of Pontiac's military psych-ops campaign against the garrison "borders on madness. The text revolves around a series of deceptions and terrifying scenes in which motive is ambiguous and the boundary between order and anarchy is unclear" (2). This psychological drama being played out in the novel, however, might be as much about forgetting as anything else, where the interfamilial revenge conflict must be replaced with the unity of the domestic sphere (the feminized man of feeling), upon which Canada can be stabilized and built. Coleman sees this at work in Richardson's follow-up to *Wacousta*, his novel *The Canadian Brothers* (1840), which has at its heart the "allegory of frater-nity" whereby bonds of brotherhood "represent the unity of the nation" (Coleman 2001, 132). What needs to be forgotten here is the fratricide that preceded the fraternity: "Thus, loyalist literature reminds its readers of what they must eventually forget: the fratricidal disturbance that explains the nation's origin and forms the central action of plot in these narratives must be 'forgotten' or sublimated as we turn our attention ... to the domestic romance of the nation's future" (Ibid., 133).

The two cultures of Rosanna Leprohon's *Antoinette De Mirecourt* (1864)

If in *Wacousta* it is the body itself which is dismembered, in gory scenes of interracial and fratricidal conflict and terror which symbolize the psychological trauma that needs to be sublimated, in Rosanna Leprohon's *Antoinette De Mirecourt* it is literally the territory of French Canada that undergoes postwar dismemberment. As the narrator writes: "The islands of Anticosti and Magdalen, as well as the greater part of Labrador were annexed to the government of Newfoundland; the islands of St. John and Cape Breton were joined to Nova Scotia; and finally New Brunswick was detached, and endowed with a separate government and the name it bears today" (36). Born in Montreal, Leprohon was a prolific poet and short-story writer, publishing in the *Literary Garland* under her maiden name, Rosanna Mullins; her first novel, *Ida Beresford* (1848), was translated into French and serialized in *L'Ordre* (1859–60). Leprohon's *The Manor House of Villerai: A Tale of Canada Under The French Dominion* was serialized in *The Family Herald* (1859–60), and translated into French in 1861; *Armand Durand; or, A Promise Fulfilled* was serialized in the Montreal *Daily News*, and published in book form in 1868 (English edition) and 1869 (French trans.). Leprohon's popularity in French Canada reveals the importance of translation in bridging Anglophone and Francophone cultures. Additionally, her early successes in the *Literary Garland* (which was established in Montreal in 1838, and ran until 1851) are indicative of the importance for women writers of this journal that also paid its contributors. Literary periodicals provided a publishing outlet and a measure of financial independence for authors; examples from across Canada include the *Amaranth* (1841–43) and *Stewart's Literary Quarterly* (1867–72), published in Saint John, New Brunswick; the *Provincial; or, Halifax Monthly Magazine* (1852–53); the *Anglo-American Magazine* (1852–55), published in Toronto; and the *New Dominion Monthly* (1867–79), published in Montreal (see Cambron and Gerson, 127).

That the idea of Canada exists in an in-between or liminal space of abjection is given symbolic form in *Antoinette De Mirecourt* by a "secret" or incomplete marriage between the French Canadian Antoinette De Mirecourt and the rakish British officer Major Sternfield. While Antoinette undertakes the Protestant form of marriage, she does not regard the process as "ratified" until she has had the relationship publicly announced with a Roman Catholic wedding. Once again, a female protagonist is positioned in an interregnum in relation to the strictures of patriarchy: she appears to be courting and thus she is publicly – if temporarily – free of patriarchal power. In the terror of this romance gone wrong, the suspension of certainties are both negative and productive: the interregnum in this novel is a culturally interpenetrated "chora", a secret space which is neither inside nor outside either culture (see Glossary).

With *Antoinette De Mirecourt* chora is also a "legal" space – sanctified but not completed, because only both cultures, at least in the novel in question, can make it whole. In other words, the conjoining of the two cultures needs to be made public to progress from the uncertainties of the liminal space. Clearly, the plot and the characters therein thus carry a symbolic charge which far exceeds the "action"; for example, the repetition of marriage, which will lead to ratification, symbolizes a desire to repeat the settlement of the Seven Years' War in "Canadian" terms, to the satisfaction, that is, of both dominant European cultures. Such cultural and political claims are what contemporary philosopher Jean-François Lyotard calls a "*differend*": a legal situation where each side has an equally valid claim. Any judgment that favours one side will inevitably hurt the other, and so it is with the loss of justice, from a French Canadian perspective, brought about by the imposition by the British of "that most insupportable of all tyrannies, martial law" (34). As the narrator continues: "Despite the terms of the capitulation, which had expressly guaranteed to Canadians the same rights as those accorded to British subjects, the former, who had confidently counted on the peaceful protection of a legal government, were doomed instead to see their tribunal abolished, their judges ignored, and their entire social system overthrown" (34). The suspension or loss of justice means that each situation is a *differend*; even the novel's rake, Major Sternfield, both abuses and is disempowered by this state of affairs.

If one factor can override the *differend* it is the state of "resemblance": identification with the Other is a compelling force. Early on in *Antoinette De Mirecourt*, a lineage narrative tells the story of Antoinette's father, Arthur De Mirecourt, who discovers that an orphaned young woman, Corinne Delorme, distantly related, has fallen in love with him. At first, the love is hidden, and his love for her is "brotherly"; she is "a dear sister" (20) and his "kind little sister" (23). But then Arthur accidentally discovers her true feelings: "Suddenly, through the half open door, his eye fell on a mirror suspended opposite him, on the wall of the library; and clearly reflected in that mirror, was the figure of Corinne Delorme seated on a low stool, apparently in the utter abandonment of grief, her face bowed over some object which she held tightly clasped in her slender fingers, and on which she was showering impassioned kisses. That object was his own miniature, a gift which he had brought his mother from France" (24). This mirror scene triggers Arthur's "mirror stage", in that he passes from being a beau to being a husband (from passion to patriarch). It is Corinne in the mirror's reflection, but more importantly, the image which she is worshipping, and which is also reflected back to Arthur, is a small portrait – the "miniature" – of himself. What is Arthur seeing here? Corinne appears to be holding Arthur's image as if it were a religious or sacred icon; such chaste love reflects the sibling terminology, not just of these two characters, but as an important facet of eighteenth-century novels: " ... as Gerard Barker has pointed out, lovers in eighteenth-century novels often have 'a pseudo-sibling relationship that conveniently sublimates the sexual realities of courtship.' [...] If a man could play the part of a good brother, it guaranteed that he would be a good husband" (Perry, 146). We also have with this scene the symbolic foregrounding of the importance of familial relations (even though with the subsequent marriage, such relations appear to be incestuous), one which will be re-created in Antoinette's later successful marriage of French and English Canada (the Other turns out to have been more closely related than was first thought – that is, the Other can be domesticated and incorporated into the same). The incest theme, so predominant in eighteenth-century literature, emerges at a time when notions of familial connections, rights and responsibilities were undergoing change. In the gothic genre, incest represents "a kind of experiment with the meaning of blood relations, a test-ing of limits" (Perry, 388), precisely those limits that were perceived to be under threat as indigenous and European nations intermixed.

An allegory of decline: William Kirby's *The Golden Dog* (1877)

The *historical* existence of New France is brought to a close in William Kirby's *Le Chien d'Or (The Golden Dog): A Legend of Québec*, a gothic romance which opens on the ramparts of Quebec in 1748. Poet, novelist, newspaper editor, and prolific letter-writer, Kirby was a founding member of the Royal Society of Canada in 1882. Kirby's loyalist beliefs were expressed across a number of genres, although he is best known for his long narrative poem *The U.E.: A Tale of Upper Canada* (1859) and *The Golden Dog*. Klay Dyer notes that "Kirby remains one of the first English-language Canadian writers to recognize the narrative possibilities in the already romanticized history of French Canada. Connecting him with such prominent 19th-century Québec writers as James McPherson Le Moine and Philippe Aubert de Gaspé, such foresight locates Kirby as an important Victorian commentator on the role of the Canadian imagination within a multicultural and bilingual nation" (581).

In the historical time-frame of *The Golden Dog* the French have recently been defeated in a major attempt to regain Louisbourg which had fallen to New England troops; at an intense sea battle off Cape Finisterre, in the Bay of Biscay, the English fleet destroyed that of the French, but peace between England and France soon followed in 1748 with the Treaty of Aix-la-Chapelle, whereby Louisbourg was exchanged for Madras. Eight years of supposed harmony preceded the beginning of the Seven Years' War in 1756; in reality, boundary disputes between Canada and New England continued unabated. *The Golden Dog* suggests that the real threat to New France lies within – indeed a sequence of interior spaces structure the novel, which concerns a double romance, between on the one hand the virtuous, doomed, Amélie de Pentigny and Colonel Philibert, and on the other the murderess Angélique des Meloises who throws over her lover for her desire to marry the Intendant Bigot. In parallel the novel portrays an interior struggle between the commer-cial activities of the peace-loving Bourgeois Philibert, who leads the business association *Les Honnêtes Gens*, and the corrupt Intendant who leads the war-profiteering Grand Company. This gothic fantasy that explores virtue and vice through the foil characters of Amélie/Angélique and Philibert (father and son)/Bigot is complicated by a mysterious woman called Caroline de St. Castin, hiding in a secret chamber at Bigot's palace called Beaumanoir. Angélique does not just see Caroline as a silent rival in her plans to marry Bigot, she also starts seeing her "eidolon" or ghost, whichever way she turns. Caroline is entombed in a gothic chamber or dungeon, one from which she will not escape, as she is eventually murdered: being poisoned and then stabbed. As with *Wacousta* and *Antoinette De Mirecourt*, characters and events carry symbolic weight, creating an allegory of the decline of New France, one which expresses the post-Confederation ideology of Kirby's authorship (Stacey, 101). But why create a narrative with a gothic chora at its heart? How does this affect the allegory of New France's inner turmoil and decline?

As seen above a New World sensibility is explored in the abjected, liminal spaces of gender reversals in the early Canadian novel; with the chora, the threat to the nation is perceived as uncanny. Therefore the interior, homely or domestic shelter is also the site of danger. Perhaps the chora, in a mirroring fashion, is "the fictions that exist at the heart of their national metanarratives" (J.D. Edwards, xix). In other words, "if a nation is imaginary, a precarious fabrication that is built upon questionable cultural narratives, then a nation is also haunted by the spectral figure of its own fabrication" (Ibid.). In wanting the domesticity of marriage with the Intendant, Angélique foregrounds the political nature of that relationship and its potential spatial existence. But the chora undermines this domesticated Eden: it is the uncanny site of murder, of death, that stands behind the public manifestation of a successful polity. The crone commissioned to murder Caroline traverses the entire gothic landscape of forests, towers, stairways, vaults and recesses, before she enters the hidden chamber; the crone figure is often the conveyor of oral history, folk knowledge, and she usually has a cross-cultural identity. Misused folklore is worse than no folklore; so the liminal gothic space becomes a nightmare world which will ultimately destroy all those who come into contact with it. And yet there is worse to come: "Montcalm, after reaping successive harvests of victories, brilliant beyond all precedent in North America, died a sacrifice to the insatiable greed and extravagance of Bigot and his associates, who, while enriching themselves, starved the army and plundered the colony of all its resources. The fall of Quebec and the capitulation of Montreal were less owing to the power of the English than to the corrupt misgovernment of Bigot and Vaudreuil, and the neglect by the Court of France of her ancient and devoted colony" (312–13).

Re-defining domesticity: immigration and gender politics in women's autobiographical settler narratives

The abjected liminal spaces of the early Canadian novel were radically re-conceived in relation to immigration, settlement and domesticity in early women's autobiographical writing. Hagiographical biographies of women were in existence in French-Canada: Father Étienne-Michel Faillon's (1799–1870) hagiographies (the lives of saints) of Madame d'Youville (1852), Margaruerite Bourgeoys (1853), Jeanne Mance (1854) and Jeanne Le Ber (1860; trans. English as *The Christian Heroine of Canada; or Life of Miss Le Ber*, 1861), were highly popular. Abbé Henri-Raymond Casgrain's (1831–1904) historical biography *Histoire de la Mère Marie de l'Incarnation* (1964) interprets personal destiny in terms of theology. Such authorized and canonized biographies tended to reinforce the status quo, which in French Canada meant the authority and power of the church. Autobiography adopts more self-reflexive, fictionalizing writing strategies to shape in meaningful ways a woman's notion of herself, and how she is embedded in, and contributes to the construction of, the surrounding society. In other words, it is not just memory that feeds into autobiographical writing, but also story (Grace, 17). From a more political perspective, this mode of writing opens up a space of writing for otherwise silenced or marginalized authors: "[T]he auto-biographical voice and eye/I are available to minorities and to groups, such as women, who have been excluded from the dominant discourse and whose stories have been dismissed as worthless" (Ibid., 14). Early Canadian auto-biographical texts in English are highly performative, as authors create deliberately entertaining, theatrical accounts of travel narratives, disasters, encounters with Natives and other nationalities and classes, to name just a few. Such a performative genre is conjectural, assembling notions of Canada from partial, fragmentary experiences, which nevertheless are heavily invested in, or are emotionally charged (see Lane 2006a).

Re-defining domestic space in the writing of Catherine Parr Traill

A prime example of the conjectural impulse is Catherine Parr Traill's (1802–99) *The Young Emigrants; or, Pictures of Life in Canada* (1826), which is constructed from letters received from family and friends, rather than from direct experience. Traill, who was born in Kent, England, was one of five sisters in a family that suffered financial hardship with the death in 1818 of their father Thomas Strickland. Writing was to be a source of income that would help the family survive, with her sisters acquiring fame, if not fortune, for their outstanding work, such as Agnes Strickland's *Lives of The Queens of England* (researched and written with her sister Elizabeth, published in twelve volumes, 1840–48), and Susanna Moodie's *Roughing It in the Bush* (published 1852 – see later). Traill's earliest publications reveal her interest in conduct manuals (books that essentially taught young women how to behave in polite society) and personal, moral growth, with texts such as *The Tell Tale: An Original Collection of Moral and Amusing Stories* (1818), *Disobedience; or, Mind What Mama Says* (1819), *Reformation; or, The Cousins* (1819), and *Little Downy; or, The History of a Field Mouse: A Moral Tale* (1822). While conduct manuals would feed into Traill's later Canadian publications, another key interest in her early life was that of natural history, her two most precious possessions being Gilbert White's *The Natural History of Selborne* (1789) and Izaak Walton's *The Compleat Angler* (1653–76). Both texts adopt a hybrid format to dig deeply into different aspects of the natural world, including drawn sketches, observational data, stories, anecdotes, poetry and descriptive prose. Gilbert White, for example, opens his book section on The Antiquities of Selborne by imagining a time when Britain "was inhabited only by bears and wolves" (291). Traill's most enduring book can be seen as emerging from these early experiments combined with the experience of emigrating to Canada with her husband Thomas Traill, whom she married in 1832. *The Backwoods of Canada* (1836) with its descriptive subtitle, *Being Letters From The Wife Of An Emigrant Officer, Illustrative Of The Domestic Economy Of British America*, combines multiple genres: it is an immigrant's/settler's conduct book and manual, a natural history, travel narrative, and autobiography. The book can be divided into four main sections: the journey (letters 1 to 7); the settlement (letters 8 to 12); the naming (letters 13 to 17); and the expectation (letter 18) (Ballstadt). While different genres dominate different sections, such as the travel narrative through which Traill writes about her journey, there is also continual discursive hybridity. James calls these "discordant discourses" and they include "discourses of femininity, domesticity, maternity, colonialism, Christianity and scientific rationalism" (2). While domesticity is certainly a discursive construct, it also serves as a central trope in the redefinition of Canada, especially the notion of what it means to write Canada into existence through prose. Traill's approach is to not just make a series of truth claims about her knowledge of Canada, but to re-claim Canadian space from a female perspective. Traill's definition of domesticity, then, filters all other aspects of Canadian existence and identity, including class, race, morality and religion.

Traill repeatedly draws upon the notion of a tabula rasa, a blank surface, to inhabit the natural world that she sees in the foreground: "As to ghosts or spirits they appear totally banished from Canada. This is too matter-of-fact country for such supernaturals to visit. Here there are no historical associations, no legendary tales of those that came before us" (153). The tabula rasa enables Traill to ignore the fact that indigenous peoples and French Canadians already did have a history concerning Canada prior to Traill's arrival. Yet later on she asserts: "If its volume of history is yet a blank, that of Nature is open, and eloquently marked by the finger of God; and from its pages I can extract a thousand sources of amusement and interest whenever I take my walks in the forest or by the borders of the lakes" (155). And yet for all that this grates with the sensibility of the contemporary postcolonial reader, Traill does something quite unique: she claims Canada as a *domestic* space, one which is *not* separate from the discourses of ethics and rationality – that is, one which does *not* allow the domestic space and its inhabitants (mainly women) to become marginalized. Domestic space is not a separate chora, but is instead configured as a contact zone "between four major cultural groups – upper-middle-class English settlers such as Traill, First Nations people, republican Americans, and, to a lesser extent, lower-class Irish and Scottish emigrants" (James, 8). In other words, domestic space is important in defining and shaping what it means to be Canadian; as Traill puts it in the introduction to her text: "Among the numerous works on Canada that have been published within the last ten years, with emigration for their leading theme, there are few, if any, that give information regarding the domestic economy of a settler's life, sufficiently minute to prove a faithful guide to the person on whose responsibility the whole comfort of a family depends – the mistress, whose department it is 'to haud [hold] the house in order'" (1). The key phrase here is "domestic economy" with its double meaning of a woman's space, and the entire economic space of Canada.

In recoding and reclaiming space, Traill creates a dialectic of hardship/ endurance and progress/joy, with a sliding scale from one to the other pole as her narrative progresses. Hardships include leaving one's family and home, the long and dangerous journey to Canada, involving illness and disorientation (even the poorly cleared road to the Traills' land appears to deposit them in the middle of nowhere), and the struggles of building a cabin and clearing land; progress is made through social strength, especially with the concept of the "bee" (the entire community clears land, or helps frame a house, etc.), moral fortitude, and personal development. Social class, while still existing, necessarily undergoes transformation: "here it is considered by no means derogatory to the wife of an officer or gentleman to assist in the work of the house, or to perform its entire duties, if occasion requires it; to understand the mystery of soap, candle, and sugar-making; to make bread, butter, and cheese, or even to milk her own cows; to knit and spin, and prepare the wool for the loom. In these matters we bush-ladies have a wholesome disregard of what Mr. or Mrs. So-and-so thinks or says" (270–71). Canada becomes a personal and social testing ground which has been gifted by God.

In a visit to a resident clergyman, Traill narrates an entire immigrant narrative in condensed and religious form; this religious family has adopted a plain style of living, with their house decorated in "Yankee" fashion. Instead of a piano dominating the sitting-room a more practical spinning-wheel is placed there, and is under use. The simple, homespun mode of dress of the entire family represents "prudence and comfort" (273). The clergyman interprets his immigrant experience via Christian biblical narrative, remembering his first open air service, with the pulpit being "a pile of rude logs", in a church which was "the deep shade of the forest" (280), his sermon being from Deuteronomy: "For the LORD your God is bringing you into a good land, a land of brooks of water, of fountains and springs, that flow out of valleys and hills; [...] a land in which you will eat bread without scarcity, in which you will lack nothing; a land whose stones *are* iron and out of whose hills you can dig copper" (Deut: 8.7 and 9). This notion of emigration being akin to exodus and arrival in a promised land can only function, however, with the con-comitant notion of Canada's indigenous peoples being a "vanishing race"; as Traill writes: "I believe it is generally considered that their numbers [Canada's

First Peoples] are diminishing, and some tribes have become nearly if not totally extinct in the Canadas. The race is slowly passing away from the face of the earth, or mingling by degrees with the colonists, till, a few centuries hence, even the names of their tribes will scarcely remain to tell that they once existed" (220). As noted earlier, the narrative of the "vanishing race" is key to naturalizing the negative impact of colonialism upon Canada's First Peoples. Yet within Traill's narrative it is a surprising statement to make because in so many other ways she reveals the local Natives to be enterprising, knowledge-able, excellent business and craftsmen and women, as well as having far more successfully managed the local environment compared with the more recent settlers. If this is a "vanishing race" then they are surprisingly vibrant and healthy, and the most Traill can do to negate their presence is to suggest that the Native men are at times childish, an observation that reveals more about her own prejudicial notions of racial difference than anything else.

Sketches from the bush: the writing of Susanna Moodie

It is not surprising that Traill's most famous Canadian work should be compared with that of her sister's – Susanna Moodie's *Roughing It in the Bush, or Life in Canada* (1852) – which, while written some time after the event, narrates her personal experiences as an emigrant and settler. Like her sister, Moodie had also married an officer, Lt. John Wedderburn Dunbar Moodie, leaving Britain just over a year later in 1832 for Canada. Unlike the Traills, the Moodies moved first to a cleared farm near Cobourg, on the fourth concession, Hamilton township, in Upper Canada. Clashing culturally with their neighbours led to a rapid breakdown of relations and a move after merely a year to Douro Township, where they were closer to the Traills, but now in possession of uncleared land. Less temperamentally suited to the life of the bush settler, Moodie narrates a very different story from that of her sister, although in terms of form, she also adopts an aesthetically complex approach, which derives in part from the multiple genres that she was familiar with from an early age, with the publication of her first book, *Sparticus: A Roman Story* (1822). Moodie's poetry was highly successful and well received in Canada, the USA and England, forming a backdrop to *Roughing It in the Bush*. Poetry by Moodie appeared in England in the *Lady's Magazine*, and in the American *Albion* and *Emigrant and Old Countryman*. Her poetry was written about, and published, in the 1834 issue of the *North American Quarterly Magazine*, and she had work commissioned for the *Literary Garland*. Moodie's patriotic poetry, written in response to the rebellion in Upper and Lower Canada in 1837, was particularly popular. But it was another literary form – that of "sketches" – that *Roughing It in the Bush* is built upon.

Lynch notes that the differences between short story and sketch are not always clear, but there is consensus that the sketch is a more personal, anecdotal genre with focus on place, person, or experience (Gerson and Mezei), and that there is often focus "on one subject (a character, a natural event)" (Lynch

2002, 1039). Humorous sketches are the lifeblood of Thomas Chandler Haliburton's (1796–1865) *The Clockmaker, or The Sayings and Doings of Samuel Slick of Slickville* (1837), which was originally published in the *Novascotian* newspaper, and went on to become an international bestseller, even if the series of books that followed did eventually lose impetus and originality. Moodie's main precursor, however, was Mary Russell Mitford's (1787–1855) *Our Village: Sketches of Rural Character and Scenery* (five volumes, 1824–32). Before emigrating, Moodie had produced her own country sketches in *La Belle Assemblée Or Court And Fashionable Magazine* (1827–29), and she continued such work in Canada, publishing her New World sketches in *The Victoria Magazine* and *The Literary Garland*. Lucas argues that these sketches constitute neither "fragments nor haphazardly-ordered fictional interludes" and furthermore, that their conscious chronological re-arrangement in *Roughing It in the Bush* "constitute an integral part of the book's formal and thematic plan" (149). Detailed analysis of the first publication of the sketches, and their place within the version of *Roughing It in the Bush* produced by the Centre for Editing Early Canadian Texts, supports this thesis (see Table 3.1).

Moodie's notion of domesticity is that it is a key site of economic production, although one conceived quite differently from that of her sister's (the intersection of travel, autobiography, moral guidance, didacticism and scientific observation); Moodie's "sketches" approach the domestic chora through the cultural interpenetration that first shocks her, and then provides her with valuable literary material. In other words, the large binary oppositions that structure her work – cultured vs. uncultured; Old World vs. New World; civilized vs. the primitive (Lucas, 149) – are eventually problematized as she acculturates to her new surroundings, even if settling is ultimately a personal failure. Thus the *hypercritical* first half of the book gives way to the even

Table 3.1

Chapters		Magazines	
1	A Visit to Grosse Isle	(6)	Sept. 1847 VM
2	Quebec	(10)	Nov. 1847 VM
4	Tom Wilson's Emigration	(4)	June 1847 LG
5	Our First Settlement{...}	(3)	May 1847 LG
8	Uncle Joe and His Family	(5)	Aug. 1847 LG
11	Brian, the Still-Hunter	(8)	Oct. 1847 LG
21	Dandelion Coffee (pp. 375{-}378)	(7)	Sept. 1847 VM
25	The Whirlwind	(9)	Jan. 1848 VM
26	The Walk to Dummer	(2)	Mar. 1847 LG
28	Adieu to the Woods	(1)	Jan. 1847 LG

The Victoria Magazine = VM
The Literary Garland = LG
Numbers in parenthesis = periodical publication sequence
(Lucas, 154; modified by Lane)

more challenging, but ultimately transformative, creation of a domestic space which is first and foremost protected by Moodie, not her husband, who leaves to join the militia. The transformation has taken Moodie some distance from her first shocking vision of her home: "I gazed upon the place in perfect dismay, for I had never seen such a shed called a house before. 'You must be mistaken; this is not a house, but a cattle-shed, or pig-sty'" (83). The "Yankee driver" she is talking to responds with "You were raised in the old country, I guess; you have much to learn, and more, perhaps, than you'll like to know, before the winter is over" (83). While towards the end of her account Moodie argues that "These government grants of land, to half-pay officers, have induced numbers of this class to emigrate to the backwoods of Canada, who are totally unfit for pioneers" (467), it is the additional, "unwanted" knowledge, that transforms the domestic space into one not just of survival, but achievement and control.

With her husband away as a captain in the militia, many of the Moodies' debts were paid not just by his salary, but by her turn to writing; Moodie, in other words, moves from a situation where she could not write while struggling in the bush, to being the new local head of the household and a writer. Her first payment for writing is described as "the nucleus out of which a future independence from my family might arise" (441). The domestic economy is suddenly booming: with sugar making (and the bartering involved), the production of preserves, and even decorative fungi sold among the officers in the militia. While this also signals the end of her life in the woods, when she does finally leave with her family, to join her husband after his appointment as Sheriff, she now describes the backwoods as "the school of high resolve and energetic action in which we had learned to meet calmly, and successfully to battle with the ills of life" (505).

The rise of the Canadian popular novel and the role of the popular press

From its beginnings, the Canadian novel had a symbiotic relationship with the popular press. In the June 10 1823 issue of the *Upper Canadian Herald*, a prospectus sought subscribers for a new novel written by Julia Catherine Beckwith Hart (1796–1867), called *St. Ursula's Convent*. Of interest is the fact that this prospectus foregrounded the suitability of Canada as the backdrop (alongside the old countries of England and France) for literary, novelistic, production:

> No country presents more interesting subjects for the pen of a Novelist, than Canada. The romantic scenery, the history, and feudal character of the early colonists, their peculiar institutions and customs, the state of society, the habits and manners of the religious orders, the Noblesse and peasantry, derived from their ancestral connexion with France, and their own colonial circumstances, and modified by the introduction of British laws, examples and intercourse, in consequence of the cession of the

Province to Great Britain, afford ample and appropriate materials for a Novel.

(Quoted in Lochhead, xxiii)

In fact it was from the presses of the *Upper Canadian Herald* that the novel would be published in 1824, its initial subscribers' names printed in the first edition. Book historians have noted how the publication of Hart's novel "was part of a burst of literary and intellectual activity ... that started in newspapers from Halifax to York (Toronto), among them Anthony H. Holland's *Acadian Recorder*, Ludger Duvernay's *La Minerve*, and William Lyon Mackenzie's *Colonial Advocate*" (Parker, 345). Newspapers would be important in strengthening Acadian culture, with the publication in New Brunswick in 1867 of *Le Moniteur acadien* (1867–1926), and the longer-running *L'Évangéline*, launched in 1887, lasting until 1982. French-language newspapers were being established across the country, such as *Le Courrier de la Nouvelle Calédonie* (est. 1856, Victoria, British Columbia), *L'Ordre* (est. 1859, Montreal), *Le Métis* (est. 1871, Winnipeg), *L'Ouest canadien* (est. 1898, Alberta), and *Le Patriote de l'Ouest* (est. 1910, Duck Lake, Saskatchewan) (Basque and Giroux, 55, 57–58). William Holland had already serialized Thomas McCulloch's (1776–1843) satirical "letters" from the fictional character Mephibosheth Stepsure during 1821–22, and in the same year that *St. Ursula's Convent* was published, George Longmore's (1793–1867) satirical poem *The Charivari or Canadian Poetics* was published by the Montreal bookseller and publisher Joseph Nickless (Parker, 346). Hart's connection with the printing and publishing world was indeed intimate: her husband, George Henry Hart, was a bookbinder and stationer, in Kingston, Ontario, where Thomson was also based.

Resemblance and misrecognition in Catherine Beckwith Hart's *St. Ursula's Convent* (1824)

Hart's mother, Julie-Louise Lebrun de Duplessis, married Nehemiah Beckwith and settled with him at Maugerville (Fredricton). The fact that her mother was Roman Catholic and her father a Wesleyan Methodist Protestant – a faith which her mother converted to upon marriage – would have some bearing on Hart's literary output, since the two different family backgrounds continued to be important to her as she grew up, and this interest forms one of the major plot devices in *St. Ursula's Convent*: the intertwining of families and nationalities both intentionally and unknowingly. Recognition and misrecognition drive this novel: identities that appear stable – a nun in a convent, an apparently deceased husband, even lineage and familial relations – are overturned and reconfigured by the novel's end, all in a complex romance narrative that unfolds through repetitions and re-tellings of various individuals' stories. Lochhead suggests that the novel is "a significant early attempt by a Canadian of French and English heritage to articulate a vision of Canada that united the best of England and France in a bilingual and bicultural nation located in North America but linked through family, social, and religious ties to its European origins" (xxxv). Additionally, the romance creates this visionary national meta-narrative through twenty-five micro-narratives or *les petit recits*, little stories that form discrete tales. The novel's structural tension arises with the question of whether the little stories constitute or form the meta-narrative of place, or if they deconstruct the very possibility of that narrative. The fact that recognition and misrecognition appear to merge in the novel suggests that *St. Ursula's Convent* does *not* simplify an already complex picture of the new Canadian culture. Rather, the novel works with some of the key themes of the long eighteenth-century novels of sensibility and the gothic – uncanny doubles, incest, events and occasions of heightened feeling and sentimental responses, the picturesque, the sublime and the uncanny – to reveal that subjectivity is not always malleable or controllable but subject to overwhelming exterior forces.

When Lord Durham meets his friend Sir Edward, he reacts strongly to seeing Sir Edward's daughter's friend Adelaide: "Lord Durham had just begun to address her, when Adelaide removing her veil, he started back, exclaiming – Astonishing! the perfect resemblance of Lady Durham; every look! every feature! her exact shape! the striking portrait of my Louisa, when I first saw her! Where, oh where, Sir Edward, did you meet with this Lady?" (69–70). This is more than just similarity: Adelaide appears to be Lady Durham's uncanny double or doppelgänger (we later find out she is her daughter). Adelaide's arranged marriage causes her unease, even though she is unaware that she is being ordered to marry her brother. The incest theme is announced later on in the novel by the nurse responsible for switching babies and causing all of the trouble: " ... when you returned from London, and I heard you were to be married to your own brother, I shuddered, and my guilty conscience knew no rest. I saw there was no alternative, I must either permit the crime of incest, or I must divulge the secret, that I had for so many years confined to my bosom!" (146). The one rock of stability in the novel appears to be the nun, Mother St. Catherine, whose melancholy tale of death and familial loss is told in the third and fourth chapters. Her fortitude and obedience to her destiny is eventually revealed to have been unnecessary; the husband she thought of as dead – leading her into the cloister – had survived shipwreck and imprisonment, but news of his state has been kept secret by an evil priest. The need to be reunited with her husband, however, should not lead to religious and cultural scandal: "I can serve the Almighty as faithfully in the midst of my family, as within the walls of a convent; but do not cause so great a scandal on our religion; which, sooner than be the occasion of, I would willingly be immured here for the remainder of my life" (159). Cross-cultural family relations succeed in the novel, but religious differences are still of great sensitivity. As much as Providence appears to control fate, so does the evil priest, who eventually repents on his deathbed. These two symbols of good and evil – the nun and the evil priest – appear to cancel one another out, leaving the little stories, the local, personal narratives, as a remainder that endures.

The first novel in Quebec: Philippe-Aubert de Gaspé's *The Influence of a Book* (1837)

Early critics were hostile to Hart's novel, wanting the grand narratives of great literature, the canonical works that already existed elsewhere, overseas in older cultures. To ignore the little or small stories is to ignore the mode of production of early Canadian literature, and its close examination of local customs, folk tales and oral stories, as well as the daily religious and economic lives of the people. It was precisely in and through the local that the distinctiveness of the Canadian popular novel emerged. The tension between good and evil seen in the two antithetical characters of the nun and the evil priest in *St. Ursula's Convent* has its counterpart in the first Quebec novel, *The Influence of a Book* (1837) written by Philippe-Aubert de Gaspé, Jr (1814–41). In his preface, de Gaspé defends not writing about "the grand, remarkable characters which have fired the imaginations of Europe's novelists for so many generations" by arguing that he has "had to be content depicting men and women as they exist in quotidian (or everyday, commonplace) life" (26). And yet what an exciting "quotidian" life that turns out to be. Using elements of the gothic genre, and a picaresque mode (an episodic narrative that follows the adventures of a likeable rogue or "pícaro"), folk tales merge with religious faith and superstition, all embedded in the overarching frame narrative of Charles Amand, a thwarted alchemist and lover of black magic.

The discourse is not entirely that of the mythological – with additional references to new pseudo-sciences such as phrenology – and the theatricality of the gothic horrors portrayed is often self-referential and foregrounded. A sense of this theatricality is found with the appearance of a murdered body: "For pure souls who have not yet become inured to thoughts of death or to the sight of it in the city's theatres, such an event can provoke violent emotions. Poor creatures! They would not have shed such tears had they, like us, been able to veil their sensibilities with the thick curtains that drop at the end of a play by Victor Hugo or Alexandre Dumas" (59). Such writing is immensely playful, the narrator's sympathies with country-folk and city-folk crossing back and forth, as do the subtly embedded ironies, whereby in the process, neither the innocence (or naivety) of small-town Canada, nor the sophistication (or jadedness) of the city-dweller, is favoured or totally denigrated. Later on in the novel, the "elements" of society are identified by the character Saint-Céran: "egotism, vanity, sycophancy and the folly of believing oneself universally admired, of mistaking derision for admiration, of tormenting oneself in the company of others and then announcing, 'Oh, what a marvellous time I had!'" (83). Similar scorn is reserved for the theatrical performances of women, the "false allure" and "ploys" (84) designed to ensnare unsuspecting men. Yet it is the men in the novel who are most intent on perverting the true course of nature and going against the authorized religion, which may be indicative of an underlying critique of patriarchy; as Amand suggests, "Genius and, more importantly, books are not wasted on mankind. Books enable us to conjure spirits from the great beyond. One might even bring forth the devil" (112).

From oral to print culture: humour and the picaresque in de Gaspé and Haliburton

Ironically, de Gaspé privileges orality, especially stories which express culture memory and/or powerful individual experiences, to produce a written book, or that which belongs to the Age of Reason; every person who goes through some kind of crucible returns, in this novel, "with strange, frightening tales" (116), yet these are precisely the tales that facilitate the transferring of popular oral culture to that of print. Scholl regards the novel as having two competing belief systems: "An enlightened mentality, embodied by Saint-Céran, struggles with a world of magic and superstition, which – as the author suggests in the last chapter – will survive as long as loneliness and isolation dominate other people's lives" (101). The productive tension between these two systems – of enlightenment and superstition – creates the frisson of the gothic, and in the hands of his father, in *Canadians of Old* (1837; see later), a gentle yet still penetrating humour.

The picaresque adventures or episodes of *The Influence of a Book* are composed via three main plot strands which are interwoven through sequentially embedded tales. As Leblanc notes, with this structure de Gaspé "is playing with the notion of containers and their contents. The most important plot contains a lesser one; this latter contains another; and so it goes until one arrives at entirely autonomous stories" (quoted in Lemire, 16). A more simple picaresque structure is apparent in the adventures of Sam Slick, written by Thomas Chandler Haliburton (1796–1865) for the *Novascotian* newspaper (September 1835), eventually appearing in book form as *The Clockmaker, or The sayings and doings of Sam Slick of Slickville* in 1837. Haliburton, born in Windsor, Nova Scotia, had a career as a lawyer and circuit judge, as well as serving on the Legislative Assembly as an elected representative, where he was renowned for his biting, satirical and sarcastic wit, something he found the perfect vehicle for with his Yankee character Sam Slick. This character might have come as a surprise to those who knew Haliburton's previous work, his *General Description of Nova Scotia* (1823) and his *Historical and Statistical Account of Nova Scotia* (2 vols, 1829), but the fact that Slick is a Yankee meant that he could speak indirectly, and humorously, for Haliburton. In other words, each episode contains biting satire, but that satire is also "contained" and made safe. Slick argues that "the folks of Halifax" do nothing but talk of progress: "They talk of steamboats, whalers, and railroads; but they all end where they begin – in talk" (14). The irony here is that Slick's own endless talking is central to the construction of his character and the picaresque novel itself.

One of the constant refrains in *The Clockmaker* is the need for a railroad, which is seen not as a solution to all of Nova Scotia's economic woes, but a way of inspiring "a spirit of enterprise" (26). Yet for all the boosterism, there is still an underlying love of the country ways, expressed perhaps best by Slick when asked for advice about a farmer's son and his ambitions: "[M]ake a farmer of him, and you will have the satisfaction of seeing him an honest, an independent, and a respectable member of society; more honest than traders, more independent than professional men, and more respectable than either" (129). While the racist and sexist language of Slick may now make readers uncomfortable, Haliburton derives much of the dynamism and sheer exuberance of his protagonist from earthy, local language, partly as a way of modelling an "authentic" Yankee (when in reality his speech is a hodge-podge of different idioms from different countries), and partly as a way of generating humour. Many of the phrases that Slick used became current in England and Canada, where the Sam Slick books were best-sellers. Examples include "spic and span" (shiny, clean, new-looking), "wamblecropt" (sick to the stomach), and "soft sawder" (soft soap, to soften someone up, to flatter). Later "Slick" books include *The attaché, or Sam Slick in England* (4 vols), and *Sam Slick's Wise Saws and Modern Instances* (2 vols). In his retirement Haliburton was a member of the British Parliament in England, an institution that welcomes witty and satirical speakers.

Historical romance and *Les Anciens Canadiens* (1863)

If the picaresque hero appears to be larger than life, then the early classic of French Canadian literature, *Les Anciens Canadiens* (1863), overthrows this notion. Its author, Philippe-Joseph Aubert de Gaspé (1786–1871), was born in Quebec, studying law at the Quebec Seminary; he eventually gained the position of High Sheriff of Quebec in 1816. In this post his financial troubles began, as he naively signed numerous promissory notes personally guaranteeing the debt of unscrupulous friends and colleagues. Retiring to Saint-Jean-Port-Joli after losing his post, de Gaspé spent fifteen years attempting to extricate himself from his deep financial distress, although he was ultimately unsuccessful, and was imprisoned in Quebec between 1838 and 1841. After his release he became part of the Club des Anciens, an informal group who dedicated themselves to "researching and recording the details of a stirring past" (Brierley, 10). It was in this atmosphere of dedicated memorialization of French Canada's past, that de Gaspé began writing his novel, with extracts published in the magazine *Les Soirées Canadiennes* in 1862. *Les Anciens Canadiens* is a historical romance, influenced by de Gaspé's interest in the novels of Sir Walter Scott. As with his son's novel, *The Influence of a Book*, the bedrock of the adventures recounted is folk or local small stories, *les petit recits*, the cultural customs, oral narratives and memories. *Les Anciens Canadiens* was very popular, given a second edition in 1864, and a dramatization in 1865 at the Collège de l'Assomption; English translations, with the title *Canadians of Old*, were produced by Georgiana M. Pennée, in 1864, Charles G.D. Roberts in 1890, and Jane Brierley in 1996.

De Gaspé discusses his approach to writing *Canadians of Old* in his first chapter which is also his preface: he says he will not write "according to popular literary tenets" (19), and instead will produce a work that is "entirely Canadian in style" arguing that "in a work of this kind I am determined to have a free hand and obey no set rules" (21). De Gaspé realizes that this will lead to generic instability: "Let the purists, the venerable *literati* whose sensibilities are shocked by such shortcomings, call this tome what they will – novel, memoir, chronicle, miscellany, pot-pourri, or hotch-potch – I don't care" (21). After this feisty preface, he plunges straight into some scene-setting and the stories begin to follow.

Sublime community in New France

The two protagonists of *Les Anciens Canadiens*, Jules d'Haberville and Archibald Cameron, are bosom buddies who will eventually find themselves fighting on different sides in the Seven Years' War. Much of their romance narrative provides a loose framework on which to hang multiple amusing adventure stories and folk tales. The society being depicted is deeply religious, and de Gaspé creates a narrative perspective which faces two ways: at the action, and at the religious context of the communities' response. The key instance of this bi-focal narration is when the character Dumais is trapped on an ice-filled river that is breaking up, and about to sweep him down a waterfall, to his death:

> It would seem wellnigh impossible to add anything to this picture of unparalleled horror and sublimity or to heighten the spectators' anguish as they looked on, petrified by the spectacle of a man who might at any moment vanish into the yawning abyss of the falls. And yet a scene equally sublime and awe-inspiring was taking place on shore: that of religious faith comforting the Christian prepared to appear before the fearsome tribunal of his Supreme Judge, and offering consolation to the soul about to cross the terrible bridge between life and death.
>
> (64)

What is interesting from a Canadian perspective about this scene, is that the sublime is generated as much by the community – the spectators – as it is by the overwhelming picture of impending death and destruction. De Gaspé thus maintains the tension between Eurocentric notions of sublime – in a Canadian setting – and this communal, religious, and intrinsically local Canadian sublime. The New World Sensibility is here defined through a split- or doubled-consciousness, where allegiances and emotions are torn, eventually symbolized in the novel by the war between the British and the French, foreshadowed by a "witch" called Marie: "Is it indeed Jules d'Haberville, bravest of the brave, whose bloody body I see being dragged over the Plains of Abraham?" (122). At the beginning of Chapter 11, the impending war is called a "darkening" of New France's horizon (140), and Locheill warns of "a government that is always wide awake to its colonies' interests, and therefore the interests of the British empire" (141–42).

Ultimately, the two protagonists do fight for different sides in the conflict, and they do go through a period of intense alienation from one another, but they are eventually reconciled, though not with the simplicity of a comedy genre-ending and a series of predictable marriages, since in this novel, an uncomfortable remainder continues to inflict itself upon the survivors of the Seven Years' War. While some of the folk humour may clash with the more serious side of the novel, its debt to Scott means that this is a historical romance that above all is readable, convincing and at times moving, yet it entirely breaks free of Scott in its local French-speaking cultural roots and its setting of one of Canada's earliest great battles. De Gaspé shows, then, that the popular novel can also articulate a political vision, yet maintain the telling of "an interesting story in a convincing fashion, through characters who took on the reality of living people" (Stevenson, 197). This would be seen just after the turn of the century with a novel that pondered Canada's place within Empire, as Canadians started to demand more autonomy yet still identified in some quarters with the British.

The imperial idea in the local setting: Sarah Jeanette Duncan's *The Imperialist* (1904)

Prior to a visit to England, Lorne Murchison, the protagonist of Sarah Jeanette Duncan's (1862–1922) novel *The Imperialist* (1904), ponders Canada's place in the Empire: "I've been reading up the history of our political relations with England. It's astonishing what we've stuck to her through, but you can't help seeing why – it's for the moral advantage" (98). Duncan, a Canadian journalist and author who spent much of her life living in Calcutta where her husband Everard Charles Cotes was Curator of the Indian Museum, was herself a firm believer in the imperial idea, and she uses the form of the popular romance novel to map out Canada's political space. Born in Brantford, Ontario, Duncan trained as a journalist, working for the *Washington Post*, the Toronto *Globe*, and as a Parliamentary correspondent for the Montreal *Star*. A highly prolific author, most of Duncan's novels have international settings, describing her travels in *A Social Departure: How Orthodocia and I Went Round the World by Ourselves* (1890), her time spent in London in *An American Girl in London* (1891), and India in *The Simple Adventures of A Memsahib* (1893), to name just a few. In *The Imperialist*, Duncan draws on her knowledge of Canadian and international politics, yet situates her story and characters in a small town called Elgin, based on Brantford, where she had grown up.

The small town focus (apart from the protagonist's trip to London, England) enables Duncan to show how the imperial idea is not a universal or abstract one, but instead impacts everyday Canadian society, businesses and local culture. This potential closer integration with the British Empire, however, is also regarded as facilitating Canadian autonomy and identity, not the subsuming of Canadian identity within that of the British. Even if the great spaces of Canada are perceived to be an "empty horizon" this is better than having none: "England has filled hers up" (110) says the character Hugh Finlay, whereas Canada's horizon is one of "faith and the future" (110). Capital in this novel is highly fluid and dynamic, following emerging markets rather than being restricted to old, static ones: "Already capital is drawing away [from London] to conditions it can find a profit in – steel works in Canada, woollen factories in Australia, jute mills in India" (123). Of course one of the most dynamic commodity producers in this period is Canada's neighbour, and the thirst for American goods is parodied in the novel; describing a typical Canadian family comfortably sitting down, the narrator says, "It is a fact, or perhaps a parable, that should be interesting to political economists, the adaptability of Canadian feet to American shoes … Though I must add that the 'rocker' was also American; and the hammock in which Stella reposed came from New York; and upon John Murchison's knee, with the local journal, lay a pink evening paper published in Buffalo" (128). When Canada imposed a twenty-percent duty on overseas imports in 1859, the British government strongly appealed against this barrier to trade, yet the will of the Canadian government prevailed. For some, this could only lead to integration with the USA: "One effect of all this was to instill in sections of the population a sense of independent status within the Empire. There were also those who had come to believe the severance of the imperial tie to be inevitable, and annexation to the United States a likely consequence" (Bailey, 130).

Problematically, the protagonist of *The Imperialist* rejects integration with the Republic in part on eugenic terms: America is a bastardized nation, the daughter of Britain "who left the old stock to be the light woman [prostitute or 'loose' woman] among nations, welcoming all comers, mingling her blood, polluting her lofty ideals" (233). In language that would be repeated later on in the century by eugenicists and extremists, such as the National Socialists in Germany, this racial interbreeding is cast in derogatory terms in comparison with the healthy racial stock of the Anglo-Saxon nations. If the pure stock of Canada and England combine, Murchison argues, then they will dominate the USA. Murchison's key imperialistic speech is also couched in terms of eugenics:

We stand for the wheat-belt and the stockyard, the forest and the mine, as the basic interests of the country. We stand for the principles that make for nation-building by the slow sweet processes of the earth, cultivating the individual rooted man who draws his essence and his tissues from the soil and so, by unhurried, natural, healthy growth, labour sweating his vices out of him, forms the character of the commonwealth, the foundation of the State. [...] The imperial idea is far-sighted. England has outlived her own body. Apart from her heart and her history, England is an area where certain trades are carried on – still carried on. In the scrolls of the future it is already written that the centre of the Empire must shift – and where, if not, to Canada?

(229)

The language of the healthy versus the exhausted body is also one of purification versus sickness; the healthy Canadian body has been purified by the "natural" processes of toil, and of productive labour. This is also a sober body, unlike the "intoxicated" Indian, described in *The Imperialist* as untrustworthy, slovenly, dirty, pathetic, trouble, and a "dying fragment" (242). Such eugenic language would be used to good effect in raising troops for the First World War (see the next chapter). But Murchison fails in his political efforts, and ironically, the winner in the novel appears to be a British immigrant, who marries into Canadian business, by winning the love of Murchison's intended. Duncan's real achievement in *The Imperialist* is to show how the language of romance and of realism, in a small-town local setting, can be used to explore the politics of nation and Canada's place within the Empire, standing side-by-side with the dominant countries of the global economy.

Affectionate irony: small-town Canada sketched by Stephen Butler Leacock

The *theatricality* of small-town Canada shows how it is a political and aesthetic space, one that would become world famous with the short stories of Alice Munro; in *The Imperialist*, much of the theatre is located in church, and at the hustings during election time. The word "hustings" derives from "house" and "assembly"; Duncan cleverly intertwines the politics of house and home, with the public spaces of democracy and morality, to show how they form a continuum. The big questions of Canadian identity are thus asked at the local level, through the vehicle of a highly readable story. Interpreted through its humorous vein, the novel becomes a national treasure, which is precisely what happened in the case of Stephen Butler Leacock's (1869–1944) *Sunshine Sketches of a Little Town* (1912). Born in England, but educated in Canada and the USA, Leacock became professor of political science at McGill University (1908–36); he published widely in his field, including *Elements of Political Science* (1906), *The Dawn of Canadian History* (1914), *The British Empire* (1940), *Canada* (1941) and *Montreal: Seaport and City* (1942). Leacock had privately published his early humorous sketches as *Literary Lapses* (1910), followed by *Nonsense Novels* (1911); both established Leacock as a popular humorist, and he was approached by the *Montreal Daily Star* with a commission for more sketches that appeared in twelve instalments between 17 February and 22 June 1912, the book version following in the fall. Leacock continued to publish political science/history books in parallel with his humorous materials, the latter appearing in book form virtually every year for the rest of his life, leading to international recognition and acclaim. Key to Leacock's humour is the creation of a speculative realm, the utopian small town of Mariposa, and the gentle, affectionate irony of his narration. For all his interest in and admiration for the early Dickens, especially *Sketches of Boz* and *The Pickwick Papers*, Leacock's satirical humour is less biting and more appreciative of the target of his humour than are European and American precursors and models, except perhaps in his darker *Arcadian Adventures with the Idle Rich* (1914). This affectionate irony, then, can be shared by Leacock's readers: laughing with him, with his characters, not entirely at them or at small-town Canada.

Leacock makes no attempt to hide his utopianism: in fact quite the opposite, he reveals its theatricality, the way in which his characters perform their identities as if on a stage. In attempting to win a court case involving after-hours drinking, the proprietor of the local hotel and bar, Mr. Smith, creates almost over night a fantasy world of imported sophisticated French culture with his café and beer cellar: "Light and cool, with swinging windows open to the air, tables with marble tops, palms, waiters in white coats – it was the standing marvel of Mariposa. Not a soul in the town except Mr. Smith, who knew it by instinct, ever guessed that waiters and palms and marble tables can be rented over the long distance telephone" (21). The jokes here are multiple: poking fun at the small town lack of sophistication so that windows that open appear the height of sophistication, as well as at the figure of Mr. Smith who knows about theatricality and artificiality "by instinct", as well as the ephemeral nature of the signs of sophistication in the small town which necessarily lags behind city fashions.

This theatricality, and naïve, enthusiastic response to it, is charming and pleasurable to read about: this is a world where disasters, when they occur, involve the puncturing of ridiculous dreams or are tame enough to laugh at. The most famous example in the novel is the "sinking" of the *Mariposa Belle*, a highly playful, circular account of an apparent disaster that turns out to be more of an inconvenience: "What? Hadn't I explained about the depth of Lake Wissanotti? I had taken it for granted that you knew; and in any case parts of it are deep enough, though I don't suppose in this stretch of it from the big reed beds up to within a mile of the town wharf, you could find six feet of water in it if you tried" (51). The stage-sets of small-town Canada can of course be rapidly changed: the sophisticated café disappears overnight when Mr. Smith wins his campaign to keep his liquor licence; the people on the *Mariposa Belle* get home with relative ease, and even a disastrous church fire leads to an insurance claim that solves a financial problem. But there is a traumatic and painful remainder to mundane events: Dean Drone has a stroke when he sees the church fire, from which he does not really recover; Jefferson Thorpe gets caught up in financial speculation, winning and losing a fortune, but with the result that he has to work harder in his barber's shop to pay off the debts other people incurred, for which he feels morally bound.

And in the last chapter, the entire town appears a fond, but deeply nostalgic dream or lost opportunity: it is the town we could have visited if we were not always too busy to do so. This nostalgia verges on melancholy and underlies the gentle satirical humour. Unlike Dickens, however, where the sentimentality is mawkish, Leacock's humour maintains a satirical edge.

Deconstructing the novel of education: Lucy Maud Montgomery's *Anne of Green Gables* (1908)

Gentle ironic humour also drives Lucy Maud Montgomery's (1874–1942) most popular of popular Canadian novels, *Anne of Green Gables* (1908), in some ways a novel that is now better known by its numerous TV and film adaptations (Lefebvre, 150). Set on Prince Edward Island, where Montgomery lived as a child (in the town of Clifton, and then the rural community of Cavendish), *Anne of Green Gables* presents an idyllic world and an ironic *Bildungsroman*, or novel of education and formation, which also subtly parodies the romance genre. Montgomery was educated at Prince of Wales College, Charlottetown, and she financed a year at Dalhousie University by working as a school teacher. From an early age Montgomery had expressed a desire to become an author, and she first published at the age of sixteen. *Anne of Green Gables*, her first novel, was immensely successful, spawning a culture and tourist industry devoted to the book and the series that followed. Such an industry has not always been aware of Montgomery's own complex writing strategies, especially the ways in which they undermine apparent certainties when discussing her work; for example, while her novels do adopt generic conventions and writing styles, they also subtly critique or undermine the politically conservative ideology of genre writing per se. The *Bildungsroman* is used by Montgomery, for example, to question why the young women of her period have to struggle so hard to acquire a meagre, basic education, compared with their male peers. Apparently used as a device to write the fictional biography of a protagonist, the *Bildungsroman* can therefore be more subversively used to critique the society within which the protagonist is embedded or trapped. As Lefebvre suggests: "By using humour and Anne's naïveté, Montgomery satirizes conventions of patriarchal romance, exaggerating them to the point of rendering them ridiculous while subtly critiquing the conventions themselves" (155). Even the landscape in *Anne of Green Gables* hovers somewhere between pastoral hyperbole and intense reverie, yet this is in itself a function of how Anne sees the world around her, in her yearning as an abandoned orphan for a world of imagination, adventure and loving or at least friendly and interesting "kindred spirits". Avonlea is a paradise that many tourists now long for, where even the brook that runs through this garden of Eden is "quiet" and "well conducted" and not "without due regard for decency and decorum" (7).

Anne herself is supposed to be an orphan boy adopted to help with farm work; instead, Marilla Cuthbert and her brother Matthew adopt her because their fondness for her develops beyond empathy, becoming instead love. Anne at first overwhelms the near-silent Matthew by revealing the imaginative vision that filters her view of Prince Edward Island: wild cherry trees become "marble halls" (19); Barry's pond becomes "the Lake of Shining Waters" (27); and the landscape that she imaginatively reconfigures is watched over by "a great crystal-white star" which "was shining like a lamp of guidance and promise" (28). This biblical imagery foreshadows the fact that while there is initially no room at the inn for an orphan girl, she will save Marilla and Matthew from years of childlessness and ultimately bless their shared home.

While for some readers reading this novel is like eating too many pancakes with maple syrup, it is also extremely seductive, and seductively transparent. The reality is that the text is far more complex than first appears. Even the setting is far more than a pastoral idyll:

Avonlea is small, but geographically it is already nationally implicated. Its province of Prince Edward Island was the "cradle of Confederation" due to the political conference held in the capital, Charlottetown, in 1864 to plan the organization of modern Canada. The novel's setting is linked even more strongly with nation and kinship through the phrase – unspoken in the novel but ubiquitous in Canada – for the politicians who had gathered to rock the national cradle: Prime Minister John A. MacDonald and his peers were known as the Fathers of Confederation.

(Dull, 170)

Anne's own confederation of friends is constituted by the "kindred spirits" who, like her, are not necessarily born and bred in Avonlea; through Anne's re-definition of "kin" in the conceptual space of the novel, we can see how an analogy is being developed with the political yoking together of diversity and difference in the constitution of Canada as a national entity. Anne's excessive imagination leads to much laughter, being almost a carnivalesque force that needs reining in or counterbalancing by the ethical voice of Marilla: "Marilla was as fond of morals as the Duchess in Wonderland, and was firmly convinced that one should be tacked on to every remark made to a child who was being brought up" (66). Such a perspective is at times undermined by Anne's exuberance which in turn represents some irrepressible intensity without which life would be extremely dull and inhuman; the novel may be asserting the need for a balance between the carnivalesque and the ethical, or it might simply be that there are generic restrictions placed on Anne's transgressive behaviour.

The speculative worlds of James De Mille: *A Strange Manuscript Found In A Copper Cylinder* (1888)

The popular novel in Canada articulates political and conceptual possibilities that would appear to be pushing at the boundaries of genre fiction; in fact critics have long noted how genre fiction has the potential to articulate issues of social and ideological concern, as well as exploring speculative worlds that are ultimately a reflection on the possibilities of our own. *The Imperialist, Sunshine Sketches of a Little Town* and *Anne of Green Gables* all engage in the politics of Canadian nation formation from a small-town perspective, as well as offering in turn the small town closely observed and dissected. The small town is also a container of speculative possibilities, the small stories that matter the most. Playing with the notion of a chora, a narrative interiority with powerful conceptual potential, is one of the most unusual of early popular Canadian novels, James De Mille's (1836–80) posthumously published *A Strange Manuscript Found In A Copper Cylinder* (1888).

Born in Saint John, New Brunswick, De Mille was educated at Acadia College in Nova Scotia, and Brown University, Rhode Island. Initially opening a book and stationery store in Saint John, De Mille switched careers when he became professor of classics at Acadia College; he was appointed professor of English and rhetoric at Dalhousie College, Halifax, in 1864, a position he held for the rest of his short life, which was brought to a premature end by pneumonia. Apart from his academic text *The Elements of Rhetoric* (1878), De Mille was known as a highly prolific writer of popular fiction, with his first novels being religious in character, including a novel written for the *Christian Watchman* called *Andy O'Hara: Or, The Child of Promise* (1861), and two historical novels called *The Martyr of the Catacombs: A Tale of Ancient Rome* (1865) and *Helena's Household: A Tale of Rome in the First Century* (1867). De Mille's two series of boys' books began in 1869 with *The "B.O.W.C." A Book for Boys*, following a Nova Scotian secret society called the Brethren of the White Cross, and the Young Dodge Club series which began in 1871, with *Among the Brigands*. De Mille had travelled with his brother Elisha to Europe for a tour of the continent in 1851, and he later drew upon these experiences with his adult fiction, parodying American tourists in the satirical *The Dodge Club: or, Italy in 1859*. De Mille wrote romantic mysteries, such as *Cord and Creese; or, The Brandon Mystery* (1869), comic novels, such as *The Lady of the Ice* (1870), and speculative fiction – *A Strange Manuscript* – often, although not always, with Canadian settings or connections. The publication history of *A Strange Manuscript* contributes to misunderstanding concerning the novel; anonymously and posthumously published in parts in *Harper's Weekly* (7 January to 12 May 1888), it appeared in book form in England and the USA in the same year. Watters suggests that this delay in publication led to the novel being thought somewhat derivative or imitative of Rider Haggard, when in fact *A Strange Manuscript* preceded Haggard's *She* and *Allan Quatermain* by seven years (viii). As Watters notes, "De Mille's *Copper Cylinder* [sic] is important, however, not because it possesses elements of fantastic adventure common also to the works of Haggard and Verne, but because of its uncommon ironic humour and powerful social satire. The antecedents to which De Mille was possibly indebted, of a class far superior to the popular fiction just mentioned, were such satirical masterworks as Swift's *Gulliver's Travels* and Samuel Butler's *Erewhon*" (viii).

Container or contained? Narrative interplay in *A Strange Manuscript*

Two main narrative strands make up *A Strange Manuscript*, the frame narrative and the contained narrative: the first involves a group of becalmed men discovering at sea a manuscript inside a copper cylinder, reading that manuscript aloud, and debating the veracity of its contents; the second involves the story of a sailor called Adam More, lost at sea until he eventually arrives at the dystopian community of Kosekin, where he finds that all of his familiar values are inverted. In Kosekin, darkness and death are sought out, while possessions, wealth, rank and title are considered a desecration of one's good name and character. Adam More's story combines multiple discourses, including that of explorers' tales, utopian and dystopian literature, and scientific/ speculative writing. The frame narrative, in attempting to work out Adam's status as a writer – is he a fiction writer or a scientific observer? – involves debates concerning language, culture, literary criticism, palaeontology, geology, geography and navigation.

While the dystopian story is in itself fascinating and varied, it is the interplay between frame and contained narrative that sets this novel above many of its competitors, offering a satirical view of contemporary society, alongside a self-reflexive interrogation of speculative fiction. What or who the target of the satire is varies from interpretation to interpretation; more recent critical examinations have seen the text as a subtle critique of colonialism and Orientalism, whereby the frame speakers are aboard a "parodic ship of state" representing "the essence of empire, composed of wealth (Featherstone), science (Dr. Congreve), and language, the latter divided into philology (Oxenden) and literature (Melick)" (Gerson 1995, 227). The subtlety arises from the fact that it is the power-knowledge discursive constructs that drive and underpin colonial exploration and expansion, not the direct tools of oppression. The potentially anti-Semitic aligning of Kosekin with Hebrew also contributes to this Orientalist / colonialist world view of the frame speakers.

Other critics regard Adam More as an unreliable narrator, veering from perceptive insight and commentary, to dense, uncomprehending observation and even obfuscation. As unreliable narration, however, the text unfolds using interrupted delayed decoding, that is to say, the experiences Adam undergoes are narrated in "real time" without heavy interpretation or meta-commentary. This has the effect, as in Joseph Conrad's (1857–1924) *Heart of Darkness* (1899, in *Blackwood's Magazine*), of drawing the reader closer into the story world. Ironically, the unreliable narrator has become one of the defining features of postmodernism, "simultaneously deconstructing the possibility of a *reliable* one" (Lane 2006b, 72); unreliability can also be equated with the linguistic turn in literary critical studies, whereby all statements are subjective and open to multiple interpretations. The fact that *A Strange Manuscript* is an unfinished, open-ended novel also contributes to this proto-postmodernity, and undermines the notion of a moral code that the novel appears to be working towards (see Lamont-Stewart). *A Strange Manuscript*, then, is a novel that critics have had to learn how to re-read: its apparent weaknesses are now celebrated and its strengths are re-confirmed. Yet there remains the hint that the critic of Canadian literature is one of the people on the becalmed yacht, attempting to explain a dystopian fiction that constantly resists precisely the act of explanation and interpretation.

Conclusion

- The eighteenth- and nineteenth-century literary notion of "sensibility" is rewritten by the Canadian novel, to forge a New World sensibility, one which articulates a double discourse: looking back to the past, and forwards to a new, autonomous future.
- The Canadian gothic recodes the Romantic notion of the sublime, and produces an uncanny mode for articulating issues of warfare, race and gender.
- The first Canadian novels are concerned with the Old World surveillance of the new colonial spaces, especially covering trade, ethnic relationships, and warfare; the New World is a space of potential gender and social transformation.
- Narcissistic doubling occurs in the first Canadian novels as the Other is given projected characteristics of similitude; the Other is a threat to colonial stability and needs to be reined in and incorporated into the same.
- Reclaiming Canada as a domestic space allows a new female perspective on what was traditionally a patriarchal domain: that of exploring, invading, and settling. As a domestic space, Canada is re-imagined and refigured from a variety of alternative perspectives, including a more liberal (although still colonialist) notion of indigenous peoples.

4   *In Flanders Fields*

Gender and social transformation in the First and Second World Wars

Overview

Transformation in society and literary expression occurs in the period of the two world wars (1914–18 and 1939–45): women gradually gained the right to vote across Canada, and they also had access to jobs that had previously been considered suitable only for men. Women also served as nurses and medical staff near battlefronts. Many men lost their lives in the trenches of the First World War, and class and nationalistic attitudes underwent re-evaluation by those who survived what appeared a senseless mass slaughter. The different attitudes towards enlistment and loyalty to Great Britain reveal a shift in Canadian identity; by the Second World War, less people felt loyalty to a distant country that was part of an Empire in decline. Still, during both wars, there was careful government control of the media and other forms of artistic communication, including literary texts. War was considered to be a proving experience, a potentially sacrificial test of one's loyalty or manhood; those authors who portrayed the war as absurd, meaningless or simply surreal appeared to be writing against the grain of government-led jingoism and national unity. Yet it is these oppositional texts that now appear more truthful in their adoption of more experimental writing modes to represent fragmented, shell-shocked or otherwise traumatized subjectivities, as well as shifts in gender roles within society. In other words, the reassessment of the Canadian literature of this period now sees the best literature as modernist or at the least proto-modernist, replacing a Victorian sensibility with one that is deeply existential and suspicious of the value of fighting large-scale battles in the modern era.

The execution or poetics of Canadian war literature: some shared themes

Three men are pointlessly executed in a Canadian novel about the Second World War: two at the beginning of the novel, and one at the end; in between these executions, other men find they have mentally broken away from the stabilities and certainties of their lives, their ethical anchors – and identities – having been destroyed by witnessing such pointless acts. In an earlier Canadian novel, about the First World War, the men at the front are likened to Isaac, led to the sacrificial site by Abraham in Genesis 22. In some early Bible *commentaries*, Isaac is slaughtered; in the Bible itself, he is saved, but only because a substituted innocent creature is killed in his stead. Either way, war is the sacrifice of innocents: a Canadian might survive the trenches, but only at the cost of another life, be it Canadian or European. Both actions – execution and sacrifice – are brought about by the men who are supposed to be on "our" side: the military leaders who demand the executions in Colin McDougall's (1917–84) *Execution* (1958), or send the men to be sacrificed at the Front in Charles Yale Harrison's (1898–1954) *Generals Die in Bed* (1928). Both actions are utterly senseless, stripping away at the ethical foundations of subjectivity, confounding the logic of the nationalistic and religious reasons for going into battle. The characters in these two novels are left in a void, one where identity is dismantled, broken into fragments, and never reconstructed again in a coherent, unified manner. The novels offer stark existential choices that reveal the absurdity of war, its surreal commands and demands, its dislocating, rupturing experience. Soldiers, in these novels, can't go on, but they must go on, regardless of shell-shock, apathy, disgust or simple rejection.

Canadian war propagandists worked hard to block the publication of such bleak, modernist texts in magazines and newspapers: "*Camaraderie – esprit de corps* – good fellowship – these are words for journalists to use, not for us. Here in the line they do not exist" (Harrison, 91). Language, at the Front (the name for the location where the fighting took place in the First World War), is shell-shocked, yet also at times crystal clear, separating itself from the façade of hyped patriotic fervour and propaganda back home.

The war poetry of John MacCrae and F.G. Scott

Acceptable ways of writing about war, from the government's perspective, would involve a language that could generate enthusiastic participation … and sell Canadian Victory Loan Bonds.

Shell-shock was a term given to men who returned from the trenches of the First World War suffering from a range of debilitating nervous disorders. Such men were initially diagnosed as being cowards or shirkers – men who were unwilling to do their duty for king and country. Equally problematic was that in relation to the gender expectations of the time, shell-shocked men exhibited symptoms of what used to be called "hysteria", a nervous disorder that was only supposed to be manifested in women. Different treatments for shell-shock included the forced application of electric shocks to the inside of the mouth and throat, to more humane counselling methods. Regardless of the means of obtaining a cure, these men were then sent back to the trenches and their almost certain deaths. Much of the research on this condition was not published until long after the war, but new psychoanalytical theories were partly developed because of this important work.

Canadian Victory Loan Bonds were a financial instrument used to raise money to pay for Canada's involvement in the First and Second World Wars. The first issue of 150 million Canadian dollars took place in November 1915 (it was massively oversubscribed); the patriotic term "Victory Bond" or "Victory Loan" was first used in the fourth issue of November 1917.

Such a literature is now well known from annual readings of the poem *In Flanders Fields* (1915): "In Flanders fields the poppies blow / Between the crosses, row on row". This simple, highly compressed sonnet by John MacCrae (1872–1918) functions now as a memorialization of lost veterans, being the words most often read aloud in Canada on Remembrance Day (11 November, when Canada's armed forces are commemorated). The poem is in part a contract, between the living and the dead: uncannily, it is the dead who *demand of the living* that they should "Take up our quarrel with the foe" – the enemy being fought in the trenches of the First World War. The imagery in the third stanza is that of school-boys playing sports or more professional men engaging in athletic competitions, such as the Olympics: "To you from failing hands we throw / The torch; be yours to hold it high". There is not really much choice involved, since those living who *will* run the race to the finish are being faithful to those who have *already* sacrificed their lives. In other words, if the living *do not* respond to this call, they have sacrificed all over again those who died for them, and have desecrated the action, and the memory, of the dead. More bluntly still, if the living "break faith" with the dead, the dead will remain forever with us, as ghosts, uncannily haunting the living.

Of course this critical response reads the poem through its conclusion or call to action, but this is a deliberate reading choice, because it is the third stanza that begins to make sense of the poem, bringing into focus the haunted landscape of the first two stanzas. The fragmented, uncanny, modernist imagery of the first two stanzas is therefore re-integrated into the ethical imperative that becomes the point of the poem. Many contemporary readers struggle with this re-integration, wanting the first two stanzas to be concluded in the vein of the famous British war poets Wilfred Owen (1893–1918) or Siegfried Sassoon (1886–1967), a "might have been" conclusion that could have expressed "a moving and powerful indictment of the use of poison gas and German militarism, or a great modernist poem about alienation, or a poem that refuses to be either, that simply and devastatingly 'describes'" (Holmes, 25). But the concluding stanza does none of these things, instead it is closer to the sentiments of Frederick George Scott's (1861–1944) poems written at the Front, called *In The Battle Silences* (1916). Scott, the father of the modern Canadian poet F.R. Scott (1899–1985), opens *In The Battle Silences* with affiliation, "O England of our Fathers and England of our Sons" (*The Crown Of Empire*); this will be the England that Canadian blood is spilled for, but only because it was perceived to really be English blood in the first place:

"The Blood which Thou didst give us is the blood we spill for thee" (Ibid.). An ethical lesson is being learnt on the battlefields of France – that sacrificial love, as embodied in Christ, is the beginning of life: "For lonely graves along the country side, / Where sleep those brave hearts who for others died / Tell of life's union with the Crucified" (*On The Rue Du Bois*); the mourner recognizes that "For Life is born of life's self-sacrifice" (Ibid.), a line that is as claustrophobic and compressed as the mass war graves and trenches reconstructed in part with decomposing bodies.

The discourse here in Scott is analogous to MacCrae's: the dead are "those brave hearts" who are *sleeping*; they died for others – for the living, and this implies an ethical imperative or task for those who are still alive. This is "The path of duty plain" (*A Canadian*) for those patriotic soldiers who travelled to the trenches from Canada "ablaze with one desire" which is to play a part "In crushing tyranny" (Ibid.). Death, amidst the vision of starry skies, is "A sudden, glad surprise" (*A Grave In Flanders*). In fact, this poem is again similar to MacCrae's, spoken from the perspective of those who are already dead, "wrapped" in the roots of tall trees; even more uncannily, the trenches themselves become graves *in advance of* death. Fussell points out that the perspective of the trenches was mainly upwards, sky-gazing with awe at literary, painterly sunrises and sunsets, or the vision of brilliant stars. He quotes a character in Ford Madox Ford's *A Man Could Stand Up –* : "the light seen from the trench seemed, if not brighter, then more definite. So, from the bottom of a pit-shaft in broad day you can see the stars" (52).

In *Requiescant*, Scott imagines the dead troops as a medieval pageant marching by: "Strange ghostly banners o'er them float, / Strange bugles sound an awful note, / And all their faces and their eyes / Are lit with starlight from the skies" (1915). This vision, in the first stanza, bursts upon Scott as he stares at the night sky; the dead are infused with romantic "starlight" and they are at peace, yet not lacking in "iron purpose" or willpower. The Christian resolution – "Dear Christ who reign'st above the flood / Of human tears and human blood, / O house them in the home of God" – appears awkward and pathetic; if Christ does not respond, will the dead forever be marching through the night skies, just as they might haunt the living in *In Flanders Fields*? And for Scott, of course the enemy cannot invoke Christ: "In vain you call upon the Lord, / Emperor!" (*Blood-Guilt*). The German empire, here, is beyond the Lord's blessing: "What god will bless the hideous flood / Which drowns the world in human blood?" (Ibid.). Scott's jingoistic poetry (ironically, the word itself derives from "jingo", a euphemism for "Jesus") was immensely popular during the War. The dead have not lost in Scott's poetry, they have won, just as the *Halifax Morning Chronicle* would report on the death of the American track and field athlete, Lt. Johnny Overton: "He put all he had into this race – his life; and won all there is – the glory of God and man" (quoted in Keshen, 131). MacCrae's concluding stanza, then, fits perfectly with the patriotic, Christian sentiments of his day. But there remains a conundrum: the first two stanzas of *In Flanders Fields* are not quite as simple, or as jingoistic, as the concluding one.

Discordant voices: *In Flanders Fields*

In many respects, the first two stanzas of *In Flanders Fields* appear conventional: a pastoral landscape of fields, poppies and larks "bravely singing" and flying is lit by the dawn sunrise and the "sunset glow". But the fields are now graveyards, with the rows of crosses signifying mass graves, and the disturbing thought that the bodies may be so disfigured that they cannot be identified. The singing birds can hardly be heard because of "the guns below", the word "below" signifying not just "beneath the sky" but some subterranean world, of graves, of trenches, of Hades. This is confirmed by the opening statement of the second stanza: "We are the Dead." Now the dead are not passively tucked away in their graveyard, or symbolically present in the flying birds – they are speaking: they are the poetic voice. The use of this voice creates a "weird dissonance" (Holmes, 19), or discordant combination of sounds, between the pastoral imagery/sounds and symbolism of the first stanza, and the spoken ghostly presence of the second stanza. There is something deeply uncanny here:

> The palimpsest quality of a traditional poem overwritten by a strange and ghostly voice is a true example of what Freud called "*das Unheimliche* [The unhomely or uncanny]." In his famous essay "The Uncanny," Freud attempts to describe the strange effect of the uncanny in life and literature. He defines "the uncanny [as] … something which ought to have remained hidden but has come to light" (217), a definition that suits the grisliness that seems to seep unbidden yet unstoppably into the poem's conventional cluster of images. […] What MacCrae has managed to do is take the mundane landscape of Flanders and the familiar literary symbolism of crosses and sunsets and make them frightening by the end of the second stanza, blotting the familiar and the hopeful with supernatural horror and chilling absence.
>
> (Holmes, 19–20)

Holmes, in a comprehensive and insightful reading, notes that the first two stanzas of the poem "de-Christianize" and "de-Romanticize" the setting, since the uncanny, ghostly voices of the dead undermine the rhetoric of the Christian, pastoral landscape (21). The uncanny, in other words, does not allow the poet of the first two stanzas to see life whole, to paraphrase the English author and critic E.M. Forster (1879–1970), since that vision of life has been shattered, fragmented, if not totally destroyed by the war.

The psychic landscape of the first two stanzas is truly ghastly because of this deconstruction of high literature using the very tropes and literary devices that are brought more powerfully into control in the third stanza (the ethical imperative; the switching of discourses to that of English schoolboys and patriotic politicians). The first two stanzas, then, are a deformation of jingoistic poetry at the Front; representation here is "about instinctual release" (Foster, 113) and the *"coupling* of two realities, irreconcilable in appearance, upon a plane which apparently does not suit them" (Ernst, quoted in Foster, 81). Such an aesthetic is deeply modernist, if not surrealist, although it could be argued that the third stanza is a sort of dialectical synthesis of unleashed modernist emotions and aesthetics, with that of the literary great tradition.

The competing perspectives of the soldier poets

Other Canadian poets who broke free of the great tradition did exist, although it is only recently that critics have more closely turned their attention to them. With reference to Frank Prewett (1893–1962), W.W.E. Ross (1894–1966) and Robert W. Service (1874–1958), Baetz notes that works "of these three soldier-poets foreground some of the essential experiments and ideas that would be central to modernist poetry in the coming decades" (8). Furthermore, "Canadian poetry of the First World War acts as the perfect site on which to stage the emergence of one of the predominant tendencies of modernist literatures: the articulation of impaired subjectivity, one that, in different ways and to different degrees, is alienated, divided, and obscured" (11). Such literary expression, while raw and uncompromising, appears closer to the uncensored archival record of experiences at the Front, than poetry such as Edgar W. McInnis's (1867–1951) *Poems Written at "the Front"*, with their cheery gusto and bonhomie, as in *Our Dug-Out*, where the soldier goes in the midst of the chaos to a warm, dry, friendly, rat-proof, rain-proof home-away-from-home full of pals having a big adventure. Ironically, for most of the war, the only dug-outs that were this well-constructed were on the German side of the trenches, but the Canadian public reading this poem could fantasize that all of their boys were snuggled up when they weren't fighting.

In Robert W. Service's *Rhymes of a Red Cross Man* (1916), the fragmented subject is juxtaposed with the patriotic discourse that readers back home in Canada quickly came to expect, creating an uneasy tension, and an uncertain hierarchy, between two different articulated perspectives, with the fragmented subject becoming more noticeable after the battle of the Somme, in which tens of thousands of troops were killed on the first day.

The battle of the Somme (1 July to 18 November 1916) is remembered in Canadian military history for the great sacrifices that took place, including the decimation of almost the entire 1st Newfoundland Regiment that fought on the first day at Beaumont-Hamel (10 per cent of the regiment were kept back in reserve, which was usual military practice at the time). On the first day of the battle, the Newfoundland Regiment accompanied the Essex Regiment onto exposed ground, whereupon 255 of the former were killed, 386 were wounded, and 91 went missing in action. Some 650,000 Allied soldiers died or were wounded during the battle of the Somme, in the process achieving the capture of 10 kilometres of enemy ground.

The Somme was a transformative event, not least in the numbers dead, wounded or missing in action; after the tragedy of the Somme – such as the failure to cut the wire or bomb the German guns that had merely been kept safe in deep bunkers – a new awareness of endless war, or the war as an autonomous entity, arose: "No road. No thoroughfare. Neither race had won, nor could win, the War. The War had won, and would go on winning" (quoted in Fussell, 13).

Rhymes of a Red Cross Man was published in the autumn of 1916, one of the first books of poetry to express a new mood, not of despair, but of impotence in the face of something so powerful. The old language here begins to give way to the new: the lark, that most favourite of literary birds (larking about in the sky like schoolboys playing in a field), is "good to hear" when one is about to die: "I am horror-haunted from the hell they found me; / I am battle-broken, all I want is rest. / Ah! It's good to die so, blossoms all around me, / And a kind lark singing in the golden West" (*Our Hero*). The irony in the phrase "it's good to die so" can of course be missed, but the intruding "horror-haunted from the hell they found me" suggests terror rather than pastoral pleasure. War is an unstoppable force, a machine within which the human subject is subsumed, incorporated, and forced to act: "*But on you charge*" is the refrain of *Wounded*: "The heavens vomit death; / And vicious death is besoming the ground. / You're blind with sweat; you're dazed, and out of breath, / And though you yell, you cannot hear a sound." Still, the machine of war continues, and the subject continues with it, as machine-like in turn: "*But on you charge.*"

Service's *On The Wire* re-codes the perspective of war from those men in terror-filled movement, or taking cover in holes in the ground, to that of modern man suspended – hung or strung-up – on the wire: "Hide from my eyes the sight / Of the body I stare and see / Shattered so hideously. / I can't believe that it's mine." In this existential suspension, where the only outcome that makes sense is suicide, the human subject is "shattered beyond repair"; the man "on the wire" becomes a metaphor for the entire war, for all human beings, at the Front or back home, men or women, whose lives are by the war suspended, made meaningless, pointless and absurd.

Popular fiction and romance: the war writing of Bertrand William Sinclair

On 3 October 1914, Canada sent 36,267 trained men from their camp at Valcartier, Quebec, towards the as then unknown horrors of trench warfare; the troops were based at Salisbury Plain in England, and sent to the Front in February 1915. Canadian ethnic and regional identity clearly had a large part to play in the rapid mobilization, especially given the fact that just over 23,000 of the first troops were British immigrants, and just over 10,000 were born in Canada (Bothwell, 290–91). In *The Inverted Pyramid* (1924), the popular fiction writer Bertrand William Sinclair (1881–1972), who specialized in romances with a socialist subtext, recreated the atmosphere of the first few days following the announcement of war in Vancouver, where troops "drilled in parks, on playgrounds. Bands marched abroad to stir men's blood" (178). Sinclair was interested in the psychological reasons that led to men signing-up for battle, noting among other reasons the strong general sense of threat that was felt along BC's poorly protected coastline:

> There was an edge of expectancy in the air, for the *Leipsig*, the *Dresden*, the *Nuremberg*, and two unknown battleships were loose in the Pacific. No one knew what truth lay in the rumor that any hour might see their shells dropping in the downtown section [of Vancouver]. There was nothing to stop them. They out-steamed and out-gunned any British Squadron in those waters.
>
> (Sinclair, 1924, 178)

The two "unknown" battleships may be a reference to the submarines that could easily hide themselves along the labyrinthine coast. Apart from this perceived threat of external attack, the people of British Columbia also feared the possible internal action of recent German immigrants, yet in Sinclair's fiction he resists such essentialist analysis. In *Burned Bridges* (1919), the rational voice of Sam Carr comments on the media stories of German brutality, saying that "The Germans are reckoned in the civilized scale the same as ourselves. I'm not ready to damn sixty-five million human beings outright because certain members of the group act like brutes ... The Allies will win this war with cannon and bayonets, but up to the present we seem to think we must supplement our bullets with epithets" (222).

This defence of the German people must be contextualized in light of the deeper, embedded racism in Sinclair's work, where Aboriginal people are marginalized and effaced, and other, non-European immigrants are portrayed via crude, degrading stereotypes. The fear of British Columbia being physically attacked linked regional identity with the European theatre of war, with the British Empire and Britain itself. As Barman notes, "Patriotism now became the order of the day ... British Columbia had the highest per capita volunteer rate in Canada at just over ninety per thousand population compared with about seventy-five in Ontario and across the prairies, just over fifty in the Maritimes, and half that in Quebec" (198–99). Analysis of the men who actually went to fight the war shows a truly complex background: "On Mayne Island many [of the volunteers] were half-breeds, elsewhere native Indians. The Japanese and Sikh communities offered to raise troops" (199). This was support given to the old colonial power, a recognition of allegiances and debts, both physical and spiritual. Yet for Sinclair, the same forces which generated such intense patriotism also generated a questioning of colonialism. In his personal correspondence, he labelled men who responded only to the propaganda of the call-up "sheep": "I wasn't overseas fighting for King and country, and I have no apologies to make to anybody therefore. If the same events arose I should be just as much of a rebel against being a sheep and tamely following the bell-wearers, as I was in 1914" (University of British Columbia, Special Collections Division). He could not present such an attitude in his fiction – the war-disfigured protagonist of *The Hidden Places* (1922) was already putting off his readership, Sinclair's publishers suggested – but he could present the questioning of the patriotic fervour:

> To Wes Thompson, concentrated upon his personal affairs, the war never became more than something akin to a bad dream recalled at midday, an unreal sort of thing ... The war aroused his interest, but left his emotions unstirred. There was nothing martial about him. He dreamed no dreams of glory on the battlefield. He had never thought of the British Empire as something to die for. The issue was not clear to him, just as it failed to clarify itself to a great many people in those days.
>
> (Sinclair 1919, 216)

The economics of war: societal profit and loss in popular fiction

Burned Bridges, Sinclair's novel about the casting aside of empty religious values in favour of a materialistic, rational existence, emphasizes the economic gains made by BC's industrialists during the First World War. As the narrator notes, "business in Vancouver was actually looking up because of the war" (217). In *Burned Bridges*, the highly successful entrepreneur, Tommy Ashe, uses his contributions to the war-effort as a front to cover his underlying profiteering. In this he is aided by the demand for ships needed to supply the Allies. Thompson notes, in discussion with Ashe, "Nobody can accuse you of profiteering ... your undertaking is both patriotic and profitable" (241). Ashe warns Thompson that if he doesn't utilize the same cover, he will be accused of being a "slacker" (232). Ultimately, unlike Sinclair, Thompson goes to war; the novel never really allows for an alternative, between the propaganda of the self-seeking city-dwelling industrialists and those who genuinely fight for their country. But even the latter leads to further ambiguity. In *The Inverted Pyramid*, the narrator says of Rod Norquay, who is in a similar position to Thompson, "He loved his native country ... But he revolted against being a pawn in the European game" (179). The phrase "native country" would seem to be Canada, but the novel also stresses Rod's familial allegiances with Britain and his regional identity as a born and bred British Columbian.

Sinclair devoted much of his BC fiction not only to a Marxist critique of the economic profits which increased during the war, but also to the question of how the men returning from the war would fit back into the BC environment. In *Poor Man's Rock* (1920) and *The Inverted Pyramid*, the protagonists return home from the war heroically strengthened in character and attractive to society in general; in *The Hidden Places*, however, the protagonist is shunned by Vancouver society because of his facial disfigurement. All three protagonists are situated in relation to the reactions they invoke from society, and to their own reactions to that society. Many veterans returned home to find that their jobs had all but disappeared. In the logging industry, war-time demands had enabled working men to raise their wages and conditions; returning veterans were often used as pawns in a game designed to destroy such aspirations. The mixture of political activism and returning veterans was explosive, leading to unionization and political organization. In *The Inverted Pyramid*, demobilization is portrayed as the beginning of a secret industrial war; the battlefields of France are transposed into scenes of strikes and strike-breaking.

The war machine: redemption and propaganda at a distance

While Sinclair uses the popular romance for political ends, at no point does he question the genre's embedded patriarchal ideology. The romance genre undoubtedly dominates Canadian First World War writing, but that is not to say that there were no subtly subversive questionings of gender roles. Two of the strongest feminist narratives are Francis Marion Beynon's (1884–1951) *Aleta Dey* (1919) and L.M. Montgomery's *Rilla of Ingleside* (1921), which, combined with the raw and powerful critique of the masculine attitudes expressed in the First World War in Charles Yale Harrison's (1898–1954) *Generals Die In Bed* (1930; excerpts in magazine form, 1928), form an important trilogy of Canadian war fiction. Earlier novels followed a predictable stultified formula, although there were some isolated instances of more complex writing.

Ralph Connor (Charles William Gordon, 1860–1937) adopts the discourse of muscular Christianity in his fiction, especially in his highly patriotic war novels, *The Major* (1917), *The Sky Pilot in No Man's Land* (1919) and *Treading the Winepress* (1926). The Christian notion of the redemptive value of war was particularly endorsed by those who did not personally see action in the trenches – or, if they did fight, they were soon behind the lines or back home. Robert James Campbell Stead (1880–1959) also published three war novels: *The Cow Puncher* (1918), *Denison Grant* (1920) and *Grain* (1926). Like Bertrand William Sinclair, Stead did not enlist, although he did receive military training, and both authors, however constrained by the formulaic and the melodramatic, introduce psychological resistances and complexity to their protagonists.

Montreal-born Henry Beckles Willson (1869–1942) did enlist – he served as Assistant Records Officer to the Canadian Expeditionary Force – but he eventually devoted his energies to collecting material for propagandistic purposes as the war correspondent for the *Daily Express*. The redemptive function of war is again central to the vision and experiences of war as narrated in Willson's *Redemption: A Novel* (1924), and the differences in attitudes towards the war, among people of different nationalities, is explored in William Benjamin Basil King's (1859–1928) *The High Heart* (1917) and *The City of Comrades* (1919). In all of these novels, the war is a huge looming presence, yet it often remains strangely off-stage. The character Frank Melbury, in *The City of Comrades*, ponders why the trauma of war cannot always be directly articulated:

> The machine of war does not vary in its working much more than any other machine, except for the drama played out in each man's soul.
>
> And of that I can say nothing. I don't know why – but I cannot. Day and night I think of what I saw and heard and did in those two years, but some other language must be coined before I can begin to speak of it.
>
> In this I am not singular; it is a rule to which I know few, if any, exceptions. I have heard returned soldiers on the lecture platform, telling part of the truth, and nothing but the truth, but never the whole truth nor the most vital part.
>
> (227)

The first person narration of *The City of Comrades*, and its assertion that war is a machine – as well as the idea that "some other language must be coined" to articulate the experience of being a part of this machine – foreshadows the modernist aesthetic revolution that would create a literature expressive of the machine-age and all of its concomitant shocks and disorientating experiences. Part of the responsibility for generic limitations with the first wave of Canadian war literature, however, may simply be pinned upon the author's lack of direct experiences of the worst horrors of the war: "They had little knowledge about life at the front, how abysmal the conditions, how great the suffering, how traumatic the experience" (Novak, 42). While this is true, the impact of war could still be explored in some depth, as did Beynon and Montgomery, who obviously did not experience the trenches firsthand, and this impact reveals much about the ways in which society as a whole underwent profound transformation.

Redefining gender performances in Lucy Maud Montgomery's *Rilla of Ingleside* (1921)

The Canadian Expeditionary Force sent to fight in the trenches was not just composed of men: women also volunteered for service overseas, as nurses, and back home, women took on occupations that were usually not open to them, such as working in munitions factories and all sorts of new charitable institutions and associated initiatives, such as the Canadian Patriotic Fund, which supplemented the difference between past civilian and current military incomes (so that Canadian families did not suffer financial hardship). Many of these new-found professional working roles would be lost to women after the war, but by then, women had become a political force to reckon with, gaining the right to vote throughout Canada in 1918 (except for in Quebec). In Montgomery's *Rilla of Ingleside*, the transformation of a patriarchal family during the war is observed from the perspective of the women, with emphasis upon the protagonist Rilla Blythe and the family cook and servant, the aptly named Susan Baker. At first the flippant denial of the importance of the impending war appears to more firmly place Rilla and Susan into their patriarchal gender performance, with Susan calling news of the Archduke Ferdinand's assassination "uninteresting, immaterial stuff" (2) compared with local newspaper jottings. Rilla is caught up in her own feckless self: "There was nothing in the world to worry about – not even freckles and over-long legs – nothing except one little haunting fear that nobody would ask her to dance" (33). Into this gentle and genteel narrative the war intrudes with a rude shock:

> Rilla drew a long breath of rapture – and caught it midway rather sharply. Jem was telling some story to Faith – something that had happened in the Balkan war.
>
> "The doctor lost both his legs – they were smashed to pulp – and he was left on the field to die. And he crawled about from man to man, of all the wounded men around him, as long as he could, and did everything possible to relieve their sufferings – never thinking of himself – he was tying a bit of bandage around another man's leg when he went under."
>
> (34)

Rilla's innocent rapture is interrupted by this narrative which both partakes of the romantic, heroic and patriotic discourse of the war (the doctor is a "hero"; he euphemistically "went under"; his "action was god-like" and he "responds to the ideal of self-sacrifice"), and remains distant from this discourse, with the framing device of an overheard conversation that reverts back to a pastoral environment separate from the ugly, if redemptive, world of trench warfare. Rilla wants to remain detached – "I don't see why we should fight England's battles" (47) she cries – but the men are already caught up in a different ideology, which initially effaces women: "And now she [Rilla] was nobody. His [Kenneth's] thoughts were full of this Great Game which was to be played out on blood-stained fields with empires for stakes – a Game in which womenkind could have no part. Women, thought Rilla miserably, just had to sit and cry at home" (47).

From this inauspicious start, the novel goes on to reject the notion that women can so easily be blanked out, re-articulating Rilla's growing sense of autonomy and self-worth to replace the word "nobody" with somebody far more complex, and far more independent. Stereotypical feminine domestic discourse is also replaced with the "terms of military tactics and diplomatic intrigue" (109), while additionally, Rilla and others learn to cope psychologically with casualty lists and blunt telegrams from war officials. Another device which subverts the pro-military discourse (mainly expressed by the male characters in the novel) is that of the image of the Pied Piper leading the young men off to war; eventually, even Rilla's brother Walter sees the Pied Piper in a vision at the Front: "I saw him marching across No-man's-land from our trenches to the German trenches – the same tall shadowy form, piping weirdly – and behind him followed boys in khaki" (257). The infantile Rilla matures emotionally and psychologically, but the men who rush to war appear younger and younger as the novel progresses, imagined here as "boys in khaki" seduced by magical folk music and dance. Walter, who was going to write the great war poem (possibly modelled on MacCrae's *In Flanders Fields*), knows he is about to die, and that he will never write the poem after all; yet he senses freedom from the fear of death, and the uncanny certainty that "it isn't only the *living* who are fighting – the *dead* are fighting too. Such an army *cannot be defeated*" (258). The uncanny dead are not just speaking, as in *In Flanders Fields*, here they are also fighting, haunting the battlefield and contributing to the success of the Allies. Rilla and Susan do more than mature in the novel: they take on jobs formerly done by the men (as noted earlier) who are now fighting. Rilla has done so much as part of her journey of development or *Bildungsroman* that her character will never be the same again: "By the end of the novel she has skilfully managed the Junior Red Cross, raised a war baby, risen above Irene's [her friend and rival] pettiness, organized a wedding, and worked at a tedious job in a store. […] Rilla learns that she does not have to be a boy to effect change" (Tector, 81).

A feminist critique of war: Francis Marion Beynon's *Aleta Dey* (1919)

Montgomery's *Bildungsroman*, however much a story of maturing female subjectivity and relative autonomy, still firmly situates Rilla in the domestic sphere, for example with the novel's war baby subplot. A more divided narrative is Francis Marion Beynon's *Aleta Dey*, which counters a romance plot with one of female political protest. Sister of the leading women's reformer and President of the Manitoba Political Equality League Lillian Beynon, Francis also played a crucial part in the passage of the women's suffrage bill (the right to vote) that was passed in Manitoba in 1916. Working for the *Grain Growers' Guide* as a journalist and political reporter gave Francis Beynon some leverage which was used to protect a clause within the suffrage bill that gave women the right to stand for political office. She also managed to work her feminist perspective into her popular section of the *Grain Growers' Guide* called "The Country Homemakers", in particular quoting extensively from Olive Schreiner's (1855–1920) *Women and Labour* (1911). However, Beynon's outspoken opposition to the war – beginning with "her report on the formation of a Women's Peace Party in the United States" (Hicks, xiii) – led to her demise, including being asked to resign from her post at the *Guide*, and exile in the USA, where she could not be persecuted by the Canadian Press Censor (although it also meant the end of her journalistic career as the Press Censor's reach extended to foreign-press publications such as the *International Socialist Review*).

   As a feminist fictionalized auto/biography, *Aleta Dey* is existentially powerful, and bleak, as we witness the destruction of the protagonist who is killed because of her pacifist beliefs. Beynon parodies the patriotic discourse of the day, the jolly-hockey-sticks approach to war, which "burst like a cloud upon our holidaying world, and set us all a-tremble and a-thrill" (163). The parody extends to those who thought the war would be but a playful romp, over by Christmas: "Germany had broken the peace of the world and plunged us into night. Very well, we would collect a few Canadians and send them over and they would settle the matter in a few months and come home, and we would give them a banquet, and allow them to die in the poor-house, as had been done to the heroes of other wars" (163). The breathlessness of Beynon's prose mimics the frenzied and hasty public plunging into patriotic fervour; with the repetition of the phrase "What days those were!" there is retrospective justi-fication for such a response, a justification that Beynon is also parodying. When Aleta's lover, McNair, enlists, she finds herself having emotions that she would otherwise abhor, desiring that other "able-bodied men" (166) would sign-up and go to war also: "That is the first of many internal hates war breeds; the first of a whole army of ugly, primitive, degrading emotions, which tend to drag humanity back to barbarism" (166–67).

McNair perceptively sees that Aleta does not believe in the righteousness of war, and from this moment she becomes far more outspoken about her anti-war beliefs; she rejects the invasive prying into the private lives of soldiers' wives, while the lives of war profiteers remain their own business. In the course of her involvement at Suffrage rallies, Aleta's anti-war sentiments are remarked upon, until she discovers her telephone is tapped; the Canadian Press Censor contacts her to warn her against speaking against the conscription measure, and after distributing pamphlets in support of freedom of speech, she is arrested and imprisoned. Aleta asks, "Since when had Canadians relinquished the right to discuss unmade legislation? Was this Prussia or Canada in which we lived?" (217). Aleta is assaulted by a soldier at a meeting and dies from her wounds, eventually becoming a martyr to the pacifist cause. The divided narratives – romance and political revolt – come together in death, with an idealistic funeral march and a burial service which synthesizes Biblical rhetoric with that of Aleta's activist writing. This fantasmatic ending can be criticized, or perceived as an alternative gender *performance* to that of the state-sanctioned public funerals held for military heroes. In other words, Beynon overlayers final patriarchal and patriotic rituals in an act of imaginative, feminist subversion.

The new language of war: absurdism in Charles Yale Harrison's *Generals Die In Bed* (1930)

Masculine ideals are also undermined by probably the most famous of all Canadian books about the war (at least, prior to the publication in 1977 of Timothy Findley's (1930–2002) *The Wars*): Charles Yale Harrison's (1898–1954) *Generals Die In Bed* (1930). The singularity of the event of war, and the experience of war as a limit or boundary situation (as Jaspers sketches this concept: "I cannot live without struggling and suffering ... I cannot avoid guilt … I must die" (178)), is constitutive of a new language: one that is stark, raw, existential. This is a novel where the language of command (and patriotism) is received as a factual absurdism: orders simply to be followed unto death, yet *not* justified by that death. Harrison is famous for having to testify to his publishers that the events depicted in his novel were based on reality, so shocked were they to see the war depicted in this way. Yet in retrospect, it is the breakdown and clearing away of high-flown rhetoric that is indicative of veracity in Harrison's prose, the war stripped bare of its baroque ornamentation, leaving nothing but ugly life, and death, and a new lunar landscape.

The opening of the second section of *Generals Die In Bed* realizes a new discursive approach to war: "We leave the piles of rubble that was once a little Flemish peasant town and wind our way, in Indian file, up through the muddy communication trench. In the dark we stumble against the sides of the trench and tear our hands and clothing on the bits of embedded barbed wire that runs through the earth here as though it were a geological deposit" (15). The absurdism is active from the start: what are these men fighting for, if the town behind the front has been reduced to a pile of rubble? What is the point of a "communication" trench that injures the troops as they pass through it? The machinery and technologies of war – here represented by the barbed wire – have become so embedded in the landscape that they are like geological deposits: something that was there before human history, with the concomitant suggestion that they will be there after humans have all destroyed one another and passed from the earth. The pastoral, in other words, has been dug up by the war, exploded, its idyllic landscapes interlaced with razor-sharp technologies. The landscape, having become dangerous, muddy and miserable, leaves the men to scurry around like the bloated, overfed rats that live in the trenches. What is absent from these sentences is as important as what is present: the communication trench leads from a pile of rubble to an unnamed place, although we surmise that going "up" means going towards the front; the men are not moving swiftly and strategically like heroic soldiers, they are literally stumbling in the dark, falling over and falling into water-filled holes. The outmoded image, "in Indian file", even confuses the sense of who these men are.

Overall, this section of the novel is highly disorienting, reducing the spatial co-ordinates to a pile of rubble and a dark, dangerous trench, one which a bit later on "rocks and sways" (23) under the impact of bombardment: "Mud and earth leap into the air, come down upon us in heaps" (23). Romanticized war narratives often present a linear account of traumatic events: the build up is followed by the event or trial, then the endurance of the trial, and finally the relief or redemptive reward when it is over. Here, the bombardment is over, then it starts again, then it stops, then it starts again and is even worse, leading the narrator to write, using the modernist device of "primitivism", that the men eventually "throw ourselves face downward on the bottom of the trench and grovel like savages before this demoniac frenzy" (25). Civilized man has been reduced to a "savage", but still the narrator can pray, before he remembers "that I do not believe in God" (26), so stripped of this last component of heroic western man, he is left with nothing but "insane thoughts": "I can find nothing to console me, nothing to appease my terror" (Ibid.). Finally, time itself, the days of the week, the seasons, appear to mean nothing: "We do not know what day it is. We have lost count. It makes no difference whether it is Sunday or Monday. It is merely another day – a day on which one may die" (27).

Harrison's language is starkly absurdist, modernist, and deeply existential: his modernist "primitivism" is apt, regardless of how contemporary readers might be disturbed by words such as "savages"; instead of heroes, we have Beckettian characters waiting for clean sheets, a meal, sex, or just death. In this world, euphemisms rule, such as the word "rest" which "is another military term meaning something altogether different" (36). The lice, not the Germans, are the real enemy, while the war is simply a repetition of the same dire experiences; the land is soaked, stinking "like a city garbage dump" (54), and the men in turn are always wet. If there is fighting, it is as likely to happen among the men themselves, who are lambs being led to the slaughter. Words continually falter and fail, being replaced by ellipses, another modernist device, seen for example in the work of the dramatist Henrik Ibsen. "Better not to ask questions. Better not to ... " (130), says Harrison's narrator, the ellipsis trailing off into multiple possibilities and subversive thoughts. Even when a literary or intertextual allusion or analogy is at work, it is left open, or undermined, by the ellipses: "here we are no more factors than was the stripling Isaac whom the hoary, senile Abraham led to the sacrificial block. ... " (131). The ellipsis is followed, on the next line, by another inde-terminate statement: "But it is better not to think. ... " (131). The reader is left to fill in the blanks, although there are some clues: Abraham, who stands in for the officers of the First World War, is "senile", undermining the sec-ondary meaning of "hoary", that of being "venerable"; the soldiers are "lads", but also they are part of a group, or a community ("striplings"). In Genesis 22 – the intertextual reference – Isaac carries his own firewood for his own sacrificial slaughter, just as the soldiers in effect dig their own graves (the trenches) and lay down the barbed wire upon which they will be killed. Isaac is saved by a substitutionary creature, the ram which is sacrificed in his place (in Adele Wiseman's (1928–92) novel *The Sacrifice* (1956), this Biblical narrative is turned into a powerful story about immigrants, gender, and madness). In the trenches, however, there is contiguity: the "ram" is simply the next man, the "everyman", who dies today, just as the one saved will die tomorrow as someone else's "substitution". As the narrator says: "it is better not to think" about this situation, one in which there appears to be no sal-vation. The ellipses also disallow for any notion of "glory" in death-in-battle; later on in the novel, the narrator writes that "To us this business of military glory and arms means carrying parties, wiring fatigues, wet clothes and cowering in a trench under shell-fire" (212). In Romantic and patriotic war narratives, glory is held high like a banner; here, the troops simply carry the materiel for their own death and destruction.

Literature of the Second World War: psychology and ethics in the Canadian war novel

The theatre of war became more varied, its geography more dispersed, during the Second World War. Once again, Canadians played a significant part, even though from the beginning an expeditionary force was decided against. With the National Resources Mobilization Act of 21 June 1940, however, substantial material – including human resources – were provided for.

Once again women played a major role in the armed forces and at home in factories and offices, and the industrial boom that occurred in the shipbuilding and airplane building industries in cities such as Vancouver provided many temporary jobs. Canadians were an active part of British Bomber Command; Canada also provided corvettes as naval escorts for Atlantic convoys which needed protection from German U-Boats, a role explored by Hugh Garner (1913–79) in his novel *Storm Below* (1949). In *A Handful of Rice* (1961), author and artist William Allister (1919–2008) examines the after-effects of the attempt to defend Hong Kong in November 1941, in this case, following a group of men held prisoner by the Japanese. In *Execution*, Colin McDougall (1917–84) follows the men who served in the Italian campaign (1943–45), which had begun with the invasion of Sicily, and rapidly turned into an extended journey up country.

What these and other Canadian Second World War novels share is a focus on psychology rather than physiology, the impact upon diverse peoples from around the world: "With the development of the tank and the armoured personnel carrier, the trench war of 1914–18 could not be repeated. And with the airplane and ultimately, the atomic bomb, the people of such cities as London, Berlin, and Hiroshima bore the brunt of the war" (Novak, 96). This shift into psychology also creates a concern with ethics rather than absurdism, no doubt still an ethics of alienation but also one where the individual soldier

The National Resources Mobilization Act was a successful attempt to provide support for Canada's military efforts while maintaining a promise to its people: that there would be no conscription (enforced participation in the war). The Act was Prime Minister William Lyon Mackenzie King's solution to this promise, since it provided for the *defence* of the nation through the registration of eligible adults, as well as giving the government the power to acquire all of the other necessary resources for this task. In parliament the question of conscription continued to be debated, leading to a plebiscite on 27 April 1942, in which King's masterfully ambiguous slogan was "conscription if necessary, but not necessarily conscription". Some 83 per cent of English-Canadians supported conscription, with 72.9 per cent of French-Canadians opposed. There was rioting in Quebec with the introduction of the ensuing Bill 80, which repealed anti-conscription law.

once more exists, "and his view of himself as a being with moral responsibility" (Novak, 96).

While the Second World War soldier (or sailor/airman) has more mobility, he is frequently situated in a liminal space, one suspended between worlds, such as we find in playwright Samuel Beckett's *Waiting for Godot*. This liminal space is less war-as-machine, and more war-by-machine, as the narrator of *Storm Below* observes, "There is no human element in submarine warfare. It is submarine against ship, then ship against submarine" (50). Subtle psychological changes occur in the liminal space of the Second World War, with Canadian authors articulating concerns of gender, race and racism. The Captain in *Storm Below* examines a photograph of a dead sailor's girlfriend, initially wondering if she is a "cheap" salesgirl or waitress, before remembering that gender roles have changed: "During the past few years girls had striven, through wearing good imitations, to confuse the average male as to their social status or their wealth. And this, in itself, was good" (43). The initial sexism in this statement gives way to approval of class mobility, and furthermore, the notion that such mobility is revolutionary: "It was part and parcel of the revolution which was taking place around them. A revolution which depended not so much on the Hitlers and Stalins, but on the small, insidious changes in thought and behaviour which were bound to make the world different at the end of the war to what it had been in 1939" (43). The issue of anti-Semitism is explored in this novel in a disturbing sub-plot of introspection and self-hatred, with a Jewish-Canadian officer called Harris not just being subject to a sustained campaign of racism, but also becoming sickened by his own Jewish-Canadian identity. As one of the characters disturbingly argues: "As far as I'm concerned a Jew's a Jew no matter if he joined up in the Commandos on September the third, nineteen-thirty-nine ... I agree with Hitler, they should be wiped off the face of the earth" (132). Invited to visit a gentleman's club in the Laurentians, Harris bets that the club will be "gentiles" only, his self-hatred leading to an angry defacing of the officer's table-cloth: "Cut into the linen, as though with a razor blade, was a swastika that Harris had made with his knife" (137).

Storm Below follows a fairly standard sea-story plot of the disasters that follow the failure to bury a dead sailor at sea, the close analysis of human beings under extreme tension emerges as a key feature shared by the best Canadian war literature. On the broad historical canvas of a war novel such as *Little Man* (1942), by G. Herbert Sallans (1895–1960), this intensity is not achieved, although there are some acute analyses of the role of the media and propaganda, which does not come as a surprise from an author who worked for the Vancouver *Sun* and became Director of Information for the Canadian army in 1942. Crossovers between journalism and war reporting were common, as with Lionel Shapiro (1908–58), who worked as a journalist and then war correspondent for the Montreal *Gazette*; his three war novels – *The Sealed Verdict* (1947), *Torch for a Dark Journey* (1950) and *The Sixth of June* (1955) – were preceded by an account of the Allied campaign in Sicily, called

They Left the Back Door Open (1944). Another significant war reporter was Ralph Allen (1913–66), who began his career in journalism working as a sports writer for the *Winnipeg Tribune*, becoming war correspondent for the *Globe and Mail*. Allen's war novel is *Home Made Banners* (1946), although he is now better known for his history of Canada between the wars, *Ordeal by Fire: Canada, 1910–1945* (1961). Intensity of existential character and situation is reached with McDougall's *Execution*, and this novel is arguably the finest achievement of Canadian Second World War fiction.

War as existential void: Colin McDougall's *Execution* (1958)

If it is a shock for contemporary readers to discover horses on the battlefields of the First World War – in fact Findley's *The Wars* starts with a description of a horse – the effect in *Execution* is part theatre, part pantomime: "Here at last, in the afternoon of their first day at war, the enemy was visible; and that enemy consisted of soldiers arrayed in blue and gold, sabres belted at their side, and mounted on horses. *Horses!*" (12). While the horses at the Front are often a sign of tragic beauty and freedom, here they remain precious, but described as if part of an imagist scene. Imagism and Surrealism are even more prevalent when the Colonel of the defeated Sicilian cavalry presents arms in surrender: "His beet-red face dripped with sweat … he looked at the sword, he looked in the Colonel's face – like an anxious egg poaching in the sunshine … he felt an irresistible urge to laugh: he wanted to split his sides laughing" (15). The complex synaesthesia here – vegetable beets and poached eggs, red and white, perhaps the silver of the sword, and the dripping sweat – includes smells, such as the smell of sweat, and the cooking egg.

Imagism and Surrealism are two modernist aesthetic movements from the beginning of the twentieth century. Imagism's most famous practitioner, the poet and critic Ezra Pound (1885–1972), believed in a pared down aesthetic, whereby language was stripped of all ornamentation to facilitate a poetic "presentation" of an image; one of the key devices used was synaesthesia, the mixing of senses, such as smell, taste, touch and sound, to make a complex image (see also the following chapter). **Surrealism** was a much longer-lasting artistic movement led by André Breton (1896–1966), who published the first manifesto of Surrealism in 1924. Surrealism attempted to bring the world of the unconscious into everyday life, creating an artistic, sexual and political revolution in the process. Its methodology included the juxtaposition of unlike images or objects, the downplaying of rational control over thought processes, for example, in the production of texts through high-speed "automatic writing", an interest in chance encounters or found objects ("objective chance"), and an obsession with the outmoded and the uncanny.

The end result is highly comic, enough to lead to the disintegration of subjectivity: not "he wanted to laugh", but the far more visceral "he wanted to split his sides laughing". This fragile subjectivity will fall apart in different ways when a totally meaningless and probably unnecessary execution of two harmless young Italians takes place. Crucially, the young men sense that as long as they make the Canadian soldiers laugh, they will remain safe; they perform, with their little cardboard suitcase, whatever theatrical acts are necessary, pretending at one moment to cook Mediterranean food: "Egged on by the surrounding men they made great play of adding imaginary spices and flavourings. They were like children on a Sunday picnic" (36). The richness of imaginary Italian cooking becomes theatre, but the men are soon re-labelled as deserters, for which they are shot.

It is the order to kill these innocent young men that finally does "cleave" or split Adam, the protagonist of the novel: "Full cognizance of the order he had received cleaved him, and left him incapacitated like a gigantic wound" (42). Three men form a close bond in the novel: Adam, Major Bazin, and Padre Doorn, and their responses to this pointless execution are held in tension, and in comparison, with the feelings of exhilaration, excitement and adventure that war can also generate. Bazin regards himself as more sophisticated than the other two, less naïve and less susceptible to shock, but still he ends up in a bizarre existential state, working through various psychical stages until he decides that it is his personal existence that prolongs the war, since "objects possess only subjective existence" (49): "It must follow as inexorable consequence that if *I* cease to exist, then the war itself will cease to exist. If I die today – *the war will be over!*" (49).

Adam attempts to cover over the void in his shattered subjectivity with extreme competence as an officer, but still the void remains, like a Conradian heart of darkness: "The emptiness was the horror" (59). The Padre appears to go insane, and spends his time searching for a true fragment of the Cross, which he believes he has finally found in a remote Italian sanctuary: "it was much more than wood, more than mere representation. ... Then for centuries it had performed miracles: given sight to the blind, life to the dead, cleansed lepers, routed demons. The object was the Son of God himself" (124). Dropping the fragment on the battlefield, another soldier retrieves it, but when the Padre returns from his temporary insanity, he finally accepts that this recovered fragment is probably "a piece of broken rifle stock" (144). Ironically it is the third execution in the novel, of an innocent young mentally disabled Canadian soldier called Jonesy, who should never have been allowed to enlist, that leads to a sense of release from the existential void; Jonesy functions as a scapegoat in René Girard's sense: he takes on the fears and anxieties of his friends, and cares for them right up to the point of his execution, lifting their burdens as they sacrifice him. This role reversal is powerful and moving, but still fitting with the absurdism of war. These men who will not shoot horses are released by the sacrificial death of Jonesy, but not in a romanticized way. The novel remains open, the existential void remains in place, and war remains senseless.

Conclusion

- As much as the literature of the First World War expressed a patriotic, fervent desire to serve Empire and God, it also expressed scepticism in the face of the mass slaughter of men and the horrors of trench warfare.
- The literature of the two world wars explores shifts in gender roles in Canadian society, during a time when women gained the right to vote and to partake, however temporarily, in the wider economy.
- Popular fiction has historical value, and many of the questioning, more complex attitudes towards war, nationalism, and the transformation of men and women's lives, can be found in popular novels and genre fiction.
- The breakdown of society, unstable subjectivity, shell-shock, and the increasing use of mechanized warfare finds a concomitant world in the new increasingly urban centres of modernity; war literature is relevant therefore not just for those directly involved, but in its searches for new modes of writing, it becomes more representative of disturbing new human experiences.

5 Canadian modernism, 1914–60

"A journey across Canada"

Overview

Recent shifts in critical understanding have led not only to a reassessment of Canadian modernism but also to an awareness that Canadian modernism took place over a significant period of time. Competing critical and literary historical narratives now exist, with important feminist research leading to different notions of the modernist canon. Recent editing and "history of the book" projects in Canada have also contributed to critical reassessment, with focus on the role of small presses and magazine/journal publications.

Marginal modernism/Imagism and the poetic imagination

Two historical narratives concerning Canadian modernism are at times over-layered: the first is largely masculinist, beginning with the First World War poets and the high modernist aesthetic engagements with Imagism and other international movements; the second, more recent narrative is largely feminist, recovering marginalized voices and women authors such as Louise Morey Bowman (1882–1944), Katherine Hale (Amelia Beers Warnock Garvin, 1878–1956), Dorothy Livesay (1909–96), and P.K. Page (1916–2010), who were at times downplayed, excluded or simply ignored by the first narrative. In many respects, it is amazing that there are any literary historical narratives at all concerning modernism in Canada, since Robert Kroetsch famously declared in 1974 that "Canadian literature evolved directly from Victorian into Postmodern" (1). Over four decades earlier, critic and poet Leo Kennedy surveyed the literary scene in his essay "The Future of Canadian Literature" (1928), arguing not only that "In poetry the Tennysonian and Wordsworthian traditions still rule" (quoted in Dudek and Gnarowski, 34) but furthermore, quoting S.I. Hayakawa, that "The bulk of poems written in Canada may be briefly classified under four heads. They are, Victorian, Neo-Victorian, Quasi-Victorian, and Pseudo-Victorian" (Ibid., 36).

How could Canadian modernism be either not there at all, or not happening as such by 1928, the year Livesay published her innovative collection *Green Pitcher*, and eight years after Jean-Aubert Loranger (1896–1942) had published his free verse poem *Je regarde dehors par la fenêtre*? One answer is that many of the early Canadian modernists published in small presses, or overseas

The Futurists, led by Filippo Tommao Marinetti (1876–1944), and **the Vorticists**, led in London by the Canadian Percy Wyndham Lewis (1882–1957), believed that art should embrace the speed of the new machine technologies of the early twentieth century, as well as the "cleansing" properties of warfare, industrialization and Fascism. Lewis theorized the "vortext" [sic] as a node through which powerful ideas would rush at great speed; in a manifesto text called "Our Vortex" (1914) the Vorticists argued that "The Vorticist is not the Slave of Commotion, but its Master" and that "We are proud, handsome and predatory. / We hunt machines … " While Futurism proclaimed a new joyous aesthetic, sensitive and receptive to the machine age, Vorticism reacted harshly against the new aesthetic of the Bloomsbury Group and their Omega Workshops in London, which were perceived as feminine and divorced from the machine world.

(mainly in the US), before they gained a more public presence with poems being reprinted in later book collections (if this happened at all – for many women poets it would be *much later*). However, the small size of a particular print-run or readership did not necessarily equate to low impact; in fact the opposite was often the case, for example with the Quebec avant-garde arts magazine *Le Nigog* (the fishing-spear), founded in 1918 by the architect Fernand Préfontaine and others, running to only twelve issues. *Le Nigog* created a platform for innovation in the arts, publishing over one hundred essays on experimental aesthetics, in the process rejecting the conservativism and utilitarian themes of the French Canadian literary establishment. Jean-Aubert Loranger, a journalist and innovative poet who was one of the founders of *Le Nigog* (and a member of the École Littéraire De Montreal), published a remarkable collection of poems in 1920 called *Les atmospheres, le passeur, poèmes et autres proses*, followed by *Poèmes* in 1922; these collections contain some of the first modernist poems in Canada. Another answer to the question of Canadian modernism's perceived absence is that even though it existed in dialogue with American and European modernist movements and key authors, its distinctiveness is still being explored and discussed in Canada today, using new critical paradigms and newly edited and published texts. Modernism in all nations is a hybrid aesthetic, one where poetry, art and performance are complemented and at times exceeded by the public impact of manifesto writing and criticism, such as the manifestos of the Surrealists in France, the Futurists in Italy, or the Vorticists in England. Canadian modernism's hybridity is still being analysed and reconsidered.

Canadian modernist manifesto writing

It is no coincidence that Arthur Stringer's (1874–1950) poetry collection *Open Water* (1914) should be as important for its critical manifesto-leaning preface, as for its poems: "This book must be seen as a turning point in Canadian writing if only for the importance of the ideas advanced by Stringer in his preface. In a carefully presented, extremely well-informed account of traditional verse-making, Stringer pleaded the cause of free verse and created what must now be recognized as an early document of the struggle to free Canadian poetry from the trammels of end-rhyme, and to liberalize its methods and its substance" (Dudek and Gnarowski, 3). Some of the earliest poets engaging in this struggle are Frank Oliver Call (1878–1956), who published *Acanthus and Wild Grapes* in 1920, Louise Morey Bowman (1882–1944), who published *Moonlight and Common Day* in 1922 and *Dream Tapestries* in 1924, and Katherine Hale (1878–1956), whose *Morning in the West* was published in 1923. Call's preface to *Acanthus and Wild Grapes* is another important manifesto-leaning document in this history of Canadian modernism; he argues that the new poets have "joined the great army of seekers after freedom" and that they "refuse to be bound by the old restrictions of rhyme and metre" (quoted in Dudek and Gnarowski, 21). While Call's poems bridge traditional (*Acanthus*) and modern (*Wild Grapes*) aesthetics, he still speculates that "The boldest of the new school [of modernist poets] would throw overboard all the old forms and write only in free verse, rhythmic prose or whatever he may wish to call it" (Ibid.).

The garden and the machine in Louise Morey Bowman's *Timepieces* (1922)

Bowman's poetry achieves this boldness of form, seen in poems such as *Timepieces* (1922) which is her intriguing dialectical meditation upon the machine or technological age. In the poem, the old house and its "three wise clocks" in the first stanza represent a previous era; they are the two Grand-father's clocks and "a very, very old Clock, on the library mantel ... ", all three being "very wise and human. ... / And faithful." But the old house is suddenly left empty and "unlighted" (stanza II), and the transition in the third section is into the garden, where an old sundial is an even more ancient machine for timekeeping. The first stanza of section three bursts into colour-ful life: "Where flowers bloom in wild riot of colour." The transition from the stately and beautiful wooden clocks to this "riot of colour" appears to mimic the transition from a past aesthetic to the modern world of free verse, this feeling confirmed in the final stanza of section three: "For we cannot read only Elizabethan lyrics and sonnets / Beside the sundial." The fourth section is mysterious, with a controlled lyricism and formality of setting ("the sunken garden") and of objects ("The sundial stands aloof as ever on its slender pedestal. ... "); moonlight in the first stanza is juxtaposed with the "vivid spray of red Autumn berries" which symbolize the permanence of love in the "old motto". In the second stanza the sundial is even more architectural, crowned with snow, lit again by moonlight, but having received the snow "From the mysterious sky that holds the Sun and the Moon." Before this phrase can fully resonate, the controlled lyricism of this formal scene is revealed in section five to be a "sketch" written "in the power-house of a great factory ... ": "Now the noise has become rhythmical. ... awesome. ... "

The poet moves from the antique house, to the empty house, and then to the garden which has become increasingly more formal and abstracted; the reader's shock of discovering that all along the poet has been inside of the machine is tempered by the poet finding shelter in rhythms and noise, whereupon she fuses the inorganic with organic worlds, creating the images of the "deep, green caverns" and "the roar of the ocean". In the second stanza of section five, poetic insight, however, is given over to the mind of the machine; while the opening lines of the stanza complete a grammatical sentence that begins in the first stanza comparing the old clocks with the "hurrying machine", the sentence break leads to an association with the second sentence and a meaning which overrides grammatical sense: "In comparison / With this hurrying, rhythmical beat of these mighty engines, / [...] I understand nothing. ... " In the poem's coda, the poet writes: "As a child writes. ... " a simple list which embodies a transition from the transcendent to the machine age, still ending with "TIME AND ETERNITY" but clearly this is now the eternal rhythm of the autonomous machine, not that of God and the heavenly spheres. Critic Wanda Campbell argues that the poet here "comes 'laboriously' and 'reverently' to realize that engines, like sundials and clocks before them, can be a means to contemplate 'TIME AND ETERNITY'" (84), an insight which also carries the additional notion that all of these machines are in effect tools with which to measure or aestheticize the immeasurable. Nonetheless, there does appear to be a transition into a new world, one where the machine does not need a human being to "wind it up" like an old clock, and where understanding resides "in" the machine.

Journeys into modernity: Katherine Hale's *Grey Knitting* (1914) and *Going North* (1923)

Bowman's achievement with *Timepieces* is to have written a poem which places the poet inside *and* outside of the machine, comparing the machine with the Victorian house and garden, and juxtaposing the machine-world of modernism with that of the architectonic world of antiques and garden sculptures/design. These historical/temporal and aesthetic domains within *Timepieces* are porous, interrelated and interpenetrated. Subjectivity is both in control and "impaired", is powerfully synthetic and yet is also "alienated, divided, and obscured" (Baetz, 11) by the machine world. Bowman's poet takes the reader on a journey, something that Katherine Hale does on a much larger scale in her groundbreaking *Going North* in her collection *Morning in the West* (1923). As Campbell notes, in *Going North* Hale "explores four central themes of international modernism – movement across social, geographic, and gender lines; postwar reflection; rising nationalism; and a renewed interest in the past – all within a Canadian setting. Hale chooses to go north, rather than south or east for her inspiration but, ironically, the journey north turns out to be a journey into modernity" (87). One of the most important aspects of *Going North* is the way in which it expresses potential liberation for women in Canada, the journey North being symbolic of the poet's freedom in comparison with those women stuck in more traditional gender roles. Yet even in Hale's earlier work, such as *Grey Knitting* (1914), traditional gender roles exceed the initial societal expectations of correct gender performance: the women knitting across Canada for the men in the trenches of the First World War produce "A web of grey" which "spreads strangely". Like the Lady of Shallott in Tennyson's poem, the women here weave in a domain separate from that of the male-dominated world of the trenches (although, as noted above, large numbers of women served in the medical corps); this knitting/weaving might appear "foolish, inadequate", followed by the powerful image and the juxtaposed deeply ironic phrase "Grey wool on fields of hell is out of fashion", yet as the men die, the poet hopes they will hear "the fairy click of women's needles" as a reminder of another world left behind, one less jingoistic perhaps, where other sacrifices are made.

Imagism in the Canadian poetic imagination: A.J.M. Smith and E.J. Pratt

Hale's image of the "Grey wool on the fields of hell" is amazingly spare, creating a powerful presence. Early Canadian modernists adapted the methods of the Imagist movement, as one important component in a complex array of new, experimental literary techniques. F.S. Flint, in his essay "Imagisme" (1913), presented the three main rules of the movement:

1 Direct treatment of the "thing", whether subjective or objective.
2 To use absolutely no word that did not contribute to the presentation.
3 As regarding rhythm: to compose in sequence of the musical phrase, not in sequence of a metronome.

(352)

Ezra Pound called these three rules "the result of long contemplation" (357) rather than dogma, which he explicitly rejected; he argued that "An 'image' is that which presents an intellectual and emotional complex in an instant of time" (356). Imagism emerged in part from the British critic and poet T.E. Hulme's theories of aesthetics, yet an important fact is that Hulme had himself been inspired by a journey across Canada: "The first time I ever felt the necessity or inevitableness of verse was in the desire to reproduce the peculiar quality of feeling which is induced by the flat spaces and wide horizons of the virgin prairie of Western Canada" (quoted in Stevens, 35).

Imagism was one of the influences on A.J.M. Smith (1902–80), for example towards the end of his poem *Fin de Siècle* (1928) where he imagines "poems, crisp and sharp and small" (quoted in Stevens, 43). A well-known poem by Smith that fuses what Hulme above calls a Canadian "peculiar quality of

The Group of Seven first held an exhibition at the Art Museum of Toronto in May 1920, with work by the artists Franklin Carmichael, Lawren Harris, A.Y. Jackson, Franz Johnston, Arthur Lismer, J.E.H. Macdonald and F.H. Varley; the theme of the exhibition was the Algonquin Landscape. Critics were outraged by the new style of painting on display, which had been influenced by Canadian artist Tom Thomson: declaring that they were painting Canada, the Group of Seven utilized a new colour palette to express Canada's Northern landscapes – "the bare Precambrian rock, the wide skies, lonely lakes and rivers, the sinuous dark pines, and the autumn colouring of the maples" (Harper, 263). Theirs was a bold and striking post-impressionist vision, partly driven by metaphysical and transcendentalist beliefs which directly affected the spiritualist colours used to portray glaciers, lakes, and vast landscapes. The British Columbia painter Emily Carr was associated with the Group, as was the Montreal artist Edwin Holgate and the Winnipeg artist L.L. Fitzgerald. Carr is now most famous for her paintings of Aboriginal villages and totem poles in the brooding Pacific Northwest rainforests on Vancouver Island, in British Columbia.

feeling" with the influences of Imagism, Romantic, Symbolist and Metaphysical poetry, is *The Lonely Land* which was first published in 1926; critics have argued that this text attempts to present an "unmediated vision" of Canada analogous to that of the Group of Seven (Darling, 20): "Cedar and jagged fir / uplift sharp barbs / against the gray / and cloud-piled sky."

Smith's poem is also in direct intertextual relationship with two poems by the American Imagist H.D. (Hilda Doolittle, 1886–1961): *Oread* and *Sheltered Garden*, but the imagery in *The Lonely Land* is ultimately resolved in the notion of an eternal strength – "the beauty / of strength / broken by strength / and still strong" – that is absent in H.D.'s *Sheltered Garden*. Furthermore, H.D. allows her images to stand for themselves, whereas Smith engages in a self-reflexive foregrounding or interpretation of his images, which, combined with the Canadian penchant for *extending* images, creates a distinctive Canadian synthesis of modernist technique and more open and extensive poetic sensibility. For example, Smith's poem *Silver Birch* (1926) initially appears to follow the "rules" of Imagism, giving a "complete imagist poem" (Stevens, 54) in the first seven lines, whereafter the poem continues in a less successful (from an Imagist perspective), more self-reflexive mode, interpreting the image already presented, aligning the "wide water" with the Romantic concept of "an infinite love". While Smith himself did not think highly of his own poem, it does reveal that Canadian modernists were often involved in synthesis and a distinctive poetic vision.

E.J. Pratt's (1882–1964) Imagist experiments in *Newfoundland Verse* (1923) feed into a grander vision that would eventually find full expression in the long poems *Titans: Two Poems* (1926) and the epic poems *Brébeuf and His*

Brethren (1940) and *Towards the Last Spike* (1952). In *The Shark*, the animal world and the machine world are powerfully fused into one, the shark's fin "Like a piece of sheet-iron, / Three-cornered"; his body is "tubular" and his eyes are "metallic grey". This killing machine appears to be more of a submarine than an organic creature, one that doesn't so much come alive in the third stanza, as become transformed through the animals of Canadian myth: "That strange fish, / Tubular, tapered, smoke-blue, / Part vulture, part wolf, / Part neither – for his blood was cold." Animal, myth and machine combine in a synthesis that reveals the Canadian perspective of "the realm of space" (*The Final Moments*), or, to put this another way, Canadian modernism in the hands of Pratt fuses the modernist fragment with the grand vision of bigger narrative forms. Pratt went on to imaginatively explore science, technology, and fantasy in parables and allegorical poetic narratives.

The Montreal Movement: "Ideas are changing"

On 21 November 1925, a new literary journal appeared in Canada called the *McGill Fortnightly Review*, founded by A.J.M. Smith and F.R. Scott (1899–1985). It's precursor was *The McGill Daily Supplement* of the university newspaper *The McGill Daily*; Smith had edited the weekly *Supplement* between 1924 and 1925, but it was the new *Review* that would be artistically and critically innovative in its two-year publication run. In an essay on "Contemporary Poetry" published in the *Review* in 1926, Smith began by defining the current age as one of rapid change with everyday life being heavily influenced by science and technology; he argues that " ... the whole world contracted almost visibly under the tightening bands of closer communications. Things moved faster, and we had to move with them" (quoted in Dudek and Gnarowski, 27). The Victorian age has given way to the modern transforming religious and philosophical ideas: "Science, again, has been the catalyst" (Ibid.) and there is a shift within Canadian society from stability to flux:

> The whole movement, indeed, is a movement away from an erroneous but comfortable stability, towards a more truthful and sincere but certainly less comfortable state of flux. Ideas are changing, and therefore manners and morals are changing. It is not surprising, then, to find that the arts, which are an intensification of life and thought, are likewise in a state of flux. Those who attended the concert given by the Boston Symphony Orchestra a few weeks ago will have noticed the influence of our changing age upon music, while post-impressionism, cubism, vorticism and half a dozen other "isms" indicate its effect upon painting. Contemporary poetry reflects it as clearly as any other art.
>
> Poetry today must be the result of the impingement of modern conditions upon the personality and temperament of the poet. Some have been awakened to a burning enthusiasm by the spectacle of a new era; others are deeply disturbed by the civilization of a machine-made age. Some

have heard music in the factory whistle; others have turned aside into solitude that they might better hearken to the still small voice.

(Ibid., 27–28)

Critical enquiry, for Smith, was as equally important as aesthetic innovation; in "Wanted: Canadian Criticism" he argues that "of criticism as it might be useful" in Canada "there is nothing" (31). Famously, he asserts in this essay, " … that our condition will not improve until we have been thoroughly shocked by the appearance in our midst of a work of art that is at once successful and obscene" (33).

In his Introduction to his 1943 edited anthology *The Book of Canadian Poetry*, Smith argued that modernism emerged from "a simplification of technique" whereby "Canadian poets turned against rhetoric, sought a sharper, more objective imagery, and limited themselves as far as possible to the language of everyday and the rhythms of speech" (quoted in Dudek and Gnarowski, 46). Smith gives a representative list of such poets and poems in his 1943 Introduction: "Some of the lyrics of Dorothy Livesay, the farm poems of Raymond Knister, Charles Bruce's stirring 'Words Are Never Enough,' the cadenced 'laconics' of W.W.E. Ross, and Anne Marriott's fine example of proletarian poetry, *The Wind Our Enemy* (1939)" (Ibid.). Livesay's *London Revisited – 1946* was later added to the expanded edition of Smith's *The Book of Canadian Poetry*, with its marvellous evocation of the eerie post-Blitz city which Livesay had witnessed on a visit as a correspondent for the Toronto *Daily Star*: " … I fell / Blundering through dark, around / No builded wall." The poet experiences "Rubble of rift and wreck / […] / And the stars flung / Up to the throne of hell: / And above, no ceiling / And below, no wall." The typical vision of the starry skies from the trench-bound perspective of World War One has been transposed and re-envisioned here, from the broken buildings of bombed out London (standing in, perhaps, for all of bomb-damaged Europe). The scene is uncanny, and symbolic of the modern poet's attempt to articulate a new fragmented world, one in which all that remains is the "Rubble of rift and wreck". Livesay imagines the city as having a face which is "Scarred and grimed by human hand". In a previously unpublished poem called *London in Retrospect* (1948), the stark skeletal city is fleshed out by organic growth and the return of "royal" colours: "If blackout paint has peeled from pillared doorways / And houses possess new fronts … / … the empty socket / Is no sodden pit, but a pocket of green / Into September paling, into michaelmas purple / Into the golden glint of the sceptre's rod" (in Irvine, ed., 83). The powerful image of "blackout paint" (used during the Second World War to make the city harder to see for incoming German bomber planes) peeling from London's surviving buildings leads to the (once again) eerie notion that the city lies safe underneath its camouflage, being merely in need of repair and time for re-growth, the organic world making up for the deficiencies of the inorganic. This symbiosis of the city machine and nature appears to gesture towards a more complex notion of time and space, machine and organic healing.

The Canadian Authors Meet (1927 and 1928)

In the *McGill Fortnightly Review*, the wide-ranging poetic approaches deployed by F.R. Scott, from traditional to experimental, reveal a restlessness, a searching for form – even in this case traditional form (Stevens, 69) – to articulate new restless ways of being in the modern world. At times Scott is highly adaptive, bending old and new voices to the Canadian cultural scene (for example, *Sweeney Comes to McGill* and *Sweeney Graduates* both in fascinating intertextual conversation with T.S. Eliot); at other times, Scott's poetic voice is more pointed, scathingly critical of contemporary notions of aesthetics, the most famous example being *The Canadian Authors Meet* (1927; revised 1928). As Stevens says of *Sweeney Comes to McGill* (1926), "It is a pastiche of [T.S.] Eliot's Sweeney poem but it is not a particularly exact pastiche. It is more in the nature of an adaptation of Eliot's form, with passing nods at Eliot's diction, in order to hit out at the pretensions and shallowness of both the bourgeois undergraduate and the system which perpetuates that shallowness" (68). Scott was appalled by the commercialization of Canadian literature, which was embodied for him by the Canadian Authors Association, an organization that promoted what the new poets and critics considered to be safe and mediocre Canadian literature. In *The Canadian Authors Meet* he called its members "Expansive puppets" and "unknowns": "The air is heavy with Canadian topics, / And Carmen, Lampman, Roberts, Campbell, Scott, / Are measured for their faith and philanthropics, / Their zeal for God and King, their earnest thought." "Canadian topics" suggests a written-to-order literature, Victorian and old-fashioned in its colonial notion of society. The English tea-party setting clearly means there is no room for the experimental or that which isn't quite genteel.

Scott originally ended the poem with himself placed in the corner, like a dunce or a little schoolboy undergoing a detention: "A rather lewd and most ungodly poet / Writing these verses, for his soul's salvation." The notion of "salvation" resonates on a number of levels: is he to be "saved" from this environment by writing this pastiche, or is he *supposed* to be absorbed into the environment, accepted back into it, and thereby "saved" from modernity? Scott eventually wrote a new final stanza, that broadens his attack:

> O Canada, O Canada, Oh can
> A day go by without new authors springing
> To paint the native maple, and to plan
> More ways to set the selfsame welkin ringing?

This shift from the original, personal salvific ending and a more general satire aimed at the Canadian literature industry appears to produce a more powerful poem, and yet it is also a withdrawal and an effacement of the person oppressed by the literary hangover of a Victorian past. Is this person projecting a masculinist, decadent perspective? Lorraine York argues that "this critique of cut-rate colonial derivativeness is a sexist broadside against the feminization of poetry that feminist critics of Canadian modernism have not been slow to notice" (160). Scott, along with the poet Leo Kennedy (1907–2000), would increase the intensity of their attack on cultural mediocrity in *The Canadian Mercury* (1928–29), and a landmark anthology that carried on the fight appeared in 1936, edited by Smith and Scott, called *New Provinces*. David Staines argues that, "This landmark collection had an effect similar to that of Wordsworth's 1798 preface to the *Lyrical Ballads*, arguing for, and exemplifying in its verse, the unadorned language of everyday speech. *New Provinces* solidified these poets as the Canadian modernists of their time" (140–41). *New Provinces* contained work by Smith, Scott, Kennedy, Pratt as well as Robert Finch (1900–95) and A.M. Klein (1909–72). Other literary historians note, however, that this collection is as significant for who it leaves out as for those it includes, probably the most significant *excluded* poet being Dorothy Livesay.

Protest, social observation and ethnicity: "King or Chaos"

Momentous changes in world economics and ongoing imperial warfare meant that social and aesthetic values were increasingly shaken up during the beginning of the twentieth century. Modernism in Canada developed during the recession (1913–15), two world wars (1914–18 and 1939–45) and the global economic depression of the 1930s, that would last for an entire decade. The government, under Prime Minister R.B. Bennett (1870–1947), reacted strongly to social and political protest, as with the harsh crackdown on the delegates to the Workers' Economic Conference in Ottawa in 1932; protesting in public in front of the Parliament, they were met in force by the RCMP, an armoured military car and the local police (Finlay and Sprague, 338). Prime Minister Mackenzie King (1874–1950), who had taken over from Bennett in 1935, came back to a job he had held before, and a nation that had profoundly changed, many people shifting to the left in their newfound socialist politics. The socialist CCF (Co-operative Commonwealth Federation) was founded in 1932–33, pressurizing Bennett to produce his New Deal programme which almost immediately fell apart. King came back into power with the slogan "It's King or Chaos" and that meant for many people that nothing would be done to help them out of their poverty. Lack of jobs also meant that immigrants to Canada were no longer welcome, especially Jewish peoples, who suffered under Canada's anti-Semitic Director of Immigration, Frederick Charles Blair (1874–1959); Blair's anti-Semitism was revealed in many ways, but no more so than in the refusal to allow to land in Canada (in 1939) over 900 Jewish refugees who were on board a ship called the *St. Louis*. In the year that Hitler began to destroy Europe, Canada had closed its doors to virtually every Jewish refugee.

Dorothy Livesay's aesthetic of commitment

Following a path of social awareness and engagement, Dorothy Livesay had witnessed social and political unrest in Paris in 1931 – where she completed a thesis at the Sorbonne on the influence of the French Symbolists and Metaphysicals on contemporary British poetry before returning to Canada, enrolling in a social work course at the School of Social Work in Toronto, and engaging in field work with the Family Service Bureau in Montreal. The lessons of her early technically innovative poetry collections, *Green Pitcher* (1928) and *Signpost* (1932), were incorporated into the literature that emerged from her experiences of Depression Canada and the USA (such as her casework in Englewood, New Jersey, and in Vancouver). Livesay also joined the Young Communist Party, which in Canada as elsewhere meant that she embarked on a very different trajectory (one which would find her living a parallel life) to those of the Canadian literary establishment. The ensuing collection of poems published in 1944 was called *Day and Night*: it won the Governor-General's Award for Poetry, as did her 1947 collection, *Poems for People*.

Critics have been divided over the relative worth of Livesay's aesthetic of commitment: some regard it as a maturing of the earlier experimental verses, others, as a reductive poetic move that was thankfully abandoned with a later return to more natural and subjective modes of expression. Paul Denham wittily suggests that for a Marxist poet, a dialectical treatment of her phases is necessary (7), a suggestion that offers an alternative notion of Livesay's aesthetic development, whereby the earlier experimentalism is sublated or incorporated into her aesthetic of commitment, both being in turn sublated in her later work (where sublation means being incorporated and lifted-up to a higher level).

The poem *Autumn*, in *Green Pitcher*, offers a good entry-point into Livesay's aesthetic; the poem presents a series of images, beginning with the desire "To recapture / The light, light air / Floating through trees / As a river through rushes". Such images fuel the transmogrified surroundings in *Day and Night* in Livesay's 1944 collection, from the opening "Dawn, red and angry" to the factory production-line-controlled rhythms of the working week, where "Light rips into ribbons / What we say". Whereas in *Day and Night* a multitude of voices express the vernacular as consumed by the profit-based capitalist machine, overriding such images, in *Autumn* the final image muddies the water, with its assertion on one line of the word "Unreal" being reminiscent of the striking last stanza of "The Burial of the Dead" in T.S. Eliot's *The Wasteland*, which opens with "Unreal City". Here, Livesay's final image of Autumn is of children "walking apart" and "Smelling the day / In brief snatches of wonder!" The single word "Unreal" appears to describe the children no longer in their usual group formation, and also the entire series of images that have both successfully expressed an autumnal moment, and yet somehow concomitantly failed in the attempt (according, that is, to the poet herself). The word "Unreal" hangs, in other words, over the entire poem, as a rejection of its own aesthetic and, paradoxically, as a hinge-word that dialectically creates a new aesthetic, one where the "unreal" is more relevant to the contemporary world as it fragments and undergoes the upheavals of the early twentieth century. This is the world of "Monition" in *Signpost*, where the human subject waits for the "footfall" of another person, but instead is startled by "the soft silken rush of a car over wet pavements"; in other words, not merely a matter of a sound disturbing her, but a psychological re-orientation: "The rush of a motor is too sudden a wind / In my mind" which "is as terrible / As Fear – surging – pounding."

In *Day and Night*, then, psychological disturbance and trauma are anchored to social and political environments: of a factory system divided between workers and bosses, of warfare, of capitalist flows that override human needs and desires. The opening stanza of *Day and Night* gives an evocative sense of these environments, painting a frightening picture, where "Scream after scream announces that the churn / of life must move, the giant arm command. / Men in a stream, a moving human belt / Move into sockets, every one a bolt. / The fun begins, a humming, whirring drum – / Men do a dance in time to the machines." There is an ambivalence here: the surface reading of human subjects reduced to machine parts, literally bolted into place, is countered by the "dance in time", puppets, perhaps, but also dancing with, as in partners. The possibility for human freedom thus remains open, even given the pummelling humanity receives in the stanzas of section two: "A writhing whack / Sets you spinning / Two steps back –". The subject is "called to love / deep in dream" and still has his or her senses: "We have ears / Alert to seize / A weakness / In the foreman's ease" and "We have eyes / To look across / The bosses' profit / At our loss." Livesay draws upon the vernacular of African American spirituals which were sung during slavery as a way of projecting a future hope, and maintaining spiritual sustenance; similarly, in the sixth section, the poet states that "Green of new leaf shall deck my spirit / Laughter's roots will spread" and eventually an "other way" of life will be found. Working-class lives become heroic, mundane tasks take on epic status, as in *Shipyard Voices*, and raw human labour is both self-destructive in bondage, but also the potential for a future world that will be built through such material struggle.

Livesay's own future poetic output was enormously dynamic and varied, and indeed Denham identifies this as a "central feature" of her literary career: "[with] a constant willingness to try out new modes, new poetic forms and rhythms, in order to accommodate new experiences and attitudes" (13). In 1950, Livesay published *Call My People Home and Other Poems*, a text which includes a radio documentary poem of Japanese-Canadian internment. Livesay's radio work was preceded by her agit-prop performance for children called *Joe Derry* published in 1933 and her radio drama *If the World Were Mine* broadcast by CBC in 1950. Later significant poetry collections include *The Unquiet Bed* (1967), *Plainsongs* (1969), *Ice Age* (1975), *The Raw Edges: Voices From Our Time* (1981) and *Phases of Love* (1981).

The image constellations of P.K. Page

The mechanized world of factory production so earth shatteringly represented by Livesay had another counterpart: that of the increasingly mechanized offices of the modern city dependent upon an increasing army of female workers including large numbers of "stenographers" (the early name for shorthand typists/secretaries before the advent of office computing which did away with many of these low-paid jobs). Access to these jobs for young women created independence yet at the same time a new form of subservience to a mainly male managerial class. For some modernist writers, such as Bertrand William Sinclair, this female workforce was a threat to the patriarchal order, as well as a manifestation of the increasing automatization of Canada's city inhabitants (the office as a machine). Other writers, such as P.K. Page, saw fertile ground for an aesthetic of acute social observation, such as her rapidly canonized poem *The Stenographers*, published in her first poetry collection *As Ten, As Twenty* (1946): "In the pause before the first draft and the carbon / they glimpse the smooth hours when they were children –."

Page was born in England and emigrated to Canada with her family as a young child; she grew up in Red Deer, Alberta, and in Calgary, where she attended St. Hilda's School. Page had first published a poem called *Moth* (1934) in *The Observer* in London, but it was the Canadian journals *Canadian Poetry Magazine* and *Saturday Night* that provided her with room to experiment, and she went on to become involved as an editor and contributor to a new journal called *Preview* in 1941 as well as publishing work in John Sutherland's *First Statement* (Orange, 2–3). Sutherland wrote a scathing critique of Page in his essay "P.K. Page and *Preview*", although this did not stop her from becoming a regional editor of the newly merged *Preview* and *Statement* (called *Northern Review*), when she moved to Victoria, BC, in 1944. Ironically, it was Sutherland's harsh review of *Poems* by Robert Finch that eventually led to Page's resignation from this post; in a letter to the editors she called Sutherland's reviewing "destructive" (quoted in Dudek and Gnarowski, 110).

Page's literary output was increasingly gaining far wider recognition: she was one of the poets anthologized in *Unit of Five* (1944), alongside Louis Dudek, Ronald Hambleton, Raymond Souster and James Wreford. In the same year she published an experimental novel called *The Sun and the Moon*, using the pseudonym Judith Cape. This explosion of creativity is matched by the explosive energy of her individual poems. Page's *Stenographers*, for example, is closely observed as image is heaped upon image to create a complex image constellation, structured in the first stanza by the "*a of b*" formula:

> After the brief bivouac of Sunday
> their eyes, in the forced march of Monday to Saturday
> hoist the white flag, flutter in the snow storm of paper,
> haul it down and crack in the midsun of temper.

Trehearne notes that "The '*a of b*' formula relies on a principle of unmediated juxtaposition between two previously unconnected concretes: '*a*' and '*b*' are usually nouns, '*b*' without an article, so the odd construction mimics the swiftness of juxtaposition in the Imagist poem" (75). The speed in which this constellation forms is closer to film than photography: the poem moves rapidly in its accumulation of images, giving the sense of motion, or, to steal a phrase from Walter Benjamin, "the work of art in the age of its technical reproducibility". Trehearne calls the constellation in Page a "fuller poetic structure", one which functions in *The Stenographers* by the contrasts between modernity (absorbed by the office machine) and pastoralism (memories of youth and freedom in the natural world), as can be seen in the third stanza: "Remember the sea where floats at high tide / were sea marrows growing on the scatter-green vine / or spools of grey toffee, or wasps nests on water." These memories achieve a "profane illumination" (see Glossary): the image constellation is a re-imagination of mundane objects (in this stanza, the floats) into an imaginary world, one which draws upon the energies of Surrealism and Symbolism. Orange notes that the early poems "gain depth when the images are repeated within a consistent context so that core images are transmuted into symbols" (23). Such a process is not linear: a constellation forms through accumulation and the creation of patterns, until a moment of insight or vision occurs.

In *The Metal and The Flower* (1954), the ephemeral nature of profane illumination is apparent in poems such as *Images of Angels* and *Reflection in a Train Window*. The mundane world is challenged by the thought of angels: even children lose their imaginative powers when overtaken by the law of the symbolic; the notary ends up locking his angels in a metal vault, the financier mocks them warily "for fear that they exist in worlds which he / uneasy, reconstructs from childhood's memory", the anthropologist cannot face giving a lecture on them to public ridicule: "Perhaps only a dog could accept them wholly". Page imagines asexual "nudes of Lawrence" meeting angels "with ease", or a child, playing with one innocently: "and all the telephone wires would become taut / as the high strings of a harp / and space be merely the spaces between strings / and the world mute, except for a thin singing." Speaking the name is enough to remove this vision of innocence, the music of the spheres coming to an end, and the realization that the discarded image is not even tenable for the child. Yet the poem has shown how this failure of the mundane world is a disaster, and as in Benjamin's *Angelus Novus*, the angel is looking at human progress and sees only the catastrophe that is a result of a disastrous lack of vision.

The creation of a complex image space occurs through the overlayering of the sacred and the profane; technically, this also occurs in *Reflection in a Train Window*, where the reflected woman overlayers all of the passing scenes, as if she were a ghost passing through a visual narrative, the "Christmas wreaths in passing houses" or the "background of mosaic". Yet the background scenes also shine through her: "shine now in eye and now in hair, in heart / How like a saint with visions, the stigmata / marking her like a martyr." She becomes "without substance" and "ectoplasmic" even "haloed with the reading lamps of strangers". This is once more a profane illumination, a surrealist vision of her tenuousness as a spectral figure, one which is still isolated and divided by a physical pane of glass. The medium (the glass window) is a screen, a mirror, and the film stock on which the passing scene merges with her image. Trehearne suggests that the "accumulative aesthetic" of this profane illumination does not proceed "through logic, expansion of emotion, or unfolding of narrative; rather, it extends the range of the subjective eye through a constellation of images, that are more or less dependent on a single central metaphor, abstraction, or initiatory incident" (79). For Trehearne, the purpose of such an extension of the "subjective eye" is the "conjunction of image accumulation and psychological interest" (80) in Page's work. The juxtaposition of Page's visual art and poetry in *Cry Ararat!* (1967) also helps with an understanding of her earlier visually powerful aesthetic, one that is revealed in Margaret Atwood's interpretive selections in *P.K. Page: Poems Selected and New* (1974).

Diasporic Intertextuality in the Jewish-Canadian modernism of A.M. Klein

The image constellation of Canadian modernism becomes more linguistically and intertextually complex and rich with the poetry of A.M. Klein, yet, paradoxically, Klein's work also signals the *end* of international modernism and the unifying voices or forces behind its fragmented and experimental texts, with the growing awareness of the Shoah: the murder of over six million Jews and other peoples by the Nazis during the Second World War. Klein's Judaism spans local identity – that is, the Jewish ghetto in Montreal where he lived, and international Jewish existence: the European pogroms, the diaspora, the Shoah, and the building of a new nation in Israel. Such dispersed ethnic existence is brought together in the grand architecture of Klein's poetry and prose; it is also expressed in the fact that during Klein's university years at McGill, while he was friends with the editors of *The McGill Fortnightly Review*, his earliest publications are to be found in *The Menorah Journal* in New York and *The Young Judaean* in Montreal. At McGill, Klein majored in law, a profession he would eventually hold in parallel with his literary and editing career (he edited *The Young Judaean* between 1928 and 1932, and the *Canadian Jewish Chronicle* between 1938 and 1955).

Involvement in theories of Judaism and politics was key to Klein's engagement as a thinker and creative writer; Zionism was a major influence on North American and European Jewish intellectuals, and Klein was involved in key debates concerning the foundation of Israel; he also ran for political office in 1949 as a CCF candidate, but with defeat imminent he withdrew his candidacy. However, in the same year he was commissioned by the Canadian Jewish Congress to investigate the condition of Jewish refugees in Europe and North Africa, including a visit to Israel; these experiences would later come to fruition in Klein's only novel, *The Second Scroll* (1951). Klein's first major poetry collection was *Hath Not a Jew ...* , published in 1940, followed by *Poems* in

1944, the same year in which he published a less successful mock-epic satire of the Nazis, based on Pope's *The Dunciad*, called *The Hitleriad*. Klein won the Governor-General's Award for Poetry with his final collection, *The Rocking Chair and Other Poems* published in 1948. The final section of Klein's novel is also mainly composed of poetry and other performative texts (see prose section later).

This relatively small body of work is labyrinthine in its intertextual influences, speaking myriad voices, adopting and adapting an enormous number of poetic techniques. Philosophical and theological influences include Spinoza, the Old Testament and the Talmud, the Jewish mystical scholarship and commentary known as Chassidism, and the Cabbala. Literary influences include the Romantics Shelley and Keats, the French Symbolists and international modernists, such as James Joyce, Ezra Pound and T.S. Eliot; Klein also drew deeply upon the western literary canon, admiring authors such as Vergil, Dante, Chaucer, Marlowe, and Shakespeare, as well as more modern poets such as Hopkins and Auden (see Golfman, 6). Klein was particularly drawn to James Joyce, eventually writing critical essays on him, but also incorporating techniques from Joyce's *Finnegans Wake* (1939) into his poems *Variations on a Theme, Sennet of Gheel, Song Without Music* and *Spring Exhibit* (see Heft). Golfman sees obvious parallels between Klein and Joyce: "Both writers inhabited a marginal culture, mythologically rich and historically victimized, surrounded and threatened by the devouring metropolitan homogeneity of Anglo-American modernism. In the 1940s, Klein abandoned Eliot's (and Pound's) universalizing thrust, and, instead, fully embraced Joyce's obsessive quest to exorcize the very culture he defined so brilliantly" (7). Klein and Joyce also share an obsession with languages: in Klein's case not just the English and French of Montreal, but also Hebrew, Yiddish, as well as the romance languages of Latin and Italian; as Golfman notes, "Hardly the spare, lean verses of his friend A.J.M. Smith, nor the plain-speaking elegant boldness of E.J. Pratt's poems, Klein's poetry and prose inhabit a densely populated world of words" (12).

The cultural trajectory of Klein's poetry springs initially from the diasporic world of international secular and orthodox Judaism, from folklore to sacred texts, brought into dialectical engagement with modernist and canonical literary frameworks and patterns; this dialectic involves the ironies of the modernist demand for "impersonality" staged precisely at the time in which Klein drew deeply upon a multifaceted Jewish "personality" (see Trehearne, 109). In *To The Jewish Poet*, the "tears / of Jeremiah" are cherished "as ancient gems", while in *Childe Harold's Pilgrimage* in *Hath Not A Jew* ... , the poet is found "Bewildered" as he sets out on his cultural journey, "Examining / A passport of a polyglot decision". Golfman notes that "Whether celebrating the victory of ancient Jews from a child's perspective ('Five Characters'), or lamenting the losses sustained by medieval Jewry ('Murals for a House of God'), Klein's voice sounds unfalteringly consistent. [...] Alert to the dangers of both anti-Semitism and Jewish self-hatred, Klein conveys a calmly reasoned objective detachment ... Thus the sculpted stanzas of his ballads and medieval narratives and the incantatory parallelisms of his best biblical verses unfold on the white spaces of his pages with a convincing regularity that often belies the anarchic terror of their subjects" (16). Such a "terror" is present even in one of the earlier modernist poems such as *Autumn* (which can also be compared with Livesay's poem on the same topic, above), where "Black crows are pecking at the carrion / of Summer" and "Worms enter themselves in dead / leaves", leaves which later on in the poem are described as committing suicide all day. Now Autumn is " ... a pious ghost, wrapt mistily / in winding-sheets, stalks onwards, onwards, on." The nightmarish image of Autumn is darker than the season would appear to warrant, suggesting something far more profound at work: the end of a season could be prophetic or at the least proleptic.

Laughter often gives way to lament in the early poems, as the voices of sacred text are re-articulated, and scenes of distress re-imagined, such as *From The Chronicles* where "a mob, in venery of heathen prey, and / purposing to put Jews to the sword, burst on Mayence"; the people and the sacred texts are equally exposed to brutality: "Some Jews were slain. Some knelt at the blessed font. / Books, writ by Talmud, were burnt in the synagogue. In sooth, / Christ's soldiers made all Jewry their loud haunt." But this is not an attack on other religions, since Klein's syncretist vision is closer to that of thinkers such as Martin Buber (1878–1965) and Franz Rosenzweig (1886–1929), especially the latter's *The Star of Redemption*, with its synthesis of Judaism, Christianity and Islam. Key words and phrases in Klein's texts may be traced across multiple secular and sacred sources, for example, the word "nothing" in the section "Of Nothing at All" in *Hath Not A Jew* ... can be read as an allusion to Shakespeare, to the Cabbala (see Fischer), or to Rosenzweig's critique of philosophy which opens *The Star of Redemption* (" ... by not allowing death to count as Aught but turning into Nought, philosophy creates for itself an apparent freedom ... Philosophy plugs up its ears before the cry of terrorized humanity" (Rosenzweig, 5)).

The so-called failure of *The Hitleriad* can be expressed technically, or in terms of its bad taste, but what this poem shares with *Poems* from the same year is a very un-Canadian impolite barely controlled rage and refusal to ignore "the cry of terrorized humanity": buried in its rumbustious transfiguration of Hitler as an eighteenth-century evil Tom Jones (a portrait of the picaresque hero as a Nazi) are moments of shock recognition: " ... it is true that in due time, he would / Incarnadine him murals with much blood", and "Go to *Mein Kampf* if you would know his trade, / And there learn how a people is unmade." Throughout the poem Klein keeps the wider international community in view: "The Jew being beaten, the world did not wince, / The vogue was shown, by flesh-barometer, / He could persist." In the twenty-second stanza the medium of "historic film" creates a surrealist montage of "crimes deployed", a montage where "the camera goes berzerk" and a close-up: "The fascist and his rods / Flogging the Jugoslavian [sic]." By the 25th and

26th stanzas, the dead need to speak of the atrocities done to them, need to avenge the crimes, coming forth as witnesses who are "ghosts / In wagons sealed in a forgotten land". The intensity of anger reaches a crescendo with the notion that " … from such evidence, such witnessing / Surely the anger of the world will burst" with the "wrath of nations" bringing the "multitude-accursed" to a final reckoning. Of course, such a reckoning never really came, even with the Nuremberg Trials (1945–46) where the Nazi leaders were judged within the rule of law that had been re-established by the Allies.

The poet's gaze: Klein's *The Rocking Chair* (1948)

The poems of *The Rocking Chair* take a step away from the world of the Shoah, almost, it appears, to the relief of readers and critics disturbed by the outrage of *The Hitleriad*. Canadian scenes and Montreal life are observed and made monumental, such as the modernist *Grain Elevator*, "A box: cement, hugeness, and rightangles" which emerges from and dominates the landscape: "Up from the low-roofed dockyard warehouses / it rises blind and Babylonian / like something out of legend. Leviathan / swamped on our shore? The cliffs of some other river? / The blind ark lost and petrified?" From the mysterious and the Biblical to the Saskatchewan prairie setting, the modernist object remains a "Josephdream", built for the bread which "is its theme, an absolute". Montreal similarly rises from the great Canadian landscape, that personal and public site which in "Montreal" the poet calls "part of me, O all your quartiers". This is the "City of reverie, nostalgic isle", which in the previous stanza is called "locale of infancy, milieu / Vital of institutes that formed my fate." In *Lookout: Mount Royal* the panoptical site enables the photographer "to click the eye on motion forever stopped". As Montreal is more and more finely, and minutely, observed (such as the environment of "the leaning fence" in *The Mountain*), the poet simultaneously fades from sight, becoming the *Portrait of the Poet as Landscape*, the final poem in the collection, where the poet is "not dead, but only ignored" (stanza II), "Set apart" suspecting that "something has happened, a law / been passed, a nightmare ordered" (stanza IV). Reading back into Klein's poetry it is possible to see hints of his impending breakdown and extended silence ("some go mystical, and some go mad", stanza III), but it is also possible to see myriad other possibilities in this most talented of poets.

Critics regard *Portrait of the Poet as Landscape* as Klein's greatest poem, yet the profound and painful texts of lamentations, after the Shoah, such as *Elegy* or *A Meditation Upon Survival*, are also highly significant works. "Where shall I seek you?" asks the poet in *Elegy*: "There's not anywhere / A tomb, a mound, a sod, a broken stick / Marking the sepulchres of those sainted ones." The poem soon comes up against the ineffable, the "things still hidden, and unspeakable more", breaking between stanzas before beginning again with the statement that "A world is emptied." Vengeance is a core desire in *Elegy*, whereas in *A Meditation Upon Survival*, the many voices of suffering and death converge upon the survivor poet creating an unbearable burden and desire for death, "my wish / for the centigrade furnace and the cyanide flood." The survivor is "bereaved and suspect", his "stuttering innocence a kind of guilt", condemned not in his death but through being passed over. The poem's opening horror – "that I must live / their unexpired six million circuits … " – is equally matched by the poet's closing "solution": "What else, therefore, to do / but leave these bones that are not ash to fill – / O not my father's vault – but the glass-case / some proud museum catalogues *Last Jew*." Brenner argues that there is connection and coherence in the Jewish-Canadian response to the Shoah, even if literary styles appear to be at odds; for example, the powerfully satiric writing of Mordecai Richler (1931–2001) is part of a Jewish-Canadian "continuum", whereby both Klein and Richler "vacillate between espousal and rejection of humanist values as operative factors in post-Holocaust social interrelationships" (66). Brenner goes on to argue that Klein and Richler also "share the desire to endorse and promote the ideal of human brotherhood; their work, however, also reflects their growing scepticism in view of man's evident proclivity to brutal victimization of his fellow man" (Ibid.).

Klein's lapse into extended silence, and his multiple suicide attempts, appear an existential response to the Shoah, as clear as Theodor Adorno's notion that there can be no poetry after the catastrophe. Trehearne has expressed this the most insightfully:

> Klein's very ability to sustain so many points of view, so many poetic personae, and to give expression to each through the gracious deferral of his own voice, is in times of communal celebration a source of his verbal richness, but in the teeth of the Holocaust may have multiplied his consciousness of suffering and given each murdered Jew a voice in his mind. This reading is indicated by those many self-portraits and portraits of others in which Klein interprets the individual Jew as the embodiment – in some cases very literally so – of the entire Jewish people from antiquity to the present. Klein's poetry is full of such figures, who become – often by persecution – the conduit of memory through which the dead remain vital and the as yet unborn become consequential. How anguished must such representative personalities be at a time when the extirpation of their entire people is possible – when not only the past must be held tangible in one's self, but the present, too, and millions in the present whose individual histories and futures have been wiped out?
>
> (125)

Canadian modernist prose: a second scroll

It was once possible to pass over Canadian modernist fiction, to scroll through the realist texts, the romances, the popular novels (many of which are now out of print), and sense a disconnect between more experimental modernist Canadian poetry and what appears to be conventional prose. The word "scroll" is useful here: in the previous sentence it is being used in its contemporary sense, meaning to scroll up or down (or sideways and across) a computer screen of digital text; however, "scroll" originally meant a rolled parchment on which ancient or sacred text is inscribed. The disjunction between these two meanings is significant: they are two very different technologies for accessing a larger amount of text than can be physically seen by a human being at one time. Canadian modernism can be thought of as the two different scrolls – here, what is apparently canonical form and more experimental content (or "construal" of that content) – combined in one narrative act. Glenn Willmott contextualizes this situation: "Canadian authors, lacking an elite market at home and disconnected from those abroad, devise their works to be able to 'pass' through the production and distribution mechanisms of a more popular print marketplace. Modernist effects … are evidenced not necessarily in unique, newly invented forms of text, but in newly invented forms of construal which these texts, when read, are programmed to demand" (2002, 41). Canadian modernism thus uniquely encompasses the Nietzschean transvaluation of all values underway at the turn of the twentieth century: the old Imperial Victorian and Edwardian world orders were giving way to industrialized and urbanized city spaces and environments (including the environments of large-scale mechanized farming, and the newly mechanized warfare) where social and class structures were being tested and transformed, and new political, artistic and psychological frameworks were beginning to replace the certainties of organized religion and other established moral codes.

There is a tension in this modern transvaluation between the loss of home – the move into towns and cities, destruction of families through the First World War, political persecution and migration, poverty in the Depression leading to population movement, the rise of Fascism leading to extensive displacement of ethnic groups, and often their death and destruction in the Shoah or Holocaust – and home as a shelter from change and uncertainty. Philosopher Gaston Bachelard thinks of the house as the central site of "integration for the thoughts, memories and dreams of mankind … the house thrusts aside contingencies, its councils of continuity are unceasing. Without it, man [sic] would be a dispersed being" (6–7). The upheavals of the early twentieth century saw the end to such "integration" as sites of stability are questioned, transformed, or simply lost.

Alienated space in Sinclair Ross's *As For Me and My House* (1941)

The protagonists' home in Sinclair Ross's (1908–96) *As For Me and My House* (1941) is grey and damp with a leaking roof and poor furniture, without the space needed to accommodate its ethnically diverse alternative family, just as it somehow cannot contain the questioning of organized religion and outdated marital power relationships. The novel appears conventional on the surface, but the increasingly alienated spaces of the Canadian prairie town, and the repetition of the modernist artistic re-imagining of this synecdochic place, rapidly undermines such a reading, leading to a deconstructed realism via a controlled disruption of form. Ross, who had grown up in the farming communities of Saskatchewan, wrote about alienation in his later novels and short stories, including *The Well* (1958), *The Lamp at Noon and Other Stories* (1968), *Whir of Gold* (1970), and *Sawbones Memorial* (1974). Willmott argues that much of Ross's modernist deconstructive force is apparent at the level of the reading experience:

> I will take it that modernist form is recognized where, in a context of historical modernization, the form of a work both (1) acts to reveal the inadequacy of conventional forms of representation ... by disorienting us in time and space, including the time and space of language in its reading, and (2) acts to create a formal, aesthetic experience of space and time, not only a concept or image, which is new – a new reading experience – and which indicates these values. [...] Modernism tends to be eccentric or oppositional to the modern world with which it is cosubstantial: it may be considered ... as a kind of compensatory formation in which sub-versive desire may be expressed, but contained in normal, specialized spheres of production and consumption. I emphasize the reading experi-ence because ... the formal effects I will ascribe to Canadian works as modernist act to create an innovative experience of incoherence for the reader, typically without the openly alternative or aggressive relationship to conventional form characteristic of canonical texts.
>
> (2002, 41)

Canadian modernist prose, then, is quietly subversive, functioning through an accumulative disorientation, one that through repetition and incremental enhancement takes the reader out of his or her canonical comfort zone, into a new time and space.

One of the opening dialectical juxtapositions of *As For Me and My House* is that of Philip's standard first sermon placed together with one of his drawings; the sermon is "stalwart, four-square, Christian", one which "nails his colours to the mast" and lets the small-town people "know what they may expect" (7). The drawing is a repetition of every other similar Main Street in every other small Canadian town that the protagonists have lived in: "It's like all the rest, a single row of smug, false-fronted stores, a loiterer or two, in the distance the prairie again" (7). The drawing would be acceptable to the narrator-protagonist (Philip's unnamed wife) if it was laughing at the scene, ridiculing its smallness and insignificance, but instead it takes the scene seriously and empathetically: " ... there's something about it that hurts. False fronts ought to be laughed at, never understood or pitied. They're such outlandish things, the front of a store built up to look like a second storey. They ought always to be seen that way, pretentious, ridiculous, never as Philip sees them, stricken with a look of self-awareness and futility" (7).

Philip's wife interprets the sermon and the drawing dialectically, as thesis and antithesis brought together in a synthesis, which for her is a symbol, or "a summing up": "The small-town preacher and the artist – what he is and what he nearly was – the failure, the compromise, the going-on – it's all there – the discrepancy between the man and the little niche that holds him" (7). And yet upon closer inspection there is here "an innovative experience of incoherence". The symbol is not adequately explained: it is not entirely clear which of his roles Philip has failed at, since the narrator has already told us that "he still hasn't learned the proper technique" (6) for small-town preaching ("to be bland" (6)), and she has described a painting that "hurts", that fails through its "understanding", its pity, its clarity of vision – that is, one that quite manifestly is not a failure. If the symbol stands in for the "discrepancy" between Philip's two roles – the gap between orthodox religion and artistic creation that would be better called a chasm – there is another type of dialectic at work in this juxtaposition, what Walter Benjamin calls a dialectic at a standstill. This is one where there is no synthesis of thesis and antithesis; instead, thesis and antithesis are temporarily held together in a potentially explosive image-space, one that creates a "rift-design" to use a phrase from the German philosopher Martin Heidegger, which "holds in tension the essential ... conflicts of being without resolving them" (Lane 2005, 140).

A dialectic at a standstill can create shock images whereby reality is convulsed, what the surrealists called the "fixed-explosive", which relates to the photographic snapshot: "reality undergoes a process of folding, convolution and involution: the uncanny is now placed in the foreground and comes abruptly to the surfaces of experience; contradictions are revealed and held in tension ... Via the fixed-explosive the otherwise smooth and homogenous surfaces of the real are broken down into ruins" (Lane 2005, 141). Philip's sermon is "homely" – it is safe and secure, non-threatening to the people of the town – but his drawing of the same town is "unhomely" (*unheimlich*): it sees past the smug exterior. This is a fragile architecture that reveals the deconstructive energies of social change and exposure to threatening external forces: later in the novel the false fronts are ripped off in a storm, and the protagonists' outhouse collapses again and again, parodying their futile attempts at propriety. In other words, the dialectical image reveals in advance the psychological vision or inner subjective actuality of the town in ruins, and it reveals a "dread" of (or angst generated by) this space.

Willmott regards Duncan's novel *The Imperialist* (1904) as the archetype of the modern Canadian novel, where "the narrative space is caught between, on the one hand, an empathic use of realist plot and perspective, which develops a sense of regional unity through the figure of a (literally representative) developing youth, and, on the other hand, a modernist distortion of this use of plot and perspective and of the agency of development itself, in the abstraction of regional into larger spaces with fluid and unpredictable proportions. So it is that an expressionist 'dread of space' asserts itself against and within a desire for realism" (2002, 59–60). In *As For Me and My House*, this dread leaches through the entire text, creative drives giving way to the town that suffocates in its smallness, such suffocation being symbolized as the town gets buried in the wind-blown dust: " … always the urge to create, the belief that he could create. Always the encroaching little town, always the train, roaring away to the world that lay beyond" (43). Freedom belongs not just to the modern technologies that will take people away from this angst-filled space, but also to the new technologies of representation, such as the ranch that the protagonists visit in a surreal plunging into a modernist painting: "Their contours [the hills], he says, are so strong and pure in form that just as they are they are like a modernist's abstractions" (60). The key phrase is "just as they are" meaning that "abstractions" becomes ironic: the modernists believed such formal experimentation more accurately represented the modern world. Once the town disappears beneath the dust, its fence posts and fences buried, it joins this modernist form.

Where is beauty to be found in this angst-ridden space? One possibility is at the railroad, or sheltering by the vast grain elevators; the railroad is exciting, as Judith, Philip's lover, expresses: "It always excited me, the glare of the headlight, the way the engine swept in steaming and important, the smoky, oily smell" (75). The grain elevators, like Malcolm Lowry's Shell Oil Refinery viewed from the North Shore of Vancouver, take on strange and spectacular form when shrouded in dust or at night, through artificial illumination:

> We walked as far as the last grain elevator again, and then sat down on the sheltered side and watched a freight train shunting up and down the yard. A man appeared with a lantern, walking like a pair of legs without a trunk. The headlight for a moment swung on him and made him whole, swung off and left him walking cut in two. The locomotive hissed out clouds of steam that reddened every time the fireman stoked. It started backing up presently, and the dead, clugging sound of car on car ran through the night like a mile of falling dominoes. El Greco all the while sat motionless, his muzzle in my lap.
>
> (172)

This remarkable scene is reminiscent of the world of no-man's-land as represented in the literature of the First World War, with its sliced and dismembered bodies still walking or moving across the artificially illuminated bombarded space. The imagery in this scene from Ross's novel is hellish, but it is also like a movie or opera set: brooding and atmospheric, architectural and theatrical. The man "cut in two" is also an allusion to André Breton's *Manifesto of Surrealism* (1924), and the "rather strange phrase" that came to him prior to sleep: "There is a man cut in two by the window" (21). Hal Foster relates this phrase to surrealist subjectivity and art: "This image suggests neither a descriptive mirror nor a narrative window, the familiar paradigms of postmedieval art, but a fantasmatic window, a 'purely interior model' in which the subject is somehow split both positionally – at once inside and outside the scene – and psychically – 'cut in two' ... the [surrealist] artist does not invent new forms so much as he retraces fantasmatic scenes" (59).

In *As For Me and My House*, this fantasmatic scene is the space of dread where the man with the lantern can be the characters of Philip (cut in two or torn apart as preacher or artist), Paul (divided in his loyalties between philology and the ranch), Judith (trapped yet free in her fantasies and desires), and the protagonist (torn between love for a man's potentiality and the man as he is in constrained form). Of all these, it is most likely Philip signified by the man "with a lantern" as this is also an allusion to the Pre-Raphaelite painting of Christ by William Holman Hunt called *The Light of the World* (1851–53; retouched 1858), which in turn illuminates a citation from Revelation 3.20: "Behold, I stand at the door, and knock: if any man hear my voice, and open the door, I will come in to him, and will sup with him" (King James Version), with further reference to "light" and "lamp" imagery from the Bible, such as Psalm 119.105: "Thy word is a lamp unto my feet, and a light unto my path" (King James Version). Ruskin called this painting "one of the very noblest works of sacred art ever produced in this or any other age" (in Parris, 119). The third artistic "allusion" (perhaps "citation" would be more accurate) comes from the name of the dog, "El Greco", explained earlier on in the novel: "when it was over [his bath] and he stood dripping and bony and drowned-looking Philip named him. El Greco – because El Greco was an artist who had a way of painting people long and lean as if they'd all been put on the rack and stretched considerably, and if he had ever painted a dog, Philip says, it would have been just such a one as ours" (107). Lassaigne notes that "El Greco's models have a strange, lost quality, they seem suspended between life and death, captured in just the moment when they are most intensely themselves" (244).

In Ross's scene, the passing headlights capture the man "cut in two" revealing that, unlike Breton's experience, it is *technology* that illuminates the moment; if the man carrying the lantern symbolizes Christ, then modern technology clashes with an older notion of illumination. It is worth mentioning that even though the Spanish El Greco lived between 1541 and 1614, his deeply mystical religious art was one of the major influences on modernist painters, especially Pablo Picasso (1881–1973). Ross has here achieved a remarkable Canadian modernist scene, set firmly in the prairie grainyard of grain elevator and railway line, steam train and worker, yet simultaneously, like Breton's image, being fantasmatic, a psychological and performative or theatrical space, whereby the sexual, social and aesthetic themes, concepts and *affects* of the novel are played out. In other words, the scene which should be the most material and realistic (the farming and communication technologies that were utilized to settle the Canadian prairies) is also a scene that is shown to be part of an imaginary construction.

In many respects, Ross's scene is reminiscent of one of Canada's most famous modern realist authors "cut in two": Felix Paul Greve / Frederick Philip Grove (1879–1948), author of *Over Prairie Trails* (1922), *Settlers of the Marsh* (1925), *A Search for America* (1927), *The Master of the Mill* (1944) and his science fiction novel *Consider Her Ways* (1947), among many other novels, as well as autobiographical and critical texts. Greve was born in Radomno, Prussia, and was educated at the University of Bonn; his first attempt at becoming a professional writer was not financially successful, although he did produce work in multiple genres, including two sprawling novels: a *Künstlerroman* (the development of an artist novel) *Fanny Eßler* (1905) and a psychological study of family breakdown called *Maurermeister Ihles Haus* (1906). Faking suicide with the aid of his wife Else, Greve emigrated to Canada whereupon he created a new identity for himself as Frederick Philip Grove, the son of Swedish-Russian parents, and a well-travelled man of the best European education, who had fallen on hard times. As critics have suggested, Greve did not entirely re-invent himself, rather he followed the more successful procedure of embellishing the truth to refashion his identity in terms of the prevailing Canadian narratives of struggle with the environment, settlement, and the building of a nation. As Kamboureli notes: "The deliberate refashioning of his subjectivity across continents and national borders, his ambiguous self-location on the edge of truth and fiction, his construction of Canada as a sign that is simultaneously desired and repudiated – these and other elements of his writing spill out of his diasporic condition" (Kamboureli, 2000, 37).

Greve / Grove is the split name, the divided personality that crosses borders and disrupts his own will-to-literary-power (Grove wanted to reinvent Canadian literature by himself); such a split directly contradicts the teleological building-of-Canada narratives that always move in a linear fashion, such as Neils Lindstedt's "pioneer dream" (J. Moss, 150) in *Settlers of the Marsh* to build a dynasty through sheer unremitting labour, or the chronicle of Abe Spalding's Promethean overreaching and subsequent fall from power in *Fruits of the Earth* (1933). But as John Moss observes about *The Master of the Mill*, "To give his continuous account a coherent form, Grove imposes rigid and arbitrary measures upon his narrative" (155). In Grove, the split or divided subject is one subject to deep psychological passions, flaws or simply blindness, such as Neils Lindstedt's naïve marriage to a prostitute, whom he eventually murders. Realism, then, imposes a rigidity of form that cannot constrain the psychological tensions inherent in a Nietzschean will-to-power or will-to-succeed.

Gendered re-visioning in Canadian modernism: Sheila Watson, Bertram Brooker and Elizabeth Smart

The nameless narrator-protagonist in *As For Me and My House* continually effaces her own female identity as she ponders the social setting and behaviouristic propriety of small-town Canada, as well as placing first her husband's career and artistic endeavours. In the moments she spends alone, or with Judith, however, her imaginative powers are unleashed. A female space or chora is thus carved out in the novel, but it is one that is in a continual tension with the patriarchal order, although ironically, by continually retreating into his study to surreptitiously produce art (the study is supposed to be the site of sermon writing), Philip is potentially feminized in his own transgender chora (he does not partake of the masculine activities in the surrounding society, but neither does he occupy himself with the legitimized exception to the masculine rule: being a minister). Similar gender tensions are found in modern novels as diverse as Sheila Watson's (1909–98) *The Double Hook* (1959), Bertram Brooker's (1888–1955) *Think of the Earth* (1936), and Elizabeth Smart's (1913–86) prose poem *By Grand Central Station I Sat Down And Wept* (1945). In each case, a chora exists – be it fleeting, spiritual, extended in time and space or dialogic – but is also at risk of being subsumed by patriarchy; in each case, it is precisely the modernist textual strategies that allow for the continuity and maintenance of the chora in time and space.

In *The Double Hook*, a regional novel of dense poetic and symbolic language, the murdered Mrs Potter initially occupies a ghostly, spiritual space through her act of fishing, traversing boundaries, fences, private property (land and water), revealing in the reactions to her unsettling and annoying presence the interconnectedness of the entire community – as much as the characters also appear, or wish to remain, isolated; the novel rapidly shifts focalization and perspective, as sexual relationships also shift, stylized like a minuet without end, in the raw settlement of dust and heat:

> As Watson explained, she aimed at defining the characters by their rela-tionships rather than by "documented history" or description, just as living people elude definition, although they are "resolutely there". Lan-guage merges with locale: " ... I wanted to fuse the dialogue with the context – the reaching toward speech – the speaking out of silence – out of space" ... Watson further fuses characters and context with language; she depicts them as "figures in a ground from which they could not be separated ... the people are entwined in, they're interacting with the landscape, and the landscape is interacting with them".
>
> (Morriss, 57)

Meaning in the novel is existentially generated: there is no grand narrative to turn to beyond the mundane actions of human relationships; the boundary-blurring space occupied by Mrs Potter empties out as she symbolically becomes the absent mother; Willmott, in an essay comparing Samuel Beckett and Watson, argues that "For both Watson and Beckett, the narrative turns upon the problem of substitutions in the empty space left by the dead or estranged mother, a space haunted by both fear and desire. But there also appears to be that which *cannot* be substituted ... in Watson's texts, it is a native place, the childhood landscapes of the short stories, or the aboriginal territory, 'In the folds of the hills / under Coyote's eye,' of *The Double Hook*" (2005, 108–9). If the chora has some irreducible residue, it is not some "primitive" or essentialist human impulses but rather the substrate of this western Canadian landscape: the indigenous culture that was in place, codifying and creating the landscape, before the settlers arrived.

In Brooker's *Think of the Earth*, the key event is one which is opposed not only to the conventions of the romance genre in which the novel is articulated, but also to the patriarchal order which so rigidly constructs the female protagonist's social world – the murder by Laura of an unwanted lover. The novel is primarily an extended meditation upon the possibility of a Nietzschean messianism that is "beyond good and evil" to use Nietzsche's phrase; the male protagonist, an English immigrant called Tavistock, has a belief in his own messianism: either he will trigger a new age with an action beyond good and evil (an "innocent" act of murder), or he will himself be murdered to the same effect like a modern-day Christ or scapegoat. Rejecting orthodox Christianity (and other religions), Tavistock is continually in debate with its representative in the novel, Laura's father, the canon of the rapidly expanding town of Poplar Plains, Manitoba; as Tavistock argues, "A man living in light is above sin and above righteousness. He becomes *innocent* of good and evil" (59). Laura is a musician, seeking other artistic visionaries, although she is disappointed in her current lover, Harry Anderson, who is shallow and egotistical. In fact it is Harry who turns upon her, for not conforming to the sexually passive role model of a woman who should be grateful for his sexual advances and ultimate promise of marriage.

The romance genre is paradoxically endorsed and deconstructed in this modern novel, for example, Laura's effect on Tavistock: "Her moist, eager eyes made him ache for life. As he looked at her the transparent, murmurous space in his mind collapsed suddenly, as though crushed like an egg-shell" (78). The romance is both stereotypically heightened and punctured at the same time: "crushed like an egg-shell" is an imagist moment, rather than one conforming to narrative expectations of overwhelming romantic love and desire. Brooker is better known for his modernist art – and his involvement in The Arts and Letters Club in Toronto – with innovative Canadian painters and thinkers, including The Group of Seven artists. While not a follower of the theosophy of The Group of Seven, Brooker's three novels are intense explorations of the messianic theme, including his pseudonymously published crime thriller about a cult leader called *The Tangled Miracle* (1936), and his later novel *The Robber* (1949) which is about a Christ-like messianic leader. The novel form, then, becomes a vehicle for Brooker's unorthodox ideas, but also an acknowledgement that for an aesthetic to be relevant to the modern world it has to encompass the crises *of* the modern world.

In *Think of the Earth*, the romance structure re-frames love and desire as a crisis point in parallel with bigger societal crises (the urbanization and industrial expansion of the town; the unsettling nomadic postcolonial world where immigrant workers follow construction projects rather than utopian settlements; the loss of faith in organized religion, etc). The protagonists have met at a crisis point: "For some reason we have met – last night – and to-night – at a crisis, apparently, in both our lives" (177). The word "crisis" comes from the Latin *decision*, and the Greek *krisis* and *krinein*, to decide; it is: "1 a crucial stage or turning point in the course of something, esp. in a sequence of events or a disease. 2 an unstable period, esp. one of extreme trouble or danger in politics, economics, etc. 3 *Pathol.* A sudden change, for better or worse, in the course of a disease" (*Collins Dictionary*). Commonly, we think of a crisis as something that suddenly occurs for the worse, and more importantly, that *we* are not usually responsible for the crisis in the first place. The "decision" is still there as such: someone else made a decision that threw our lives into crisis, or we might have inadvertently made a "bad" or "wrong" decision (taken the wrong turning); often, we think of our decision as the one that will take us out of crisis and back into normality. Sometimes, we seek the "period of instability" by interjecting, deliberately, crisis into our lives: for example, we leave a secure job for one that appears less secure, or we move countries, or we leave a secure but stifling relationship. All of these actions involve generating potential crisis, if not actual crisis: and from it we seek something new, exciting and something with the potential to help us "grow". Allan Megill argues that

> The more usual interpretation of crisis comes out of the continental philosophical tradition and out of the theology connected with that tradition. Typically, interpreters of this tradition tie crisis to the collapse of the "God of the philosophers" and of the "God of the Bible" which they see as occurring in Kant's First Critique and in the Biblical criticism of David Friedrich Strauss ... In this view, the loss of the transcendent dimension, prompted by the notion of *Kritik* as a pervasive power, leads to modern man's homelessness in the world. This is the crisis. It is the loss of authoritative standards of the good, the true, and the beautiful to which reason has access, coupled with loss of the Word of God in the Bible.
>
> In my interpretation, crisis arises not out of the early but rather out of the late nineteenth century. Specifically, I see it as connected with the collapse, circa 1880–1920, of historicism and of the faith in progress that was the widely diffused, vulgarized form of historicism. In the "theological" view, the dominant metaphor for crisis is the abyss ... In my "historical" reading of crisis, the dominant metaphor is that of the break. This presupposes something to be broken, namely, history ...
>
> (xii–xiii)

Brooker's "crises", then, blast at the Nietzschean transvaluation of all values, and appear to suggest that modern messianism is both a desire and a mistake; Brooker explores a "homeless" humanity, but he also adopts the notion of the "break", suggesting in *Think of the Earth* that the past can be sacrificially and symbolically overturned and broken free of, and this includes developing the beginnings of a feminist project, however limited, in Brooker's vision.

Smart's *By Grand Central Station I Sat Down And Wept* is a novel about a love-triangle where longing or heterosexual desire itself is presented as an intense crisis, while simultaneously creating at a higher level of tonality what critic Anne Quéma calls a "rhetoric of the sublime that constitutes her contribution to the polyphony of modernism" (2005, 278). Through utilizing *and* deconstructing the discourse of Biblical text, here The Song of Songs, as well as a prevalent genre in Canadian modern fiction, the *Bildungsroman* or novel of development, the chora created within this text is thus ultimately counter-discursive. As such, Quéma argues that "Smart's novels and diaries ... herald Hélène Cixous's concept of *écriture feminine* [see Glossary] in an attempt to reclaim the power of feminine sexuality, reproduction, and maternity" (2005, 279). *By Grand Central Station I Sat Down And Wept* has biographical origins, as does her second novel *The Assumption Of The Rogues And Rascals* (1978), a psychological journey into despair, passion and creativity; crises can be caused as much by action as by *inaction*, as these novels show. Smart's *écriture feminine* – a feminist mode of writing that is non-patriarchal, allowing space for the Other – is far more experimental and dynamic than any other Canadian modernist produced, partly because her novel occupies a liminal site or threshold between prose and poetry, text and music. As with The Song of Songs, the resistance to a realist reading (its allegorical structure) is countered by the passion expressed at a personal, bodily level, one which is intensely erotic and transgressive.

Smart refuses the notion of the chora as a separate space: it is a female matrix, one of creativity, birth and pre-Symbolic forces (it is outside the law of the Father), yet it is not a separate space, instead, patriarchal time and space are to be encompassed, incorporated and transformed, by chora. Female desire is thus constitutive, a new moment of origin that replaces the phallogocentric (patriarchal/the law of the symbolic phallus expressed through logocentricism) beginning in the word/logos: "What is going to happen? Nothing. For everything has happened. All time is now, and time can do no better. Nothing can ever be more now than now, and before this nothing was" (43). The re-telling of stories becomes central in this new originary narrative; the re-describing of mundane existence through the "rhetoric of the sublime" continues the modernist obsession with "profane illumination". Biblical discourse and subjects – the lovers, the angels – are re-imagined as epiphanic creatures of a profane world: "This is the state of the angels, that spend their hours only singing the praises of the Lord. Just to lie savouring is enough life. Is enough" (45). Smart's angelic voices reject any *teleological* narrative of a forthcoming messianic state: the *jouissance* of the present, of the moment, *is* the angelic state.

Biblical discourse is thus inhabited from within, reinscribed as an *écriture feminine*, seamlessly integrated into the text in an act of intertextual weaving, using what Walter Benjamin called quotation without quotation marks. For example, the quotation from The Song of Songs 8.6 that ends the third part of the novel: "Set me as a seal upon thine heart, as a seal upon thine arm, for love is strong as death" (47). The constant foregrounding of the writerly act reveals the possibility that this novel is a *künstlerroman* (a novel of artistic development) rather than simply a *Bildungsroman*, with additional evidence being that "the novel exists in a paratextual relation to Smart's early journals, which retrace her development as a young writer" (Quéma 2009, 303). As Quéma continues in her discussion of exile and dispossession related to this question of the *künstlerroman*: "Like H.D., Djuna Barnes and Jean Rhys, Smart struggled to define herself as a writer in a masculine context. The story of *By Grand Central Station* concerns the passion, in the Christian sense of the term, that the female protagonist has to undergo in her struggle to become an artist in a society historically defined in patriarchal terms" (Ibid.).

The polysemic word: from Smart to Klein's *The Second Scroll* (1951)

Smart's *écriture feminine* gives new meaning to the modernist break with the past: the reinscription of desire and reproductive metaphors in a new literary language reveals that "the word" is now to be conceived as polysemic. Similarly, in a text that would appear to be very different from Smart's – Klein's *The Second Scroll* – the polysemic word is also foregrounded, which as modernist poet and critic Miriam Waddington (1917–2004) points out, leads to an exceeding of the Judaic doctrinal content of the novel. In fact Waddington continues this project of multiple signifiers and voices, unfolding "the sign of Judaism to display its polysemic possibilities of ethnic, linguistic, cultural, intellectual, religious, and secular ways of being" (Rifkind, 258).

The Second Scroll tells the story of "Uncle Melech", a Jewish "everyman" who survives a pogrom in Russia, becomes a communist, abandons this ideology when Soviet Russia and Germany agree to a pact during the Second World War, and then witnesses the massacre of the Jews at Kamenets-Podolsk, in the Ukraine. Approximately 23,000 Jews were killed here in 1941 by the Nazi *Einsatzgruppen* (mobile killing units) and by other German military and police leaders. In *The Second Scroll*, Uncle Melech is accidentally buried alive in a mass grave, rising from this hellish place like the longed-for Jewish Messiah. En route to the safe haven of the newly formed Israel, Uncle Melech visits the Jewish ghetto or *mellah* of Casablanca where he visits those who exist in a state of degradation; eventually, he arrives in Israel, where he becomes revered, but he is also ultimately murdered. The narrator of *The Second Scroll* follows as far as possible in Uncle Melech's footsteps, in some ways becoming his double, with a double goal: "my twofold mission: the discovery, among Israel's speeches, proclamations, fervours, grumblings, and hopes, of the country's typical poetic statement, and the recognition ... of Uncle Melech" (74).

Being a type of "everyman" Uncle Melech's image becomes universal, sharing the suffering of all of the Jewish peoples alive and dead; this impossible burden on one man creates the hint of his transcendent status, which is immediately undercut by his shabby murder. Yet Uncle Melech has "already" risen symbolically from the dead, almost as if he were a Christ-figure in reverse; he represents the hope of the newly born nation, a continuation of the desire for a Davidic king to come and revenge the victims of the Shoah. This messianic reading already contains its own ironic undercutting: looking for the one man, the one messiah, and the one voice, Klein's narrator finds the Jewish people in their ethnic and linguistic diversity, survivors and eccentrics who all remind him of Uncle Melech. The lesson is that "They were not members of literary societies, the men who were giving new life to the antique speech, but merchants, tradesmen, day labourers" (84). As with Malcolm Lowry's modernist prose in novels such as *Under The Volcano* (1947) and *October Ferry To Gabriola* (1970), it is the language of advertising that creates "Inspired metaphor": "There were dozens, there were hundreds of instances of such metamorphosis and rejuvenation. Nameless authorship flourished in the streets" (84).

Semi-autobiographical in nature, *The Second Scroll* "glosses" each chapter with a series of poems, an extract from a letter and an extract from a play, all of which are gathered in the final section of the novel. This Talmudic structure can be read as mimetic of the Jewish faith texts, or, once again, the polysemic nature of the modern world, even at the founding of Israel. As with Smart's prose-poem, Klein's glosses do not so much resolve the main prose chapters of his novel, as dissolve their linearity, the doubled journey to the Holy Land which is ultimately revealed to be a gathering of remnants and fragmented peoples. Both Smart and Klein re-articulate origins, beginnings, and reveal the polysemic nature of "the word" in their reworking of Biblical text; Smart's intense exploration of female desire and writing (or writing-in-the-feminine), and Klein's search for the messianic subject and voice, lead the reader back into the mundane world of everyday lives, journeys, relationships and the new media which will become the substrate of modernism's progeny: the postmodernists.

Conclusion

- Feminist scholarship has revealed a very different literary historical narrative concerning the role of key women modernists in Canada, leading to a reassessment of the canon, alongside a reassessment of the key critics and editors in the modernist movement(s).

- Canadian modernism partakes of an international aesthetic movement, while being uniquely located in terms of site and conceptualization; in many respects, the latter is more noticeable in prose fiction than poetry, since Canadian modernist prose is often subtly subversive, occupying and deconstructing more traditional genres, such as the *Bildungsroman*.

- Ethnic diversity and social change are key factors in Canadian modernism, from Livesay's social observation and political critique to Klein's ethnic ghettos observed in Montreal and across the world, following the horrors of the Shoah; the waning of the power of organized religion in Canada is explored through the use of new, competing philosophies and theories of existence, such as the ideas of Friedrich Nietzsche and Karl Marx.

6 Feminist literatures

New poetics of identities and sexualities from the 1960s to the twenty-first century

Overview

Feminist literature in Canada has developed hand-in-hand with feminist social, political and literary-theory movements; the figure of the chiasmus – a crossing back and forth – applies to this dialogic interplay, whereby creativity and theorizing speak to, or inform one another, with a downplaying of hierarchy in favour of collaborative exchange. Beyond gaining the right to vote in all of the Canadian provinces in 1920, women were highly restricted in family, social and political life for much of the first half of the twentieth century; in 1966, the Fédération des femmes du Québec and the Committee for the Equality of Women in Canada were formed to redress this situation, leading to the Pearson government's 1967 Royal Commission on the Status of Women, which reported in 1970, making 167 recommendations covering issues as diverse as birth control, pensions, family law and the Indian Act. Many of the recommendations were put into place, except for some of the more radical proposals, such as a national day-care programme, guaranteed income for the heads of single-parent families, or universal access to affordable abortion (see O'Neill). Creative artists and writers were key in the exploration of women's rights, offering alternative perspectives and ideologies to those sanctioned by the government.

Gender and creativity in Margaret Atwood's fiction

One of the best-known Canadian authors has played a significant role in the development of a literary and critical feminist discourse: Margaret Eleanor Atwood was born in 1939 in Ottawa, and was educated at Victoria College, University of Toronto, Radcliffe College, Cambridge, and Harvard University. Atwood's *Survival: A Thematic Guide to Canadian Literature* (1972) continues to be read and debated by scholars around the world. Reflecting upon her first published novel, *The Edible Woman* (1969), Atwood argues that the book is "protofeminist rather than feminist" (Introduction, np) because "there was no women's movement in sight when I was composing the book in 1965 ... though like many at the time I'd read Betty Friedan and Simone de Beauvoir behind locked doors" (Ibid.). Atwood ponders the two choices available to her novel's protagonist: a dead-end career or marriage, and she suggests that ten years later, nothing much has changed for women in Canada: "The goals of the feminist movement have not been achieved, and those who claim we're living in a post-feminist era are either sadly mistaken or tired of thinking about the whole subject" (Ibid.). This bleak assessment needs to be tempered with a further three decades of feminist action and publication in Canada: in the 1980s, authors often embraced the feminist theories that Atwood is so cautious of in her introduction, and Atwood's own ongoing literary output has in turn engaged with the entire gamut of social and scientific theories of new and/or alternative subjectivities across a wide range of genres. *The Edible Woman*, however, is set in a much more static society, described early on in the novel with the symbolic "organizational structure" of the company in which the protagonist, Marian, works:

> The company is layered like an ice-cream sandwich, with three floors: the upper crust, the lower crust, and our department, the gooey layer in the middle. On the floor above are the executives and the psychologists – referred to as the men upstairs, since they are all men – who arrange things with the clients; I've caught glimpses of their offices, which have carpets and expensive furniture and silk-screen reprints of Group of Seven paintings on the walls. Below us are the machines ... Our department is the link between the two: we are supposed to take care of the human element, the interviewers themselves. As market research is a sort of cottage industry, like a hand-knit sock company, these are all housewives working in their spare time and paid by the piece. They don't make much, but they like to get out of the house. [...] Because our department deals primarily with housewives, everyone in it, except the unfortunate office-boy, is female.
>
> (19–20)

The ironies of this societal snapshot are multiple: the core Group of Seven artists were all men, and their paintings very quickly graced the walls of the male-centric bastions of corporate Canada; Marian occupies a sort of "soft centre", women being excluded from the machinery of governance and often from the machinery of production (the accounting and print shop beneath her). Market research is portrayed here as "women's work" which means part-time, badly paid or not paid at all, on the margins of the proper profession (from a patriarchal perspective) of being a housewife. In the novel Marian becomes increasingly alienated from this patriarchal society, shifting from being a consumer of products to feeling instead like a consumer object; her resulting anorexia and rejection of her fiancé's sexist attitude towards her is resolved in her offering of a symbolic substitute woman made of cake which he refuses to devour, freeing her from the relationship and her loss of appetite.

In Atwood's *Surfacing* (1972), a postmodern novel (see Chapter 8) with an unnamed narrator-protagonist and a shape-shifting plot, the female characters resist becoming sexual objects, in particular in a film called *Random Samples* that the male characters are producing. The novel is partly about a search in Quebec for the protagonist's missing father, as well as being an ecological, feminist journey of awakened awareness and consciousness as the "unreliable" (from a narratological perspective) narrator-protagonist gradually replaces her fake memories with the real ones of her past affair and abortion. In *The Canadian Postmodern*, Linda Hutcheon notes that *Surfacing*'s narrator is an "artist-figure": "as are the protagonists of [Michael Ondaatje's] *Coming Through Slaughter*, [Audrey Thomas's] *Intertidal Life*, [Timothy Findley's] *Famous Last Words*, and so many other Canadian postmodern novels" (145). The artist-figure is central for feminist fiction in the 1960s and 1970s, since she allows for the exploration of the aesthetic and political frameworks that can either block or facilitate alternative modes of communication and representation. As Hutcheon notes, in *Lady Oracle* (1976) "Atwood further and more explicitly explores the artist as both the instigator of the creative process and, indeed, as a product of her own art" (145).

Gender roles in *Lady Oracle* are re-imagined through the protagonist's adoption of the gothic mode, and its undercutting through her use of surrealist automatic writing to create more revealing poetry. In fact genre and gender are co-constituents of Atwood's exploration of the artist-figure, and this may be a mimetic re-enactment of Atwood's feminist genre-shifting project. For example, she utilizes the "problem novel" in *Life Before Man* (1979) where an impending divorce between the protagonists parallels the separatism of the Parti Quebecois and their attempt to "divorce" English- and French-speaking Canada (Palumbo, 79); *Bodily Harm* (1981) deconstructs the thriller novel in its account of a journalist who becomes increasingly politicized; and *The Handmaid's Tale* (1985) adopts the genre of the dystopia, to explore a fascistic future society where women's reproductive rights are abrogated and controlled in a disturbing new religious caste system.

Even at this early stage, Atwood had created a powerful body of work interrogating the systems and societies that controlled, or attempted to control, women's representational and reproductive realities. Her own artistic output resists systematic closure because of her deconstructive adoption and adaption of popular fiction genres. Thus her use of speculative fiction is in the tradition of feminist science fiction authors, and it is returned to in her later novel *The Blind Assassin* (2000) where it forms the innermost embedded story; the romance genre is repeatedly parodied, dismantled and reconstructed, across Atwood's entire oeuvre, and in *The Blind Assassin* the various science fiction futures are offered as romantic possibilities that are repeatedly rejected, interconnecting with the second embedded story, the romance between Laura and her lover. Shifts in perspective – such as the intratextual movement across embedded stories – are a narrative tool that Atwood uses to such good effect, that ultimately a postmodern incredulity towards metanarratives (that is, universal or transcendent ways of seeing the world) dominates her texts. As oppressive metanarratives are suspended or entirely abandoned, a more dynamic textual space of subjectivity and possibility is created. But this also involves re-examining power relations between women, as seen in *Cat's Eye* (1988), *The Robber Bride* (1993) and *Alias Grace* (1996), and the intersection/interrogation of genre and discourse: the discourse of string theory and science in *Cat's Eye*, the discourses of New Age theories and history in *The Robber Bride*, and the discourse of psychoanalysis in *Alias Grace*.

All three novels also engage in trauma and the recovery and/or exorcism of that trauma: the protagonist of *Cat's Eye*, Elaine Risley, relives her childhood experiences of bullying, especially at the hands of her friend and "abject twin" (Palumbo, 82) Cordelia, whereas the three protagonists of *The Robber Bride*, Tony, Charis and Roz, have to overcome the influence and traumatic involvement with a fourth character, Zenia, who each feels has ruined their lives; in *Alias Grace*, Grace herself is the indeterminate subject or site of psycho-sexual trauma, as a potential "murderess" in a society that is titillated and appalled by her apparent actions. Atwood so enmeshes Grace in a series of competing perspectives and fantasies about her actions and identities, that it is clear that Grace's "guilt" is massively overdetermined and superimposed.

In more recent fiction by Atwood, this perspectivism spans two interconnected dystopian novels (the first two novels of a projected trilogy): *Oryx and Crake* (2003) and *The Year of the Flood* (2009). The commodified body in contemporary media and pornography is a central, mind-numbing obsession of *Oryx and Crake*'s protagonists. Written in the "last man" genre, this novel depicts Snowman's world of genetic engineering run amok, his companions being the engineered "Crakers" and his rapidly fading memories of a dystopian world where authentic human emotions and cultures are degraded and despised. In *The Year of the Flood*, the same dystopia is depicted from the perspective of "the pleeblands", with the protagonist Toby pondering her role in "God's Gardeners", an eco-cult that has attempted to restore the urban wastelands with organic gardens, long since destroyed in the novel's narrative present.

Atwood's achievement in the first two instalments of her dystopian trilogy is to reveal how the commodification of the female body is not an isolated process: in a globalized world in which all natural objects (and subjects) can be turned into commodities which have the potential to be manipulated at a genetic or informational level, feminist resistance becomes more, not less, relevant. Canadian feminism has its roots, however, precisely in global cultures, whether it be in response to government multicultural policy, a sense of shared experiences of the injustices imposed upon ethnic minority groups inside and outside of Canada, or in empathic relation to colonial injustices to indigenous or native peoples around the world.

Margaret Laurence: decolonization and writing in Africa

Margaret Laurence (1926–87), famous for her Manawaka cycle of books – *The Stone Angel* (1964), *A Jest of God* (1966), *The Fire Dwellers* (1969), *A Bird in the House* (1970) and *The Diviners* (1974) – is a key example of a globally situated author who writes her way back to Canada after her time spent living in, and writing about, Africa. Born in Neepawa, Manitoba, Laurence began her writing career as an undergraduate at United College, Winnipeg, publishing in student magazines, before progressing to professional journalism, writing for the *Westerner* and the *Winnipeg Citizen*. It was moving to Somaliland in 1950 (now Somalia), with her husband who was an engineer, that gave Laurence the distance she needed to artistically re-engage with small prairie town life: "[M]y view of the prairie town from which I had come was still too prejudiced and distorted by closeness. I had to get farther away from it before I could begin to see it" (Laurence 1976, 14). Getting "farther away" involved deep immersion in African culture, first that of Somaliland and then the Gold Coast (now Ghana), publishing her own highly respected translations of Somali poetry and mythology in *A Tree for Poverty* (1954), her first novel, *This Side Jordan* (1960), a collection of short stories called *The Tomorrow-Tamer* (1963) and a memoir called *The Prophet's Camel Bell* (1963). Another important work of non-fiction from this period is Laurence's *Long Drums and Cannons: Nigerian Dramatists and Novelists, 1952–1966* (1968).

Laurence experienced a postcolonial Africa: the British administration in this part of Africa was in the process of being dismantled, and Laurence's translations, fictional and critical works, can be regarded as being part of the decolonization process. In *This Side Jordan*, the end of Empire is revealingly sketched, as in a scene later on in the novel at "The Club": "The Club was the last sanctuary of whitemen, yet even here the present climate of change was apparent" (140); the club is haunted by "The long-dead tamers of a continent" who appear more real "than the living, who drifted spectre-like up the steps and along the corridors" (140). The novel presents both sides of what was known as the "Africanization" process, whereby White persons' jobs were being handed over to indigenous peoples; focusing on the fictional company of Allkirk, Moore and Bright, Laurence examines the tensions and contradictions in this process, as the colonial class hold out in disbelief at the impending independence of Ghana. The liminal state that Laurence charts becomes uncanny and uncertain, reflected in an overheard conversation in the club:

– if they let the blacks in, I'll resign my membership –
– every bush cocoa-farmer will be able to come in and raise hell –
– they say the government's got plans for a road through this exact spot,
  if we don't allow Africans –
– I've no objection to educated Africans, but –
– they're all the same, they're all bush –

– you should have seen it before the war –
– everything's different – everything's changed ...

(140–41)

The image of the road which will go straight through the "whiteman's" club is highly symbolic: decolonization represents the progress that the British are holding up; as the club members fantasize about African "primitivism", the modern Africa is impatient to clear these people out of the way.

Laurence's highly significant postcolonial writing is sometimes not critically considered in relation to her Manawaka Cycle, meaning that, as Stovel argues, "the important connections between the two bodies of work, and indeed the influence of her African writing on her subsequent Canadian fiction, have not been fully appreciated" (7). Stovel's thesis is that Laurence's African experiences facilitated her postcolonial notion of Canada, and that from a feminist perspective, "her observation of African women led her to perceive how women can be colonized under patriarchy. Writing of emerging independence in her African fiction inspired her to write about the self-empowerment of women in her Canadian fiction" (7). Stovel backs up this argument by looking at the influence of Dominique-Octave Mannoni (1899–1989) on Laurence's thought, in particular his monograph *Prospero and Caliban: The Psychology of Colonization* (1950). From this perspective, *The Stone Angel* is the intellectual and political midpoint between Laurence's African and Canadian works.

Margaret Laurence's Manawaka Cycle (1964 to 1974)

The world of the small prairie town fictionalized in the Manawaka Cycle is what in *Heart of a Stranger* Laurence calls "an amalgam" (15) of the many Canadian towns of her youth. In "Where the World Began", the final essay in *Heart of a Stranger*, Laurence describes the strangeness of her hometown: it was "A place of incredible happenings, splendours and revelations, despairs like multitudinous pits of isolated hells. A place of shadow-spookiness, inhabited by the unknowable dead. A place of jubilation and of mourning, horrible and beautiful" (213). As she shockingly starts the following one line paragraph: "It was, in fact, a small prairie town" (213). The protagonist of *The Stone Angel*, Hagar, is named after the Biblical character in Genesis, a servant woman who is the mother of Abraham's son Ishmael, eventually banished from their home by his wife Sarah. Hagar fears the death of her son in the desert: God sends an angel to comfort her and to promise his survival. Hagar is also a Somali word meaning "thornbush" (Stovel, 15), and in The Koran, Ishmael receives God's blessing, not Isaac.

With this one name – Hagar – Laurence brings together competing cultures and religions, alternative narratives and readings, and she begins the process of myth-making that is the Manawaka Cycle: "The Manawaka novels invent and rediscover lost histories of Canada that are contained in both geographies of the land and of the body. This myth-making is part of a Canadian modernist movement that is intricately connected to a feminist Canadian movement in the late 1960s and 1970s" (Dudek, 24). As an elderly woman, Hagar resists death, remembering the relationships and resistances in her life that have contributed to her forging of a strong personal identity, one which she now needs to be released from. The image of the stone angel is powerful: it is a frozen figure, perhaps the Victorian "angel in the house" which Hagar became for a time, even though she had initially chosen the sensuality of her husband Bram as a way of escaping from the patriarchal world of her father; at each stage in her life, freedom becomes a new form of imprisonment, until Hagar finally lets go of the past.

A Jest of God and *The Fire Dwellers* present multiple perspectives of the lives of two sisters: Rachel, who is a schoolteacher living alone in *A Jest of God*, and Stacey, a married mother who attempts to realize her identity within a restrictive domestic sphere in *The Fire Dwellers*. As a potential eccentric (see Godard) when viewed from a patriarchal small-town perspective – i.e., she should be engaged or married/a mother – Rachel "is victimized by a myth of normalcy, which women are expected to enact within strict specifications dictated by patriarchal structures" (Dudek, 75–76; see, also, Kearns). The pressure of this "normalcy" leads to her alienation and, again from a patriarchal perspective, her inner fragmentation and "hysteria", yet her body and sexuality also become crucial sites of resistance. Dudek aligns Rachel's "crisis of identity" with that of the era: "Canada in the 1960s and early 1970s was a country that was experiencing a crisis of identity based upon its desire to leave behind traditions and institutions that linked its identity to another country – either Great Britain or the United States – and to create a new identity based on its own distinct characteristics. [...] A gynocentric Canadian literary modernism emerged from this climate of change. *A Jest of God* is a product of this modern condition, and Rachel Cameron's hysterical subjectivity is symptomatic of a divisive, unsettled national atmosphere" (78). Rachel eventually leaves Manawaka, but her sister Stacey has already moved to Vancouver finding a new form of entrapment in her own family home, where she also suffers from intense anxiety concerning the threat of nuclear warfare.

The Fire Dwellers is a much more experimental novel in that Stacey's fragmented subjectivity is shown through a playful graphical surface (with different typefaces used for different inner voices), and emphasis upon dream and fantasy narratives. Movement through time and space disrupts linearity, producing a modernist simultaneity, although this disruption is something that occurs, via the different handling of memory, in all of the Manawaka texts. *The Diviners* foregrounds simultaneity as a major component of *écriture féminine*, the protagonist Morag Gunn and her Métis daughter called Pique shifting the focus of the cycle to class, ethnicity and history. Drawing upon Métis mythology, *The Diviners* goes beyond the Anglo-Celtic backgrounds of the Manawaka characters to create a more syncretist notion of identity. The semi-autobiographical short story collection *A Bird In The House* covers much of the same territory as the four novels in the cycle, staging or performing the auto/biographical subject in more straightforward ways than in the novels, but it is crucial to recognize, as Kristjana Gunnars argues, that "all of Laurence's fictional worlds are politically imbued. Her women protagonists are enmeshed in politics, and their attempt to speak, in fact to rejoice, is in and of itself a political act" (126).

A change of scenery/*Dépaysement*: the nomadic fiction of Gabrielle Roy

In early twentieth-century women's writing political perspectives can be subtly masked or existentially and/or spatially embodied. A striking example is found with the work of Gabrielle Roy (1909–83) whose first, and most political, novel, *Bonheur d'occasion* (1945; translated as *The Tin Flute*, 1947), develops a spatial dynamic whereby a simple act – in this case, walking through the working-class neighbourhood of Saint-Henri, in Montreal – creates a deeper social and psychological consciousness. Born in Saint-Boniface, Manitoba, Roy's family originated from Quebec; Roy was educated at the Winnipeg Normal Institute, and worked as a teacher before moving to London, England in 1937, where she studied at the Guildhall School of Music and Drama (see Hoy). Returning to Canada in 1939, Roy settled in Montreal, although "settled" does not begin to describe her highly observant city walks in which she gathered the materials for her journalism and eventually her first novel. In these walks Roy became a feminist *flâneur* (someone who wanders, strolls, or aimlessly proceeds through a city, voyeuristically observing and being observed in turn as a spectacle); in fact she takes over the masculine, modernist act of *flânerie* and re-appropriates it to purposefully observe the harsh everyday social conditions of working-class women.

The *flâneur* is a highly mobile, endlessly moving observing eye; she is "a figure in perpetual motion – there is no safe and stable perspective from which to behold events, but only a series of briefly held positions offering glimpses of a world in flux" (Gilloch, 244). As Gilloch explains, the *flâneur* is "the privileged physiognomist [someone who analyses the surface or face of a person or object] of the urban setting, transforming the city into a locus of reading and remembering" (214); she is a sensitive person who can appreciate "a secret counter-history of the city" (222), and "the prototypical sociologist" (243). In Roy's hands, *flânerie* led to four articles or written walking tours through Montreal for *Le Bulletin des Agriculteurs* (all published in 1941), and one of the best-selling novels in Canada – *Bonheur d'occasion* – focused on a mother, Rosa-Anna Lacasse, and her daughter Florentine (who becomes pregnant through her relations with the character Jean Lévesque, yet only finds support by marrying another more mundane man called Emmanuel Létourneau). Roy balances the claustrophobia and depressing poverty of the working-class district in which lives and destinies appear to be repetitively re-played, with the restless psychological dreams, fantasies and linguistic journeys that find creative expression in part through the use of *joual*, or the French

Canadian street language. The central irony in this realistic novel is that escape is only provided for the young men by the Second World War, another type of journey that for many soldiers ended in death.

Journeys interior and exterior, imagined and real, structure almost all of Roy's books. Her characters, whether anchored in place because there is no role for them in society beyond, say, being housewives and mothers, are nonetheless highly mobile in terms of family migration, memorable past journeys, and hoped for or future projected lives. Actual journeys are often taken by male characters, and younger female characters visiting family or grasping at newfound independence and autonomy. As Lewis notes, such characters are all essentially "antithetical, nomadic creatures" (818), and "In every novel and short story characters do make numerous and significant voyages" (820). Notably, Luzina Tousignant follows annual journeys to give birth in *La Petite Poule d'eau* (1950; trans. *Where Nests the Water Hen*, 1951), whereas the local priest has a "nomadic life of freedom as he travels throughout northern Manitoba" (Lewis, 817). In Roy's works, characters often feel imprisoned by the city or the townscape, especially when they are on the edge of an urban settlement and in view of wide-open prairies. Journeys to the countryside are a way of escaping this feeling of imprisonment, such as those found in *Rue Deschambault* (1955; trans. *Street of Riches*, 1957) and *La Route d'Altamont* (1966; trans. *The Road Past Altamont*, 1966), whereas the novel that was published in between, called *La Montagne secrète* (1961; trans. *The Hidden Mountain*, 1962) recounts a journey North and then on to Paris, as well as involving "an aesthetic journey toward the perfect work of art" (Lewis, 817). *La Rivière sans repos* (1970; trans. *Windflower*, 1970) creates a tension and journeying between cultures North and South, while *Cet Eté qui chantait* (1972; trans. *Enchanted Summer*, 1976) returns to the journey as a sort of rural *flânerie*. Nomadism, departures and arrivals in uncanny places prevail in *Un Jardin au bout du monde* (1975; trans. *Garden in the Wind*, 1977) and *Ces Enfants de ma vie* (1977; trans. *Children of My Heart*, 1979).

From a feminist perspective, what these nomadic and adventurous journeys (or yearnings for journeys) signify can be grasped through the example of *The Road Past Altamont*, where multiple journeys lead to uncanny experiences that shift matrilineal power relations as creative powers are passed on from generation to generation. In the opening story, "My Almighty Grandmother", the journey to a village in Manitoba shifts the child's perspective to that of her Grandmother's: other young relatives arrive and depart in what seems like seconds, in a whirlwind of noise and dust; they are gone before Grandmother can offer them a drink or a moment of conversation. In a moment of boredom Grandmother makes a doll, weaving in to its creative production past names, family history and the geography of her life: "I began all over again here in Manitoba what I'd already made back in Quebec, made once for all, I thought – a home. That is work" (15). The doll is uncannily real, and Grandmother is awesome and god-like in her creative powers that also bring the past to life in the act of passing on the family history from a woman's perspective. In the closing story, "The Road Past Altamont", the protagonist's mother is as old as Grandmother at the start of the book, and it is now Christine who starts to realize her own creative powers. Strangely, these are manifested in an uncanny journey, a disorientating yet creative act of drifting or *dérive*, while driving in Manitoba: "I refused to choose [which way to drive] and let myself be guided by caprice or intuition" (113). The end result is that Christine discovers the Pembina Mountains, a range of hills in Southern Manitoba, which remind her mother of her childhood in Quebec. Christine asks herself: "Did the hills really give Maman back her joyous childhood heart? And why is it that a human being knows no greater happiness in old age than to find in himself once more the face he wore as a child?" (119).

This magical discovery of the past in the present, and the hills among the otherwise flat prairies, is a "challenge to rational causality" (Foster, 19): found through abandoning logical maps or grids, the road is invisible to the uncles who lack imagination; "Maman" calls the discovery and the place "marvelous" (120). This Surrealist term signifies what Breton called "objective chance": the sudden encounter whereby we realize that "the marvelous *is* the uncanny – but projected ... away from the unconscious and repressed material toward the world and future revelation" (Foster, 20). The repetition compulsion in objective chance also points to the loss of the mother: in "The Road Past Altamont" the marvelous uncanny encounter with the Pembina Mountains also foreshadows Christine's journeying away from her mother, and her mother's death. The paradox, then, is that in giving her mother back her childhood paradise, Christine is also losing her mother, or driving herself away. Christine's creativity as a writer is embedded in her nomadism, a desire "to go beyond and undo an emergent order" (Williams, J., 65) to put it into Deleuzian terms. As a female writer, Christine resists "univocal" discourse and space and instead she creates a "multivocal" aesthetic, which can be understood via Deleuze's theories of difference: "The argument depended on what he called a nomadic distribution whereby space was said to be defined by the individuals that distributed themselves in it, as opposed to a sedentary distribution where the individuals could only be identified by a prior definition of the space in which they have to be distributed. So, instead of the question 'Where does this go?', Deleuze advocates the priority of the questions 'What space does this draw up?' and 'How is space continuing to be transformed by individuals?'" (Williams, J., 190). What this means is that Roy's nomadic characters, who embody a mobile identity across space and time, are far more politically radical than might first appear; her sociological vision continues through psychological and aesthetic perspectives and the traversing of multivocal space.

Alice Munro's visionary short stories

Small-town Canada is most famously written about by Alice Munro (b. 1931), whose "double vision" – which Howells defines as realism "juxtaposed with fantasy and romance" (200) – presents a homely surface that overlayers uncanny depths. In her only novel (although it is constructed like a series of short stories) *Lives of Girls and Women* (1971), the protagonist Del Jordan describes people's lives in the small town of Jubilee, Ontario, as being "dull, simple, amazing, unfathomable, deep caves paved with kitchen linoleum" (249). The uncanny resides in the odd or shocking detail, the quirkiness that goes beyond acceptable levels of eccentricity or simple humanity; Del's ambition to become a writer is described in the "Epilogue" as beginning at the time "when all the books in the library in the Town Hall were not enough for me ... I saw that the only thing to do with my life was to write a novel" (240). Such a novel will not be a simple charting of local history, or an entirely abstracted fantasy: the "Epilogue" recounts the subtle tension between real-life and its fictionalized account whereby the town of Jubilee becomes "an older, darker, more decaying town" (243), one that no amount of documentary list-making can contain: "no list could hold what I wanted, for what I wanted was every last thing, every layer of speech and thought, stroke of light on bark or walls, every smell, pothole, pain, crack, delusion, held still and held together – radiant, everlasting" (249). The closely observed uncanny moment can also lead to – or become – an epiphany, through which broken threads are gathered back together again, or individual stories suddenly cohere in a wider, more organized pattern of vision and insight.

Born in Wingham, Ontario, and educated at The University of Western Ontario, Munro's first publication was the short-story collection *Dance of the Happy Shades* (1968); she returned permanently to this genre after *Lives of Girls and Women* with two short-story collections, *Something I've Been Meaning To Tell You* (1974) and *Who Do You Think You Are?* (1978), the latter described by Gerald Lynch as "a wonderfully well wrought short story cycle, arguably Munro's best book" (2001, 161), which he places in a wider Canadian tradition:

> *Who Do You Think You Are?* is in fact a supreme example of a con-
> temporary story cycle of character wherein place as small town, Hanratty, is
> recovered to play a definitive role in the formation of character and, later, the
> affirmation of identity. [...] *Who* remains ... like [Emily Carr's] *Klee Wyck*,
> the story cycle's version of female künstlerroman, being about the growth of
> Rose the actress, and not Hanratty per se. The stories are about Hanratty
> secondarily and only in so far as that place is germane to understanding the
> development and maturity of Rose. In the context of Canadian short story
> cycles of character, *Who* can be seen as part of a tradition that begins with
> [Frederick Philip] Grove's *Over Prairie Trails*, and includes such other works
> as *Klee Wyck*, [Margaret] Laurence's *A Bird in the House*, Clark Blaise's *A
> North American Education*, and [Thomas] King's *Medicine River*.
>
> (2001, 160)

The fragmentation of modern subjectivity – seen in the unspoken ellipses of Laurence's writing of *jouissance* – also occurs in Munro's stories, with the gaps or missing pieces in character portrayal, what Lynch calls in a neat turn of phrase "fragmented coherence" (Ibid., 161).

While there is continuity to Munro's fictional exploration of complex modern subjectivity, some literary experimentation occurred during the 1980s and 1990s, with her collections *The Moons of Jupiter* (1982), *The Progress of Love* (1986), *Friend of My Youth* (1990), *Open Secrets* (1994) and *The Love of A Good Woman* (1998). Critics have pointed to an increased use of intertextuality (for example, in the story "Spaceships Have Landed" – see Martin and Ober) and a move beyond realism. In *The View From Castle Rock* (2006), historical fictionalizing about Munro's ancestors – the Laidlaw family from Scotland – is intertwined with more contemporary memoir-type stories, while *Too Much Happiness* (2009) contains one historical story concerning the nineteenth-century Russian mathematician and novelist Sophia Kovalevsky. From a feminist perspective, Munro's life-long observation of mother–daughter relationships (as well as her subtle exploration of female autonomy and creativity within socially constraining societies) has contributed to a positive re-evaluation of the importance of the short-story genre to women's writing in Canada.

"Scandalous bodies": gender recoding and auto/biographies from Aritha Van Herk to Kerri Sakamoto

In Aritha Van Herk's (b. 1954, in Calgary) *Judith* (1978), the protagonist returns to rural Canada to start her own pig farm: she escapes from the memories of her father's practical knowledge by doing everything herself, taking her own direction. While she does eventually find a lover, the relationship develops on her terms, not his (unlike the relationship with the lover she left behind in the city, her domineering office boss). Judith's gender performance disturbs the local farming community as she replaces the law of the father with her own laws of self-creation and her occupation of traditionally masculine roles. Put more bluntly, it is Judith's corporeal presence that is scandalous: the pioneer narratives of men and women settlers carving out habitable land in Canada foregrounds the bodily presence of the heterosexual *family*, whereas Judith is female, single, and resolutely independent. She takes on tasks that are considered by the local community too challenging for a woman's body (such as the highly symbolic castration of the pigs), yet as the novel shows, she performs many of these tasks with speed and precision.

Van Herk's female protagonists bodily re-occupy Canada, in a mimetic process of re-occupying and re-coding male-dominated spaces, from the gender shifting J.L.'s job in a mining camp in the North in *The Tent Peg* (1981), the nomadic wandering and exploring of Arachne Manteia in *No Fixed Address: An Amorous Journey* (1986), to the genre-blurring and boundary-crossing essays that constitute *Places Far From Ellesmere: A Geografictione* (1990), *In Visible Ink: (crypto-frictions)* (1991) and *A Frozen Tongue* (1992). In *Restlessness* (1998), the protagonist, Dorca, an international courier has become so dislocated that the only future she can envision is her suicidal encounter with an assassin; even in this encounter, however, movement overcomes stasis. Overall, in re-occupying the Canadian West, and refusing to be pinned down, van Herk's female protagonists also revise and recode the genre of the western where women rarely had an active role outside of the family homestead (although there are of course notable exceptions, for example, with the westerns of Bertha M Bower (1871–1940), the first wife of Canadian author Bertrand William Sinclair).

Japanese-Canadian internment and historical silences in Joy Nozomi Kogawa's *Obasan* (1981)

The same year in which van Herk's *Judith* was published, Joy Nozomi Kogawa (b. 1935, in Vancouver) published "Obasan" in the *Canadian Forum* (1978), a short story that would form the basis for her best-selling novel *Obasan*, published in 1981. Kogawa explores the ways in which history is not only written on the body, but, counter-culturally, can be reconceived through the female body, the latter being the "scandal" which "lies not in the body's unknowingness, but in its very knowing" (Kamboureli 2000, 180). *Obasan* is a personal journey through a bleak chapter in Canadian history: the internment of Japanese-Canadians during the Second World War. Twenty-two thousand Japanese-Canadians had their property confiscated and lost their right to live in British Columbia after the War; it was not until 1949 that the exclusion order was lifted, and not until September 1988 that a formal apology from Prime Minister Brian Mulroney was delivered, alongside a more substantial financial compensation package for those involved.

Obasan takes the reader back to the trauma of internment and displacement, with the novel's protagonist, Naomi Nakane, suffering from the loss of her mother (who cannot return to Canada from Japan), and her father, who is in a work camp. Naomi is initially forced to live in Slocan, BC, and then at a sugar-beet farm in Granton, Alberta. The novel uncovers this painful past from the perspective of the narrative present of Naomi's life as a schoolteacher; looked after by her aunt Obasan and her uncle Isamu, Naomi starts to re-examine the past, with the help of her politically active aunt Emily, after the death of her uncle. Shockingly, Naomi reveals not just the history of Japanese-Canadian mistreatment, but also a personal story of childhood sexual abuse. The novel, in its journey through memories of trauma, also develops a political consciousness, focused on "social reformation" (Ueki, 7), one which Kogawa explores in her follow-up novel on the Japanese-Canadian redress movement, called *Itsuka* (1982). The sexual abuse that Naomi has suffered is revealed in a four-page sequence in *Obasan*; in her third novel, *The Rain Ascends*, sexual abuse is also the focus, in a story about an Anglican minister abusing his choristers, based upon a real-life case in Kingston, Ontario.

Critics (see Miki) have differed as to how far *Obasan* is a novel that leads to a cathartic sense of ending, and potential redress ("resolutionary" readings) and those that maintain that a sense of difference, of otherness, and unresolved tensions lead to a more politically activist notion of the text ("revolutionary" readings). Naomi's materialist historiography asserts that the "state of emergency" declared during the Second World War impacts the body, especially the female body; Smaro Kamboureli picks up on this materialistic approach and refuses to smooth out or synthesize that which remains unresolved and traumatic in the novel(s): "Neither in *Obasan* nor in its sequel, *Itsuka*, does Naomi seem to overcome the histories she embodies" (2000, 176). Naomi is thus a character who articulates Walter Benjamin's concept of "history as a montage":

> The dialectics of inside and outside, laughter and fear, speech and silence, form the correlates of Naomi's subjecthood. It is important to note that she does not align herself with either of the two sides in these binary constructions, but locates herself in the spaces between them. As "Canada and Japan do not afford the reader symmetrical discourses" in the novel (Brydon 1987, 98), so is there no satisfying balance between the silent Naomi and the Naomi who is the loquacious narrator. Absence, displacement, humiliation, deferral, desire, and the disfiguration of the maternal body – literal or figurative – are at the centre of her story. These conditions determine her silence, but they also show that silence to be ambivalent, to both sustain and traumatize her. Naomi's childhood memories help us to understand how this asymmetrical relationship of silence to speech is brought about, and how it relates to the history of her community in Canada.
>
> (Kamboureli 2000, 177)

The auto/biographical elements of *Obasan* – Kogawa and her family endured many of the privations narrated – are important for a feminist reading of the novel. In fact auto/biography (the "slash" in the word signifying a more theoretically inflected notion of this genre involving an understanding of the fictionalizing strategies of historical and biographical narratives) is a widely used genre for modern Canadian women writers. In many respects, contemporary theories of auto/biography articulate postmodern and gendered notions of subjectivity without effacing corporeality, developing a traditional mode of women's writing in Canada (see Buss).

Postmodern auto/biography in the work of Carol Shields

Postmodern auto/biography and feminist theories of corporeality converge in the fictions of Carol Shields (1935–2003), with her novels *Small Ceremonies* (1976), *Swann* (1987), *The Stone Diaries* (1993) and *Larry's Party* (1997). Born in the USA, Shields emigrated to Canada in 1957, where she studied at the University of Ottawa. A poet, dramatist and critic, Shields is best known for her intensely self-reflexive novels. The biographer in *Small Ceremonies*, Judith Gill, is torn between her reconstruction of the life of Susanna Moodie and her obsession with her landlord's unpublished manuscripts which are full of the private salacious details that she feels that biographies should leave out. In *Swann*, a murdered and dismembered woman's life is obsessively recreated by a group of academics; this absent protagonist, who "in unwitting conspiracy with the Death of the Author" (Briganti, 178), has been violently removed from the scene of writing, is now subject to problematic reconstruction and fictionalization. While the reader does get a living protagonist in *The Stone Diaries* – the fictional auto/biography of Daisy Goodwill Hoad Flett – mundane life appears to be illuminated and dispersed or decentred by family photographs and other archival data, such as recipes, grocery lists, letters, genealogies and even "a scrap of embroidered linen on her kitchen wall" (12) with religious writing on it. The closer the reader gets to Daisy, the more mysterious is her inner life: the photographs used in the novel are "fake" (that is, the reader demands their veracity even though this is a fictional text), the rapid shifts in the novel between first and third person narrators appear to give the text multiple speakers when in fact Shields has said that all of these voices "are filtered through Daisy – she's always imagining what other people think of her" (quoted in Werlock, 18–19), and the reader never actually finds out the date of Daisy's death, her lifespan being given in the novel as "1905–199-". This biographical indeterminacy may be elusive, but it gives Daisy a vitality and interest that reveals that it is in the mundane that people's authentic lives are lived, and that the bodily realm of birth, illnesses and death creates a lasting image. As Briganti argues: "beyond the decentring of the subject, what is genuinely postmodern in this autobiography is the reclaiming of the maternal body and the elaboration of its relation to language in a genre that has traditionally banished the body from representation" (185). In *Larry's Party*, mundane life is represented as labyrinthine, this image structuring the entire text, while the shock of her daughter dropping out of university and sitting on a Toronto street corner with a sign that says "GOODNESS" causes protagonist Reta Winters, in Shields's last novel, *Unless* (2002), to re-evaluate her philosophy of unreflexive domesticity.

A "politics of location" in Daphne Marlatt and Dionne Brand

Daphne Marlatt (b. 1942, in Melbourne, Australia) recreates the labyrinthine images of other women's lives in two novels: *Ana Historic* (1988) and *Taken* (1996), the former depending upon slender archival evidence, the latter upon photographic and televisual images (see Sprout). In *Ana Historic*, the exclusion of women from historical narratives is overturned as the protagonist, Annie, uncovers fragments of a life of a nineteenth-century woman called Mrs Richards, while doing archival research for her husband; these fragments form the basis of a much bigger imaginative project to write women back in to history, including for Annie memories of her mother's life. The novel is, however, highly disorienting in its experimental form, with its chronological palimpsest (layering of different times and places) challenging the reader to cast aside normative, linear notions of biographical writing in favour of a complex psychology of uncovering, remembering, and fabulation. Similarly, in *Taken*, the trope of the photographic image is as important for its absences, its "negatives", as the presencing of image space. Set during the first Gulf War, the protagonist Suzanne has quarrelled with her lover Lori over the war itself, televisual images invading and disrupting their lives, although as Sprout argues, "For Suzanne ... this disruption is potentially productive: it forces her to consider this relation between the war *there* and her life *here*, a West Coast island" (89). Remembering her mother's life in Penang and Melbourne triggers a postcolonial critique of war and patriarchal gender roles.

The recognition in Marlatt's novel of a *globalized* environment of warfare which cannot remain separate from personal and familial histories (and relationships) is part of a new Canadian literary "politics of location" that articulates ethnic differences, although as Peter Dickinson has argued, this necessitates "a more fluid definition" of such a politics, since otherwise hegemonic notions of centre and margin continue to be applied to minority authors (156). Dickinson quotes poet, film-maker and novelist Dionne Brand (b. 1953, in Trinidad) with her "destabilizing and dislocating response" to questions of ethnic positioning: "I don't consider myself on any 'margin,' on the margin of Canadian literature. I'm sitting right in the middle of Black literature, because that's who I read, that's who I respond to" (quoted in Dickinson, 156).

In the 1990s and early twenty-first century, ethnically diverse women's writing in Canada had a significant impact upon postcolonial notions of identity and belonging. Brand's *In Another Place, Not Here* (1996), divided between Toronto and the Caribbean, and two characters Verlia and Elizete, explores sexual and class oppression through two narratives, one of subjugation (Elizete's life as a sugarcane worker) and one of activism (Verlia's life in the Black power movement in Toronto in the 1970s and her union work after she returns to the Caribbean). Elizete is an orphan who comes from a place named "Nowhere" (20), and yet is twice told to "go home" (44–45; 230); the history of Caribbean slavery suggests that such a command is more complexly ironic than first appears, just as Verlia realizes in Toronto that her relations are "fleeing" from their own Black identities. Verlia's continual movement, flight, and concomitant resistance to any mode of stasis leads to her freedom and her death, whereas Elizete's eventual flight to Toronto, in a neat chiasmus or crossing of two subjects sharing the same lover, leads to a new "nowhere" in which "she has to name both self and space in order to create places of be/ longing for herself" (Freiwald, 52).

Movement, or "drifting", is crucial for Brand's *At the Full and Change of the Moon* (1999), a wide-ranging novel of slavery from the 1800s to the late twentieth century. "Drifting" as a trope signals a rejection of colonial notions of belonging and home, as well as a feminist recuperation of highly mobile desiring subjectivities; both impulses have been criticized in Brand's writing, but she has defended her imaginative and political vision of difference, embedded in "diasporic narratives" that are about "decentred, transnational

The Situationists were an artistic and political group loosely organized by Guy Debord (1931–94), author of *The Society of the Spectacle* (1967). Situationism was an anti-capitalist movement that derived much of its impetus from anarchism and avant garde poetics; its main precursors were Dada, Surrealism and Lettrism. One of the Situationists' main practices for the restructuring (or at least re-imagining) of society was that of "drift" (*dérive*): regulated city spaces were perceived as oppressive capitalist constraints that could be creatively restructured by engaging in them in radically different ways, for example attempting to find the fabled Northwest Passage by creating a new route from the Left Bank to Aubervilliers in Paris.

connections" (Goldman, 26). In *What We All Long For* (2005), Brand contrasts the different experiences of first and second generation immigrants living in Toronto, with greater mobility for the latter group as they resist both the constricted lives of their parents, and the stereotypical labelling of the Toronto police and other hegemonic forces. Occupying the marginal and dynamic city spaces, such as the Paramount nightclub, the second generation characters re-map the urban environment, in a contemporary act of "*flânerie* or psychogeography" (Johansen, 56) in a way analogous to the Situationists, who used creative new passageways through city spaces as a political re-mapping, re-coding and claiming of the environment.

Psychogeography in Canadian Asian writing

In *What We All Long For*, psychogeography is portrayed as a tentative decolonization process, and this is a pattern repeated in a large number of contemporary Canadian Asian novels and short-story collections, many of which re-map the city-spaces of Vancouver, BC. Glenn Deer regards Evelyn Lau (b. 1971, in Vancouver) as a precursor to this new generation of authors, her debut auto/biographical book being *Runaway: Diary of a Street Kid* (1989; film version 1993), followed by the short-story collections *Fresh Girls and Other Stories* (1993), *Choose Me* (2000) and her memoirs *Inside Out: Reflections on a Life So Far* (2002). Lau has been attacked by critics for *not* articulating a politics of resistance to the urban lifestyle of prostitution and drug addiction that she narrates in her auto/biographical postmodern flat narrative style; yet Lau's finely portrayed observations of hedonistic, sadomasochistic relationships – especially those between older, wealthy men and younger women – critically articulate uncomfortable and unstable power relations between the sexes, as well as the commodification of the female body.

The harsh capitalist urban environment does not allow any sense of "civic historical recuperation" (Deer, 119) for the new wave of Asian Canadian writing such as Madeleine Thien's (b. 1974) *Simple Recipes* (2001) and *Certainty* (2006),

Nancy Lee's (b. 1970) *Dead Girls* (2002), and Larissa Lai's (b. 1967) *When Fox is a Thousand* (1995) and *Salt Fish Girl* (2002). As Deer argues:

> What is gained by grouping these writers together for the purposes of analysis is an enhanced understanding of the emerging spatial consciousness of a recent generation of Asian Canadian writers, a group that has been able to speak from greater socially mobile positions than their predecessors. Such an analysis also reveals how they are moving beyond some of the earlier preoccupations with historically racialized enclaves in order to address important contemporary phenomena such as group diasporas and the breakdown of traditional family structures across many ethno-cultural groups (Thien), the gendered spaces of street violence (Lee), the contemporary cults of celebrity ([Kevin] Chong) [in his *Baroque-a-nova* (2001)], and the future trajectories of globalization and technology (Lai).
> (119)

Family history is thus reconfigured alongside such new mobility, yet even in novels and short-story collections which take a more historical and biographical approach, such as Sky Lee's (b. 1952) *Disappearing Moon Café* (1990) and *Bellydancer* (1994), Hiromi Goto's (b. 1966) *Chorus of Mushrooms* (1994), *The Kappa Child* (2002) and *Hopeful Monsters* (2004), and Kerri Sakamoto's (b. 1960) *The Electrical Field* (1997) and *One Hundred Million Hearts* (2003), dynastic or familial continuity is in continual tension (if not downright conflict) with the new world, younger generation of Asian Canadians. In almost all of these novels and short-story collections there is a search, however, back through genealogical time, to make sense of origins, mysteries, and family relationships. The doubled consciousness of Asian Canadian women writers thus maintains ethnic and familial continuity as well as a profound critique of more static modes of community and place.

Feminist poetry: an alternative space of writing (or, being Other)

In one of her most famous early poems, *Riel: In the Season of his Birth*, Erin Mouré (b. 1955, in Calgary) writes of Riel's death as a new beginning: the birth of a counter-cultural and historical voice that cannot be denied, the merging with the landscape of an indigenous body that will be renewed, and a voice "wild and liquid" which is "focused / as grass reborn / to breathe in the white spring / of prairie rivers" (in *Empire, York Street*, 1979). While being a major achievement in its own right, "Riel: in the Season of his Birth" also develops some of the artistic and theoretical impulses of Mouré's later feminist work: an attention to gender and the body, the fluidity of the semiotic (using Kristeva's definition of this term), a deconstructive approach to the patriarchal "real" or symbolic, with the creation of "supplementary" poetic/theoretical texts (meta-textual commentary that ironically and paradoxically undermines hegemonic or meta-textual thought), and the creation of an ethics

Feminist Poetics – "Feminism has given us critical methods for understanding gendered reading and writing practices. But now there are new questions – about identity formation, cultural appropriation, and forms of oppression based on race, class, and sexuality. Who speaks for whom? What is the poet's relation to community? How do new subjects gain visibility? How do race, class, and sexuality impact poetic practice?" (Pauline Butling and Susan Rudy, viii)

of difference and alterity, or *being other*. Such a range of theoretical approaches to feminist poetics is reflected more widely in the 1970s and 1980s in Canada, through the exchange of ideas and practices between English- and French-speaking poets and academics.

Marie Carrière argues that feminist poets/theorists in Quebec in the early 1980s – including Louky Bersianik, Nicole Brossard, France Théoret, Madeleine Gagnon, Jovette Marchessault, Suzanne Lamy, Carole David, Louise Desjardins, Louise Dupré, Denise Desautels, Louise Cotnoir – had an "Anglophone equivalent" in the mid-1980s, namely Daphne Marlatt, Gail Scott, Erin Mouré, Marlene Nourbese Philip, Di Brandt, Lola Lemire Tostevin, Dionne Brand, Ann Diamond, Betsy Warland, Smaro Kamboureli, and Claire Harris (3). As Carrière suggests, "Although feminist literature written in English was not a novelty at this point of Canada's literary history ... here were new efforts put into literary collaborations and writers' and critics' conferences, as well as the intention to forge a distinct, radically new, theoretical and feminist aesthetics" (3). Key conferences in which these crossovers and collaborations were forged include The Dialogue Conference, York University (1981), Women and Words / Les Femmes et les mots, Vancouver (1983), Tell It: Women and Language Across Cultures, Simon Fraser University (1988), and Women's Writing and the Literary Institution, at the Towards a History of the Literary Institution Conference, the University of Alberta (1989).

Theorizing feminist collaborative and communal writing in the 1980s and 1990s

Collaborative writing can point towards the importance of new forms of communal living, for example, in lesbian communities that reject the

Feminist Consciousness – " ... I am consciously working through and into women's relationship in and to language. I think I approach language with a feminist consciousness, consciousness of the history of women, how women are sited" (Erin Mouré, in Butling and Rudy, 51).

normative family units of patriarchal society. This more social and political concept of collaborative/communal writing – with the further play on new modes of commonality, communism, and a secular, sexualized communion – features in much of the theoretically inflected poetry from the 1980s and 1990s. For example, Daphne Marlatt and Betsy Warland's *Double Negative* (Gynergy Books, 1988; reprinted in 1994 in *Two Women In A Birth*) mimetically reconceives and incorporates a key collaborative theory text for Canadian feminist poets: Hélène Cixous and Catherine Clément's *The Newly Born Woman* (1975, trans. 1986), with its playful title in French being *La Jeune Née*, two of the word/ sound plays being *Là je n'est* (There I, a subject, is not) and *Là je une nais* (There I, a subject, a feminine one, am born). This multiple avowal and disavowal produced in a collaborative text offers an alternative space of writing that resonates for feminists such as Marlatt and Warland. In *Double Negative* the space is both open and cramped, sheltering and oppressive; this space is a train, a bed, a tomb, which as Lorraine York points out is "by no means politically neutral or an unquestioned ideal" (146). York also observes that Marlatt and Warland create a communal space via intertextuality, quoting and incorporating Jane Rule's *Desert of the Heart* (1964) and Nicole Brossard's *Mauve Desert* (1987).

For Marlatt, language is always already "collaborative" in the sense that it is a "living body" ("Musing with Mothertongue" in *Touch to My Tongue* (1984), 45), the "matter" which signifies and is material, as well as being "by extension mother", "a part of the speech and a part of the body" (46). Marlatt poetically evokes a language that takes issue "with the given, hearing the discrepancy between what our patriarchally loaded language bears (can bear) of our experience and the difference from it our experience bears out – how it misrepresents, even miscarries, and so leaves unsaid what we actually experience" (47). Rejecting male experience, hierarchy and legality which translates for her into patriarchal language, Marlatt quotes instead Julia Kristeva and her notion that each of the sexes has its own unconscious and its own language; as Marlatt says:

> i [sic] link this with the call so many feminist writers in Quebec have issued for a language that returns us to the body, a woman's body and the largely unverbalized, presyntactic, postlexical field it knows. postlexical in that, as Mary Daly shows, with intelligence (that gathering hand) certain words (dandelion sparks) seed themselves back to original and originally-related meaning. this is a field where words mutually attract each other, fused by connection, enthused (inspired) into variation (puns, word play, rime at all levels) fertile in proliferation (offspring, rooting back to *al-*, seed syllable to grow, and leafing forward into *alma*, nourishing, a woman's given name, soul, inhabitant).

(48)

In Erin Mouré's "The Acts" (in *Furious*, 1988), women's language must necessarily articulate the physical body: "Not truncated, not synecdoche, but the physical image speaking directly the entire body at once" (85). Mouré rejects patriarchal logic, aiming for a poetics of "pure reason" (87) or that which is beyond logic and sign-systems, replacing logic with love and desire, with a relational "touching" rather than phallocentric singularity (98), defying pre-inscribed notions of reality: "(The 'real-' that women have never inhabited as whole beings: it has never been formed by our desire, Irigaray says)" (92).

Embodying theory from postmodernism to postcolonialism: feminist conceptions of translation, textuality and corporeality

Marlatt's and Mouré's theorizing, appended to, yet also integrally part of, their poetic texts, draws upon the Quebecois turn to French structuralist and poststructuralist theory in the aftermath of the fiercely nationalist poetics that dominated the 1950s and 1960s. In 1965 a new journal, *La Barre du jour*, was founded by Nicole Brossard, Marcel Saint-Pierre, Roger Soublière and Jan Stafford, with a remit to explore formal and theoretical issues in contemporary aesthetics. Brossard re-launched the journal in 1977 as *La Nouvelle Barre du jour* shifting the focus to more creative work which synthesized aesthetics and theory, in other words a more "literary practice" which Brossard called "fiction théorique" (Carrière, 19). Receptivity in Anglophone Canada to this formalist and theoretical shift of focus that occurred in Quebec was in part due to the poetic experimentalism of the 1960s, and the shift to a language-based postmodernism in the 1970s and 1980s. Of note is the *Tish* group of poets in Vancouver (George Bowering, Frank Davey, David Dawson, James Reid and Fred Wah), who were interested in the aesthetic experimentalism of the Black Mountain poets in the USA; the journal *Tish* was published between 1961 to 1969, and it supported an energetic, powerful "spoken" poetry that was constructed via oral rhythms. Marlatt's interaction with the *Tish* group, for example, led to her interest in the graphical surface, including typographical and etymological playfulness. Steve McCaffery (b. 1947) is another key poet exploring a more theoretically inflected practice, one striving for non-referentiality, for example his sound poetry ensemble with poet bpNichol (Barrie Philip Nichol, 1944–88) called *Four Horsemen* (1970), and his collaborative founding of and contributions to the parodic and theoretically astute Toronto Research Group in 1973. McCaffery was also a key contributor to the American language poetry magazine called $L = A = N = G = U = A = G = E$. The intersection of theoretical and creative experimentation in language writing "anticipated" a similar process of theoretical incorporation in the work of more radical Anglophone feminist poets, especially drawing upon Jacques Derrida's (1930–2004) notion of *différance*, or the continual, necessary dispersal of meaning through spacing and through time, which "has become crucial in the exploration of textual alterity and polysemy in writings in the feminine" (Carrière, 26). But where the feminist poetic differs from what soon became mainstream postmodernism, is the continual focus on gender, the female body, the act and trope of mothering, as well as a re-inscription of a "semiotic" or "imaginary" rather than "symbolic" language, and a new concern for an ethical mode of writing which acknowledges or creates a space for the Other (an ethics of alterity).

Theoretical and aesthetic crossovers between French- and English-speaking Canada also occurred because of a new vitality in translation. Founded in 1969 at The Université de Sherbrooke, the journal *Eclipse* was an important venue for the translation of English Canadian and Quebecois poetry. As Delisle and Gallichan note, "The journal instigated a new mode of poetry translation in Canada, creating a space for dialogue and networks of sociability between pairs of literary writers from the two main linguistic groups, such as Gaston Miron and F.R. Scott. In the 1970s a truly bilingual community arose among authors and translators, particularly feminists, with Anglophones translating francophone novelists and theorists" (54). Explosive growth in the number of translations followed the creation of the Canada Council's translation grants in 1972 (Ibid., 55). One translator in particular – Barbara Godard (1941–2010) – was a significant driving force in the translation of Quebecois feminist theorists and authors, as well as writing key critical essays that have contributed to the bridging of feminist cultures in Canada. Educated at The University of Toronto, Université de Montréal, Université de Paris VIII, Vincennes, and the Université de Bordeaux, Godard translated Quebecois authors such as Nicole Brossard, Antonine Maillet (b. 1929), Louky Bersianik (b. 1930), Yolande Villemaire (b. 1949) and France Théoret (b. 1942), leading critic Smaro Kamboureli to assert that Godard generated "a vibrant dialogue between Anglophone Canadian literature and Quebec writers, especially women" (2008, 17). Godard argues that the more theoretically inflected "emergence of a feminine subject" (99) in Quebec and elsewhere led to a feminist interrogation of discourse and representation, especially in light of poststructuralist notions of the "death of the author", and the concomitant feminist need to re-assert agency and existence. Translation plays a key role in such interrogations, especially as it "traffics in power" in its "double movement" (205):

> In the double movement of interanimation that is translation, languages, subjectivities, are exchanged, relativized. Such "dialogism" points to the incompleteness of all languages, to the absence of any homogenizing master language, not to posit the transcendence of the need to translate in some theological moment of signification or "pure language" but, on the contrary, to insist on the dynamic interaction and contamination of languages in the continuous *movement* of transformation in the making and unmaking of hierarchies. There is nonetheless a difference in the effect of such commerce in languages depending on where one is positioned within the axes of power, and on the direction of the transfer – downwards, upwards, or horizontally – along the hierarchy, whether one "translates"

the self into the perspective of the other, or translates the other in the language of the sovereign subject, or meditates on the difficulties of passage.

(205)

Contributing to such "commerce in languages" from a feminist perspective meant being involved in the formation of "a new literary genre, the 'théorie-fiction/ fiction-theory' featured in [the bilingual feminist magazine] *Tessera*" (312). The Tessera Collective, founded in 1984 by Barbara Godard, Daphne Marlatt, Kathy Mezei and Gail Scott, facilitated the production of such newly conceived notions of gender in translation.

The literary-theoretical turn recognizing being Other in Francophone and Anglophone feminist poetry involves a return to the body, and a concomitant re-evaluation of mother–daughter relationships, leading to the concept of "being (m)other". Karen Gould points to the title of a special issue of *La Barre du jour* (1977) which "draws attention to feminist theorizing on the physicality of women's language and to the emerging poetics of the female body as text" (43); the title is threefold:

le corps
(body)
les mots
(words)
l'imaginaire
(imaginary).

The traditionally patriarchal logos or Judeo-Christian "word" is pluralized, and placed in between the body and the imaginary. All of the terms are doubled, with the two official languages of Canada side by side, except in this case there is a reversal of hierarchy, whereby the dominance of English is reversed by being situated in parentheses. Gould argues that this title is non-linear, and can be read from top to bottom, or bottom to top; with the former, "the vertical, nonlinear distribution of three key concepts in Quebec's *écriture au feminine* exemplifies a new mode of conceptualizing the female body as a generator of women's words and of the feminine imaginary", whereas when read in the opposite way "the body is the inscribed result of the feminine imaginary put into words" (43).

This rejection of logocentrism in favour of writing the body has its precursors in the critique of Catholic attitudes to family and women's reproductive sexuality, in the writing of key women authors such as Claire Martin, Marie-Claire Blais and Anne Hébert (Ibid.). The new feminist poets, however, are far more assertive in creating an autonomous voice. The need to not only re-conceive of male–female but also mother–daughter relations as part of a rejection of patriarchy starts with the dismantling and reconstruction of language itself.

Recoding the symbolic mother: Nicole Brossard's *These Our Mothers* (1977) and *Picture Theory* (1982)

Arguably, the key text in which familial relations are theorized is Nicole Brossard's *These Our Mothers, Or: The Disintegrating Chapter* (1983), first published in 1977 as *L'amèr ou le Chapitre effrité*. Brossard's writing directly confronts the mechanisms of normative language, re-schematizing not just frameworks of linguistic sense-making mechanisms, but rebuilding them from a lesbian-feminist perspective. As she writes in *These Our Mothers*: "If it weren't lesbian, this text would make no sense at all" (16). Brossard argues that for women, survival depends upon becoming "recognized as symbolic mother" (17), but this is not a simple replacement of one symbolic code with another, since Brossard writes through paradox and the occupying of multiple subject positions: the mother–daughter relationship is agonistic and incestuous, murderous and loving, recoded through the writing of a lesbian imaginary which is "where the code of the species is preserved at its best" (94). Perhaps the most powerful moment in *These Our Mothers* is the re-writing of the Lacanian mirror-stage recognition, and other mirror scenes in canonical women's writing:

> A woman in front of the mirror looks for her identity. And sees there only an allusion. Illusion, metamorphosis: the gaze of the other. Obsession or juxtaposition of her bodies, mother's and woman's. No, she hasn't thrown her head back because of the bliss of orgasm. She was completely bowled over at the very idea that difference cut her in two.
> The difference is what is left. The result of subtraction.
>
> (38)

The specular image is doubled, not just woman per se, but the mother–daughter reflection; also, the reflection is not simply a returned gaze, but it is corporeal. Difference appears related to *jouissance*, but it is also a "subtraction" or the cut of the mother–daughter relationship. Winfried Siemerling argues that here "the question of self and other is posed explicitly in the image of a paradoxical mirror that reveals more than one image" (17); the gaze into the mirror is returned, "both the gaze of the other and an other gaze" (Brossard, 179).

What Brossard resists is the notion of the mirror reflecting back the identity of woman as the patriarchal object, fixed in place by the male gaze; instead, she offers a subversive image of female relationships (subversive in the sense that this is the mother–daughter relationship perceived outside of the structure of the heterosexual family). The father's gaze is figured in the text as scientific, taking place in a laboratory; ironically, it is the scientific highly theoretical approach of the early issues of *La Barre du jour* that led Brossard to reinvent her own approach to feminist writing, creating a new holographic theory of character in highly charged poetic prose in her "novel" *Picture Theory* (1982).

Picture Theory interrogates the specular scene via which women are written into existence, offering a way of reconstructing both the fragmented, objectified patriarchal notion of the female body, and the utopian strategically fragmentary vision of lesbian-feminist deconstruction; this may initially appear essentialist, but in fact it is "holographic" or beyond "mimetic representation" (Thompson, 23), producing a "virtual image" (Ibid., 28) only in the minds – and memories – of a reader who has returned to the text over and over again. In effect, the reader brings together the holographic light beams, and the reader becomes immersed in the hologram, in the "flash of recognition, as the semiotic chain of meaning halts, temporarily, anchoring itself to some body for an instant" (Ibid., 29). In *Picture Theory* this is the "knowledge braided" of the "global feminine": "working on architecture, time, I/her force familiar in becoming. Identity in the trajectory of the body, a condensation of inscriptions: celebrates the her/i/zon" (Brossard, 99).

The feminist-deconstructive poetics of Lola Lemire Tostevin

In Anglophone writing in the feminine, the importance of the body and the mother–daughter relationship(s) have been explored by Lola Lemire Tostevin (b. 1937, in Timmins, Ontario) and Di Brandt (b. 1952, in Winkler, Manitoba). Tostevin's *Color of Her Speech* (1982), *Gyno-text* (1982 within *Color of Her Speech*; published separately in 1985), *Double Standards* (1985) and *'Sophie* (1988), foreground the experiences and existential reality of the female body, through a rich intertextual wordplay, especially referring to formative writers and theorists such as Brossard. In *'Sophie*, Brossard is cited almost from the beginning: "as *These Our Mothers* have said we cannot hide / from ourselves the fictional character ... " (10). Tostevin expresses the magnitude of the feminist task when it comes to expressing desire through the reinvention of what she calls "the world", pondering further "how she came to this place between writing the body / and writing as erasure of the body" (22). The contradiction here is that in writing the feminist poet can "make a name for herself / then loses it in the writing" (23). This is a feminist-deconstructive logic, one where phallogocentric writing needs to be occupied from the inside, but with an awareness that the concepts deconstructed also continue to carry metaphysical weight and meaning.

Tostevin's main strategy to resist reincorporation into the patriarchal order is to create a doubled language, for example, introducing French into English poems, or to put this another way, interjecting her "mothertongue" into the language of colonization. In *Gyno-text* the rhythms of the pregnant body structure the entire poem in a mimetic production of thirty-seven poems (reflecting thirty-seven weeks of pregnancy). The intertextual reference is to Kristeva's concept of the *geno-text* (Lane 2006b, 188) or the maternal affects that are constitutive of the semiotic chora or matrix. In "by the smallest possible margin", her essay on attending Derrida's seminar on The Political Theology of Language, Tostevin articulates a maternal infrastructural possibility: "Derrida has pointed out via Schelling, that both religion and philosophy are lacking a mediator, an interpreter, or some semiotic sign and I propose to give him one by the way of the amniotic. Thin membrane that surrounds all beginnings. The pregnant pause as conceptual space" (Tostevin, 47). At the seminar, Derrida rapidly agrees with Tostevin's comments, as a way, Tostevin suggests, of marginalizing a woman's voice; but Tostevin has already utilized this metaphor throughout her writing, regardless of other theorists' opinions. Her insightful "proposition" is of course an attack on the law of the deconstructive father – Jacques Derrida himself.

"Between command and defiance": mothers and daughters in the poetry of Di Brandt

Di Brandt articulates mother–daughter relationships through the problematic triangle of mother–daughter and law-of-the-father, both her actual father, and the father's discourse of Christianity. In *questions i asked my mother* (1987), the barrier between mother and daughter is in fact the word/law of the father: "what do you think my father says this verse means if it's not about the end of the world look that's obviously a misreading i say ... " (4), the stream of reported speech forming a continuum that the poet continually upsets and interrupts through her disturbing comments and questions. Some of the disruptive energy of the poet derives from her auto/biographical journey away from the site of the word/law of the father, adolescent bodily urges to know sexual truths being interdicted by Mennonite religious strictures: "we could understand for example that hair was an unruly item best kept under kerchiefs and hats its dangerous tendency to shine in the sun and spring provocative curls sometimes without prompting" (8). The parody of the religious command to cover female hair works far more powerfully than a direct criticism, the phrases "we could understand" and "its dangerous tendency" working both with and against the interdiction.

Beauty is "altogether a disturbing category for Mennonites" argues the poet, writing of the shock of "mistakenly" going to an art gallery instead of a museum, and entering a room full of nudes: "our first glimpse of the shape our own bodies were destined to become i would have liked to stay in this room awhile and sort out the strange emotions aroused by this totally new vision of the world but for the sake of our education we rushed on" (11). Again, parody and ironic language ("for the sake of our education ... ") undercut the religious command that it is sinful to see paintings of female nudes. The visit to the art gallery is followed directly by an erotic poem where self-awareness of female sexuality and desire is in contradiction with a "head full of lies", the phrase "your great empty nothing" (12) potentially indicating a sexist notion of the female mind, or the female womb when not pregnant. The poet repeats the phrase "despise despise the Word of God is the Word of God" in a mantra that is more complex than first appears: is it the *logos* that is being despised because it is transcendent, or because it cannot be interpreted, or belong to, any one else? In *mother, not mother* (1992), the poet writes "today i spit out God and Jesus / for the last time", and "how sick i am of these / pieces of Godhead" (27). As Tanis MacDonald notes, "Brandt shows the mother's problematic complicity in this belief system, obeying the father's commands even as 'her / body is shouting *No! No!*' This tension between men and women, between command and defiance, between violence and love, thrives upon the silence that surrounds it, and Brandt asserts that the price exacted for silence is profoundly painful" (xi). In an autobiographical essay, "you pray for the rare flower to appear", Brandt situates her poetry in a cultural Mennonite context as well as referring to technical and aesthetic liberation; she writes that "I am grateful to have come to poetry in a time when the spirits of experimentalism and postcolonialism and feminism were at a height in Canada, in the 1980s, a hundred years after my ancestors arrived on this continent, frightened, destitute, garrisoned" (50). Rejecting postmodernism, Brandt foregrounds and celebrates her writing of poetry "as a woman and as a mother" (51).

Diasporic doubled consciousness: Dionne Brand's postcolonial Canada

If for Brandt the postcolonial is a struggle to move away from inherited patriarchal, religious modes of living, for Dionne Brand, postcolonial Canada is a place of exile and racism that needs to be combated through a militant poetic counter-discourse. Born in Trinidad, Brand emigrated to Canada in 1970, the diasporic immigrant theme being enormously important in much of her poetry and prose writing (see earlier). In *No Language Is Neutral* (1990), she writes how "language / seemed to split in two" (31), the doubled consciousness of a Black Canadian creating a dialectic without synthesis or resolution. Whiteness is often symbolized in Brand's poetry through descriptions of harsh Canadian winters, "In this country where islands vanish, bodies submerge" (*Land To Light On*, 1997, 73). For Brand, the "heart of darkness" is not some kind of primordial Africa, as envisioned in Conrad's famous novella, but, paradoxically, this snow-blanketed place: "the heart of darkness is these white roads, snow / at our throats" (Ibid.). The female subject, however, is dispersed, alienated and interpellated through racist vision, from the White cop "looking at aliens" (Ibid.) when simply gazing in at "Three Blacks

On Representation – "If I wanted my life represented, and I could choose a shape for its representation, I would choose poetry. [...] A lot of young Black women have seen the film I've worked on [*Long time comin'*] and they say to me, oh, I really loved that. I sense their relief and thankfulness at being able to watch themselves or people like themselves in a film. And I recognize film as a modern medium ... But if I want my life represented in its fullness and its beauty then it takes the shape of poetry" (Dionne Brand, in Butling and Rudy, 87).

in a car" (Ibid.), to the woman who "One year sat at the television weeping, / no reason, / the whole time" (*Inventory*, 2006, 21), the poem revealing a despair for global peoples subjected to colonial interventions and political unrest.

Performing gender/feminist theatrical subjectivities

The origins of feminist theatre in Canada are intricately connected with the development of an anti-colonial, anti-mainstream theatre profession, one which Denis Johnston sketches by tracing back in time: "[O]ne can see gay and feminist theatres of the 1980s breaking off from alternative theatres of the 1970s, which in turn were a reaction to the original theatre network created primarily in the 1960s" (225). While the regional theatres that led to the theatre network had been built upon community theatres, little theatres and workers' theatre groups were also important, especially during the depression years. Yvonne Hodkinson notes that "In the 1930s, women like Dora Smith Conover and Leonora McNeilly of the Canadian Women's Press Club, saw the importance of producing a national drama. Through the establishment of the Playwright's Studio Group in Toronto in 1932, these women forged an important stronghold through which Canadian drama could flourish. The Studio Group also became a place for female playwrights to discover an aesthetic consciousness" (9–10). Core members were Dora Smith Conover, Rica McLean Farquharson, Leonora McNeilly, Lois Reynolds Kerr, Virginia Coyne Knight, Marjorie Price and Winnifred Pilcher.

Foundational feminist drama from the 1930s to the work of Gwen Pharis Ringwood

Lois Reynolds Kerr's (1908–2001) satirical plays *Among Those Present* (produced 1933), based on the title of a silent movie, *Nellie McNab* (produced 1934), and *Guest of Honour* (produced 1936) explore the world of journalism – and marriage – from a feminist perspective. Plays of the Depression, such as Kerr's *Open Doors* (1930), Dorothy Livesay's *Joe Derry* (1933), the collectively produced *Eight Men Speak* (1934) by Oscar Ryan, E. Cecil-Smith, H. Francis (Frank Love) and Mildred Goldberg, and Gwen Pharis Ringwood's *Still Stands The House* (1938), are historically and politically important. For example, the agitprop play *Eight Men Speak* is based on a prison riot in 1932, in Kingston Penitentiary, whereupon the Canadian Communist Party leader Tim Buck and seven other imprisoned compatriots were fired on by a guard; the play depicts an imaginary situation whereby the state authorities and capitalism are put on trial, prosecuted by the Canadian Labor Defense League (CLDL). As James Doyle observes, "Significantly, CLDL is represented as a woman, a reflection of the feminist influences in the Communist literary community that made this milieu so congenial to writers like Dorothy Livesay and *New Frontiers* editor Margaret Gould" (131). Ostensibly about the men involved in the riot and their subsequent standing in for larger forces in society explored in the play, the central role of this symbolic female character reveals how workers' theatre did at times intersect with feminist concerns. Social realism also offered technical innovation at a time when playwrights were searching for new ways of representing the harsh experiences of economic and social deprivation.

Gwen Pharis Ringwood's (1910–84) prairie realism developed in *Still Stands The House* reveals not just psychological isolation and breakdown, but an entire landscape haunted by patriarchal oppression, also the driving force of Ringwood's following play, *Dark Harvest* (1939). Ringwood, who was born in Anatone, Washington, had direct experience of the vast open spaces of Montana and Alberta. Her extensive contribution to Canadian theatre includes writing over sixty plays. Hodkinson argues that "In a modern context, Ringwood's plays provide a foundation for feminist thought in Canadian drama, and suggest the need for a transformation of women's place in the patriarchal tradition" (11). This foundation includes Ringwood's later exploration of Aboriginal women and society, in *Lament for Harmonica* (1959), *The Stranger* (1971) and *The Furies* (1980), plays which mix a postcolonial concern for indigenous people with Greek mythology and modernist dramatic form.

The 1970s and 1980s: new environments and dramatic re-telling of women's stories

In *The Lodge* (1975) and *Garage Sale* (1981), Ringwood gives autonomy and strength to elderly women; similarly, Beverley Simons's (b. 1938) *Crabdance* (1969), *Green Lawn Rest Home* (1973) and Betty Jane Wylie's *A Place On Earth* (1982) all engage with elderly women coming to the end of their lives. Simons's dark existential plays stage and in effect evacuate social rituals of all meaning as death approaches her protagonists; Wylie's seventy-two-year-old female protagonist, called Peggy, is sensitively and claustrophobically encased in her apartment, fearing the pressures and dangers of the outside world. Yet these women are not just vulnerable: they are powerfully critical of an ever-increasing violence and aggression in society. However, their isolation is highly symbolic of the prison-house of domesticity, especially within an urban or suburban environment, as explored in Elinore Siminovitch's *Tomorrow and Tomorrow* (1972), Mary Humphrey Baldrige's *Bride of the Gorilla* (1974), Judith Thompson's *The Crackwalker* (1980), Sharon Pollock's *Doc* (1984) and Pamela Boyd's *Inside Out* (1985).

Feminist playwrights in the 1970s and early 1980s also re-assessed women's roles in history:

> Diane Grant's *What Glorious Times They Had* (1974) recalls the feminist crusades of Nellie McClung; Carol Bolt's *Red Emma* (1974) brings the passionate 19th century American feminist, Emma Goldman, to the stage, and Wendy Lill's *Fighting Days* (1984) portrays the moral vision of the Manitoban suffragette, Francis Beynon. In *Blood Relations* (1980)

Sharon Pollock reinterprets the 19th century legend of Lizzie Borden, accused and later acquitted of murdering her father and stepmother. Ann Henry's *Lulu Street* (1972) attempts to understand the female experience within the context of the 1919 Winnipeg General Strike. [...] Plays such as these express the historical entrapment of women in a male-oriented society, but do so in an attempt to comprehend female experience in a modern context.

(Hodkinson, 13–14)

While Rina Fraticelli's report called "The Status of Women in the Canadian Theatre" (1982) had revealed "the relative absence of women from the power structure of the profession" (quoted in Burton, 3), the creative explosion of new feminist drama in the 1960s, 70s and 80s suggests that this artistic form was highly valuable for exploring the consequences of societal transformation.

Carnival and the picaresque heroine in Antonine Maillet's *La Sagouine* (1971)

In re-coding the picaresque from a female perspective in her play *La Sagouine* (1971; trans. 1979), Antonine Maillet (who was born in Bouctouche, New Brunswick) draws upon Acadian folklore, and creates a new profane illumination in the gritty world of working-class poverty, prostitution and disempowerment. Sagouine, a cleaner who ponders her life with great verve and wit, reminds her audience of the Acadian expulsion when she says she wants to go back to Prince Edward Island to find her family and get together with people: " ... 'n to recognize each other; 'n slap on an ol' man's shoulder 'n call him by his first name ... 'n find fr'm a distance a person that looks like you, 'n speaks yer language, 'n does yer same work, 'n wouldn' look down on you cause yer not'n but a scrubwoman that ain't never done not'n 'n never seen not'n" (19). Sagouine's piercing insight into human and social relations comes from her biting wit and ironic reversals, such as her notion of the depression being a good time because then she suffers poverty less since society "invented relief" (106). As she argues, "The worst time fer poor folks is when not'n happens: no war, no floods, no ecumenic crash ... not'n to remind the world some folks don't got not'n to eat" (106). Religious dogma dissolves through her carnivalesque vision: "The thing I und'stand the least is on the one hand, the Good Lord says it ain't easy fer a rich man to go to heaven; but on the other hand, seems to me it ain't easy fer a rich man not to get there" (125). Yet Sagouine's identity is always under threat. In "The Census" she goes through a whole list of possible nationalities, including "*Acadjens*": "Well, them censors didn' wanna write down that word on their list. The way they sees it, seems *L'Acadie* ain't a country, 'n *Acadjen* ain't a nationality, cause of the fact it ain't written in Joe Graphy's books" (165). Finally, then, the censors make up their own minds: "So, I think they put us down with the Injuns" (166).

Maillet's earthy humour may in part be traced to her interest at university in Rabelais, her PhD thesis being *Rabelais et les traditions littéraires en*

Acadie (1971); Rabelais' *Pantagruel* also appears in her play *Les drôlatiques, horrifiques et épouvantables aventures de Panurge, ami de Pantagruel* (1983). In Maillet's fiction and drama, the carnivalesque emerges through the figure of the strong female picaresque heroine, who may be in exile, but is always irrepressible in spirit, expressed through the vernacular or "mother tongue": "The Acadian dialect in the play represents the articulation of female identity, as mother tongue is linked to ancient origins and the retracing of a forgotten vision. La Sagouine's dialogue is an expression of emotional and personal experience which she brings into the world of theatre" (Hodkinson, 120).

Sharon Pollock and Margaret Hollingsworth: alternative worlds

The alternative world of the picaresque is also a liminal space, sometimes one in which the heroine occupies a threshold between sanity and insanity, the socially acceptable and the frowned-upon, the legitimate and the illegitimate voice. This alternative world has attracted feminist playwrights, such as Sharon Pollock (b. 1936, in Fredericton, New Brunswick) whose play *Blood Relations* (produced as *My Name is Lisbeth* in 1976; revised production 1980) stages a play-within-a-play interpretation of Lizzie Borden's life, a woman acquitted of an axe murder in 1892. Even though Pollock had already produced a mature body of work prior to *Blood Relations* – with historical plays such as *Walsh* (1973), about the North West Mounted Police and the Sioux chief Sitting Bull; *The Komagata Maru Incident* (1976), concerning the racist and inhumane denied entry to Vancouver of a boatload of Sikh immigrants; and *One Tiger to a Hill* (1980), which explores a hostage-taking event at New Westminster penitentiary in BC – her study of Lizzie Borden represents a shift into more specifically feminist work. Diane Bessai calls *Blood Relations* a turning point in Pollock's aesthetic, leading to a focus away from the broad historical canvas to a more intimate, problematic space of female domesticity, which also involves a shift in form: "The difference from the other histori-cally-based plays is *Blood Relations'* metaphoric rather than causal focus on the present, for which the vehicle is organically theatrical" (130–31). The play-within-a-play structure facilitates a relationship between Lizzie and an unnamed actress who is in effect her double in that she is representing her; the framing and crossings of play and "reality" leads to a more subtle approach to historical material, what Bessai calls "anti-documentary" or "an implicit critique of documentary drama's basic assumption that the truth can be demonstrably discovered in an investigatory dramatic structure" (132).

In *Blood Relations*, the key feminist move is to reverse the charge of Lizzie's innocence which was based upon the patriarchal notion that a properly brought up young woman could not be capable of murder: as "The Defense" says, "[D]o you believe Miss Lizzie Borden, the youngest daughter of a scion of our community, a recipient of the fullest amenities our society can bestow upon its most fortunate members, do you believe Miss Lizzie Borden capable of wielding the murder weapon?" (363). Lizzie, then, has the strength, under certain conditions, to no longer be a "puppet" (394), yet that is not to say that the play simplistically offers a reading of her guilt, since the accused is the society within which she is embedded.

Margaret Hollingsworth (b. 1940, in Sheffield, England) also explores this liminal space of accusation, innocence and guilt, in her play *Alli Alli Oh* (1977), which was first produced by the feminist Redlight Theatre. Intriguingly, the character of Alli, who is attempting to recover from an oppressive marriage and a nervous breakdown, begins to identify with one of the cows at the farm where she is being looked after by a woman called Muriel; Alli's descent into madness is thus also a journey away from a constricting notion of human subjectivity and female "productivity". In the follow-up play, called *Islands* (1983), the relationship between Alli and Muriel is complicated by the presence of Muriel's mother, Rose, who is visiting Muriel's island farmhouse which is now devoid of animals. Rose's conventional marriage is compared with the choices Alli has made in rejecting convention within her relationships; both modes of intersubjectivity can lead to a form of madness. Cynthia Zimmerman argues that "these [two plays] can be seen as companion pieces about the separateness of each person, about isolation and islands both physical and psychic. The plays are a variation on Hollingsworth's ongoing themes, presenting ... both the yearning for a home and intimate connection, and its obverse: the claustrophobia, the sense of invasion, or the loss of self, when home comes to feel like a prison" (108). Both plays can be productively read alongside Hollingsworth's *Mother Country* (1980) in which a domineering woman creates the oppressive conditions from which her children need to break free; at an allegorical level, the play is about Canada's relationship with the "mother country" of Great Britain, and the need for independence.

Psychodrama and "the violent woman" in feminist theatre in the 1980s and 1990s

A reintegration of historical "documentary"-style drama with that of focused identity-based "psychodrama" can be seen emerging among key women dramatists in the 1980s and 1990s, including Betty Lambert's (1933–83) plays about female sterilization, called *Jennie's Story* (produced 1981), and the kidnapping of a young girl called *Under The Skin* (1987) and Wendy Lill's (b. 1950) hard-hitting plays about political feminist activist Francis Beynon in *The Fighting Days* (1985), gender and racial relations in *The Occupation of Heather Rose* (1986), Canadian author Elizabeth Smart in *Memories of You* (1988), the Aboriginal residential school system in *Sisters* (1991) and contemporary "witch-hunting" for potential child abusers in a day-care centre in *All Fall Down* (1994). Lill also adapted Sheldon Currie's (b. 1934) short story "The Glace Bay Miners' Museum" (1976) as the radio and stage play *The Glace Bay Miners' Museum*, which premiered in 1995 at the Eastern Front Theatre (founded by Mary Vingoe, Gay Hauser and Wendy Lill in 1993). Lill has also written plays about the treatment of disabled people, in *Corker* (2000), and stem-cell research, in *Chimera* (2007).

Shelley Scott identifies "the violent woman" as a new focus of artistic interest – and a new character type – in late-twentieth-century feminist drama, suggesting that "The very idea of a woman who kills disturbs our most basic beliefs about gender" (7). Scott traces this interest back through the history of Canadian drama to 1933, and Ringwood's *Still Stands The House*, suggesting that the knowledge that the protagonist Hester has – that she has sent her brother and sister-in-law out into a blizzard without oil in their lamps – is tantamount to their murder. Pollock's *Blood Relations* is the strongest dramatic precursor from the 1980s, while Pollock's play about the American Indian Movement activist Anna Mae Pictou Aquash, called *The Making of Warriors* (1991), is a more contemporary example. Scott also surveys Carol Bolt's (1941–2000) *Famous* (1997), Joan MacLeod's (b. 1954) *The Shape of a Girl* (2001), and feminist "Revenge Tragedies" such as the Anna Project's (Suzanne Odette Khuri, Ann-Marie MacDonald, Banuta Rubess, Maureen White) *This is For You, Anna* (Nightwood Premier, 1985), Lorena Gale's (1958–2009) *Angélique* (1995) and Marie Clements's *The Unnatural and Accidental Women* (2000). In *The Making of Warriors*, originally a radio play, Nova Scotian MicMac activist Anna Mae Pictou Aquash crosses multiple boundaries: those of traditional passive gender roles in favour of active political engagement, and those of national and ethnic domains, as a Canadian working for an American indigenous movement (one whose peoples existed before colonialism imposed new maps and borders). Other Canadian female "warrior" plays include Sally Clark's (b. 1953) *Jehanne of the Witches* (produced 1989), a play about Joan of Arc, and Sonja Mills's *The Danish Play* (2002) concerning World War Two resister Agnete Ottosen, who was Mills's great aunt.

Perhaps the most controversial play in this entire cluster is Bolt's *Famous*, concerning Karla Homolka, who, along with her partner Paul Bernardo, was involved in the rape and murder of a series of young women in Scarborough, Ontario, beginning in 1990 with her own sister. *Famous* creates a fictional framework to distance itself from, yet still indirectly comments upon, the Homolka case; for example, through some astute plea-bargaining and with-holding of key video evidence, Homolka's lawyers had managed to get her a reduced sentence for manslaughter, the sadistic and pornographic video materials (since destroyed) inevitably becoming objects of intense fascination for journalists and the public. In her play, Bolt devises a character called Sheila who is a videographer, to address the issues raised in the real-life case and in relation to the voyeuristic televisual journalistic furor that followed.

Another controversial real-life court case involved the murder of a teenage-girl called Reena Virk in 1997, in Victoria, BC; MacLeod's *The Shape of a Girl* is – indirectly – about her life and the gang of teenage girls who had bullied and murdered her. Again, a fictional frame enables distance and reflection on the real-life case: "The character of Braidie acts as a kind of conduit, negotiating the terrain between audience experience and real-life events, and is a crucial device in the way MacLeod guides the spectator towards the subject matter" (Scott, 47). If audiences (and the general public) are morally shocked and simultaneously voyeuristically attracted to female murderers, murder as an act of female revenge is even more disturbing. *This is For You, Anna* utilizes multiple, collectively produced scenes, as well as all of the actors playing the protagonist Marianne, to holographically depict the protagonist's revenge killing of her daughter's murderer; *Angélique* portrays the oppression of a Black slave in New France, who eventually uses arson as a way of avenging her mistreatment, although she is hanged for her actions; *The Unnatural and Accidental Women* follows the real-life case of a Vancouver barber who murdered at least ten women in the Hastings Street neighbourhood – the play uses dark humour in bringing the murdered women back to life, with Rebecca, the daughter of one of the women, avenging her mother by the end of the play (Lane 2003, 272–74).

Dramatic sites of desire: lesbian theatre in Canada

Dramatic explorations of sexualities have long been tied in to issues of national identity, although Rosalind Kerr suggests that with lesbian theatre, it is the urban environment in Canada that has nurtured "new alternative sexual and cultural communities" (2007, 221). Lesbian drama directly tackles "heterosexualizing norms" (Kerr 2006, iii) through a variety of strategies, including the decentring of heterosexual subjectivities and sites of desire. In a groundbreaking anthology called *Lesbian Plays: Coming of Age in Canada* (2006), Kerr creates a genealogy of Canadian lesbian drama, beginning and ending with key coming-out narratives: transgender dramatist Alec Butler's *Black Friday* (1989), Shawna Dempsey and Lorri Millan's *Growing Up Suits, Parts I and II* (1994 and 1995), and *Object/Subject of Desire* (first full performance 1989), Vivienne Laxdal's *Karla and Grif* (1991), and Corrina Hodgson's *Privilege* (2004). Hodgson critiques the notion of coming-out as a "pathological state" that needs to be addressed in adolescence, through the imaginative powers of her protagonist, Ginny, who creates a series of counter-discursive sexualized scenarios based around her counsellor and other adults who try and cure her of her sexuality.

Historical narratives of lesbian desire and potentiality are explored in Lisa Walter's *Difference of Latitude* (1995), Kathleen Oliver's *Swollen Tongues* (1998) and Natalie D. Meisner's *Life and A Lover* (1999); each of these plays examines role-playing and gender performance, from an escape from domesticity by going to sea in *Difference of Latitude*, cross-dressing and transvestism in *Swollen Tongues*, and the love affair between Virginia Woolf and Vita Sackville-West mediated through the androgynous figure of Orlando in *Life and A Lover*. Set in contemporary society, three plays articulate more recent concerns: Susan G. Cole's *A Fertile Imagination* (1991) is about a lesbian couple who wish to have a child, written with fast-paced wit and double-edged humour, beginning with the opening scene as the protagonists Rita and Del are in search of a sperm-donor (as Del says, "I want to keep an eye on the guy I don't want to see" (in Kerr, 2006, 170)); Kerr argues that "By representing all the difficulties that arise when lesbians try to participate in the most sacrosanct of heterosexual rituals, Cole forces us to look closely at the kinds of exclusionary rules that reward traditional family structures" (163). Diane Flack's *Random Acts* (1999) occurs on the eve of the Millennium, opening with the Biblical Sarah's laughter at the knowledge that she has been able to conceive at the age of ninety, and a monologue about the contradictory chaos and order of interconnected society; the protagonist, Antonella Bergman, engages with her recent disability and the ironies of her situation as a self-help guru in a world which appears beyond help. Alex Bulmer's *Smudge* (2001) intertwines the onset of blindness with the breakdown of a lesbian relationship in a play which is both comic and deeply poignant.

Conclusion

• Feminist authors in Canada have gained national and international recognition for their work, including the early novelists and short-story writers who have now entered the mainstream.
• A dialogic approach to theory and creativity marks much of the literary output of feminist writers, especially in the case of the Quebec poets, who developed a "writing in the feminine" through a synthesis of radical poetics and structuralist and poststructuralist literary theory.
• The rise of postcolonial theory and an awareness of oppression within a global context has been important for feminist writers from Margaret Laurence onwards; more recent work on ethnicity, race and gender continues to develop this key strand of feminist writing.
• While early feminist writing emerged from "small-town" Canada, more contemporary alternative writers imagine city spaces and urban Canada, for example, lesbian drama, and Black and Asian poetics. The malleability of city spaces functions at social and sexual levels.

7 Contemporary indigenous literatures
Narratives of autonomy and resistance

Overview

The oral narratives of Canada's First Peoples are a living legacy, one that has been transmitted through the generations to the present day. During colonial times, this oral culture came under attack, through a whole host of degrading measures, including the appropriation of aboriginal land, the loss of political autonomy, the criminalization of religious practices and rituals, and the taking control of Aboriginal education, mainly through the residential school system. The colonial narrative of the "vanishing Indian" has since been revealed to be false, and in fact First Peoples have regained a significant measure of cultural and political autonomy, leading to a renaissance in indigenous arts and belief systems. In the late twentieth century, an exciting new hybrid form of Aboriginal writing brought together the techniques of oral, performance based culture with innovative modes of indigenous literary expression. Going from strength to strength, Aboriginal literature is now one of the most vibrant and successful art forms in Canada.

New venues, new voices: indigenous publishing in the 1960s

Part of the highly successful "moving away" from colonial systems and values involved finding new political and aesthetic voices. The 1960s were crucial years in the establishment of alternative venues of publication, seeing the launch of many newspapers and periodicals, including *Indian Outlook* (est. 1960), *The Micmac News* (est. 1965), *Kainai News* (est. 1968), *Akwesasne News* (est. 1969), *The Indian Voice* (est. 1969), *The First Citizen* (est. 1969), *The Saskatchewan Indian* (est. 1970), *Tepatshimuwin* (est. 1976) and *The National Indian* (est. 1977). While some of these publications were relatively short lived, they represent the beginnings of a new wave of Canadian indigenous writing in English, one in which orature and written texts cross-over and intersect. Non-literary formats were very important in this period, including biographical, autobiographical and other modes of reflective writing, such as Wilfred Pelletier's (1927–2000) *Two Articles* (1969), an examination of the differences between White and indigenous education and organization, or the biographies of the Cree Chief Payepot, *Payepot and His People* (Abel Watetch, serial publication, 1957), and Kwakwaka'wakw Charles James Nowell (1870–?), *Smoke from Their Fires: The Life of a Kwakiutl Chief* (1941, with a popular reprint in 1968). Textualized orature includes Ojibwa Norval Morriseau's *Legends of My People, the Great Ojibway* (1965) and Nuuchah'nulth George Clutesi's *Son of Raven, Son of Deer* (1967).

Significantly, the first anthology of Aboriginal literature in English appeared in 1969, called *I Am An Indian* (edited by Kent Gooderham). The year 1969 is crucial in Aboriginal writing since this was also the date of the publication of *The statement of the Government of Canada on Indian Policy*, a government White Paper that advocated the end of special status for Canada's First Peoples: "This reflected Prime Minister Pierre Trudeau's belief that special status for a special group was fundamentally wrong in a democratic society. Aboriginal rights were not recognized, and the significance of treaties was challenged" (Dickason, 377). The White Paper had the effect of unifying indigenous oppositional movements and voices, and the subsequent attempt by the government to employ a Cree lawyer, William I.C. Wuttunee, to support the White Paper from an indigenous perspective completely backfired. Wuttunee's account of this situation was published in 1971 as *Ruffled Feathers: Indians in Canadian Society*, the same year in which the White Paper was formally retracted. Other more critical responses to the White Paper include the essays collected by the Anglican Church in *Bulletin 201* (1970) and Harold Cardinal's *The Unjust Society: The Tragedy of Canada's Indians* (1969). Powerfully anti-colonial texts published in this era include Willfred Pelletier's *No Foreign Land* (1973) and Howard Adam's *Prison of Grass* (1975).

Indigenous readers became a focus in the late 1960s and early 1970s as more and more First Peoples called for autonomy in education and the provision of reading materials on the reservations, in properly funded and stocked libraries. One of the earliest indigenous organized and maintained libraries was that of the Dene Nation Library in Yellowknife, set up by the Dene-Métis Negotiations Secretariat in conjunction with the Métis Nation in the mid 1970s (Edwards, B.F.R., 504). Other First Nations followed suit, but

Assembly of First Nations – while the Indian Act had been used to suppress the formation of indigenous political groups, regional and national movements did come into existence, including the short-lived League of Indians – organized in 1918 by Mohawk Frederick Ogilvie Loft (1861–1934) – and the North American Indian Brotherhood, which existed during the 1940s. The National Indian Council, formed in 1961, represented a significant number of First Peoples and Métis People, but not the Inuit. The group split in 1968, with Métis and Non-Status Peoples forming the Native Council of Canada, and Treaty and Status Peoples forming the National Indian Brotherhood, which in 1982 became the more representative Assembly of First Nations.

improvements to Aboriginal education depended upon the government shifting from a parochial system, whereby a narrow set of mainly white Canadian pedagogic materials were offered for use, turning instead to a needs-driven system, whereby indigenous peoples selected suitable educational tools that worked for their local communities. The National Indian Brotherhood policy paper called *Indian Control of Indian Education* (1972) argued that "radical changes were needed to render Indian education relevant to the philosophy and needs of First Peoples. Among the recommendations were calls to provide reading materials appropriate to the experiences of Native children, as well as to foster literacy in Aboriginal languages, encourage literary expression, and adapt traditional oral languages to written forms" (Edwards, B.F.R., 504). These recommendations were adopted, leading to a revolution in indigenous education, the establishment of indigenous friendship centres – which also became centres of literacy – and a remarkable increase in journalism, political writing, and literary production.

Anthologization: recollecting and innovating

The anthologization of Aboriginal literature reflects its explosive resurgence in the 1960s and early 1970s, and subsequent popularity up to the present day. *I Am An Indian* draws together earlier collected stories as well as illustrations, photographs and Native art. In some ways it would be more accurate to say that the book documents indigenous writing rather than literature, such as extracts from Loucheux Edith Josie's newspaper column in *The Whitehouse Star* called "News From Old Crow", describing day-to-day life in the Arctic Circle, or part of a speech at York University, Toronto, delivered by Ojibway Lloyd Caibaiosai, arguing against racial integration in Canada. A major anthology of Aboriginal poetry was published in 1977, called *Many Voices: Contemporary Indian Poetry*, edited by David Day and Marilyn Bowering; subsequent anthologies include *First People, First Voices* (1983), edited by Penny Petrone; *A Gathering of Spirit: A Collection by North American Indian Women* (1984), edited by Beth Brant; *Seventh Generation: Contemporary Native Writing* (1989), edited by Heather Hodgson; *Our Bit of Truth: An Anthology of Canadian Native Literature* (1990), edited by Agnes Grant; *Writing the Circle: Native Women of Western Canada* (1990), edited by Jeanne Perreault and Sylvia Vance; *All My Relations: An Anthology of Contemporary Canadian Native Writing* (1990), edited by Thomas King; *An Anthology of Canadian Native Literature in English* (1992), edited by Daniel David Moses and Terry Goldie; *Voices: Being Native in Canada* (1992), edited by Linda Jaine and Drew Hayden Taylor; and *Steal My Rage: New Native Voices* (1995), edited by Joel T. Maki. It is of note that the first editions of the *Canadian Anthology* (1955), edited by Carl F. Klinck and Reginald E. Watters, and *The Oxford Anthology of Canadian Literature* (1973), edited by Robert Weaver and William Toye, contain no Aboriginal literature whatsoever. It would now be inconceivable to have an anthology of

Canadian literature devoid of Aboriginal writing, and this in itself is a measure of the transformation of the Canadian literary scene from an indigenous perspective.

Contemporary Aboriginal writing/performance in English

One of the great successes of Aboriginal writing is the production of hybrid modes of discourse: prose, poetry and drama draw great vitality from orature, indigenous humour, narratives of historical struggles (defeats and successes), and perhaps most importantly of all, performative modes of action and representation drawn from indigenous ritual. Such a "translation" of orature into written forms has been regarded as a mode of decolonization, working at two levels: that of "the English language and its genres of literary expression" (Schorcht, 30). Internationally, Aboriginal drama first received the intense acclaim and recognition that has since been extended to other genres. While Aboriginal drama does not begin or end with the Cree playwright and novelist Tomson Highway, there is no doubt that his play *The Rez Sisters* (premiered 1986) has been enormously influential in spreading awareness of indigenous writing and performance.

The hybrid drama of Tomson Highway

The Rez Sisters builds upon another earlier famous play in the history of Canadian theatre: Michel Tremblay's (b. 1942, in Montreal) *Les Belles-Soeurs* (1968), which focuses on "the dislocation and placelessness experienced by … Quebecois women living in the east end of Montreal – dislocation in terms of their families, their futures, and their society within the larger realm of Canadian politics" (Gilbert and Tompkins, 47). The two plays share a relationship not only between their respective settings and analyses of social and ideological displacements, but also a story, based upon the desire to find a way out of bleak personal and societal situations through winning at bingo. Both plays are extremely funny, much of the humour coming from a sophisticated and witty use of the vernacular – or, everyday local dialect or language (the language of the streets and/or the reservation). Dickinson elaborates upon the shared contexts of the Highway/Tremblay plays:

> … Tremblay's "Belles-Soeurs cycle" of east-end Montreal plays (of which there are twelve in total) alternates between the "Main" tenderloin of drag queens and prostitutes and the kitchens and back-alley "balcons" of working-class families, using both "as sites for exploring the fears, insecurities, and damage wrought to the colonized psyche" of Quebec … Similarly, Highway's own cycle of plays (of which there are a projected seven in total) uses the mythical Wasy Hill Reservation to document Native Canadians' very different experiences of the legacy of imperialism. Moreover, as with Tremblay's use of *joual*, Highway frequently uses the

Cree and Ojibway languages in his plays to subvert the hegemony of English-Canadian literary discourse. Finally ... both playwrights "que(e)ry" representative norms of masculinity, linking "crises" in gender and sexuality to the process of decolonization.

(183)

Highway encounters *Les Belles-Soeurs* most obviously and markedly with the "Ode to Bingo" parallels. The "Ode to Bingo" is a powerful moment in *Les Belles-Soeurs*, where a blackout allows time for the women to line up at the edge of the stage: Rose, Germaine, Gabrielle, Therese and Marie-Ange all speak in an ensemble, while the others call out bingo numbers. The focus in *Les Belles-Soeurs* is on the excitement of the game itself. In *The Rez Sisters*, while the women love the bingo game, they are frustrated that the rewards are getting smaller and smaller, made especially clear with the comic observation that the dollar is getting weaker. The solution to community woes in *The Rez Sisters* is not ultimately the empty promise of gambling and game playing, but Nanabush, a mediating trickster figure who offers empathy and catharsis.

As Highway says in his "Note on Nanabush" in *The Rez Sisters*: "Some say that 'Nanabush' [Trickster] left this continent when the whiteman came. We believe he is still here among us – albeit a little the worse for wear and tear – having assumed other guises. Without him [her or it] – and without the spiritual health of this figure – the core of Indian culture would be gone forever" (xii). Nanabush mediates in a spatial and temporal sense: there is always the desire for a return to a more straightforward past, but Nanabush also firmly looks to the future hope of the community. Nanabush translates and transforms personal desire into something far more powerful and beneficial for the community as a whole.

Trickster is one of the key archetypal figures of Aboriginal orature, featuring in many stories across Canada, the USA and beyond. Native Canadian dramatist Tomson Highway argues that Trickster, who takes many names – such as Raven, Coyote, Nanabush, and Weesageechak – is "as pivotal and important a figure in our world as Christ is in the realm of Christian mythology" (xii). In "The Raven and The First Men", Haida artist Bill Reid and Canadian poet Robert Bringhurst tell the creation story of Trickster finding human beings in a giant clamshell: "So the Raven leaned his great head close to the shell, and with the smooth trickster's tongue that had got him into and out of so many misadventures during his troubled and troublesome existence, he coaxed and cajoled and coerced the little creatures to come out and play in his wonderful, shiny new world" (28). Highway calls Trickster a teacher and mediator, who connects the spiritual and earthly worlds; in a more theoretical account, Native American critic Gerald Vizenor calls Trickster "a liberator and healer" (187).

Les Belles-Soeurs, for all its bleak and dark humour, is a play without the hope that is found in *The Rez Sisters*; Highway's encounter with *Les Belles-Soeurs*, in other words, involves finding hope at the deepest and darkest moments, not in an idealistic and impractical sense, but through direct re-engagement with individuals who are also embedded in the community. Highway followed *The Rez Sisters* with *Dry Lips Oughta Move to Kapuskasing* (premiered 1989) which, while set on the same fictional Wasaychigan Hill Indian Reserve, shifts to a male perspective and the Canadian male obsession with Hockey; Nanabush gender crosses into the guise of the spirit of Gazelle Nataways, Patsy Pegahmagahbow and Black Lady Halked. Audiences were shocked by a controversial rape scene in the play, as well as finding the dream-like structure confusing, but Highway's exuberant synthesis of surreal fantasy with harsh descriptions of emotional and sexual brutality are part and parcel of his notion of the history of indigenous experience in Canada, especially as suffered in religious-based residential schools, which is one of the main topics of Highway's novel *The Kiss of the Fur Queen* (1998).

Highway's artistic achievements are considerable, both as an individual, and as a committed community member, which can be seen in his decision to drop his early career as a classically trained concert pianist in favour of working with Aboriginal community and arts groups. Highway worked with Aboriginal theatre company Northern Delights in Sioux Lookout, Ontario, before joining the De-Ba-Jeh-Mu-Jig Theatre Company on Manitoulin Island, Ontario, where he wrote/directed the satire *A Ridiculous Spectacle in One Act* (1985) and first workshopped *The Rez Sisters*. At Native Earth Performing Arts Company, where Highway was the Artistic Director between 1984 and 1992, he joined forces with his brother, who was a choreographer and dancer, for productions of *New Song ... New Dance* and *The Sage, the Dancer and the Fool*; he also wrote a play called *Aria* (1987) for the Inuit actress Maria Kleist. *The Rez Sisters* and *Dry Lips Oughta Move to Kapuskasing* are the first two plays in a projected seven-play Rez cycle, the third being *Rose*, which was workshopped by the combined forces of the National Arts Centre, the Manitoba Theatre Centre and the Canadian Stage Company in 1994, and given its premier at a student performance on 21 January 2000 at The University of Toronto. *Rose* is a commanding and sprawling play, which incorporates thirteen songs (drawing upon different musical genres from cabaret to opera), dance and abrupt theatrical contrasts, such as tragic violence juxtaposed with comic surrealism. The play explores financial greed, the role of indigenous treaties, and the ongoing battle between the men and women of Wasaychigan Hill Indian Reserve.

The Kiss of the Fur Queen is a semi-autobiographical novel that ponders deeply cultural, gender and sexual performance; the novel is on the same artistic continuum of Highway's other artistic productions, drawing upon fantastic dreamworlds, Aboriginal belief systems and oral stories, as well as the abuses of the Aboriginal community through the residential school experience. Highway's ongoing interest in exploring the ramifications of different conceptions of land title, treaties and colonial invasion and settlement continues with his play *Ernestine Shuswap Gets Her Trout* (2004), commissioned in 2000 by Western Canada Theatre and the Secwepemc Cultural Education Society. The play telescopes one hundred years of contact between Whites and the Shuswap, Okanagan, and Thompson First Nations in British Columbia. A fascinating document that Highway worked with is the Laurier Memorial, presented to Sir Wilfrid Laurier in 1910 on the occasion of his visit to Kamloops, BC; the Memorial is a transcript by James A. Teit which was dictated to him by Shuswap, Okanagan, and Thompson Chiefs, covering grievances against colonial settlers and the colonial legal system that favours Whites at the expense of indigenous rights. Also, the document notes that the expected treaty and reserve system as promised had not been negotiated. In the play, four women prepare for Sir Wilfrid Laurier's visit, only to have their resources and hospitable giving increasingly constrained and limited as they symbolically lose their rights under the impact of contact and the subsequent colonialism.

Aboriginal drama in the 1970s and 1980s

The excitement felt about Highway's plays – still some of the most widely performed Aboriginal productions throughout the world – is reflective of the enthusiastic response to the new wave of Aboriginal drama in English in Canada. Notable plays from the 1970s and 1980s include Nora Benedict's *The Dress* (1970), Duke Redbird's *Wasawkachak* (1974), George Kenny's *October Stranger* (1977), Minnie Aodla Freeman's *Survival in the South* (1980), Maria Campbell's *Jessica* (1981; rewritten 1986) and William S. Yellow Robe's *The Independence of Eddie Rose* (1986). Métis author Maria Campbell (b. 1940), famous for her moving autobiography about Métis life and culture, called *Halfbreed* (1973), had worked collaboratively with playwright and actress Linda Griffiths (b. 1956) on *Jessica*; the resulting tensions and issues that resulted were elaborated upon in *The Book of Jessica: A Theatrical Transformation* (1989).

Collaborations: Maria Campbell and Linda Griffiths negotiate *The Book of Jessica: A Theatrical Transformation* (1989)

The Book of Jessica is a doubled text, simultaneously playing or performing two overarching narratives: one narrative, is that of Griffiths's colonial appropriation of Campbell's identity and stories; the other narrative is Campbell and Griffiths's transformational journey, away from notions of appropriation and into a gift-based economy of knowledge, spiritual power and friendship (with all the colonial and personal tensions still in place, however). Because these two narratives are simultaneously overlaid, the text is extremely elusive and slippery: at any one point in the text, the signs of appropriation, for example, are also the signs of having learnt the lessons that Campbell is teaching Griffiths. For example, the "give-away" concept is a lesson that has been learnt – that is, that gifts have spiritual power.

Critics have argued extensively over the two apparently opposing readings (of appropriation and learning), but there is a sense in *The Book of Jessica* that both are available, the latter suggesting that Griffiths has entered, to whatever degree, the sacred space of Campbell's understanding and experience of authentic – hybrid, modern – Métis existence, and the former telling the reader that this is impossible, dangerous, and simply a repetition of the acts of colonialism. In this doubled performance, Griffiths's revealing of ceremonial secrets, for example, is thus both a violation of trust, and a cultural performance "directed to multi-ethnic audiences" to use Susan Roy's phrase (62). As Roy argues: "While much scholarship emphasizes how intercultural events serve the interests of dominant society, commentators should not lose sight of the fact that Aboriginal peoples autonomously 'confer meaning on the circumstances that confront them'" (62). In other words, Griffiths's mimetic re-enactment of her spiritual experience performs both an unauthorized colonialist revealing and a "framed", authorized encounter with indigenous spiritual forces.

The *staging* of *The Book of Jessica* is precisely a two-way conferring of meaning. But this is still to ignore the ways in which the coincidence of claims concerning native authenticity and modernity in the text leads to a reworking of form: Griffiths and Campbell do not just create a doubled text, they also *ritualize* the western genres of autobiography, meta-textual commentary or interpretation, and drama, in other words, they take linear, progressive time and the appropriative space of western master-narratives, and they transform them into symbolic time/space. "I thought it was over," says Griffiths (13), but of course it is never "over", since the symbolic charge of *The Book of Jessica* always overrides western conceptual attempts at closure and commodification.

The residential schools explored through theatre: Oskiniko Larry Loyie, Vera Manuel and Joseph A. Dandurand

One of the most powerful aspects of Aboriginal drama is the way in which historical events are reconceived and re-performed, sometimes as a way of re-living otherwise marginalized issues and events, and sometimes as a way of gaining deeper understanding or even community catharsis, to name just a few possibilities. The residential school experience is the subject of two plays published together in 1998: *Ora Pro Nobis (Pray for Us)* by Oskiniko Larry Loyie (b. 1933) and *Strength of Indian Women* by Vera Manuel (b. 1948). Loyie, a Cree writer from northern Alberta, structures his play via two frames: the narrative present and past, with the latter being composed of shared stories about the residential school, from the perspective of the children. The children initially survive the emotional and physical abuse meted out by the priests and religious "sisters" in charge of them through humour and a parodic undercutting of the religious code that they are supposed to live by, such as the time a boy is knocked out by a "sister" hitting him for causing trouble: the following line is spoken by another child in the school: "Ola, just like Joe Lewis, the Brown Bomber, the heavyweight champion of the world" (57). Loyie relates much of the anger and violence to a revenge motive: for the torture and murder of the Jesuits when they were first trying to convert indigenous peoples; however, in the play's narrative present George, a guest speaker at a Native meeting, argues that "the sins you see on the streets are directly the fault of the churches and the government residential school" (68). George concludes his talk, which concerns empathy and healing, with the statement "we are a fighting people and we can and must defeat our problems" (69). Manuel, a Secwepemc and Ktunaxa author, opens her play with Sousette and her granddaughter Suzie examining a photo of a residential school, pondering the irony of the fact that it is the only building in their community that was built to last; the female characters take a circular route to the traumatic memories of sexual and physical abuse. Manuel also braids the gradual recollection of traumatic events with stories of survival and achievement, as the older women pass on this knowledge to the young woman in the play, called Suzie. As Manuel writes: "The responsibility we hold in passing on these stories is to role model a healthy lifestyle for our children, who are always watching us for direction" (76).

Kwantlen poet and dramatist Joseph A. Dandurand (b. 1964), in *Please Do Not Touch The Indians* (2004), also examines sexual abuse at the hands of religious authorities, alongside a self-reflexive addressing of the question of the aestheticizing of Aboriginal identity and history; the play shockingly leads up to the death of the indigenous characters, exploring the trauma and abuse that leads each one of them to choose such an extreme escape route from the world. As Sister Coyote puts it: "They kept me in that school, they kept me until I decided that I had had enough. I had had enough of being beaten and kicked around. I am a Coyote, I would scream at them but they would laugh and kick me some more" (49).

Monique Mojica's *Princess Pocahontas and the Blue Spots* (1991)

An enduring play from the early 1990s is Monique Mojica's (b. 1954 in New York) *Princess Pocahontas and the Blue Spots* (1991), published along with Mojica's radio play, *Birdwoman and the Suffragettes* (1991). *Princess Pocahontas* aligns personal and cultural transformation as key images and stereotypes of indigenous women are explored, satirized and deconstructed. Ric Knowles argues, "What is at issue for Mojica in these plays, among other things[,] is a contestation of ownership over the representation of Native women by those who have exploited those representations for political purposes ranging from the colonialist and nationalist through to the feminist and the academic" (248).

The satirical humour of Drew Haydon Taylor and Daniel David Moses

Powerful satirical humour is also found in Ojibwa Drew Haydon Taylor's (b. 1962) plays, such as *Toronto at Dreamer's Rock* (1990), *Education is Our*

Right (1990), *Someday* (1993), *Only Drunks and Children Tell the Truth* (1998), *alternatives* (2000), *Girl Who Loved Her Horses/The Boy in the Treehouse* (2000), *400 Kilometres* (2005) and *In A World Created By A Drunken God* (2006). Taylor's blues quartet is a farcical, fast-paced exploration of racial stereotypes; the plays are: *Bootlegger Blues* (1991), *Baby Blues* (1997), *The Buz'Gem Blues* (2002) and *The Berlin Blues* (2007). Native humour is central for the dramatic vision of Delaware dramatist and poet Daniel David Moses (b. 1952), in *Almighty Voice and His Wife* (1992), *The Indian Medicine Shows* (1995 – comprising two plays parodying the western genre), *Coyote City* (1990), *Big Buck City* (1991), *Kyotopolis* (1992), *City of Shadows* (1995) and *A Song of the Tall Grass* (2007). Moses subtly interweaves indigenous knowledge with the contemporary human condition.

In *Coyote City*, the entire dramatic action is punctuated by the telling of one story: how Coyote attempts to get his wife from the land of the dead. The story makes sense of the current situation in which the protagonist Lena, whose boyfriend Johnny has called her on the telephone six months *after* he died in a bar, is convinced that he is still somehow alive. Coyote finds that people in the land of the dead are "made out of darkness, out of different bits of shadow" (43), just as Lena and Boo, her sister (as well as their mother Martha), are having to deal with the "bits" of darkness that still pervade their lives. Coyote mimetically reproduces the actions of a spirit in the land of the dead, appearing to temporarily bring into reality this other world through his performance: "Coyote watched the spirit and imitated it, you know, putting his hand to his mouth as if he was eating berries, smacking his lips as if he had a mouth full of sweet juice, as if he was being fed" (954).

The story divides into two: first, Coyote regains his wife, but only if he never touches her again. He eventually kisses her, and she "turned into smoke, turned back to the land of the dead" (95). Boo's second version of the story is that Coyote can't see the spirit world which is all around, and instead he ends up "pretending under the hot sun to be eating berries and watching horses" never to see his wife again (103). The real crux of the story may be found in the phrase that Johnny utters: "My granddad, he'd stop here, you know, all the time, letting us get the picture, shadow man and Coyote there at the door to the lodge of the dead" (74). In other words, the story is handed on and halted at the same time, for the listener to make sense of it in his or her life situation.

The lack of communication between all of the characters in the play can only be healed once they start listening to the old stories and making sense of them through their own acts of re-telling. Symbolically, Boo calls the modern world of telecommunications "disembodied" (23) and a bit later she argues with Lena that the real side of Johnny was not his sexuality but his sharing of the "old stories" (29). The best compliment in the play is "You tell it almost like my Grandad" (93). Juxtaposed with the old indigenous Coyote story is a parodic re-telling of the Christian narrative of redemption; the minister in the play soon turns out to be a hypocrite: an alcoholic who quickly falls back into his old ways of sinful behaviour. The re-telling of Coyote's story is the main act of authenticity within the play, but its healing powers are only available to those who let the story speak to and make sense of their own lives.

Interrogating colonial history and its societal impact: the rise of the Aboriginal novel

Aboriginal prose in English underwent similarly explosive growth to that of drama. Again, Native humour is one of the central elements of this writing, along with the re-telling of historical events from alternative perspectives. Beginning with Métis writer Beatrice Culleton's/Mosioner's (b. 1949) story of reclaiming Métis women's history *In Search of April Raintree* (1983), the novel has become a powerful force questioning, among other things, non-Native notions of history and society; Okanagan poet and novelist Jeannette Armstrong's (b. 1948) *Slash* (1985) is another early, groundbreaking fictional account of indigenous political and spiritual awakening. Thomas King (b. 1943), who has identified his nationality as the threefold Cheroke, Greek and German, was born in America, but moved to Canada, where he has become a highly successful novelist, radio dramatist, and critic; his novels are widely read and studied, including *Medicine River* (1989), *Green Grass, Running Water* (1993) and *Truth and Bright Water* (1998). King uses a postmodern flat narrative prose style in which much of the humour and irony depends upon allusions and subtle jokes, puns and cross-cultural references.

Thomas King's *Green Grass, Running Water* (1993)

Green Grass, Running Water appears on the surface to have a relatively straightforward plot interspersed with playful, deconstructive accounts of Christian and Native creation stories and historical intervention on the part of four elders who constantly escape their institutional home. At the level of allusion, however, the novel is labyrinthine and complex. Its main Native characters are embedded in non-Native discursive representations of stereotypical "Indians": Lionel works at Buffalo Bill Bursum's appliance store where "cowboy and western" movies play on a screen in the background, Charlie works in a law company, and Alberta at a university teaching Native Studies. Only Latisha seems to have initially subverted such stereotyping through acts of self-parody and humour at the Dead Dog Café. The *form* of King's writing is key in understanding his work:

> Much of King's work relies on the comic premise of inversion and incorporates elements of paradox, irony, and parody to undermine some of the standard clichés about Native peoples. As the creator of his own "trickster discourse," King invokes and alters Eurocentric narrative conventions in a deliberately provocative manner, which moves to dismantle

the hierarchical relationship between Natives and non-Natives living in Canada and the United States, and to displace perceptions of "difference" onto the dominant population. He also demonstrates how powerful certain negative images of Indians have become, even within Native communities.

King's comic inversions do not merely involve replacing Eurocentric perspectives with Native alternatives (e.g., God with a Native female goddess, citizenship with tribal identity). Instead, King's texts cultivate a sustained interaction between these conflicting perspectives, a strategy that conveys the complexities of being located "in-between" non-Native and Native worlds. [...] The act of combining and making connections, as well as recognizing differences between diverse points of view, allows writers like King to challenge the supremacy of Western paradigms in an overtly comic manner.

(Davidson, Walton and Andrews, 35–36)

Green Grass, Running Water is thus subversive at the level of language (the Biblical Adam is renamed "Ahdamn") and at the level of narrative, for example, the Aboriginal Elders "attempt to tell counter-na(rra)tive versions of the [Biblical] creation story" (Davidson, Walton and Andrews, 53). As with many North American Native novels, the event of colonial-indigenous "contact" is also re-imagined.

Aboriginal fiction surveyed: the 1980s and 1990s

Other key novels in the 1980s and 1990s are Ruby Farrell Slipperjack's *Honour the Sun* (1987), *Silent Words* (1992) and *Weesquachak and the Lost Ones* (2000), Jordan Wheeler's *Brothers in Arms* (1989), Joan Crate's *Breathing Water* (1990), Richard Wagamese's *Keeper 'n Me* (1994), Richard van Camp's *The Lesser Blood* (1996), Eden Robinson's *Monkey Beach* (2000) and Jeannette Armstrong's *Whispering in Shadows* (2000). Short fiction also emerged as an important interrelated genre, such as Beth Brant's *Mohawk Trail* (1985) and *Food and Spirits* (1991), Thomas King's *One Good Story, That One* (1993), Richard G. Green's *The Last Raven and Other Stories* (1994), Eden Robinson's *Traplines* (1996) and Lee Maracle's *Sojourner's Truth and Other Stories* (2000).

Intertextuality and the native gothic in Eden Robinson's *Traplines* (1996) and *Monkey Beach* (2000)

Intertextual connections between the Canadian Aboriginal short story and novel genres can be illuminated by examining Haisla author Eden Robinson's (b. 1968) *Traplines* and *Monkey Beach*, where the latter novel develops the short story "Queen of the North". In *Monkey Beach* much of this short story is integrated within the larger narrative present in which the Haisla protagonist Lisamarie is searching for her missing brother Jimmy. The entire structure of the novel has a progression forwards from this narrative present, as Lisamarie decides to take a boat down to the fishing grounds where Jimmy disappeared. But interspersed with this progressive movement, there are a large number of flashbacks, which take us back to Lisamarie's early childhood and key events and emotions that she experienced as she grew up. These events and emotions include experiences with her immediate family, the trials and tribulations of early puberty, connecting with her grandmother Ma-ma-oo and her activist uncle Mick, and her attempts to understand her powers of connecting with the spirit world, especially her ability to predict hardship or death. Lisamarie also describes the geographical and historical context of her Haisla community, and how things have changed during colonialism.

However, this is not a narrative of total despair, because part of Lisamarie's growing-up involves learning the indigenous old ways from Ma-ma-oo, and becoming a "warrior" in attitude and toughness through her relationship with Mick and through life experiences. Does the novel, then, simply conform to a standard *Bildungsroman* (a novel of personal education and development)? While Robinson is writing in Canadian English, and adopting the genre of the *Bildungsroman*, she also suggests that many of the experiences that her protagonist goes through are anchored in Native identity, and the reader therefore needs to learn about the Haisla way of living to relate to Lisamarie's development. The form of the novel – Native Canadian Gothic – is also deeply uncanny.

Freud argued that what was so profoundly unsettling about the uncanny was the fact that ultimately it is a slippage from the *heimlich* to the

Native Canadian Gothic – in the Canadian Gothic, Nature (and its associated uncanny monstrous forms) is a sublime threat to human rationality and order; the Canadian Gothic, in other words, is a "haunted wilderness" to use Margot Northey's phrase (1976). If in Europe, the Gothic had been located in uncanny castles, dungeons, and haunted houses, with a frightening, sexually predatory male threatening to seduce the young, female heroine, in Canadian Gothic, it is the Other which is threatening: Native peoples, dangerous animals, and the harsh deadly weather. The female protagonist, in the Canadian Gothic, is usually roughing it in the bush, to steal the title of Susanna Moodie's "gothic autobiography" (Edwards, J.D., xxviii). The **Native Canadian Gothic** reverses this mode of Canadian writing, so that instead of Nature, it is the colonial urban landscape that has become the site of danger, and instead of wild beasts and ghosts, predatory White teachers and priests in Aboriginal residential schools are a threat to emotional and sexual order. Native Canadian Gothic can be used as a way of reclaiming cultural autonomy, refusing to portray indigenous culture in European terms, yet also writing-back to the European Gothic, drawing upon its energies and its vitality for indigenous purposes.

unheimlich; in other words, from the homely to the unhomely. Put another way: what is so frightening about the uncanny is not some outside Other, but what is inside the home, the community, the subject. Critics argue that the European settler/invaders misidentified the Gothic uncanny with the outside, with the wilderness, including Native peoples, myths and monsters. Robinson reverses this to reveal that what was uncanny all along, was within the White Canadian community, and was also an effect of the clash of two cultures: the indigenous and the White European settler/invaders.

Robinson takes the uncanny even further: she realizes that Freud's slippage from the homely to the unhomely, from the familiar to the strange, reveals that there also needs to be self-analysis of the indigenous community. As Jennifer Andrews puts it: "*Monkey Beach*, like many Gothic novels ... can be read as a response to 'cultural disorder' ... But Robinson rewrites this disorder ... [in the novel] Haisla viewpoints dominate, and Robinson's narrative conveys the sense that whatever disorder or confusion the characters experience is a result of their negotiating the often jarring juxtapositions of Native and non-Native viewpoints. The characters are preoccupied with evil because many of them have had to face the impacts of Eurocentrism on their communities and identities. The novel pays special attention to the role of the residential school system, the transition from matriarchal to patriarchal socio-political structure, and the long-standing history of government attempts to wipe out Native populations in Canada and the United States through relocation and legal regulation" (10).

Robinson uses Lisamarie as a point-of-contact between the spirit world and the world of western popular culture; she is visited by premonitions and spirits prior to people's deaths, but she cannot control the process of contact with the spirit world. Lisamarie makes connections, also, for the reader, for example, between the characters Jimmy and Karaoke, and Karaoke and Uncle Josh. What is uncovered in the process is the widespread network of sexual abuse from the residential school days, a network that becomes replicated within the community, as the effects linger and are reproduced. Andrews thus suggests that "By making Lisamarie the centre of the novel, Robinson complicates the usual Gothic pairing of dark villain and perfect heroine. She creates a protagonist who reflects on the nature and origin of evil through her relationship to the spirit world and whose subconscious continually haunts her, forcing her to negotiate her supernatural connections and desire to be ordinary. But the return of the repressed – a crucial aspect of Gothic texts – takes on a larger political significance in Robinson's novel, in which evil is primarily associated with Eurocentric interventions in the Haisla community rather than individual Native characters, a strategy that creates a more ambiguous and complicated vision of evil than those in many Gothic novels" (12).

Power relations in Eden Robinson's *Blood Sports* (2006)

Robinson utilizes the strategy of developing another one of her short stories – "Contact Sports" – into a novel called *Blood Sports* (2006), which explores the uneven and abusive power relations between two young men, Tom and Jeremy Bauer. Robinson's work here addresses two main audiences: those who recognize the events of the novel which are set in Vancouver's drug scene as being representative of what can happen to young Aboriginal men and women who are surviving in the downtown Vancouver Eastside (as well as the novel being an allegorical tale representative of the unequal power relations between Whites and Natives) and those who read the novel as a postmodern account of the North American street scene. What is clever about this approach is that it is often the reader-response that generates the Native stereotyping, and this can lead to a self-reflexive analysis of how indigenous peoples are portrayed in Canadian literary and non-literary texts.

Globalized Aboriginal literature

Critic Penny van Toorn suggests that "Today, Indigenous publishing is beginning to go global" (43). Indigenous novels and short-story collections continue to grow in popularity and strength, with new works including Lee Maracle's *Daughters are Forever* (2002) and *Will's Garden* (2002), Richard van Camp's *Angel Wing Splash Pattern* (2002), Robert Alexie's *Porcupines and China Dolls* (2002) and *Pale Indian* (2005), and Richard Wagamese's *A Quality of Light* (2002), *Dream Wheels* (2006) and *Ragged Company* (2008). Indigenous authors have always drawn deeply upon multiple genres, especially via oral modes of cultural story-telling, and such multimedia intertextuality and versioning of aboriginal literature continues to be a noticeable feature of contemporary texts. For example, Thomas King's popular CBC radio series "The Dead Dog Café Comedy Hour" (1995–2000 and 2006), in which he stars, is first mentioned in his novel *Green Grass, Running Water* (it is the name of Latisha Morningstar's restaurant); similarly, Richard van Camp's short story "Mermaids" was turned into a CBC radio play which aired on 23 May 1998.

"Words are memory": contemporary Aboriginal poetry – new beginnings

The editors of *Many Voices: An Anthology of Contemporary Canadian Poetry* (1977), David Day and Marilyn Bowering, write in their short introduction that "We believe there is a cultural revival occurring among Canadian Indians and have gathered here a representation of their many voices" (np). Native poetry of the 1970s often describes engagement in political and cultural projects to regain an indigenous identity; known more generally as "protest poetry" this counter-cultural aesthetic was made famous by Chief Dan George (1889–1981), of the Sleil Waututh First Nation, who read his *A Lament for Confederation* at the Vancouver City centennial celebrations in 1967, stating that "in the long hundred years since the white man came, I have seen my freedom disappear like the salmon going mysteriously out to sea". Key foundational texts of the new indigenous poetry of the 1970s include the poetry and drawings by Sarain Stump, *There is My People Sleeping* (1970), Ben Abel's *Wisdom of Indian Poetry* (1972), Chief Dan George's *My Heart Soars* (1974), and *My Spirit Soars* (1982; published posthumously), George Kenny's *Indians Don't Cry* (1977) describing life on Lac Seul Reserve, Daniel David Moses's *Delicate Bodies* (1978), Rita Joe's deeply moving *Poems of Rita Joe* (1978) and Peter Blue Cloud's *White Corn Sister* (1979). During the late 1960s and 1970s, indigenous poets also published individual poems in alternative presses and publications such as "*The National Indian* (Ottawa, National Indian Brotherhood), *Indian Record* (Winnipeg, Indian and Métis) and *Nesika* (Vancouver, Union of BC Chiefs)" (Armstrong 2001, xvii). Jeannette Armstrong narrates how she used to find poems in flyers and handouts at indigenous political gatherings during this period: "I recall reading a very small poem by Skyros Bruce in one such flyer and being so utterly thrilled with the beauty of her poem that I searched for flyers from everywhere to read her work" (Ibid., xviii).

Painter and poet Sarain Stump (1945–74), of Cree, Shoshone and Salish backgrounds, directed the Indian Art Program at Saskatchewan Indian Cultural College (now the Saskatchewan Indian Cultural Centre) between 1972 and 1974; he writes of his people "SLEEPING / SINCE A LONG TIME" in his poem *For the Death of the Araucans*, writing that dreams are "THE OLD CARS WITHOUT ENGINE / PARKING IN FRONT OF THE HOUSE" (in Day and Bowering, 53). Stump's texts juxtapose poetry with images: drawings, symbols that create a rich graphical surface. Skyros Bruce/Maharra Allbrett (b. 1950), of the Sleil Waututh Nation, replies to Stump in her poem *Marriane Marianne*:

in
dian

we are north americans
he said
and made me feel
ashamed   that i was not wearing
beads at my throat

(in Day and Bowering, 77)

In her first poetry collection published in 1978, Rita Joe (b. 1932) juxtaposes Mi'kmaq and English language as part of a cultural reclaiming process that she describes as "comment, protestation or even a correction aimed at history" (quoted in Armstrong and Grauer, 13). In *Your buildings*, Joe argues that cultural relearning "is not difficult, / Because those trails I remember / And their meaning I understand." At the age of nine years old, Lee Maracle (b. 1950) began her own "relearning" project by describing her struggles with the English alphabet, those symbols of a written culture that make demands upon a people from an oral society, in Maracle's case that of Métis and Salish stories; writing of the English letters Maracle says: "They hated me. They said it was because / I didn't understand them." Maracle would later recover this poem which was saved by her mother, and annotate it (and/or supplement it) with her description of befriending and cajoling the English alphabet whereby she "persuaded them for years / to make them behave" (*Bent Box*).

Daniel David Moses (b. 1952) emerged as one of the key Aboriginal poets and dramatists of the eighties with his collection *Delicate Bodies* (1980), which can be seen with his early, intensely evocative poem *Near Chiefswood* that draws intertextual resonances from Bliss Carmen's *Low Tide on Grand Pré* (1886), while claiming these allusions for his own vision: "the stir of our paddles. So / deftly do they dip, they make / no more wake than do the fins / that occasionally break / the calm, slick surface" (29). Moses interfuses lyricism with surrealist indigenous dreamworlds, perhaps most profoundly found in his poem *The Persistence of Songs* (1986, revised 1990), where "The people feed from the river and conceive songs." Two significant collections in the 1980s blend poetry and prose: Mohawk critic and author Beth Brant's (b. 1941) *Mohawk Trail* (1985) and Lee Maracle's *I Am Woman* (1988). Exploring indigenous lesbian identity, Brant writes from a third space, one that continually crosses sexual and racial boundaries. Maracle's poetry also explores personal and political identity, such as the empathic image of Nelson Mandela in prison, triggering thoughts of indigenous identity, imprisonment and freedom.

Innovative and powerful poetry collections in the 1980s include Peter Blue Cloud's *Sketches in Winter, with Crows* (1981), Duke Redbird's *Loveshine and Red Wine* (1981), Beth Cuthland's *Horse Dance to Emerald Island* (1987), *Voices in the Waterfall* (1989), Rita Joe's *Song of Eskasoni: More Poems by Rita Joe* (1988) and Joan Crate's *Pale as Real Ladies: Poems for Pauline Johnson* (1989). Heather Hodgson edited *Seventh Generation: Contemporary Native Writing* (1989), giving readers an exciting resource for the study and enjoyment of Aboriginal poetry.

Personal and public history becomes an intense preoccupation in this decade, such as Greg Young-Ing's *Vancouver (a history lesson)*, Jeannette C. Armstrong's *History Lesson*, and Lenore Keeshig-Tobias's *I Grew Up*. Young-Ing (b. 1961) writes from a Cree perspective, of the first European settlers of Vancouver being a people themselves "rejected, dispossessed / arriving with nothing / but hope" (in Hodgson, 50). These settlers, however, soon take over Native land that is already in use: "Vancouver: / encroached upon / Salish, Squamish and Musqueam land" and the city buildings "implant themselves / on ancient fishing grounds" (50–51). Armstrong re-imagines contact at the time of Christopher Columbus, out of whose ship "a mob bursts / Running in all directions / Pulling furs off animals / Shooting buffalo" (in Hodgson, 54). Again, the natural land is destroyed by the machine and urban culture that the settlers build: "The colossi / in which they trust / while burying / breathing forests and fields / beneath concrete and steel" (55).

Anishnaabe author Keeshig-Tobias (b. 1950) articulates the reserve not as a place of cramped despair, but from a child's perspective as "the most / beautiful place in the world" (in Hodgson, 68). What is important about this shift in point-of-view is that it enables a close-up of a beauty that might otherwise be missed – or simply not articulated by an adult – such as the child "watching the wind's rhythms / sway leafy boughs / back and forth // and rocking me as / i snuggled in the grass" (68). In *I Grew Up* the children "laugh at teachers / and tourists who referred to / our bush as 'forests' or 'woods'" (69), suggesting instead that the reserve is a reality not just for these childhood games, but for development and maturity in making judgements.

Aesthetic/poetic growth in the 1990s and twenty-first century

As with drama and prose, Aboriginal poetry underwent explosive growth, lagging slightly behind the other genres perhaps, but with substantial achievements in the 1990s and into the twenty-first century. Key texts are Marie Annharte Baker's *Being on the Moon* (1990) and *Coyote Columbus Café* (1994), Daniel David Moses's, *The White Line* (1990) and S*ixteen Jesuses* (2000), Jeannette Armstrong's *Breath Tracks* (1991), Connie Fife's *Beneath the Naked Sun* (1992) and *Speaking through Jagged Rock* (1999), Garnette Ruffo's *Opening in the Sky* (1994) and *At Geronimo's Grave* (2001), Louise Bernice Halfe's *Bear Bones and Feathers* (1994) and *Blue Marrow* (1998), Joseph A. Dandurand's *burning for the dead and scratching for the poor* (1995), *Looking into the Eyes of My Forgotten Dreams* (1998) and *Shake* (2003), Rita Joe's *We Are the Dreamers: Recent and Early Poetry* (1999), Lee Maracle's *Bent Box* (2000), Joan Crate's *Foreign Homes* (2002) and Jeannette Armstrong's and Lally Grauer's edited collection *Native Poetry in Canada: A Contemporary Anthology* (2001). A key digital resource is Heather Pyrcz, ed., *Native Poetry (1960–2000), A Digital History of Canadian Poetry* (1999–2008) (<http://www.youngpoets.ca/native_poetry_1960_2000>, <http://www.youngpoets.ca/?q=digital_history_of_canadian_poetry_0>).

There is often a playful disruption of western forms of poetic writing, and looser more readerly interpretive effects in Aboriginal poetry, making for a democratic openness. Jeannette Armstrong's *Breath Tracks* is one of the pre-eminent examples of this dynamic approach, alongside her self-reflexive pondering of the English language used in a Native context: "Words are memory / a window in the present / a coming to terms with meaning" (*Words*, 17). In Armstrong's poems, the singular voice is always part of a wider community, thus words are "a piece in the collective experience of time / a sleep in which I try to awaken / the whispered echoes of voices" (17). The act of awakening communal voices and memories cannot always be controlled, as Armstrong suggests in *Threads of Old Memory*, to speak in the colonial language of settler-invaders "is dangerous" and when she does speak "history is a dreamer / empowering thought / from which I awaken the imaginings of the past" (58). Armstrong is acutely aware how the English language was "meant to overpower / to overtake" the old ways of speaking and expressing songs which are now "hidden / cherished / protected" (58). The poet, then, both creates or engenders and facilitates the old stories, voices and peoples. It is no coincidence then that metaphors of life and creation are foregrounded in Armstrong's feminist writing, since the female poet rejects the racist notions of the "Indian Woman" and instead carries "seeds / carefully through dangerous / wastelands" to "give them life / scattered / among cold and towering / concrete" (*Indian Woman*, 107).

A key event that received considerable artistic attention at the beginning of the 1990s was the stand-off between Mohawks and the Canadian government at Oka in Quebec, following indigenous resistance to appropriation of their land for a golf-course expansion. Ojibway comic, critic and media writer Drew Haydon Taylor (b. 1962) calls Oka the event "Where past treatment meets current reality" (137). In Kwakwaka'wakw artist David Neel's (b. 1960) photomontage "Life on the 18th Hole" (1991) the artwork privileges the indigenous, not the colonial or postcolonial centres of power; it is an art-work that doesn't hide the raw wielding of power and its effects upon the lives of thousands of people. Neel has commented upon his work:

> The Mohawk warrior symbolizes an individual pushed to his limit and having the will to stand his ground ... The struggle of the Mohawk people is symbolic of the struggle of all First Nations people. The "10 little policemen" [around the edges of the photomontage] is a play on the nursery rhyme "1 little, 2 little, 3 little Indians," allowing the viewer to see the ethnocentric and racist roots of this ... [rhyme and symbolizing] the Canadian government's inaction in dealing with the issues leading up to the Oka crisis and the following militarization. The Circle is the circle of life, the arrows the four directions, four being the number of balance and completeness. The red dots represent the blood of man, one for each race: the red, the yellow, the black, and the white man. Jointly these remind us of the common bond of all men. The barriers between men and between races are erected, not inherent. Clearly, it is up to individuals, not governments, to dismantle these barricades and work together to the benefit of all.
>
> (Neel, 131)

Armstrong argues that Oka led to a desire to protect "what is sacred" and that this triggered "an era of literary proliferation reinforcing an appreciation of Native cultural diversity" (xx). Cree author and poet Beth Cuthand (b. 1949) writes of a "Post-Oka Kinda Woman" who " ... don't take no shit. / She's done with victimization, reparation, / degradation, assimilation" (132, in Armstrong and Grauer). Dynamic and on the move, this is an indigenous subjectivity that has lost patience with systems of oppression, and with living a life that does not allow for personal, syncretist expression: "She drives a Toyota, reads bestsellers / sweats on weekends, colors her hair, / sings old songs, gathers herbs" (132). Such a mobile indigenous subjectivity is aggressive and ready for a fight: " ... she'd rather leave / her kids with a struggle than a bad settlement" (133). Armstrong argues that Lee Maracle, in her book of poems *Bent Box* (2000), sums up the decade's indigenous struggles and modes of representation. Language is a powerful tool to escape the enslavement "to white / parasite / culture" or " ... the agony / of colonial / paralysis" (*Paralysis*); in *Streets*, Maracle re-imagines city spaces, since "Buried beneath them are old pathways, / safe trails which brought my grandmothers from birth to elderhood." In the same poem, she apologizes for "not coming sooner, to free your eyes, / to re-craft the images below, / to raise my voice in resistance." *Bent Box* is a poetry of lament for oppressed peoples the world over, yet it is also an uncovering: of the indigenous stories, pathways, and peoples, that offer a different kind of power in resistance and cultural continuation.

Conclusion

- A new wave of Aboriginal literature building upon nineteenth-century precursors, as well as the new indigenous politics of autonomy in the 1960s and 1970s, has led to exciting new novels, short stories, poems and plays from a wide range of indigenous authors such as Eden Robinson, Tomson Highway and Thomas King.
- Early political writing in the 1960s and 1970s based on journalistic discourses has developed in highly performative ways, revealing how indigenous writing draws strength from its hybridity and integral relationships with (and expressions of) oral culture.
- Shifts in educational practices, and a move towards cultural autonomy, have contributed to the explosive growth of Aboriginal literature in the late twentieth and early twenty-first centuries; the Indian Act is still a barrier to self-governance and cultural recovery.

8   Canadian postmodernism
Genre trouble and new media in contemporary Canadian writing

Overview

In *The Postmodern Condition*, a book which originates from a request by the Conseil des Universités of the Government of Quebec to produce a report on knowledge, Jean-François Lyotard (1924–98) famously argues that postmodernism can be defined as an "incredulity towards metanarratives" – that is to say, the grand narratives of truth and reason are no longer believed in, or regarded, as universals, and are replaced by local expressions, little stories or narratives (*les petit recits*), that do not attempt to totalize or oppress others. Canadian media guru and critic Marshall McLuhan recognized in *The Medium is the Massage* that the shift from metanarratives to *les petit recits* was in part technological, generated by the move from a print culture to one of "electric circuitry" (63). The anti-hierarchical screen or televisual world of postmodernism – surface rather than depth, democratic horizontality rather than vertical hierarchy – is also one which critiques what theorists call "phallogocentrism": a worldview dominated by the law of the father, the symbolic phallus, and the Christian "logos" or Word. In Canadian postmodernism, Nietzsche's death of God is translated into the death of the father, whereby deconstructive father quests, from Margaret Atwood's *Surfacing* (1972), Robert Kroetsch's *Badlands* (1975) to William Gibson's *Pattern Recognition* (2003), probe deeply into myth and traditional narrative structures, revealing new non-patriarchal modes of being. The idioms of popular culture now replace or interweave with the centuries-old canonical strata of "great works" and Biblical intertexts, with the additional sense (or sensation) that the new media will be forever generating more information, based upon the infinite code of fashion changes, sampling, cutting and pasting, permutational logic, and randomly generated narrative units, to name just a few informational processes. As McLuhan says, "Information pours upon us, instantaneously, and continuously. As soon as information is acquired, it is very rapidly replaced by still newer information. Our electrically-configured world has forced us to move from the habit of data classification to the mode of pattern recognition" (63).

Beginnings, or, deconstructive voices: Margaret Atwood

At a narratological level, it is Margaret Atwood's "unreliable narrator" in *Surfacing* who is one of the earliest representatives of the new world of post-modernism (see Lane 2006c), her multiple versions or stories concerning her own identity undermining any one stable narrational point of view. This unnamed protagonist-narrator constantly looks for patterns, as she searches for her missing father in Quebec; her friends who have come on this journey with her are producing a movie, called "Random Samples", applying a new visual logic to the landscape, one which derives from film, television and the discourses of tourism (the documentary-style film of Canada's National Film Board gives way in the novel to a more popular and media-savvy approach, just as Canada created the Canadian Film Development Corporation in 1967 to subsidize and promote new feature films). Yet Atwood remains ambivalent about this new visual logic, since the filmic gaze in *Surfacing* is portrayed as being patriarchal, with the character Anna forced to strip for the camera, and the unnamed female protagonist-narrator eventually destroying the film stock. The (dead) father is eventually found, in the process the protagonist-narrator dissolves her old multiple selves to begin the work of forging a new feminist mode of being. The environment speaks as loudly in *Surfacing* as the characters, its destruction and pollution presenting issues concerning Canadian and American identity: while the "two solitudes" of Quebec and English-speaking Canada remain, in many respects, the blurring between English-speaking Canada and American culture appears in the novel as a highly problematic self-reflexive critique of the "invasion" of a potentially pristine space.

Linda Hutcheon has noted how this "feminist and anti-consumerist" (140) vision is found from Atwood's first novel, *The Edible Woman* (1969), where even the notion of being in love is problematized through "the possession motifs of the novel" (Hutcheon, 142). In *The Edible Woman*, patriarchal binaries are deconstructed, especially those of the romance: "Marriage is presented as owning, as entrapment, even as consuming: Marian [the prota-gonist] walks 'slowly down the aisle, keeping pace with the gentle music' ... but the aisle is not the expected one of church, but rather that of the super-market" (Hutcheon, 142). Atwood develops a postmodern self-reflexivity: that is to say, her novels are written using the discourses of popular culture – such as science fiction, for example her dystopian novels *The Handmaid's Tale* (1985), *Oryx and Crake* (2003) and *The Year of the Flood* (2009) – and they foreground commentary that reflects upon the artifice of the aesthetic object *as it is being produced*. In other words, Atwood, like popular culture theorist Jean Baudrillard, is deeply sceptical of the direction that popular culture is moving in. Atwood's writing is subsequently subversive, playfully destabilizing the certainties of realism and popular genres such as the romance, but as with so many other postmodern novels, her writing also destabilizes more traditional notions of subjectivity, found in biographical, autobiographical or historical narratives. In other words, postmodern self-reflexivity extends from the individual text to wider notions of the writing of self and history (Wyile, 140), where there is a suspicion that an objective, factual account of the past can ever be produced, and the concomitant understanding that all we really have are narrative versions or interpretations of a fictionalized past. Hutcheon famously calls this "historiographical metafiction":

> The shift in emphasis, in Hutcheon's terms, is from representing history as product to representing it as process; historiographical metafiction thematizes or allegorizes "the act of *enonciation*, the interaction of textual production and reception, of writing and reading." Such a shift implies a number of concerns on the part of contemporary novelists writing of history: the scepticism about objectively representing the past, the recognition of the mediation of the past in historiography and fictional discourse, and the struggle to find an appropriate form for addressing historical and historiographical issues. Key strategies for addressing these concerns in contemporary Canadian novels include foregrounding the act of researching and writing history and/or providing surrogates of the reader and underlining the act of selection, interpretation, and construction behind representations of the past.
>
> (Wyile, 141)

In Atwood's *The Journals of Susanna Moodie* (1970), and *Alias Grace* (1996), the historical accounts of two lives are deconstructed and reconfigured via different techniques of postmodern historiographical metafiction: in the former, via a poetic and artistic collage-based re-imagination of Susanna Moodie's encounter with the Canadian landscape, and in the latter, via the quilting together of multiple discourses concerning a woman called Grace Marks convicted of murder. In fact, Susanna Moodie also commented on Grace Marks, which creates an intriguing bridge between these two postmodern narratives. Rigney notes how in *Alias Grace*, "Atwood weaves fiction in between court records, sketches of the defendants, ballads written around the events of the murders, and newspaper accounts, many of which were fiction as well, as Grace maintains throughout her story and Atwood also believes was the case" (159). In almost all of her poetry and fiction, Atwood explores versions of the past through postmodern "memory-narratives" (Lane 1993, 64) that forge identity without unifying it, such as the aesthetic versioning in *Cat's Eye* (1988), the strategic telling of stories as a trauma survival activity in *The Robber Bride* (1993), or the intertextual recycling of John McCrae's experiences of war in "Poppies: Three Variations" in Atwood's *Good Bones* (1992). Atwood's "recycling" of anecdotal, memorial, and biographical/historical materials is in itself a postmodern aesthetic, where pastiche becomes the recognition that there is no longer an "original" text, rather all texts are entirely composed of fragments of other texts, what French theorist Roland Barthes (1915–80) calls a tissue of quotations. Other Canadian authors from the sixties and seventies who adopt such compositional techniques include George Bowering (b. 1935, in Penticton, BC), Leonard Cohen (b. 1934, in Montreal), Jack Hodgins (b. 1938, in Comox, BC), Robert Kroetsch (b. 1927, in Heisler, Alberta), Michael Ondaatje (b. 1943, in Ceylon (Sri Lanka)), Susan Swann (b. 1945, in Midland, Ontario) and Rudy Wiebe (b. 1934, in Speedwell, Saskatchewan). Like Atwood, many of these authors either had careers writing poetry and prose (and composed hybrid texts, such as Atwood's prose poems), or began with poetry and eventually developed experimental prose fiction (see Rae).

The historiographical metafiction of George Bowering

George Bowering asserts that "The first time some Vancouver poets heard the term 'postmodern' it was from the American poet Charles Olsen [1910–70], and appeared to be a continuation of the New World's westward drift away from Europe" (121). Bowering is referring more generally to the "projective verse" experiments of the *Tish* poets in Vancouver (Bowering, Frank Davey, David Dawson, James Reid and Fred Wah), who were responding to the aesthetic experimentalism of Olsen's Black Mountain poets in the USA, as well as a specific textual instance: Olsen's letter of 1951 to Louiz Martz where he first uses the term "postmodern". Bowering also reminds his readers that there are other genealogies of historiographical metafiction than that put forward by Linda Hutcheon, such as Olsen's Black Mountain lectures in 1956, called "The Special View of History". But most importantly, the notion of process is foregrounded by Bowering, for example in the "instantism" of postmodern poetry, where compositional decisions are made *in situ*, becoming part of the fabric of the poetry and leading to a rejection of authority and authorial opinions that usually precede the writing act. These creative decisions necessarily need to be made fast, leading to poetry "that races to elude the authority of the poet herself. Not poems made to express the poet's point of view. Poems trying to trace their own autonomy" (Bowering, 130). While such a task becomes like trying to escape from one's own shadow, a new spatiality of "free placement" does disrupt linearity and the conventional graphic surface.

Bowering worked on a larger scale with serial poems such as *At War with the U.S.* (1974) and the serial novel *Autobiology* (1972); in *A Short Sad Book* (1977), a title alluding to Gertrude Stein's *A Long Gay Book* (1933), Bowering produces a text that is "Part detective story, part poetry, and part literary criticism", as well as being devoid of the conventional markers of realism, such as plot and character (Rae, 161). In many respects *A Short Sad Book* is a Pacific Northwest parody and critique of the Eastern Canadian dominance of canon formation and literary history. As such, it deconstructs the desire to stabilize and project a seamless, chronological, cultural progression in Canadian literary production. *A Short Sad Book* is the literary historian's worst nightmare, because it breaks the boundaries, and dissolves the ground, of literary history. Literary and critical targets include Hugh MacLennan's *Two*

Solitudes (1945), Atwood's *Surfacing* and her critical work *Survival: A Thematic Guide to Canadian Literature* (1972), as well as loosely veiled literary and artistic characters such as Al Purdy and Tom Thomson (Rae, 162–63). The reader is directly addressed throughout the book, beginning with a short note:

> Dear Reader Reading:
> 1. Please take your time.
> 2. Also there is one dream in the following pages.
>   You should be able to find it
>
> (np)

History throughout the novel is alluded to, repeated and recycled in different disorientating permutations; Bowering also humorously decentres the narrational voice or perspective: "We say back east and back east they say down east and back east they say out west ... [...] This is if you are from out west or rather the west coast. In the east, as they say on the radio, they say the west coast if you are no longer in Alberta. They think all the mountains are the Rockies" (22–23). Landscape is observed from different angles: a line of trees at Naramata, BC, becomes a diagonal when the narrator moves, and from an airplane, "it was a rug of trees" (25). Trees in Acadia will be cut down for the paper industry, "and converted into dialog" (39). Canadian symbols are both deconstructed, yet also trigger amusing associative chains, for example when pondering the patriotic song "The Maple Leaf Forever" which was written by Alexander Muir (1830–1906) in the year of Confederation (1867), Bowering's narrator begins by saying, "We used to sing that song" (60) which may be a personal memory, or a reference to the fact that it long served as Canada's unofficial national anthem, until replaced by "Oh Canada!" (composed by Calixa Lavallée in 1880), in an authorized version in 1980 ("God Save The Queen" is the *royal anthem* of Canada). Thoughts about maple leaves playfully interact in this chapter, including the narrator saying "I got it mixt up with the maypole dance", while Charles G.D. Roberts appears, getting up from the ground with a maple leaf impressed on his back, folding "his little volume of poetry, a leaf prest [sic] in the middle of Tantramar" (61). Reflecting on the contents of the chapter, the narrator says "I made that up and now it's there. How are you going to unmake it?" (62). In some ways this question presents the methodology of *A Short Sad Book*: "unmaking" of Canada's historical (including literary-historical) narratives needs to proceed before a non-hierarchical notion of Canada's identity can be reached, one where history and poetry merge, and Canada's particularities are acknowledged.

History, for Bowering, is "myth", a notion more specifically worked through in his trilogy *Burning Water* (1980), *Caprice* (1987) and *Shoot!* (1994). Winner of the 1980 Governor General's Award for Fiction, *Burning Water* is a historiographical metafiction that reconstructs Captain George Vancouver's journey to the Pacific Northwest with a parallel self-parodic journey made by the author, who heads in the opposite direction to write the text. Authorial distance leads not to objectivity, but to parodic subjectivity and caricature, especially in the case of colonial attitudes to contact with indigenous peoples, which in turn deflates the grand rhetoric of European discovery narratives. Postmodern techniques are here put in the service of postcolonial criticism of the European obsession with the mapping and charting of indigenous space – yet this serious way of putting it betrays the fact that Bowering has a lot of fun in his novel, with the rivalry between Vancouver and the shipboard botanist Archibald Menzies, the imagined homosexual relationship between Vancouver and Bodega y Quadra, as well as contact narratives that imply indigenous knowledge of western people prior to Vancouver's arrival. Ultimately, Vancouver appears a hollow man, ill in spirit and body, with a colonial consciousness that cannot see the wood for the trees, detached from Menzies' Enlightenment project, with nothing much to stand in its place except for the naming and claiming of the waterways and the land for a future invader/settler nation. With Bowering's *Harry's Fragments* (1990), the contemporary version of exploring – international travel – becomes a semiotic interpretive quest, one where signs are constantly dispersed and disseminated across time zones and political space. The protagonist, who appears to be a spy, does not so much gain insight as he travels the globe, but leaves fragments of his understanding and self behind, until he is almost completely disseminated and dispersed. In this novel, the acts of spying and textual interpretation intersect, blur, and become indistinguishable: both are posited as impossibilities, the protagonist's desired resolution and certainties being continually undermined by indeterminacy and deconstructive dissemination or simply *movement*.

Metafictional parodies in the writing of Leonard Cohen and Robert Kroetsch

Canonical writing is clearly an intertextual source of much postmodernism, especially, as noted above, in the shape of the quest form, be it spiritual or mythological. Two early Canadian postmodernists – Leonard Cohen and Robert Kroetsch – both engage with a metafictional parody of the quest, the spiritual journeys or exercises of St. Ignatius Loyola (1491–1566) being parodied and reversed in Cohen's *Beautiful Losers* (1966), and the search for a palaeontological past and a dead father being deconstructed in Kroetsch's *Badlands* (1975), with Kroetsch's similar labyrinthine deconstruction of the detective quest in the search of the ultimate collectible objects taking place in *Alibi* (1983) and *The Puppeteer* (1992). Both authors share a scatological vision, which is carnivalesque in its playfulness and earthiness (that is, overturning hierarchy and authority), and both authors invite the reader into a more active, participatory role: "Postmodern metafiction, including Cohen's, implicitly posits a new role for readers: we are not simply to identify with characters, but to acknowledge our own role in co-creating the text being read" (Hutcheon, 27).

The scatological vision is one which punctures metaphysical pretensions in favour of bodily functions, especially those of sexuality, reproduction and

The Carnivalesque derives from Mikhail Bakhtin's (1895–1975) study of François Rabelais (1494–1553), published as *Rabelais and His World* (1965; English trans. 1968). Carnival is the subversion of authority and hierarchy by a theatrical and ritualistic reversal of all values: those high in society become low, and vice versa. More profoundly, carnival in the genre of the grotesque (parodic, low or earthy humour) can provide a coded, ongoing critique of those in power, be they in the church, representatives of the state, or in Bakhtin's time, Stalinist oppressors.

excretion, in other words, replacing the transcendental with the human, fleshly body.

In *Beautiful Losers* – a novel which playfully echoes and extends the writerly themes and obsessions of Cohen's autobiographical *The Favourite Game* (1963) – desiring games predominate, holding together the novel's two narrators, the Anglophone "I" and the Francophone "F" as well as the story of the Blessed Catholic Mohawk, Catherine Tekakwitha (1656–80); the love triangle in the story is between I, his Wife Edith, and F, leading to a pornographic outpouring of language and lust.

By eroticizing the story of Catherine Tekakwitha, and trying to reclaim her narrative from that of the Jesuits, Cohen creates an ironic reversal that reveals the inherent eroticization of colonial history; this reclaimed biography, however, cannot be turned into a new grand narrative, since the novel works through dispersal rather than concentration, a traversing rather than the imposition of a narrational or authorial vertical hierarchy.

While Kroetsch uses a less obscene discourse, the scatological carnivalesque is an important component of his postmodernism, and, like Bowering, he brings together a Canadian *and* American notion of postmodernism, in Kroetsch's case from his time at Binghamton, S.U.N.Y., where he founded, with William V. Spanos, *boundary 2: a journal of postmodern literature*.

The Blessed Catherine (Kateri) Tekakwitha (1656–80) was the daughter of a Mohawk Chief and an Algonquin mother who was a Roman Catholic. Tekakwitha lost her entire family due to a smallpox outbreak when she was four years old. At the age of twenty, Tekakwitha's baptism into the Christian faith led to her becoming an outcast; she made her way to the Catholic mission of St. Francis Xavier, Sault Saint-Louis, near Montreal, where she eventually took her vows in 1679. She died at the age of twenty-four having impressed many of her friends with her sanctity and devotion. The Catholic Church declared her venerable in 1943 and she was beatified by Pope John Paul II in 1980. She is a patroness for ecology.

Kroetsch makes an important contribution to Canadian postmodernism with his concept of autobiography as archaeology, developed in his poetry – for example, *The Ledger* (1975), *Seed Catalogue* (1977) or *Completed Field Notes: The Long Poems of Robert Kroetsch* (1989; revised edition 2000) – as well as in his novels, most obviously with *Badlands*. Archaeological writing unmoors itself from previous cultural anchors and contexts, such as European mythology, to explore new ways of mapping the Canadian imagination, in seed catalogues, almanacs, oral stories by indigenous peoples or those who live outside of Canada's main cities, or in remote locations such as the North, and through the semiotics of physical landscapes (the prairies, rivers, bluffs, lakes, hotsprings and mountains), sketched most often via field notes of the sort that open *Badlands*: "God help us we are a people raised not on love letters or lyric poems or even cries of rebellion or ecstasy or pain or regret, but rather hoards of old field notes. Those cryptic notations made by men who held the words themselves in contempt but who needed them nonetheless in order to carry home, or back if not home, the only memories they would ever cherish: the recollections of their male courage and their male solitude" (2). This is not to say that Kroetsch merely turns to an empirical reality to write his poetry and prose, rather, the archaeological method shows how reality is always already constructed discursively. An empirical real outside of the text is usually, for Kroetsch, a fantasy, desire, or fetish, that drives the narrative (the quest, the sexual economy) of postmodern writing.

In *Alibi*, the protagonist, Dorf, is in search for a spa that will give his employer Jack Deemer eternal life; in the mirrored or doubled novel *The Puppeteer*, the ultimate collectible object is the face of God, an icon which is rumoured to show God's true face as a woman. The aesthetics of iconography are transformed by Kroetsch into a puppet show, a screen existence and consciousness that may indeed have a puppeteer, but only a human one. The apparently transcendental icon "exists in the novel only through the traces of other narratives; the face/trace of God remains just that: a play of absence and presence" (Lane 1997, 39–40). In both novels, gender roles are overturned through transgressive sexuality and cross-dressing, and the quest for meaning continually bogs down in scatological existence. Another way of putting this is to suggest that the scatological digression is not an unimportant aside, but is precisely where (and through which) meaning is generated; the parataxis or placing side by side of such digressions is, in other words, the logic of postmodernism.

In *A Likely Story: The Writing Life* (1995), Kroetsch explores this logic via the scrapbook, where fragments of text and images are juxtaposed "in such a way that they suggest a possible meaning without insisting on it" (146). The digression or "interrupted story", Kroetsch suggests, "tells us what the main line of narrative cannot accommodate; it tells the reader what is being left out in order to make the story hang together" (Ibid.). Keeping a scrapbook, then, is not a peripheral activity for Kroetsch, since it is the events on the periphery – be they prairie farm, Northern river, or a stormy lake – that are important; this "geographical" creative form becomes for Kroetsch "an important literary act" (Ibid.). Similarly, the commonplace book (a book in which the reader inserts mementos, notes, scraps of paper, postcards, photographs, other texts and objects) in Michael Ondaatje's (1943–) *The English Patient* (1992) is doubly paratactical: the commonplace book is Herodotus's *The Histories*, which functions by placing anecdotal and elaborate historical narratives side by side, and within the pages of this book in *The English Patient* are all of the additional juxtapositions created by the character Almásy's inserted images and texts: " ... Herodotus, his guidebook, ancient and modern, of supposed lies. When he discovered the truth to what had seemed a lie, he brought out his glue pot and pasted in a map or news clipping or used a blank space in the book to sketch men in skirts with faded unknown animals beside them" (246). The fantasmatic tales of Herodotus map the desert more accurately for Almásy than any other form of knowledge, but by interweaving different discourses together, Almásy creates a textual constellation where no one item corresponds with an outside reality: this constellation *produces* reality, it doesn't just mimetically reflect it.

The postmodern "freak shows" of Susan Swan and Jack Hodgins

It is intriguing that the most important book of history within one of the most successful Canadian postmodern novels (which is also a highly successful film) is Herodotus's *The Histories*, as well as being suggestive of the importance of founding or originary narratives for Canadian literature in general. Postmodernism facilitates the critique and re-writing of founding narratives, as well as the reversal or recovery of what was once marginal (the histories of women, natives, minority ethnic or religious groups, etc.). Susan Swan makes central women's narratives, in three novels: *The Biggest Modern Woman of the World* (1983), *The Last of the Golden Girls* (1989) and *The Wives of Bath* (1993). Reacting against repressive notions of the body and female sexuality, Swan re-imagines and re-codes dominant ideologies, such as that of the early 1960s women's boarding schools and colleges in *The Wives of Bath* (film version *Lost and Delirious*, screenplay Judith Thompson, directed by Léa Pool, 2001), or that of Maritime giantess Anna Swan in *The Biggest Modern Woman of the World*.

Compositionally, the hybrid discourses used to construct this novel undermine the notion of a single truth-telling voice: "the discourse is disrupted by testimonials, documents and letters by relatives and associates – a technique also used by Carol Shields vis-à-vis Daisy Goodwill in *The Stone Diaries* (1993)" (Steenman-Marcusse, 180). Anna Swan's sexuality, the subject of male fascination, is always that which eludes the men who project their own desires and fantasies onto her, especially those of her impotent husband. Victorian discourses of reproduction, evolution and female sexuality are all rejected by the oppositional and individual personhood of Anna Swan, even if she is literally situated as a "freak" in P.T. Barnum's travelling circus. As such, the truth-claims of historiographical metafiction become clear: "Susan Swan challenges the 'truthfulness' of the autobiography by reconceptualizing the past through the voice of a female freak. This fictionalized Anna, who shares her emotions with the reader, achieves greater credibility – I am tempted to say a greater 'truth' – than the historical Anna who remains a fossil" (Steenman-Marcusse, 180).

The "freak show" becomes everyday society in Jack Hodgins' short story cycle *Spit Delaney's Island* (1976) and first novel *The Invention of the World* (1977), where "folk moments" (Ricou, 93) – scraps of local culture, myth, dialect, and gossip – structure the narrative more so than plot. The two framing stories of *Spit Delaney's Island* – "Separating" and "Spit Delaney's Island" – map the emotional and geographical space of Vancouver Island in the 1970s, through the perspective of a man who works in a mill, with his true love: Old Number One steam locomotive. Fascinated by the transient hitch-hikers who wait for rides outside his property, Spit Delaney's own static marriage and life fall apart as he is struck by the metaphysical question "*Where is the dividing line?*" (14). Rejecting Aboriginal myth that could answer this question, or a young man's descriptive account of the continental divide, Spit takes refuge in a painting and sound-recording of his steam engine. Poetry and danger burst in upon him in the closing narrative, which he ultimately rejects in favour of safety and security, but he does regret not sharing in further "folk moments": "There was a lot I could offer. I could've told her [the poet] all about the Doukhobor colony that lived across the road once, behind that high picket fence. A religious colony that didn't believe in marriage. Maybe she'd have got a poem out of that. I could've told her about them, and about the mountain she was going to. I could've told her what to expect there, the distance to the timber line, and what she would find in the alpine meadows" (233).

The eccentricities of local cultures explode with the full force of Magic Realism in *The Invention of the World*, a novel that parodies the utopian communities of Vancouver Island, with a doubled plot: that of the Irish Revelations Colony of Truth, led by Thomas Keneally, and that of the contemporary Island community living in the aftermath of Keneally's death. Strabo Becker's character is a self-reflexive parody of the obsessional historian, collecting fragments which fail to cohere into a logical whole unless certain gaps and contradictions are papered over, while the alternative patterns and rhythms of oral history function successfully to convey the collective popular history of the colony. The most experimental section of the novel is the scrapbook, that medium which Kroetsch argues transforms us "into historians, into journalists, into gossips, into storytellers, into autobiographers" (*A Likely Story*, 129). In *The Invention of the World*, the scrapbook contains newspaper cuttings, the editorial, letters to the editor and typed-up oral accounts, all in the local idiom of small town and rural British Columbia.

Hodgins shifts from a negative view of the utopian community, to one of redemption and hope in *The Resurrection of Joseph Bourne; or, a Word or*

Two on Those Port Miracles (1979), but still with an underlying sense of irony, as the town of Port Annie is reborn via a tidal wave. Hodgins' intense interest in other historical periods drives the historiographical metafictions of *The Honorary Patron* (1987), *Innocent Cities* (1990) and *Broken Ground* (1998), the latter merging the horrific landscape of the First World War with the clear-cuts and fires needed to break the ground in new Canadian farming communities.

"The politics of settlement": giving voice to community in the postmodern fiction of Rudy Wiebe

Mennonite religious community is the focus of Rudy Wiebe's first novel *Peace Shall Destroy Many* (1962), and Christian re-awakening in *First and Vital Candle* (1966). But it was publication of *The Blue Mountains of China* (1970), *The Temptations of Big Bear* (1973) and *The Scorched-Wood People* (1977), that revealed Wiebe's strengths in postmodern historiographical metafiction. The Mennonite diaspora is the wide-ranging subject of *The Blue Mountains of China*, while the following two novels focus on two important indigenous leaders: the Cree and Ojibwa chief Mistahimaskwa or Big Bear (1825–88) and Métis Louis Riel. Big Bear was famous for rejecting the restrictive terms of Treaty Six, one in a series of treaties designed to extinguish Native title or right to the land, although Treaty Six did include provision of a "medicine chest" which would eventually form the basis for free health care for all Natives in Canada (Dickason, 261). Big Bear held out signing until 1882, when conditions for his people had so deteriorated that he had no other choice. Louis Riel is known primarily for his role in the Red River Rebellion, and his resistance to the transfer of lands from the Hudson's Bay Company to the new dominion of Canada. Instead Riel issued his "Declaration of the People of Rupert's Land and the Northwest" on 8 December 1869, establishing a provisional independent government at Red River on 27 December (Dickason, 248), one which was overturned by Canadian government forces. Riel would eventually be hanged for his role in setting up another provisional government in 1885, leading to bloodshed in an armed uprising and the violent suppression that followed. *The Temptations of Big Bear* and *The Scorched-Wood People* re-imagine these leaders from postmodern and postcolonial perspectives, suggesting that they were great orators with prophetic insight into the future colonial attempt at destroying indigenous peoples in Canada. Both novels also re-situate what Foucault has called the "politics of settlement" or "*peuplement*", that is to say, "literally to people, populate, or stock – [a word which] is more effective than 'settlement' in evoking the numerous discursive mechanisms that imperialism mobilized to regulate and monitor female sexuality and, hence, colonial reproduction" (Higginson, 174).

Wiebe begins to open up an alternative history for indigenous and White women in this period, although it is not until the co-authored (with Yvonne Johnson) *Stolen Life: The Journey of a Cree Woman* (1998), that an indigenous woman's voice becomes central for him, in this case the auto-biographical voice being that of Big Bear's great great granddaughter. While it might appear that with *Stolen Life: The Journey of a Cree Woman* the postmodern has merged with, or become, the postcolonial, the text utilizes "documentary-collage" (Jones, 210) to create a hybrid re-performance of native-colonizer relations. Johnson had contacted Wiebe from within prison, where she is serving a life sentence for murder, and it was her initiation of, and desire to go ahead with this project, that reveals her determined agency for not just a public voice, but a well-publicized and circulated *reception* to her hybrid, collaborative text.

Genre trouble and new media technologies: Michael Ondaatje's *The English Patient* (1992)

Caravaggio, in *The English Patient*, sneaks into the abandoned Tuscan villa where the patient and his nurse, Hana, are temporarily in residence; eventually, they will be joined by Kip, a bomb-disposal expert who becomes Hana's lover. Caravaggio's task is to discover if the "English" patient is really the Hungarian Count Almásy, a man suspected of murdering a British intelligence officer – Geoffrey Clinton – and possibly his wife, while working for the Nazis during the Second World War. Clinton, masquerading as a scientific explorer of the North African deserts, has really been taking aerial photographs: "[H]e was keeping an eye on your strange group in the Egyptian-Libyan desert. They knew the desert would someday be a theatre of war" (252). Nobody is what they seem to be: Almásy appears to hover between being English or German when he is really Hungarian – and Katherine Clifton's lover; Caravaggio, the thief, also works for the Allies, stealing information for the intelligence services, until the day his own image is surreptitiously taken, or perhaps "stolen":

> Really I was still a thief. No great patriot. No great hero. They had just made my skills official. But one of the women had brought a camera and was snapping at the German officers, and I was caught in mid-step, walking across the ballroom. In mid-step, the beginning of the shutter's noise making me jerk my head towards it. So suddenly everything in the future was dangerous.
>
> (35)

Caught not just once by modern technology – here, the camera, creating a network of surveillance images, like Clinton's aerial photography – Caravaggio is caught again when he attempts to steal the photograph back: "A car beam ... lights up the room he is in, and he pauses once again in mid-step, seeing that woman's eyes on him ... And she has seen, he knows, even though now he is naked, the same man she photographed earlier in the crowded party, for by accident he stands the same way now, half turned in surprise at the light that reveals his body in the darkness" (36). This doubled scene is a repetition with a difference: the first technology that captures Caravaggio is that of photography; the second technology is the beam of light from a passing car, another machine that here facilitates the unwanted production of an image.

Walter Benjamin observes that the first photographs ever produced are incomparable because "they present the earliest image of the encounter of machine and man" (678). In *The English Patient*, the machinery of photography appears to have a power of its own, whereby "a new reality unfolds" (Ibid.). The text itself is cinematographic: full of jump cuts between intense images, with montage and parataxis being the logic of the narrative. More importantly, the human subjects in *The English Patient* appear to occupy virtual realities: not separate from "the real" but a media productive of new realities, identities, relationships and understandings. Caravaggio is caught both times "in midstep" as he emerges from his shadowland, the *félhomály* or "semidarkness, dusk, half-light, [or] twilight" (De Zepetnek, 116). The "mid-step" image reveals what the human eye does not normally see, and immediately the image becomes autonomous, something out-of-control, a virtual reality that he cannot "steal" back.

When Caravaggio loses his thumbs – they are cut off at the instigation of his Nazi interrogators – the importance of the visual becomes foregrounded even more; image and human become symbiotic as vision and the visual, the gaze and the resulting visual surface, merge into one. Image fragments – snapshots – link Ondaatje's works: "Just as *Coming Through Slaughter* [1976] and *Running in the Family* [1982] have historical protagonists who remain beyond the scope of definitive knowledge, the Patient's past is ultimately indeterminate, produced through snapshot-like fragments of time and place" (Orr, 60). Caravaggio doesn't want his fluid and malleable identity fixed by old-fashioned negative film technologies; he doesn't want this pattern or constellation frozen (a man walking across a shot of people at a party) since this chance event becomes what Benjamin calls the "smallest gestalt" (867), making the image potentially dangerous and explosive. *The English Patient* thus appears to dwell in modern image technologies – painting, photography, film – but it functions philosophically and theoretically at the level of postmodern digital virtuality, what Baudrillard calls the *hyperreal*. In other words, Ondaatje shows how postmodern aesthetics are already contained and configured in the very earliest mass-reproducible image technologies. Theoretical knowledge of new media technologies in Canada derived in part from a substantial group of cultural theorists: Northrop Frye, C.B. Macpherson, George Grant, Marshall McLuhan, Marcel Rioux and Fernand Dumont. As early as 1949, the government had created The Royal Commission on National Development in the Arts, Letters and Sciences (known as the Massey-Lévesque Commission), and as Davies notes, "[T]he death of Harold Innis just one year after the Massey/Levesque commission's report left us with a series of manuscripts on culture and communications that were to preoccupy cultural theorists for the next 30 years. This is not to say that Massey/Levesque called cultural theory into existence, but rather that it provided the climate of opinion within which such concerns were taken seriously. The emergence of publicly funded institutions devoted to aspects of the culture thus made theorizing about culture (indeed almost any kind of theorizing) of central significance in public discourse" (9).

Tele-vision: Catherine Bush's *Minus Time* (1993)

One of the ironies explored within Canadian postmodernism is the way that new technologies can bring people closer together, and yet also push them further apart. Screen technologies, tied-in with visual surveillance, would appear to make the entire world transparent, open to voyeuristic observation, while communication technologies theoretically bring people closer together. The reality is a great surge in loneliness and people who hide behind fake identities – such as virtual reality avatars – for myriad reasons. In Catherine Bush's (b. 1961, in Toronto) *Minus Time* (1993), technology is dangerous (e.g., creating the industrial pollution which is destroying the Great Canadian Lakes and the fresh drinking-water supply) and yet it also facilitates new careers for women, in this case for the protagonist's mother, called Barbara, who is an astronaut working in an orbital space station. Barbara's daughter, Helen, remains on earth, in Toronto, with a schizophrenic identity that communication technologies have both created and continue to facilitate. In a more general sense, Canadians have long been suspicious of communication technologies that have the potential to negatively affect Canada's cultural and political autonomy. Ironically, the telephone – one of the most ubiquitous of communication devices, in its various guises – was invented in Canada, in 1874, by Alexander Graham Bell (1847–1922), who went on to found the Bell Telephone Company. In more recent years, the cell phone (or "mobile phone" in the UK) represents the shift from terrestrial or "landlines" to digital, satellite communications. At the end of the 1970s, the Canadian government argued that "satellite communications have greater significance for Canadian sovereignty than for that of any other country" (in Stokes, 91); the proximity and power of the USA is clearly increased by the ability to beam direct satellite signals into people's homes, yet this anxiety now seems strange given the information revolution brought about by the internet and its anarchic networked structure, which nation states cannot control or transcend (a case in point being the website WikiLeaks).

In *Minus Time*, Bush meditates upon the paradoxes that occur as communication distances both collapse (the world as global village) and increase in scale (virtual realities can become divorced from material existence); secretly watching the Space Shuttle launch from a distance with her brother, Helen notices that NASA have produced a simulacrum of her, her brother and her absent father to fulfil the televisual and societal expectation that they would be happy, and together as a family, celebrating the launch: "'It's a TV re-creation,' she said. Her heart kept speeding. 'The only difference is that they didn't re-create everything, they just re-created us. I mean, that other family was actually there, watching the launch. They didn't fake that'" (13). Helen has noticed something about the "fake": that it was an actual event; the simulacrum is produced via actual people, who really are present. This is what makes the "fake" event so successful, and so uncanny, because the fake family function as doubles. Later on in the novel, when the press discover Helen's secret life as an eco-activist and protestor, the "fake" Helen will be spotted all over town, like an uncontrollably proliferating doppelgänger. What, then, and *where* is the "real" Helen?

Minus Time explores the cost of keeping one's true identity a secret, as well as what can be gained by resisting the total surveillance of postmodern screen culture, one which Barbara is subject to on the Space Station. Ironically, even though Barbara is permanently the subject of this televisual surveillance, she isn't always to be seen: "the picture would keep switching from camera to camera, room to room, although if you were in phone contact with one of the astronauts, the astronauts could choose to still it" (41). Because she has been a celebrity, Helen and her brother Paul are used to seeing her on TV, but this distance feels different to Helen. Helen tells her mother she is studying Garbology – "It's a way to study contemporary societies through an examination of their garbage" (68) – when in reality she is secretly working and getting involved in activism.

While Barbara is a role model for all women, Helen remains suspicious of technology and the breakdown of the family, arguing that "we have to change things here" (245). The cult of celebrity makes Helen feel like a "hostage" (258) to her name, which is really her mother's name, and she needs to create her own identity to turn her role in televisual screen culture into something active, counter-cultural and positive. While "lines of spoken and visual communication are *fractured*" in *Minus Time* (Lane 1999a, 49), women's gender roles and gender performance remain central, minutely examined from potential utopian and dystopian sides of postmodern technologies. As with the evasive dynamism of Aritha van Herk's protagonist, Arachne Manteia, in *No Fixed Address: An Amorous Journey* (1986), Helen refuses to be pinned down, her identity being formed through resisting societal expectations and her mother's over-ambitious planning for her future. Arachne goes through a process of learning how to wear a middle-class disguise, even though her favourite game, while driving the prairies as an underwear salesperson, involves complete sexual freedom. When disguised she thinks of her "natural inclination to dissemble" as helping, "She is not so much an actress as a double agent, an escaped criminal who has survived by relying on what slender veneers are available" (114). Helen is not a *femme fatale*, but she does choose, like Arachne, when to wear her disguise and when to liberate herself; while Arachne ultimately disappears, becoming a missing person, Helen's schizophrenic identity, while being her choice, suggests a post-feminist perspective, one where she eventually makes public her alternative lifestyle.

Hyperreal Canada and digital domains: postmodern journeys into fear and the virtual worlds of William Gibson

One of the paradoxes of Canadian postmodernism is the shift from an actual, material location to a hyperreal virtuality, a utopian place of possibility, be this the internet envisioned in different ways (such as the concept of cyber-space), the morphing of the Canadian environs into televisual or film loca-tions that are indistinguishable from other places on the planet, or more embodied synthesized cyborg/cyberpunk existence. In each case, Canada becomes the location of *image production*, such as Stan Douglas's (b. 1960, in Vancouver) or William Gibson's (b. 1948, in Conway, South Carolina) Vancouver, even if the image produced is part of a global media network. With Stan Douglas's *Journey into Fear* (2002), the book itself is a multimedia package, composed of film installation stills, a screenplay by Douglas and Michael Turner (1962–), photography, and critical/theoretical essays; the film installation has randomly permutational picture and dialogue tracks (Lane 2009, 143). In the film installation, the setting is a container ship heading into the port of Vancouver, BC, controlled by a "supercargo" (an individual who deals with the passage of sensitive, dangerous or simply extremely valuable goods) called "Möller", and a pilot called "Graham". The narrative is an intertextual construction, based upon two novels – Herman Melville's (1819–91) *The Confidence-Man: His Masquerade* (1857) and Eric Ambler's (1909–98) sus-pense thriller *Journey Into Fear* (1940) – and two film versions of *Journey Into Fear*, the first produced by Orson Welles in 1943, with a 1975 remake directed by Daniel Mann. What all of these texts share is a sense of inde-terminacy: in Melville's novel, the Confidence Man appears in various guises, whereas in Ambler's novel, no one is who they first appear to be (apart from the protagonist, Graham, an engineer and arms dealer, and even he surprises himself with his heroic escapade at the end of the novel). Douglas's *Journey Into Fear* draws upon the permutational identity of *The Confidence-Man*, and the claustrophobic ship-bound journey of Ambler's novel, where in the latter Graham is fleeing an assassination attempt, only to discover his assassin and other undercover agents on board the ship. Melville and Ambler both pose metaphysical questions about human beings caught up in forces that are out-side of their control; in Douglas's text, metaphysics and capitalism intersect, as notions of transcendence and universal truths are undermined by market forces and expediency; Graham and Möller debate the uncertainties of the journey they have undertaken, with the postmodern inevitability that it is the intensity of the discussion, not a final answer, that drives the text.

Other Canadian postmodern multimedia texts include Douglas Coupland's (b. 1961, Baden-Sollingen, West Germany) *Generation X: Tales For An Accelerated Culture* (1991) and Michael Turner's (b. 1962, Vancouver) *The Pornographer's Poem* (1999), both novels exploring in some respects a fear of mortality, and both being hybrid or multimedia texts that offer the reader immersion in a postmodern environment. In Turner's novel, the content and form both draw upon television and film, especially the subcultural popular genre of pornographic movies. In *Generation X*, Coupland appears to go back to slightly older media, such as photocopying, comics, and cheesy advertising slogans, to create a graphic surface that is ahead of its time, pointing towards the typical networked internet computer screen of today, and playing with the adjacency of multiple frames of data and images that are now seen on a typical website, or on cable/digital television news. In Coupland's novel, the side-bars, the blocks, the cartoons, the mimetic doubles of Roy Lichtenstein (1923–97) prints, the allusions to Andy Warhol's (1928–87) art in the age of mechanical reproduction, to use Walter Benjamin's phrase, are all postmodern image-based productions that have as much authority as the textual narration itself. Marshall McLuhan theorized such image-based productions in 1962 in his book *The Gutenberg Galaxy: The Making of Typographic Man*, a text which is composed of footnotes to an absent book, "that of The Book itself, rendered culturally marginal, according to McLuhan's theories, in the electronic era" (Cavell, 2007, 89). In *Generation X*, McLuhan's absent book is partly represented by a graphical block that sits in the middle of the first page at the beginning of each chapter, filled only with lightly drawn clouds. Art magazines such as *C* (Toronto), *Parallelogramme* (Toronto), *Parachute* (Montreal) and *Vanguard* (Vancouver) were also important publications for exploring the new media graphical surfaces, as well as "the various debates between fine art and video, virtual reality, [and] performance art and music" (Davies, 13).

Conceptually, however, the most commanding text of the multimedia postmodern generation is William Gibson's *Neuromancer* (1984), a science-fiction novel in which he invented the word "cyberspace". *Neuromancer* does not experiment in form, rather it radically reconceives at the level of content the entire science fiction genre through its representation of the merging of human and computer information systems with a global urbanism or street-credibility. In other words, in *Neuromancer* cyberspace meets cyberpunk, where "Cyberpunk's characters are people on the fringe of society: outsiders, misfits and psychopaths, struggling for survival" (Cavallaro, 14). The protagonist of *Neuromancer*, Case, a cyberspace hacker or "cowboy", has a damaged nervous system inflicted upon him by a betrayed employer (who used a biological nerve agent on Case), which he eventually has repaired by

Postmodern Environment – "The concept of 'environment' was of considerable importance to McLuhan in the work he produced after *Understanding Media*, insofar as it was the domain of interfaces and had an orientation towards the material, embodied context of artistic (including media) production. With this term, McLuhan sought to convey the notion that the world around us, and the lived experience of it, had become artifactual through the effects of media, such that nature could be said to have collapsed into culture" (Cavell, 2003, 170).

working for a frontman called Armitage, so that he can rise above being mere "meat" or bodily flesh (6). The repair job is not just an extrapolation of the present-day blurring of the boundaries of medical science and computing technologies, it suggests that corporations and individuals need to maintain an informational edge to remain successful in the information age; as the character Molly says: " ... he's gonna pay these nerve boys for fixing you with the program he's giving them to tell them how to do it. He'll put them three years ahead of the competition. You got any idea what that's worth?" (29). Molly has surgically implanted lenses giving her cyborg status, the prosthesis not just being an attachment to her body, but an integral part of her identity. After many fast-paced adventures, it becomes clear that the entity behind Armitage is an artificial intelligence called Wintermute, one which eventually transcends the networked data of cyberspace only to discover traces of other transcendent entities deep in space. Critic Douglas Ivison, editor of the *Dictionary of Literary Biography* volume 251 (on Canadian Fantasy and Science-Fiction Writers), observes that *Neuromancer* paints a complex picture of cyberspace, "or the matrix, that nonmaterial realm defined by the interaction of computer systems, which Gibson developed after watching Vancouver teenagers playing video games. [...] What makes Gibson's portrayal of cyberspace so effective is precisely its lack of technical limitation; cyberspace is a transcendent, dreamlike space, populated by ghosts and gods, though the degree to which Gibson's portrayal of cyberspace approaches the mystical is only hinted at in *Neuromancer*, in the artificial intelligence Wintermute, and in Wintermute's unification with its double, Neuromancer" (100).

Gibson's conceptual and artistic innovations are found in experimental form in his short stories, eventually collected in *Burning Chrome* (1986); the stories also trace Gibson's development as a writer, bringing together his first story, "Fragments of a Hologram Rose" (*Unearth*, 1977), with his next four groundbreaking stories published in 1981: "Johnny Mnemonic" (*Omni*; film version *Tristar*, 1995), "The Gernsback Continuum" (*Universe 11*), "The Belonging Kind" (written with American SF author John Shirley, *Shadows 4*) and "Hinterlands" (*Omni*). "The Winter Market" (*Vancouver*, 1985) is not only set in Vancouver, but it meditates upon Vancouver's role as "Hollywood North", or the way in which place can be morphed into any other place in the process of generating multi-media products. The story features an editor called Casey who is a psychic engineer, editing psychic visions into a media product which is a hybrid of music, virtual reality, dreamworld, desires and televisual and film technologies; the star who produces this creative mix is Lise, her cyborg body being held together by an exoskeleton that supplements and supports her degenerating flesh. She eventually transfers her being into a computerized, virtual existence. The story contains key cyberpunk components: street culture, the recycling of outmoded technologies for cutting-edge appli-cations, intensity of emotions, and people at the margins of society, yet with skills and talent that society craves and is willing to pay for. At the heart of cyberpunk then is a strange tension between counter-cultural, anti-capitalist forces enmeshed with the commodification of every aspect of human existence, from fashion to spare body parts. Gibson further develops this world in the sequel to *Neuromancer,* called *Count Zero* (1986), and in his *Mona Lisa Overdrive* (1988).

Gibson, who had collaborated with various authors writing his short stories, also worked on a novel with Bruce Sterling, called *The Difference Engine* (1990), and a self-deconstructing computer disc version of a poem with etchings by Dennis Ashbaugh, called *Agrippa (A Book of the Dead)* (1992). *The Difference Engine* is a fascinating "steampunk" account of how history would have changed if the Victorians had actually completed the building of a steam-driven brass computer called The Difference Engine, designed by Charles Babbage (1791–1871) and finally built in 2002 (Difference Engine No. 2, at the Science Museum, London, England). Babbage's designs were fully functional, but the building of his first computer was disrupted by the enormous cost, arguments with his machine engineer and political disagreements over government funding (it was cheaper to build an entire steam locomotive). Steampunk synthesizes earlier mechanical, steam-driven machines with that of later computerized digital technologies; in Gibson and Sterling's hands, it leads to speculation on history, technology and society. These two collaborative texts clearly inspired Gibson's shift away from science fiction into mainstream postmodernist writing, with the satirical *Virtual Light* (1993), the exploration of Japanese media and virtual culture with *Idoru* (1996) and *All Tomorrow's Parties* (1999), which critics largely panned (see Ivison, 105). *Pattern Recognition* (2003) is a highly sophisticated analysis of contemporary viral multi-media which brings together the world of design and that of cult internet images, sites and blogs. The plot cleverly moves from cynicism (of the commodified image) to awe (of the artistic image), hinting at the close relationships between the two modes of image delivery. *Spook Country* (2007), with a complex, interweaving espionage plot, also develops Gibson's notion of "locative art", whereby actual geographical locations are interpenetrated by superimposed virtual reality projections of events.

Mediatized/postmodernism performance

If Canadian literature is seen as beginning with oral forms of expression, it is fitting that in some of its most recent manifestations, virtual, cybernetic, and digital realms of textualization should prevail. At the cutting edge are alternative theatre sites and modes of performance, as well as exploration of these technologies in a more conventional theatre setting, such as Theatre Gargantua's *e-DENTITY* (2005 premier, Artword Theatre, Toronto), where the "material world ... collides with the electronic world, as that which is pre-recorded and pre-programmed clashes with real-time and improvised performances" (Papoutsis, 18). In *e-DENTITY,* there is an uncanny reversal of worlds, where bodies become screens, words appear to be literally eaten by performers, and relationships are disembodied via web-cam and internet technologies, being brought together only as culminating fetishistic acts. With "The Einstein's Brain Project" <http://people.ucalgary.ca/~einbrain/new/main.html> a collaborative group of artists and scientists have been exploring "the visualization of the biological state of the body through the fabrication of environments, simulations and installations" (Dunning and Woodrow, 46). On the overview webpage, this is what the group call the "technological colonization of the body". The *Body Degree Zero* (2004, International Festival of Electronic Art, Rosario, Argentina and Ciber@rt, Bilbao, Spain) performance space is visually and aurally compelling:

> Two participants are wired to various bioelectrical sensors, ranging from electrodes that track brain waves to sensors attached to the skin that record galvanic skin responses. The sensors track the participants' activity and bioelectrical output and visualize this in real time in the form of synthesized and manipulated images that are back projected onto two large screens in front of the participants. Accompanying the images are sounds generated from the activity of the participants. Local environmental conditions are monitored and streamed into the system, where they modify the participants' data. As the resulant mix becomes more and more complex … it becomes increasingly uncertain what is being represented … as the participants' identities are lost in the ensuing environmental data storm.
>
> (Ibid., 49)

The postmodern "data storm" can be perceived as a frightening or liberating transformation of the literary into a digital, synesthesic textuality, one in which alternative notions of the body–mind dualism and other more complex notions of subjectivity can be explored.

Conclusion

- Canada has produced some of the world's leading theorists and practitioners of postmodernism, including media guru Marshall McLuhan, science fiction author William Gibson, and one of Canada's best-known writers, Margaret Atwood.
- The multi-media world of postmodernism has spawned key media industries in Toronto, Montreal and Vancouver; the intertextual and multi-media basis for postmodern texts means that crossovers exist in the art, television, film and literary worlds – for example, in the works of Stan Douglas.
- It is fitting that multiple versions of the genesis of Canadian postmodernism should exist, such as those discussed by Linda Hutcheon and Robert Kroetsch; postmodernism eventually creates its own concept of fictionalized history, as illuminated by George Bowering in his self-parodic *A Short Sad Book*.

- Postmodern historiographical metafiction has been used as a post-colonial and a feminist device for interrogating canonized historical narratives, ones which in the past have marginalized or excluded women, ethnic minorities or highly politicized voices.
- Alternative postmodern Canadian performance spaces are some of the most recent manifestations of transformations in our understanding of literature and textuality; mediatized performances dwell upon the internet and digital domains of contemporary society.

9 Concluding with the postcolonial imagination

Diversity, difference and ethnicity

Overview

The postcolonial paradigm, while widely contested and intensely debated, is one of the dominant modes of the production and reception of contemporary Canadian literature. Postcolonial authors and critics often re-read the Canadian canon – and Canadian history – through this highly critical lens, leading to new interpretations of the past and a transformed notion of present-day society. While postcolonial Canadian literature adopts many of the strategies of postmodern authors (e.g., historiographical metafiction), there is often a more focused target of critique (contact, major colonial historical episodes, oppressive state institutions, and so on). Indigenous authors and critics such as Lee Maracle and Thomas King explicitly reject the postcolonial label, and these and other writers have developed alternative descriptors or theoretical paradigms to understand the agonistic, counter-colonial literature that has emerged in Canada, often from an indigenous or ethnic minority perspective.

The postcolonial paradigm: contested understandings and alternative models

Laura Moss notes that Canada's postcolonial status is in itself debated: it is a settler-invader nation (like Australia or New Zealand), but it is also a nation that disrupted and oppressed indigenous peoples. Breaking free from its Imperial masters, Eurocentric values still prevail in many parts of Canadian society. Moss argues that the concept of postcolonialism "may be roughly defined as a concern with a series of issues including: cultural imperialism; emergent nationalisms within a nation and between nations; negotiating history and the process of decolonization; hierarchies of power, violence, and oppression; censorship; race and ethnicity; multiculturalism; appropriation of voice; revising the canon and 'writing back' to colonial education; and Indigenous languages and 'englishes' [sic] versus Standard English" (4).

At the "Is Canada Postcolonial?" conference at the University of Manitoba (2000), critics came together to debate this question. A common concern is articulated by Diana Brydon: "If postcoloniality has been primarily

Tribal literature is community or tribe based, usually written in an indigenous language; **Polemical** literature is about the clash of indigenous and non-indigenous cultures, or, asserts the benefits of indigenous ways of being; **Interfusional** literature blends oral and written narratives; **Associational** literature is primarily focused on indigenous life, utilizing a flat narrative style which gives equal value to community members.

concerned with 'the decolonization of representation' ... then postcolonial modes of representation often find themselves embroiled within the same exotifying structures that they seek to resist" (2003, 51). A highly self-reflexive criticism is called for, one that is aware of colonial complicity in the narratives of methodological progress that may simply be another form of Eurocentric thinking (the postcolonial industry, that in some cases has little to say about decolonization or indigenous rights, for example). Judith Leggatt argues that postcolonialism is "a process, an ongoing attempt to find means of cross-cultural communication that escape the repressive hierarchies of colonial encounters" (111). This means that when indigenous peoples explicitly reject the post-colonial paradigm, then some serious reflection is called for, for example, in relation to two essays written by indigenous authors and critics: Lee Maracle's "The 'Post-Colonial' Imagination", and Thomas King's "Godzilla vs. Post-Colonial". As Leggatt notes, "King argues that post-colonialism is not applicable to Native literature, and that the label itself reinscribes many of the ideas of colonialism. Maracle sees *post*-colonialism as a luxury which her people cannot afford, since they continue to live under colonial conditions, both in their material lives and in their artistic expressions" (112–13). King advocates the use of four categories of indigenous writing: tribal; polemical; interfusional; and associational. Maracle models the cross-cultural colonial/post-colonial encounter as the negative image of the colonial fort, and the positive image of the arc or bridge that exists in a dreamspace (Leggatt, 113).

Leggatt addresses two possibilities in her analysis of Maracle and King: first, that the alternative indigenous theories put forward by Maracle and King are in fact analogous to postcolonial theories, for example, the Manichean work of Frantz Fanon and Abdul JanMohamed, or the hybrid, syncretist work of Wilson Harris and Homi Bhabha, and second, that Maracle and King are correct, and that their perspectives need to be understood and respected:

> My earlier desire to read Maracle's and King's essays through the lens of post-colonialism could betray a desire to see their theories in terms of the relationship between colonizer and colonized. I seem to have ignored the fact that Maracle's dreamspace and arc traverse more boundaries than those between colonizer and colonized; they also traverse land and water, life and death, past, present and future. Similarly, King's categories focus

more on the continuation of Native traditions than the transformation of those traditions. In focusing on how these theories parallel specific models of cross-cultural communication in post-colonial theory, I may have completely missed their main points, mistranslating them and misrepresenting them.

(119)

Maracle's novel *Ravensong* (1993) and King's *Green Grass, Running Water*, both adopt writing strategies that may exceed the epistemological limits of postcolonial theory: in Maracle's novel, there is a mimetic possibility in which the critic "invades" Aboriginal territory in attempting cross-cultural communication, and in King's novel, various pitfalls await unsuspecting academic readers: "The academic brings a set of critical tools to the narrative, but these tools tend to be inadequate to deal with a tradition stemming from oral forms and trickster narratives" (Leggatt, 124–25).

Analogous resistances to interpretation can be seen at work in Kwantlen author Joseph A. Dandurand's play *Please Do Not Touch The Indians* (2004), in which two sculpted "wooden Indians" are the protagonists that a series of tourists want to photograph, capturing their stereotypical image of an "Indian" frozen into some mythological time and space. The "wooden" protagonists slowly come alive during the play, subverting attempts at pinning them down through photography, that is to say, resisting attempts at interpreting them through external, or other notions of what they signify; gradually, the "wooden Indians" tell stories and share visions, moving from monologue to dialogue, the significance of these indigenous stories and visions being clarified by Sister Coyote, Brother Raven, and Mister Wolf. As a Mountie and the tourist dressed in a blue U.S. Cavalry outfit attempt to take photographs, the audience realizes that they are witnessing both personal and historical stories; the tourist becomes a sexually abusive priest and a movie director, which makes it even more clear that he represents the entire range of Western interpreters and oppressors of indigenous culture (see Lane, 2010, 158–64).

Theorizing "Trans.Can.Lit"

Another interpretive model that incorporates postcolonial theory and related critical approaches to Canadian literature, offering a dynamic and culturally specific methodology, is called "Trans.Can.Lit" with extensive exploratory discussions at the "TransCanada: Literature, Institutions, Citizenship" conference (2005) in Vancouver, the name being a homage to artist, poet and writer Roy Kiyooka (1926–94), whose collected works called *Pacific Windows* (1997) was edited by Roy Miki, and whose *Transcanada Letters* (1975; 2004) and *Pacific Rim Letters* were edited by Smaro Kamboureli, the initiators of the Trans.Can.Lit project. The first TransCanada conference was followed by TransCanada Two (2007), at the University of Guelph, and TransCanada

Three (2009), at Mount Allison University, New Brunswick. Miki and Kamboureli argue that "Since the national, multicultural, and postcolonial idioms are affected by globalization in ways that make it imperative we confront how citizenship … is controlled and performed today, it was important to make citizenship one of the operative terms in our proposed investigation of CanLit" (xiii). New notions of knowledge-communities in Canada include the prioritization of aboriginality, globalization and citizenship, yet these are not homogenous or stable concepts as Diana Brydon points out: "[T]he TransCanada project offers the Penelopean metaphor of 'unravelling the nation.' I read this as a call to recognize that the creation of any imagined community is a continuous work in progress, involving making and unmaking, learning and unlearning, aiming not to fix boundaries but to encourage movements across them" (2007, 13).

A powerful example of this "Penelopean" process is offered by Lee Maracle, who rejects western notions of textual or story interpretation in favour of a Salish perspective, where studying a story involves attempting to "understand the obstacles to being that it presents, and then to see ourselves through the story, that is, transform ourselves in accordance with our agreement with and understanding of the story" (55). Using Leggatt's approach sketched above, postcolonial theorists can read Maracle's essay in comparative terms, and in and for "itself" (that is, as a writing mode engaged in caring for First Nations community); in comparative terms, a Salish First Nations methodology is deeply phenomenological, intersubjective, and in dialogue with the Other: "The goal of study is to see a being or phenomenon in and of itself and for itself with the purpose of engaging it in a relationship that is mutually beneficial" (Maracle, L., 61). Opening oneself to Maracle's own voice is to resist mistranslating or misrepresenting what she is saying using western terms. Direct citation is necessary, but also a willingness to learn from the text:

> We attempt to story another being/phenomenon's behaviour and commit to its journey, its coming into being and going out of being, to this story. We then alter our conduct, our behaviour, to facilitate a common journey alongside of the being/phenomenon without interrupting its physical or cultural continuum, and we story that up. We commit ourselves to social structures, which lend themselves to creative, re-creative formation and transformation. This is how oratory is born. Oratory is a painting; it is about the freedom between beings and about cherishing the distance between them; it is about relationship, and as such it is about life. Oratory is comprised of the complex relations between disparate characters in their concatenation or their lack of it. It is the story of patterned events. Oratory is a human story in relation to the story of other beings, and so it is fiction, for it takes place in, while engaging, the imagination of ourselves in relation to all beings. Oratory informs the stories of our nations in relation to beings of all life.

(64)

Re-conceiving the Canadian canon: postcolonial possibilities and allegorical resistances

Re-conceiving the Canadian canon from a postcolonial perspective offers a host of possibilities, not least being a renewed understanding of how Canadian literature has engaged with questions of nationality, ethnicity, gender and religious identity. Building on postcolonial critic Stephen Slemon's work (1987), Barbara Pell re-reads the Roman Catholic novelist Hugh Hood (1928–2000) through the trope of allegory "as a postcolonial strategy of resistance" (Pell 2001, 53). Allegory is traditionally thought of as belonging to the criticism of canonical texts: it derives from attempts to read a deeper spiritual or moral message encoded within a narrative. Thus allegory reveals two texts: the visible, surface text (say, a simple story), and the invisible, hidden text (the spiritual or moral meaning of the story). Such a methodology would appear to "belong" to a colonial perspective, but as Slemon and others have argued, postcolonial texts work counter-discursively to pluralize and open-up colonial thinking precisely through new uses of allegory.

Pell argues that while Hood's novels are Christian, through his Catholicism he also "resacralizes a land desacralized by the European colonizer's myth of nation" in the process subverting "the dominant Protestant historical and geographical mythology with an allegorical counter-discourse that is sacramental, inclusive and transformative, rather than materialistic, manichaean and utilitarian" (2001, 54–55). Thus Canada, in Hood's work, is a sacred postcolonial site, expressed through the allegorical mode, rejecting psychological characterization in favour of "large metaphoric structures" which are embedded in parables (such as his novel *White Figure, White Ground* [1964], about artistic and spiritual crisis), romances (such as his novel about the film industry called *The Camera Always Lies* (1967)), and fantasy narratives (Pell 2001, 56). But it is in Hood's The New Age series, consisting of twelve volumes, that the allegorical trope is most powerfully at work.

The series begins with *The Swing in the Garden* (1975) and ends with the posthumously published *Near Water* (2000). *The Swing in the Garden* allegorizes the biblical fall, whereas the second novel in the series, *A New Athens* (1977), allegorizes the concept of the new Athens and a new Jerusalem, as the protagonists settle away from the metropolitan centres of Canadian life on a lake near the town of Athens. Canadian "wilderness" is envisioned as heterogeneous, not belonging to any one ethnic or religious group. The entire New Age series is narrated by the central character Matthew Goderich, and written using interlinked stories and characters, dramatic shifts in time and space, and a variety of genres and narratological techniques. The third novel, *Reservoir Ravine* (1979), tells the story of Matthew's parents, continued in the fourth novel, *Black and White Keys* (1982), which is set in Nazi Germany, where Matthew's father rescues a Jewish philosopher called Georg Mandel from a death camp. The "marriage group" – *The Scenic Art* (1984), *The Motor Boys in Ottawa* (1986), *Tony's Book* (1988) and *Property and Value* (1990) – explores relationships in light of the Ten Commandments; the last four books in the series – *Be Sure To Close Your Eyes* (1993), *Dead Men's Watches* (1995), *Great Realizations* (1997), and *Near Water* (2000) – cover five generations of family relationships, "Theologically connecting history to personal allegory" moving "allegorically from human sin and suffering to sacred grace" (Pell 2010, 262).

This series of novels, Proustian in its breadth yet attentive to personal memory and feeling, even has a character in *Property and Value*, Linnet Olcott, who stars in a film production of Proust's *Remembrance of Things Past*; *Dead Men's Watches* explores acts of care and the re-evaluation of homophobia as Matthew attends to his friend Sinclair, who has AIDS. Hood once called himself a "transcendentalist allegorist" which is a deeply unfashionable role to adopt in a postmodern age, yet through an awareness of the postcolonial force of Hood's Catholic allegorical imagination, his work clearly partakes of a return to a more ethnically diverse notion of the sacred that critics have identified elsewhere. As Marie Vautier argues:

> In several recent postcolonial texts, irony, the mode of marginality, gives way to earnestness, the mode of spirituality. Thus, contemporary postcolonial novels investigate childhood memories of Catholicism even as they flaunt the uncertainties of memory, the slipperiness of *l'identitaire*, and the generative power of *l'imaginaire*. All these elements are interwoven in complex ways in these texts. Using Slemon's model of the complicity/resistance dialectic in *Postcolonizing the Commonwealth* ... it is possible to temporarily separate out some of the ways in which catholicity is apprehended as "an axis of domination" that is resisted, before looking at the ways in which Catholicism in postcolonial texts is read as contributing to the "elements that comprise a discursive formation" ... and to the formation of a generative *imaginaire de l'identitaire*.
>
> (272)

Vautier reads Ann-Marie MacDonald's (b. 1959, Baden-Baden, West Germany) *Fall on Your Knees* (1996), Sergio Kokis's (b. 1944, Rio de Janeiro, Brazil) künstlerroman *Pavillon des Miroirs* (1994; trans. in 1999 as *Funhouse*), Tomson Highway's *Kiss of the Fur Queen* and Lola Lemire Tostevin's *Frog Moon* (1994) as examples of contemporary novels that critique Catholicism yet at the same time are "complicit" (276) with it. For example, the protagonist of Tostevin's *Frog Moon*, Laura, creatively utilizes a Catholic discourse, and memories of her Catholic past, as part of a new syncretist identity which also includes French Canadian folklore and Cree imagery and language. Vautier suggests that *Frog Moon* is a "transcultured, postcolonial novel" which "carries out complex investigations of postcolonial side-by-sidedness, addressing thorny questions of memory, identity, and religion" (278). Similarly, Cape Breton Catholicism is part of the melange of identity in MacDonald's *Fall on Your Knees*, whereas different modes of iconography are at work in

Highway's and Kokis's work, the picture of Abraham Okimasis and the Fur Queen in the former, and the self-portraits in the latter.

Reconceiving the canon through African-Canadian perspectives

Postcolonial approaches to the canon necessitate a backwards glance, not just re-interpreting the canon, but opening it up, extending its range and/or legitimizing texts that have been previously excluded or simply ignored. The TransCanada project in many respects represents such a process, tentatively mapped out in relation to African-Canadian or Black Canadian writing by Winfried Siemerling, who argues that non-fictional and transcultural texts, while known to historians and "specialists", need to be included in "standard literary histories and biographies" (2007, 137). Siemerling foregrounds 1852 – the year in which Susanna Moodie published *Roughing it in the Bush*, Catherine Parr Traill published *Canadian Crusoes* and, in the USA, Harriet Beecher Stowe responded to the 1850 Fugitive Slave Law with *Uncle Tom's Cabin* – noting further that "This law made it legally binding for authorities in the non-slavery northern states to enforce southern slave ownership and assist slave catchers, the reason behind most Black emigration to Canada West at the time. In connection with this development, 1852 also saw the *First Report of the Anti-Slavery Society of Canada*, Mary Ann Shadd's *A Plea for Emigration, or, Notes of Canada West* (1852), and her planning, as the first Black female editor in Canada, of the *Provincial Freeman* (1853–60), which published its first issue in the following year and entered into competition with Henry Bibb's *Voice of the Fugitive* (founded in 1851)" (Siemerling 2007, 137). Added by Siemerling to this list of texts is Martin Robert Delany's *Blake, or the Huts of America* (serialized 1859–62), Canada's first Black novel, "produced in a Canada–US cross-border context" (Ibid. 2007, 138). In fact, while there are no extant copies, a newspaper had been established for the African-Canadian community – called the *British American* – as early as 1845 (Williams, D.W., 41).

George Elliott Clarke also argues that transcultural texts have been effaced from Canada's literary history – for example, the slave narratives that are considered part of *American* literary history: "[T]he slave narrative, whether or not indigenous or imported, seems literally out of place, always exilic, always exotic. It is a silently painful wound, an anthology of the unspeakable that cannot enter into our anthologies" (14). Both Siemerling and Clarke observe that almost all of the reasons given for excluding Black Canadian texts from Canada's literary history, such as overseas publication, international mobility or fluid citizenship of author, and so on, are usually not applied to mainstream or canonical Canadian authors (such as Rohinton Mistry (b. 1952, in Bombay), whose *Tales from Firozsha Baag* (1987), *Such a Long Journey* (1991) and *A Fine Balance* (1995) all brilliantly explore Parsi community life, mainly set in India). This different standard of "entry" into the canon which discriminates against Black Canadian literary history and a wider conception of Black Canadian textuality can also be seen in the history of Black drama. For example, the dramatic version of Harriet Beecher Stowe's *Uncle Tom's Cabin*, called *The Tom Show*, was widely performed in the mid- to late nineteenth century, with the character of Tom drawing upon the racially degrading stereotyping of minstrelsy, popular among White audiences throughout Upper and Lower Canada. *The Tom Show* and minstrel performances were thus acceptable forms of "Black" performance in White Canada, although ironically, as Robin Breon notes, "the overwhelming majority of the actors were white who would 'black up' with burnt cork or greasepaint and proceed to swagger across the stage in the grossest form of caricature and mimicry" (2). Such White actors not only performed "Blackness", they claimed to speak for Black Canadians, the tradition of "blacking up" continuing in Canada until 1960 (Winks, 294). But Black Canadians were not passive consumers of this ongoing travesty: in Toronto, Black Canadians petitioned City Hall from 1840 to 1843 to have such demeaning performances prohibited. Also, Black Canadian theatre groups, such as The Toronto Coloured Young Men's Amateur Theatrical Society, offered more serious fare than minstrel shows, in this case performances in 1849 of scenes from Shakespeare and Thomas Otway's (1652–85) *Venice Preserved* (Breon, 2).

In recent years, postcolonial writing strategies have led to a re-enactment and re-memorialization of the history of Black Canada. In introducing a significant collection of critical essays on African-Canadian Theatre (2005), Maureen Moynagh argues that such postcolonial strategies "are to be found in African-Canadian drama and theatrical practice. Plays such as [Lorena] Gale's *Angélique* [1998], [George Elliott] Clarke's *Beatrice Chancy* [1999], [George Elroy] Boyd's *Consecrated Ground* [1999], and [George] Seremba's *Come Good Rain* [1993] rework a historical moment in order to challenge historical oppressions, exclusions and atrocities through enactments of cultural memory. Similarly, plays like [Andrew] Moodie's *Riot* [1995], [M. NourbeSe] Philip's *Coups and Calypsos* [1996] and [Djanet] Sears's *The Adventures of a Black Girl in Search of God* [2001] employ specific historical moments ... as points of departure for the themes these playwrights address" (xii). *Angélique* and the verse drama/opera *Beatrice Chancy* both represent Black Canadian slavery: in the former, the play is based on the real life Montreal slave Marie-Joseph Angélique (1710?–1734) who was hanged for

---

Canadian Blackness – " ... Canadian blackness is a complex identity, rich with contradictions and fissures. Certainly, the danger in talking about 'Canadian Blacks' is that one can elide the real differences among, say, a Vancouver Rastafarian, an Anjou Sénégalaise, and a 'Scotian' African Baptist. [Additionally] ... the centuries-old African-heritage populations in the Maritimes, Québec, and southwestern Ontario are jealously insisting upon recovering and rejoicing in their histories" (Clarke, 281).

her alleged role in setting light to her owner's house (and subsequent wide-spread conflagration), in the latter, the opera is based on the historical figure of Beatrice Cenci (1577–99), a young Roman woman who was hanged for her part in murdering her sexually abusive father, the story being transposed to a slavery setting in nineteenth-century Nova Scotia.

Consecrated Ground is set on the verge of the destruction of the African-Canadian settlement of former slaves at Africville, Bedford Basin (Halifax, Nova Scotia). As early as 1945, the City Council initiated plans to redevelop Africville, which essentially meant rezoning the community as industrial land prior to removing the inhabitants with very little financial compensation; it wasn't until the early 1960s, however, that the clearance of over four hundred inhabitants actually took place, the settlement being completely demolished in 1965. *Come Good Rain* is about one man's experiences of terror and oppression in President Idi Amin's (1925–2003) Uganda in the 1970s. More recent events are the subject of *Riot*, which is about American and Canadian responses to the Rodney King beating by the LAPD in 1992; *Coups and Calypsos* follows the claustrophobic moments after the attempted 1990 coup in Trinidad and Tobago, as a doctor and a professor are forced to stay in their beach house during a curfew, and *The Adventures of a Black Girl in Search of God* is partly about the attempt to protect the name of the community called Negro Creek.

Another postcolonial strategy is to rewrite key canonical, colonial texts which produce and/or perform Blackness, perhaps the most influential being Shakespeare's *Othello* (1604); as the young protagonist of Black Canadian dramatist and author David Nandi Odhiambo's novel *Kipligat's Chance* (2003) says about studying *Othello* at school "It's the first time we've studied a book with a black character, and I'm stoked" (54). Djanet Sears' *Harlem Duet* (1997) is a significant re-writing of the play from the perspective of Othello's first wife, Billie, the setting being transposed into the years prior to Emancipation (1860–62), the Harlem Renaissance (1928), and the present day (Kidnie, 40). John Thieme argues that "Relocating her response to *Othello* in Harlem allows Sears to situate it in an all-black context, but the play's representation of Harlem is in no way essentialist" (85). Othello, according to Thieme, is "exorcised" from the play with the shift of focus onto Billie; the interweaving of modern-day Black music and allusions to historical and celebratory Black American figures creates a tapestry that unsettled some of the play's first audiences and critics, proving that Sears' recoding of the canon has the power not only to shock but to upset normative notions of performing racial and ethnic difference. "Rewriting" texts, however, is not an activity limited to the literary canon; the great attraction of historical fiction, for example, lies partly in the possibilities generated when colonial historical narratives are critiqued and reformulated. Such reformulation of history becomes a central trope in contemporary Black Canadian fiction, as critics have noted: "Lawrence Hill's *Some Great Thing* [1992] deploys the figure of the amateur historian as a community chronicler of didactic intent; Mairuth Sarsfield's *No Crystal Stair* [1997] resorts to the sentimental by portraying a single mother of two struggling to make a living in war-torn Canada; and George Elliott Clarke creatively invigorates the dry documents that tell the tale of two petty criminals in *George and Rue* [2004]" (Cuder-Domínguez, 116). In Clarke's hands, for example, Africville returns fully fleshed, and the actuality of African Canadian history is brought back to life.

Conclusion

- The postcolonial paradigm has led to an explosion of texts that "rewrite" and "write-back against" colonial notions of history. This has occurred in new works of literature, but it has also led to a renewed understanding of the canon.
- Canada occupies a postcolonial position within a global context, yet many indigenous peoples still feel "colonized" by White Canadians. Subsequently, postcolonial theories which appear liberating from a White perspective are often rejected by First Peoples as being one more attempt to appropriate indigenous cultures.
- The postcolonial metaphor facilitates a more comprehensive revision of textuality and history – for example, in the return to, and recovery of, Black Canadian narratives.

Glossary of terms

Abject, the is, as theorist Julia Kristeva suggests, the object which must be expulsed to maintain normally functioning subjectivity, but it is also therefore (paradoxically) something that constitutes subjectivity.

Bildungsroman is the term used for a novel of development and education, deriving from eighteenth-century German literature. The protagonist of a *Bildungsroman* is usually a young person whose journey to maturity can symbolize or allegorize the growth of an idea, a nation or a political system; on each stage in the individual's journey key episodes may have greater or wider significance.

Chora, the is a pre-linguistic, maternal space, which Julia Kristeva equates with the semiotic: "Though deprived of unity, identity, or deity, the *chora* is nevertheless subject to a regulating process [*réglementation*], which is different from that of symbolic law but nevertheless effectuates discontinuities by temporarily articulating them and then starting over, again and again." (26). The semiotic chora thus disrupts and re-articulates the symbolic, but it also provides a sheltering space of subject formation away from the symbolic law-of-the-father.

Dialectics at a standstill is a concept developed by the critic and thinker Walter Benjamin, who argued that dialectical movement (thesis, antithesis, and then a synthesis of the two previous positions or terms) could be halted, generating a potentially explosive, revolutionary charge. The concept is best thought of through the process of montage: the juxtaposition of radically different images on one surface, causing a shocking new way of perceiving the world.

Écriture feminine as theorized by Hélène Cixous is a mode of writing that allows space for the Other – not just to hear the Other, but to facilitate the coming-into-being of other or different modes of expression. As a way of writing outside of the strictures of patriarchy and Judeo-Christian logocentrism, *écriture feminine* is necessarily feminist, experimental, dynamic, transgressive and always on the move. Cixous regards patriarchal writing as an investment that demands a return, whereas *écriture feminine* is a form of gift-giving, thus existing in a different economy to that of Western capitalism. The French Canadian theorist and author Nicole Brossard developed an analogous term with some important differences; her term is *écriture au feminine*, literally "writing in the feminine". This term avoids some of the ambiguities of Cixous's phrase – such as claims that "feminine writing" is essentialist, or the problematic notion of defining "feminine" writing in the first place – while still indicating "that female will be the contextual default" (Knutson, 195).

Flat narrative style is used primarily by postmodern writers to express or show the flattening of artistic and linguistic hierarchies. In flat narratives, the tone stays level throughout the story, regardless of the action (or lack of it), representing the way in which the media now represents virtually all stories on one continuum of repetition and recycling (for example stories on cute animals being presented with the same level of attention and seriousness as stories about murder or political issues). Postmodern narratives are hybrid, composed of quotes and intertextual samples from popular and high culture, levelling both genres so that they are of equal status.

Gothic, the is a genre that came into fashion in the late eighteenth century and early nineteenth sentury, parodied brilliantly by Jane Austen in *Northanger Abbey* (1818), and manifesting itself in different varieties (such as the female or feminist gothic, the Native Canadian gothic, and so on) up to the present day. The gothic presents a psychological landscape and architecture of ruins, haunted castles, dungeons, mansions and country houses, usually with secret passages or labyrinthine construction. The young, virginal female protagonist of the typical gothic novel exists in a heightened emotional and sexual state; she is usually a divided subject, expressing a transgressive sexual attraction while having threatened status (the protagonist may be subject to abduction and attempted sexual assault, whether real or imaginary), but by the end of the gothic novel, a return to normality is usually the order of the day. The gothic novel facilitates the expression of female emotions and sexuality within a patriarchal society, and thus it is modified and developed by feminists, for example, in Charlotte Perkins Gilman's short story "The Yellow Wallpaper" (1892).

Hybridity is a key concept in postcolonial studies, emerging from the theoretical writings of postcolonial theorists such as Homi K. Bhabha; hybridity is a term that describes diasporic and borderline communities and subjects, such as immigrants, their descendants, and different ethnic groups and/or classes within colonized nations. Such subjectivities are composed of multiple (and at times contradictory) allegiances and cultures, creating dynamic notions of identity and ethnicity. Hybrid migrant cultures, according to Bhabha, are highly resistant to appropriation and assimilation.

Intertextuality is a concept derived from the poststructuralist thinker Julia Kristeva who argues that all texts are "intertextual" in the sense that they produce the values of the systems within which they are embedded; resistance to such production is possible, at the level of what Kristeva calls "the semiotic", signs which draw upon bodily rhythms, maternal relations, and other expressive forces which have not been constrained by the symbolic law of the father. More literally, "intertextuality" implies that texts are constructed via incorporation of other texts (be they social, political or textual) through dialogic allusion, citation, deliberate plagiarism or creative incorporation and/or critique.

Metanarratives are literally higher narratives. Postmodern theorists use the term for narratives that are traditionally perceived to express universal truths concerning aesthetics, ethics, or religion. From a postmodern perspective, universality as a concept is discredited, in favour of all narratives being considered cultural constructs. Totalizing philosophical systems, transcendent religious beliefs, or canonical texts expressive of artistic and cultural values are all cast under suspicion for their claims to meta-narrative status; postmodernism flattens vertical hierarchies in favour of a democratic levelling of textual expression. In other words, all texts are considered to have equal value.

Mimetic desire, also known as "triangular desire", is theorized by critic René Girard in his book *The Scapegoat* (French 1982; English 1986), where he argues that the object of desire is precisely that which another person already desires. Mimetic desire is believed to lead to social violence unless a symbolic figure can be found who can be sacrificed in a cathartic release of violent tension and impulses; such a sacrificial figure is called a "scapegoat".

Mirror stage, the comes from the work of the psychoanalyst and theorist Jacques Lacan, who argued that all human subjects need to progress from the realm of the Imaginary (an undifferentiated pre-linguistic state whereby young children identify with the apparently seamless world around them) to that of the Symbolic (a differentiated, linguistic world of culture, rules and regulations, dominated by the law-of-the-father). This progression takes place in part through the mirror stage, in which the infant realizes or perceives his or her separateness or individual identity.

Modernism is an aesthetic movement from the beginning of the twentieth century, which forged a break with the Victorian and Edwardian past. Modernists rejected literary realism and figurative painting arguing that new forms were needed to articulate the contemporary world of machines, industrialism, urbanization and mechanized warfare. New theories of the psyche, such as Sigmund Freud's early essays and books on psychoanalysis, informed the modernist sensibility, especially in the area of sexuality and shifting attitudes towards outmoded gender roles. The rise of feminism was an important contributing factor to modernism, for example, with the writings and paintings of the Bloomsbury Group – notably Virginia Woolf and her sister, the artist Vanessa Bell. New writing techniques include stream of consciousness and interior monologue, which are two related modes of expressing raw inner emotions, thoughts and feelings in real time; in painting new approaches include the fragmented canvases of Cubism, celebration of war, speed and machines in Futurism and Vorticism, and the exploration of the unconscious in the uncanny books, paintings and sculptures of the Surrealists.

Picaresque, the is a type of episodic narrative which features a likeable rogue or *pícaro* (Spanish). The *pícaro* goes on a series of adventures in which the surrounding society is subject to satirical critique, although much of the subsequent humour is generated by the *pícaro*'s own human failings and mistakes. The most famous picaresques are the anonymous *La vida de Lazarillo de Tormes* (1554), Mateo Alemán's *Guzmán de Alfarache* (two parts, 1599 and 1604), Hans von Grimmelshausen's *Simplicissimus* (1669) and Henry Fielding's *Tom Jones* (1749).

Picturesque, the is an aesthetic term developed in the eighteenth century, being synonymous for "graphic" or "vivid" literary or artistic style; later, the concept of the picturesque broadened to include Romantic landscapes.

Postcolonialism is a term that covers broad territory. In literary theory it emerges from the study of Commonwealth literatures in the 1960s, and key critical works such as Edward Said's *Orientalism* (1978), Gayatri Spivak's "Can the Subaltern Speak?" (1988), Bill Ashcroft, Gareth Griffiths and Helen Tiffin's *The Empire Writes Back: Theory and Practice in Post-Colonial Literatures* (1989) and Homi K. Bhabha's *The Location of Culture* (1994). With the turn to psychoanalytical, structuralist and poststructuralist theory in the 1960s, 1970s and 1980s, the study of literary texts that were mainly written in English in colonized or postcolonial countries generated a highly theoretical discourse and a new domain of study. Some cultures reject the "postcolonial" label (mainly because it defines them, belatedly, after colonialism and implies they did not exist before colonialism came along), and some critics argue that western theorizing of any sort is merely a new mode of intellectual colonization. Nonetheless, postcolonialism as an area of study and as a methodological approach, with its specialized discourse, has meant that many western people have a deeper awareness of the impact of colonialism around the world, and the types of resistances and hybrid indigenous aesthetics that have since emerged.

Postmodernism rejects the intellectual and spiritual seriousness of modernism in favour of a turn to popular culture, the media and a suspicion of metanarratives (narratives that claim to offer universal or transcendent truths). Within postmodernism, there is a flattening of intellectual and artistic hierarchies, to present a democratically equal continuum of cultures and modes of representation. Postmodern texts are often highly self-referential, foregrounding their own constructed status, implying that all values and systems of thought are socially constructed (and thus subject to change or replacement). While the television screen was once seen as a key image of postmodernism – especially that of continual televisual cable feeds – the internet is now a more appropriate model, with hyper-text links and multi-media environments offering user-created virtual worlds. Some critics argue that postmodernism is merely a form of late capitalism; others theorize that it is liberating, allowing consumers to take creative control of their artistic worlds. Jean Baudrillard suggests that postmodernism is a powerful force through which the real is destroyed and replaced by the hyperreal: virtual worlds that are intrinsically shallow and false.

Profane illumination is a term that Walter Benjamin draws from the work of the Surrealists. Benjamin argues that through aesthetic techniques such as montage being applied conceptually to create new patterns of thought ("critical constellations"), powerful insights could be reached that had revolutionary potential. Such moments of profane illumination are not epiphanies or moments of spiritual insight; rather, they have a direct connection with the material world and the revolutionary disruption of capitalist and fascistic notions of progress.

Protagonist, the is the main character in a narrative; the word derives from the Greek, which literally translated means "first actor".

Stanza in poetry is a group of lines – preceded and followed by a blank space – which usually have some kind of structurally unifying form, be it a rhyme scheme or with more experimental free verse a particular graphical layout.

Sublime, the is a key aesthetic concept from nineteenth-century English and German Romanticism; it is an experience of Nature that overwhelms rationality – the human capacity to reason about events, experiences and concepts. In Romantic poetry or painting the Sublime is often represented by human beings encountering raging waterfalls, vast mountain ranges or raging seas. As rationality is overwhelmed, it is replaced temporarily by a feeling of awe, an uneasy thrill which is (paradoxically) both terrifying and pleasurable. Eventually, reason returns, but profoundly modified or transformed by the Sublime experience. The German philosopher Immanuel Kant, who theorizes the Sublime in his *Critique of Aesthetic Judgment*, argues that the Sublime is not any particular object in nature, but the experiencing of the event, the state of mind or attunement, thereby attained. Sublimity can be likened to a transcendent or spiritual force, one which is uplifting and powerful in its triggering of creative capacities.

Symbolism is an aesthetic movement that creates evocative private symbols, that resonate suggestively across poetic texts; symbolists attempted to produce a higher reality through creating a poetic tonality or musicality that blurred the boundaries between the senses. Key practitioners in the nineteenth century were Charles Baudelaire, Arthur Rimbaud and Paul Verlaine; in Canada, the main Symbolist movement was the Groupe-des-six-éponges, founded in Montreal in the 1890s; the group renamed themselves the École Littéraire De Montréal in 1895, and continued until 1935. Symbolism had a significant impact upon other modernist poets who followed a more hybrid approach.

Uncanny, the is that which is frightening, shocking, haunting and unsettling, usually because it is accompanied by the realization that something which should be kept outside (of the home, one's life, one's subjectivity) has appeared from within. Uncanniness often involves subtle shifts in appearance or status – for example, inanimate objects such as dolls or machines exhibit signs of autonomy and life. Another phenomenon that creates uncanny feelings is that of the double: an individual who is identical to another, to the extent that he or she might be a clone or twin. The double is perceived as an uncanny threat and a harbinger of death, or at the least, loss of autonomy and control over one's life.

Unreliable narrator, the is a term derived from narrative theory which describes a narrator who cannot be trusted to be telling the truth. The unreliable narrator is usually a first-person narrator who exists within the story world (an intradiegetic narrator); he or she presents to the reader a highly subjective depiction of that story world, one which is subject to emotional distortion, self-delusion and the usual blindspots that people tend to have. The unreliable narrator can be compared with the third-person narrator who exists outside of the story world (an extradiegetic narrator), with an "omniscient" (Godlike, all-seeing, all-knowing) vision, usually sharing objective knowledge with the reader. The distance between the third-person narrator and the story world allows for judgement and ironic commentary; the immersion and immediacy of the world portrayed by the unreliable narrator creates indeterminacy and clouded judgement.

Guide to further reading

Biographical, reference and historical works

Bothwell, Robert. *The Penguin History of Canada*, Toronto: Penguin Group, 2006.

Cook, Ramsay, et al., eds. *Dictionary of Canadian Biography*, 13 volumes to date, Toronto: University of Toronto Press, 1966–.

Currie, Noel Elizabeth. *Constructing Colonial Discourse: Captain Cook at Nootka Sound*, Montreal and Kingston: McGill-Queen's University Press, 2005.

Dickason, Olive Patricia. *Canada's First Nations: A History of Founding Peoples from Earliest Times*, Don Mills, Ontario: Oxford University Press, 2002.

Dickinson, John and Brian Young. *A Short History of Quebec*, Montreal and Kingston: McGill-Queen's University Press, 2003.

Finlay, J.L. and D.N. Sprague. *The Structure of Canadian History*, Scarborough, Ontario: Pearson Prentice-Hall, 2000.

Francis, Daniel. *National Dreams: Myth, Memory and Canadian History*, Vancouver: Arsenal Pulp Press, 1997.

Gough, Barry M. *Historical Dictionary of Canada*, Lanham: Scarecrow, 1999.

Harper, J. Russell. *Painting in Canada: A History*, Toronto: University of Toronto Press, 2000.

Harris, Cole. *Making Native Space: Colonialism, Resistance, and Reserves in British Columbia*, Vancouver: UBC Press, 2002.

Hayes, Derek. *Historical Atlas of Canada: A Thousand Years of Canada's History in Maps*, Vancouver: Douglas and McIntyre, 2002.

Jones, Joseph. *Reference Sources for Canadian Literary Studies*, Toronto: University of Toronto Press, 2005.

Moore, Brian. *The Revolution Script*, Toronto and Montreal: McClelland and Stewart, 1971.

Morrison, R. Bruce and C. Roderick Wilson, eds. *Native Peoples: The Canadian Experience*, Don Mills, Ontario: Oxford University Press, 2004.

Steckley, John L. and Bryan D. Cumming. *Full Circle: Canada's First Nations*, Scarborough, Ontario: Pearson Prentice-Hall, 2008.

Wallace, W. Stewart and William Angus McKay, eds. *The Macmillan Dictionary of Canadian Biography*, 4th Edition, Toronto: Macmillan, 1978.

Winks, Robin W. *The Blacks in Canada: A History*, Montreal and Kingston: McGill-Queen's University Press, 1997.

Wright, J.V. *A History of the Native People of Canada*, 3 vols., Hull, Quebec: Canadian Museum of Civilization, 1995, 1999 and 2004.

Literary histories and encyclopaedias

Benson, Eugene and William Toye, eds. *The Oxford Companion to Canadian Literature*, Don Mills, Ontario: Oxford University Press, 1997.

Blodgett, Edward D. *Five-Part Invention: A History of Literary History in Canada*, Toronto: Toronto University Press, 2003.

Howells, Coral Ann and Eva-Marie Kröller, eds. *The Cambridge History of Canadian Literature*, Cambridge: Cambridge University Press, 2009.

Keith, W.J. *Canadian Literature in English*, 2 vols., Ontario: Porcupine's Quill, 2006.

Kröller, Eva-Marie, ed. *The Cambridge Companion to Canadian Literature*, Cambridge: Cambridge University Press, 2004.

New, W.H., *A History of Canadian Literature*, Montreal and Kingston: McGill-Queen's University Press, 2003.

New, W.H., ed. *Encyclopedia of Literature in Canada*, Toronto: University of Toronto Press, 2002.

Nischik, Reingard M., ed. *History of Literature in Canada: English-Canadian and French-Canadian*, Rochester, New York: Camden House, 2008.

Tougas, Gerard. *History of French-Canadian Literature*, trans. Alta Lind Cook, Westport, Connecticut: Greenwood, 1976.

Aboriginal/First Peoples literary criticism

Appleford, Robert, ed. *Aboriginal Drama and Theatre*, Toronto: Playwrights Canada Press, 2005.

Armstrong, Jeannette, ed. *Looking at the Words of Our People: First Nations Analysis of Literature*, Penticton, BC: Theytus, 1993.

Brant, Beth. *Writing as Witness*, Toronto: Women's Press, 1994.

Eigenbrod, Renate. *Travelling Knowledges: Positioning the Im/Migrant Reader of Aboriginal Literatures in Canada*, Winnipeg: University of Manitoba Press, 2005.

Groening, Laura Smyth. *Listening to Old Woman Speak: Natives and alterNatives in Canadian Literature*, Montreal and Kingston: McGill-Queen's University Press, 2004.

Gruber, Eva. *Humor in Contemporary Native North American Literature: Reimagining Nativeness*, Rochester, NY: Camden House, 2008.

Hoy, Helen. *How Should I Read These? Native Women Writers in Canada*, Toronto: University of Toronto Press, 2001.

King, Thomas, Cheryl Calver and Helen Hoy, eds. *The Native in Literature*, Montreal: ECW Press, 1987.

Murray, Laura J. and Keren Rice, eds. *Talking On The Page: Editing Aboriginal Oral Texts*, Toronto: University of Toronto Press, 1999.

Petrone, Penny. *Native Literature in Canada: From the Oral Tradition to the Present*, Don Mills, Ontario: Oxford University Press, 1990.

Rymhs, Deena. *From The Iron House: Imprisonment in First Nations Writing*, Waterloo, Ontario: Wilfrid Laurier University Press, 2008.

Schorcht, Blanca. *Storied Voices in Native American Texts: Harry Robinson, Thomas King, James Welch and Leslie Marmon Silko*, London and New York: Routledge, 2003.

Early Canadian literature: critical approaches

Bentley, D.M.R. *The Confederation Group of Canadian Poets, 1880–1897*, Toronto: University of Toronto Press, 2004.

Blair, Jennifer, Daniel Coleman, Kate Higginson and Lorraine York, eds. *ReCalling Early Canada: Reading the Political in Literary and Cultural Production*, Edmonton: The University of Alberta Press, 2005.

Coleman, Daniel. *White Civility: The Literary Project of English Canada*, Toronto: University of Toronto Press, 2006.

Dean, Misao. *Practising Femininity: Domestic Realism and the Performance of Gender in Early Canadian Fiction*, Toronto: University of Toronto Press, 1998.

Gerson, Carole. *A Purer Taste: The Writing and Reading of Fiction in English in Nineteenth-Century Canada*, Toronto: Toronto University Press, 1989.

Gerson, Carole and Gwendolyn Davies, eds. *Canadian Poetry from the Beginnings Through the First World War*, Toronto: McClelland and Stewart, 1994.

McMullen, Lorraine, ed. *Re(Dis)Covering Our Foremothers: Nineteenth-Century Canadian Women Writers*, Ottawa: University of Ottawa Press, 1990.

Murray, Heather. *Come, Bright Improvement! The Literary Societies of Nineteenth-Century Ontario*, Toronto: University of Toronto Press, 2002.

Steenman-Marcusse, Conny. *Re-Writing Pioneer Women in Anglo-Canadian Literature*, Amsterdam: Rodopi, 2001.

Vincent, Thomas B. *Narrative Verse Satire in Maritime Canada: 1779–1814*, Ottawa: Tecumseh Press, 1978.

Warkentin, Germaine, ed. *Canadian Exploration Literature*, Toronto: Dundurn Press, 2006.

Drama criticism

Benson, Eugene and L.W. Conolly, eds. *The Oxford Companion to Canadian Theatre*, Don Mills, Ontario: Oxford University Press, 1989.

Bessai, Dianne. *Playwrights of Collective Creation*, Toronto: Simon and Pierre, 1992.

Brask, Per K., ed. *Contemporary Issues in Canadian Drama*, Winnipeg: Blizzard, 1995.

Burnett, Linda, ed. *Theatre in Atlantic Canada*, Toronto: Playwrights Canada Press, 2010.

Filewood, Alan. *Collective Encounters: Documentary Theatre in English Canada*, Toronto: University of Toronto Press, 1987.

Grace, Sherrill and Albert-Reiner Glaap, eds. *Performing National Identities: International Perspectives on Contemporary Canadian Theatre*, Vancouver: Talonbooks, 2003.

Kerr, Rosalind, ed. *Queer Theatre in Canada*, Toronto: Playwrights Canada Press, 2008.

Knowles, Ric. *The Theatre of Form and the Production of Meaning: Contemporary Canadian Dramaturgies*, Toronto: ECW Press, 1999.

Knowles, Ric and Ingrid Mündel, eds. *"Ethnic," Multicultural, and Intercultural Theatre*, Toronto: Playwrights Canada Press, 2010.

Knuston, Susan, ed. *Canadian Shakespeare*, Toronto: Playwrights Canada Press, 2010.

Maufort, Marc and Franca Bellarsi, eds. *Siting the Other: Re-Visions of Marginality in Australian and English-Canadian Drama*, Brussels: Lang, 2001.

Moynagh, Maureen, ed. *African-Canadian Theatre*, Toronto: Playwrights Canada Press, 2005.

Nothof, Anne, ed. *Theatre in Alberta*, Toronto: Playwrights Canada Press, 2009.

Ratsoy, Ginny, ed. *Theatre in British Columbia*, Toronto: Playwrights Canada Press, 2009.

Salverson, Julie, ed. *Popular Political Theatre and Performance*, Toronto: Playwrights Canada Press, 2010.

Scott, Shelley. *The Violent Woman As A New Theatrical Character Type: Cases From Canadian Drama*, Lewiston, NY: Edwin Mellen, 2007.

Wagner, Anton. *Establishing Our Boundaries: English-Canadian Theatre Criticism*, Toronto: University of Toronto Press, 1999.

Wallace, Robert. *Producing Marginality: Theatre and Criticism in Canada*, Saskatoon: Fifth House, 1990.

Zimmerman, Cynthia. *Playwriting Women: Female Voices in English Canada*, Toronto: Simon and Pierre, 1994.

Poetry criticism

Bentley, D.M.R. *Mimic Fires: Accounts of Early Long Poems on Canada*, Montreal and Kingston: McGill-Queen's University Press, 1994.

Brandt, Di and Barbara Godard, eds. *Wider Boundaries of Daring: The Modernist Impulse in Canadian Women's Poetry*, Waterloo, Ontario: Wilfrid Laurier University Press, 2009.

Brown, E.K. *On Canadian Poetry*, Toronto: McClelland and Stewart, 1977 (first published 1943).

Butling, Pauline and Susan Rudy. *Writing in Our Time: Canada's Radical Poetries in English (1957–2003)*, Waterloo, Ontario: Wilfrid Laurier University Press, 2005.

Carrière, Marie. *Writing in the Feminine in French and English Canada: A Question of Ethics*, Toronto: University of Toronto Press, 2002.

Cook, Méira. *Writing Lovers: Reading Canadian Love Poetry by Women*, Montreal and Kingston: McGill-Queen's University Press, 2005.

Dudeck, Louis and Michael Gnarowski, eds. *The Making of Modern Poetry in Canada: Essential Articles on Contemporary Canadian Poetry in English*, Toronto: Ryerson, 1967.

Glickman, Susan. *The Picturesque and the Sublime: A Poetics of the Canadian Landscape*, Montreal and Kingston: McGill-Queen's University Press, 1998.

Hurst, Alexandra J. *The War Among the Poets: Issues of Plagiarism and Patronage Among the Confederation Poets*, London: Canadian Poetry Press, 1994.

Kamboureli, Smaro. *On The Edge of Genre: The Contemporary Long Poem*, Toronto: University of Toronto Press, 1991.

Trehearne, Brian. *Aestheticism and the Canadian Modernists*, Montreal and Kingston: McGill-Queen's University Press, 1989.

——*The Montreal Forties: Modernist Poetry in Transition*, Toronto: University of Toronto Press, 1999.

The novel: criticism

Chapman, Rosemary. *Siting the Quebec Novel: The Representation of Space in Francophone Writing*, Bern: Lang, 2000.

Gould, Karen. *Writing in the Feminine: Feminism and Experimental Writing in Québec*, Carbondale: Southern Illinois University Press, 1990.

Green, Mary Jean. *Women and Narrative Identity: Rewriting the Quebec National Text*, Montreal and Kingston: McGill-Queen's University Press, 2001.

Heidenrich, Rosmarin. *The Postwar Novel in Canada: Narrative Patterns and Reader Response*, Waterloo, Ontario: Wilfrid Laurier University Press, 1989.

Howells, Coral Ann. *Private and Fictional Words: Canadian Women Novelists of the 1970s and 1980s*, London and New York: Methuen, 1987.

Moss, John. *A Reader's Guide to the Canadian Novel*, Toronto: McClelland and Stewart, 1981.

Purdy, Anthony George. *A Certain Difficulty of Being: Essays on the Quebec Novel*, Montreal and Kingston: McGill-Queen's University Press, 1990.

Rae, Ian. *From Cohen to Carson: The Poet's Novel in Canada*, Montreal and Kingston: McGill-Queen's University Press, 2008.

Steenman-Marcuse, Conny, ed. *The Rhetoric of Canadian Writing*, Amsterdam and New York: Rodopi, 2002.

Wyile, Herb. *Speculative Fictions: Contemporary Canadian Novelists and the Writing of History*, Montreal and Kingston: McGill-Queen's University Press, 2002.

——*Speaking in the Past Tense: Canadian Novelists on Writing Historical Fiction*, Waterloo, Ontario: Wilfrid Laurier University Press, 2006.

The short story/short fiction

Davis, Rocío G. *Transcultural Reinventions: Asian American and Asian Canadian Short-Story Cycles*, Toronto: TSAR, 2001.

Dvořák, Marta and W.H. New, eds. *Tropes and Territories: Short Fiction, Postcolonial Readings, Canadian Writings in Context*, Montreal and Kingston: McGill-Queen's University Press, 2007.

Gadpaille, Michelle. *The Canadian Short Story*, Don Mills, Ontario: Oxford University Press, 1988.

Kruk, Laurie. *The Voice is the Story: Conversations with Canadian Writers of Short Fiction*, Oakville, Ontario: Mosaic, 2003.

Lynch, Gerald. *The One And The Many: English-Canadian Short Story Cycles*, Toronto: University of Toronto Press, 2001.

Lynch, Gerald and Angela Arnold Robbeson, eds. *Dominant Impressions: Essays on the Canadian Short Story*, Ottawa: University of Ottawa Press, 1999.

Nischik, Reingard M., ed. *The Canadian Short Story: Interpretations*, Rochester, New York: Camden House, 2007.

Critical themes

Cabajsky, Andrea and Brett Josef Grubisic, eds. *National Plots: Historical Fiction and Changing Ideas of Canada*, Waterloo, Ontario: Wilfrid Laurier University Press, 2010.

Calder, Alison and Robert Wardhaugh, eds. *History, Literature, and the Writing of the Canadian Prairies*, Winnipeg: The University of Manitoba Press, 2005.

Chambers, Jennifer, ed. *Diversity and Change in Early Canadian Women's Writing*, Newcastle: Cambridge Scholars Press, 2008.

Clarke, George Elliott, ed. *Eyeing the North Star: Directions in African-Canadian Literature*, Toronto: McClelland and Stewart, 1997.

——*Odysseys Home: Mapping African-Canadian Literature*, Toronto: University of Toronto Press, 2002.

Coleman, Daniel. *White Civility: The Literary Project of English Canada*, Toronto: University of Toronto Press, 2006.

Concilio, Carmen and Richard J. Lane, eds. *Image Technologies in Canadian Literature: Narrative, Film, and Photography*, Brussels: Lang, 2009.

Deer, Glenn. *Postmodern Canadian Fiction and the Rhetoric of Authority*, Kingston: McGill-Queen's University Press, 1994.

Delany, Paul, ed. *Vancouver: Representing the Postmodern City*, Vancouver: Arsenal Pulp Press, 1994.

Dickinson, Peter. *Here is Queer: Nationalisms, Sexualities and the Literatures of Canada*, Toronto: University of Toronto Press, 1999.

Doyle, James. *Progressive Heritage: The Evolution of a Politically Radical Literary Tradition in Canada*, Waterloo, Ontario: Wilfrid Laurier Press, 2002.

Edwards, Justin D. *Gothic Canada: Reading The Spectre Of A National Literature*, Edmonton: University of Alberta Press, 2005.

Fiamengo, Janice. *Other Selves: Animals in the Canadian Literary Imagination*, Ottawa: University of Ottawa Press, 2007.

Flotow, Luise Von and Reingard M. Nischik, eds. *Translating Canada, Charting the Institutions and Influences of Cultural Transfer: Canadian Writing in Germany*, Ottawa: University of Ottawa Press, 2007.

Godard, Barbara. *Canadian Literature at the Crossroads of Language and Culture*, Edmonton: NeWest, 2008.

Goldman, Marlene. *Rewriting Apocalypse in Canadian Fiction*, Montreal and Kingston: McGill-Queen's University Press, 2005.

Grace, Sherrill. *Canada and the Idea of North*, Montreal and Kingston: McGill-Queen's University Press, 2002.

Grekul, Lisa. *Leaving Shadows: Literature in English By Canada's Ukrainians*, Edmonton: The University of Alberta Press, 2005.

Hazelton, Hugh. *Latinocanadá: A Critical Study of Ten Latin American Writers of Canada*, Montreal and Kingston: McGill-Queen's University Press, 2007.

Heble, Ajay, Donna Palmateer Pennee and J.R. (Tim) Struthers, eds. *New Contexts of Canadian Criticism*, Peterborough, Ontario: Broadview, 1997.

Hutcheon, Linda. *The Canadian Postmodern: A Study of Contemporary English-Canadian Fiction*, Toronto: Oxford University Press, 1988.

Irvine, Dean, ed. *The Canadian Modernists Meet*, Ottawa: University of Ottawa Press, 2005.

Ivison, Douglas, ed. *Canadian Fantasy and Science-Fiction Writers*, Dictionary of Literary Biography, Volume Two Hundred Fifty-One, Detroit: The Gale Group, 2002.

Kamboureli, Smaro. *Scandalous Bodies: Diasporic Literature in English Canada*, Oxford: Oxford University Press, 2000.

Kamboureli, Smaro and Roy Miki, eds. *Trans.Can.Lit: Resituating the Study of Canadian Literature*, Waterloo, Ontario: Wilfrid Laurier University Press, 2007.

Keefer, Janice Kulyk. *Under Eastern Eyes: A Critical Reading of Maritime Fiction*, Toronto: University of Toronto Press, 1987.

Kerber, Jenny. *Writing in the Dust: Reading the Prairie Environmentally*, Waterloo, Ontario: Wilfrid Laurier University Press, 2010.

Leandoer, Katarina. *From Colonial Expression to Export Commodity: English-Canadian Literature in Canada and Sweden 1945–1999*, Uppsala: Acta Universitatis Upsaliensis, 2002.

Leroux, Jean-François and Camille R. La Bossière, eds. *Worlds of Wonder: Readings in Canadian Science Fiction and Fantasy Literature*, Ottawa: University of Ottawa Press, 2004.

Lucking, David. *The Serpant's Part: Narrating the Self in Canadian Literature*, Bern: Lang, 2003.

Moss, Laura, ed. *Is Canada Postcolonial? Unsettling Canadian Literature*, Waterloo, Ontario: Wilfrid Laurier University Press, 2003.

Mount, Nick. *When Canadian Literature Moved to New York*, Toronto: University of Toronto Press, 2005.

Neuman, Shirley and Smaro Kamboreli, eds. *Amazing Space: Writing Canadian Women Writing*, Edmonton: Longspoon/NeWest, 1986.

Novak, Dagmar. *Dubious Glory: The Two World Wars and the Canadian Novel*, New York: Peter Lang, 2000.

Pivato, Joseph. *Contrasts: Comparative Essays on Italian-Canadian Writing*, Montreal: Guernica, 1985.

Rak, Julie, ed. *Auto/biography in Canada: Critical Directions*, Waterloo, Ontario: Wilfrid Laurier University Press, 2005.

Reimer, Mavid, ed. *Discourses of Children's Literature in Canada*, Waterloo, Ontario: Wilfrid Laurier University Press, 2008.

Ricou, Laurie. *The Arbutus/Madrone Files: Reading The Pacific Northwest*, Edmonton: NeWest, 2002.

Saul, Joanne. *Writing The Roaming Subject: The Biotext In Canadian Literature*, Toronto: University of Toronto Press, 2006.

Stacey, Robert David, ed. *RE: Reading the Postmodern: Canadian Literature and Criticism after Modernism*, Ottawa: University of Ottawa Press, 2010.

Sugars, Cynthia, ed. *Home-Work: Postcolonialism, Pedagogy and Canadian Literature*, Ottawa: University of Ottawa Press, 2004.

——*Unhomely States: Theorizing English-Canadian Postcolonialism*, Peterborough, Ontario: Broadview, 2004.

Sugars, Cynthia and Gerry Turcotte, eds. *Unsettled Remains: Canadian Literature and the Postcolonial Gothic*, Waterloo, Ontario: Wilfrid Laurier University Press, 2009.

Thompson, Dawn. *Writing A Politics of Perception: Memory, Holography, and Women Writers in Canada*, Toronto: University of Toronto Press, 2000.

Ty, Eleanor and Christl Verduyn, eds. *Asian Canadian Writing: Beyond Auto-ethnography*, Waterloo, Ontario: Wilfrid Laurier University Press, 2008.

Waterston, Elizabeth. *Rapt in Plaid: Canadian Literature and Scottish Tradition*, Toronto: University of Toronto Press, 2001.

Author criticism

Appleton, Sarah A., ed. *Once upon a Time: Myth, Fairy Tales and Legends in Margaret Atwood's Writings*, Newcastle: Cambridge Scholars Press, 2008.

Comeau, Paul. *Margaret Laurence's Epic Imagination*, Edmonton: University of Alberta Press, 2005.

Connor, Carl Y. *Archibald Lampman: Canadian Poet of Nature*, Ottawa: Borealis, 1977.

Davidson, Arnold E., Priscilla L. Walton and Jennifer Andrews, eds. *Border Crossings: Thomas King's Cultural Inversions*, Toronto: University of Toronto Press, 2003.

De Zepetnek, Steven Tötösy, ed. *Comparative Cultural Studies and Michael Ondaatje's Writing*, West Lafayette, Indiana: Purdue University Press, 2005.

Dragland, Stan, ed. *Duncan Campbell Scott: A Book of Criticism*, Ottawa: Tecumseh, 1974.

Dudek, Debra Lynn. *Creative Displacement And Corporeal Defiance: Feminist Canadian Modernism In Margaret Laurence's Manawaka Novels*, Dissertation, University of Saskatchewan, 2000.

Dvořák, Marta and Manina Jones, eds. *Carol Shields and the Extra-Ordinary*, Montreal and Kingston: McGill-Queen's University Press, 2007.

Eden, Edward and Dee Goertz, eds. *Carol Shields, Narrative Hunger, and the Possibilities of Fiction*, Toronto: University of Toronto Press, 2003.

Everett, Jane, ed. *In Translation: The Gabrielle Roy–Joyce Marshall Correspondence*, Toronto: University of Toronto Press, 2005.

Ferri, Laura, ed. *Jane Urquhart: Essays on Her Works*, Toronto: Guernica, 2005.

Fischer, G.K. *In Search of Jerusalem: Religion and Ethics in the Writings of A.M. Klein*, Montreal and London: McGill-Queen's University Press, 1975.

Gammel, Irene, ed. *The Intimate Life of L.M. Montgomery*, Toronto: University of Toronto Press, 2005.

Grace, Sherrill. *Making Theatre: A Life of Sharon Pollock*, Vancouver: Talonbooks, 2008.

——*Strange Comfort: Essays on the Work of Malcolm Lowry*, Vancouver: Talonbooks, 2009.

Gunnars, Kristjana, ed. *Transient Questions: New Essays on Mavis Gallant*, Amsterdam and New York: Rodopi, 2004.

Hengen, Shannon. *Margaret Atwood's Power: Mirrors, Reflections and Images in Select Fiction and Poetry*, Toronto: Second Story, 1993.

Hoffman, James. *The Ecstasy of Resistance: A Biography of George Ryga*, Toronto: ECW Press, 1995.

Hurley, Michael. *The Borders of Nightmare: The Fiction of John Richardson*, Toronto: University of Toronto Press, 1992.

Kattan, Naïm. *A.M. Klein: Poet and Prophet*, trans. Edward Baxter, Lantsville, B.C.: XYZ, 2001.

Keith, W.J. *God's Plenty: A Study of Hugh Hood's Short Fiction*, Emeryville, Ontario: Biblioasis, 2010.

Knutson, Susan. *Narrative in the Feminine: Daphne Marlatt and Nicole Brossard*, Waterloo, Ontario: Wilfrid Laurier University Press, 2000.

Kuhn, Cynthia G. *Self-Fashioning in Margaret Atwood's Fiction: Dress, Culture, and Identity*, New York: Lang, 2005.

La Bossière, Camille R. and Linda M. Morra, eds. *Robertson Davies: A Mingling of Contrarieties*, Ottawa: University of Ottawa Press, 2001.

Loriggio, Francesco, ed. *The Last Effort of Dreams: Essays on the Poetry of Pier Giorgio Di Cicco*, Waterloo, Ontario: Wilfrid Laurier University Press, 2007.

Macpherson, Heidi Slettedahl. *The Cambridge Introduction to Margaret Atwood*, Cambridge: Cambridge University Press, 2010.

McMullen, Lorraine, ed. *The Lampman Symposium*, Ottawa: University of Ottawa Press, 1976.

Nischik, Reingard M., ed. *Margaret Atwood: Works and Impact*, Rochester, NY: Camden House, 2000.

Panofsky, Ruth. *The Force Of Vocation: The Literary Career Of Adele Wiseman*, Winnipeg: University of Manitoba Press, 2006.

Pivato, Joseph, ed. *Mary Di Michele: Essays on Her Works*, Toronto: Guernica, 2007.

Siemerling, Winfried. *Discoveries of the Other: Alterity in the Work of Leonard Cohen, Hubert Aquin, Michael Ondaatje, and Nicole Brossard*, Toronto: University of Toronto Press, 1994.

Staines, David, ed. *Margaret Laurence: Critical Reflections*, Ottawa: University of Ottawa Press, 2001.

Stouck, David. *Ethel Wilson: A Critical Biography*, Toronto: University of Toronto Press, 2003.

——*As For Sinclair Ross*, Toronto: University of Toronto Press, 2005.

Stovel, Nora Foster. *Divining Margaret Laurence: A Study of Her Complete Writings*, Montreal and Kingston: McGill-Queen's University Press, 2008.

Strong-Boag, Veronica and Carole Gerson. *Paddling Her Own Canoe: The Times And Texts Of E. Pauline Johnson (Tekahionwake)*, Toronto: University of Toronto Press, 2000.

Thacker, Robert, ed. *The Rest of the Story: Critical Essays on Alice Munro*, Toronto: ECW Press, 1999.

Tierney, Frank M., ed. *The Isabella Valancy Crawford Symposium*, Ottawa: University of Ottawa Press, 1979.

Wiesenthal, Christine. *The Half-Lives Of Pat Lowther*, Toronto: University of Toronto Press, 2005.

Works cited

Alfred, Taiaiake. *Peace, Power, Righteousness: An Indigenous Manifesto*, Don Mills, Ontario: Oxford University Press, 1999.

Altfest, Karen C. *Canadian Literary Nationalism, 1836–1914*. Dissertation, New York: City University of New York, 1979.

Andrews, Jennifer. "Native Canadian Gothic Reconfigured: Reading Eden Robinson's *Monkey Beach*", *Essays on Canadian Writing*, 73 (Spring 2001): 1–24.

Arch, Stephen Carl. "Frances Brooke's 'Circle of Friends': The Limits of Epistolarity in *The History of Emily Montague*", *Early American Literature*, 39.3 (2004): 465–85.

Armstrong, Jeannette C. *Breath Tracks*, Stratford, Ontario: Williams-Wallace, 1991.

——"Four Decades: An Anthology of Canadian Native Poetry from 1960 to 2000", in *Native Poetry in Canada: A Contemporary Anthology*, Jeannette C. Armstrong and Lally Grauer, eds., Peterborough, Ontario: Broadview, 2001, xv–xx.

Atwood, Margaret. *The Edible Woman*, London: Virago, 1992.

Bachelard, Gaston. *The Poetics of Space*, Boston: Beacon, 1969.

Backscheider, Paula R. and Hope D. Cotton. "Introduction", *The Excursion*. By Frances Brooke, ed. Paula R. Backscheider and Hope D. Cotton, Kentucky: The University Press of Kentucky, 1997, ix–xlvi.

Baétz, Joel. *Battle Lines: English-Canadian Poetry Of The First World War*, Dissertation, Toronto: York University, 2005.

Bailey, Alfred G. "The Historical Setting of Sara Duncan's *The Imperialist*", in *The Canadian Novel Volume II: Beginnings, A Critical Anthology*, John Moss, ed., Toronto: New Canada Publications, 1980, 129–42.

Ballstadt, Carl. "Catherine Parr Traill (1802–99)", in *Canadian Writers and Their Works*, Fiction Series, Robert Lecker, Jack David, and Ellen Quigley, eds., Toronto: ECW Press, 1985, volume 1, 149–93.

Barman, Jean. *The West Beyond The West: A History of British Columbia*, Toronto: University of Toronto Press, 1993.

Basque, Maurice and Amélie Giroux. "Minority Francophone Communities", in *History of the Book in Canada, Volume Two: 1840–1918*, Yvan Lamonde, Patricia Lockhart Fleming and Fiona A. Black, eds., Toronto: University of Toronto Press, 2005, 54–59.

Benjamin, Walter. *The Arcades Project*, trans. Howard Eiland and Kevin McLaughlin, Cambridge, Massachusetts and London, England: The Belknap Press of Harvard University Press, 1999.

Bentley, D.M.R. "Introduction" to Isabella Valancy Crawford, *Malcolm's Katie: A Love Story*, D.M.R. Bentley, ed., London, Ontario: Canadian Poetry Press, 1987, xi–lxi.

——*The Confederation Group of Canadian Poets, 1880–1897*, Toronto: University of Toronto Press, 2004.

Berton, Pierre. *The Invasion of Canada 1812–1813*, Toronto: McCelland and Stewart, 1980.

Bessai, Diane. "Sharon Pollock's Women: A Study in Dramatic Process", in *Amazing Space: Writing Canadian Women Writing*, Shirley Neuman and Smaro Kamboreli, eds., Edmonton: Longspoon/NeWest, 1986, 126–36.

Beynon, Francis Marion. *Aleta Dey*, London: Virago, 1988.

Blair, Jennifer, Daniel Coleman, Kate Higginson and Lorraine York, eds. *ReCalling Early Canada: Reading the Political in Literary and Cultural Production*, Edmonton: The University of Alberta Press, 2005.

Bothwell, Robert. *The Penguin History Of Canada*, Toronto: Penguin Group, 2006.

Bowering, George. "Vancouver As Postmodern Poetry", in *Vancouver: Representing the Postmodern City*, Paul Delany, ed., Vancouver: Arsenal Pulp Press, 1994, 121–43.

Brand, Dionne. *No Language Is Neutral*, Toronto: Coach House, 1990.

——*In Another Place, Not Here*, New York: Grove, 1996.

Brandt, Di. *questions i asked my mother*, Winnipeg: Turnstone Press, 1987.

Brandt, Di and Barbara Godard, eds. *Wider Boundaries of Daring: The Modernist Impulse in Canadian Women's Poetry*, Waterloo, Ontario: Wilfrid Laurier University Press, 2009.

Brenner, Rachel Feldhay. "A.M. Klein and Mordecai Richler: Canadian Responses to the Holocaust", *Journal of Canadian Studies*, 24.2 (Summer 1989): 65–77.

Breon, Robin. "The Growth and Development of Black Theatre in Canada: a Starting Point", in *African-Canadian Theatre*, Maureen Moynagh, ed., Toronto: Playwrights Canada Press, 2005, 1–10.

Breton, André. *Manifestoes of Surrealism*, trans. Richard Seaver and Helen R. Lane, Ann Arbor: The University of Michigan Press, 1972.

Brierley, Jane. "Introduction" to Philippe-Joseph Aubert de Gaspé, *Canadians of Old*, trans. Jane Brierley, Montreal: Véhicule Press, 1996, 9–16.

Briganti, Chiara. "Fat, Nail Clippings, Body Parts, or the Story of Where I Have Been: Carol Shields and Auto/Biography", in *Carol Shields, Narrative Hunger, and the Possibilities of Fiction*, Edward Eden and Dee Goertz, eds., Toronto: University of Toronto Press, 2003, 175–200.

Brooke, Frances. *The History of Emily Montague. In Four Volumes. By the Author of Lady Julia Mandeville*, London: Printed for R. and J. Dodsley in Pall Mall, 1769.

——*The History of Emily Montague*, Toronto: McClelland and Stewart, 1995.

Brooker, Bertram. *Think of the Earth*, Toronto: Brown Bear Press, 2000.

Brossard, Nicole. *These Our Mothers, Or: The Disintegrating Chapter*, Toronto: Coach House, 1983.

Brown, E.K. *On Canadian Poetry*, Ottawa: The Tecumseh Press, 1977.

Brydon, Diana. "Discovering 'Ethnicity': Joy Kogawa's *Obasan* and Mena Abdullah's *Time of the Peacock*", in *Australian/Canadian Literatures in English: Comparative Perspectives*, Russell McDougall and Gillian Whitlock, eds., Melbourne: Methuen, 1987, 94–110.

——"Canada and Postcolonialism: Questions, Inventories, and Futures", in *Is Canada Postcolonial? Unsettling Canadian Literature*, Laura Moss, ed., Waterloo, Ontario: Wilfrid Laurier University Press, 2003, 49–77.

——"Metamorphoses of a Discipline: Rethinking Canadian Literature within Institutional Contexts", in *Trans.Can.Lit: Resituating the Study of Canadian Literature*, Smaro Kamboureli and Roy Miki, eds., Waterloo, Ontario: Wilfrid Laurier University Press, 2007, 1–16.

Burton, Rebecca. "Dispelling the Myth of Equality: A Report on the Status of Women in Canadian Theatre", *Canadian Theatre Review*, 132 (Winter 2007): 3–8.

Bush, Catherine. *Minus Time*, London and New York: Serpent's Tail, 1995.

Buss, Helen M. "Canadian Women's Autobiography: Some Critical Directions", in *Amazing Space: Writing Canadian Women Writing*, Shirley Neuman and Smaro Kamboureli, eds., Edmonton: Longspoon/NeWest, 1986, 154–64.

Butling, Pauline and Susan Rudy. *Poets Talk: Conversations with Robert Kroetsch, Daphne Marlatt, Erin Mouré, Dionne Brand, Marie Annharte Baker, Jeff Derksen, and Fred Wah*, Edmonton: University of Alberta Press, 2005.

Cambron, Micheline and Carole Gerson. "Literary Authorship", in *History of the Book in Canada, Volume Two: 1840–1918*, Yvan Lamonde, Patricia Lockhart Fleming and Fiona A. Black, eds., Toronto: University of Toronto Press, 2005, 119–34.

Campbell, Wanda. "Moonlight and Morning: Women's Early Contribution to Canadian Modernism", in *The Canadian Modernists Meet*, Dean Irvine, ed., Ottawa: The University of Ottawa Press, 2005, 79–99.

Cappon, James. *Roberts and the Influences of His Time*, Toronto: William Briggs, 1905.

Carrière, Marie. *Writing in the Feminine in French and English Canada: A Question of Ethics*, Toronto: University of Toronto Press, 2002.

Cavallaro, Dani. *Cyberpunk and Cyberculture*, London: Athlone, 2000.

Cavell, Richard. *McLuhan in Space: A Cultural Geography*, Toronto: University of Toronto Press, 2003.

——"Marshall McLuhan and the History of the Book", in *History of the Book in Canada, Volume Three: 1918–1980*, Carole Gerson and Jacques Michon, eds., Toronto: University of Toronto Press, 2007, 88–90.

Clarke, George Elliott. "'This is no hearsay': Reading the Canadian Slave Narratives", *Papers of the Bibliographical Society of Canada*, 43 (2005): 7–32.

Clements, William M. *Native American Verbal Art: Texts and Contexts*, Tucson: The University of Arizona Press, 1996.

Coleman, Daniel. "The National Allegory of Fraternity: Loyalist Literature and the Making of Canada's White British Origins", *Journal of Canadian Studies*, 36.3 (fall 2001): 131–56.

——*White Civility: The Literary Project of English Canada*, Toronto: University of Toronto Press, 2006.

Concilio, Carmen and Richard J. Lane, eds. *Image Technologies in Canadian Literature: Narrative, Film, and Photography*, Brussels: Lang, 2009.

Crawford, Isabella Valancy. *Malcolm's Katie: A Love Story*, D.M.R. Bentley, ed., London, Ontario: Canadian Poetry Press, 1987.

Crow, Brian and Chris Banfield. *An Introduction to Post-Colonial Theatre*, Cambridge: Cambridge University Press, 1996.

Cuder-Domínguez, Pilar. "The Racialization of Canadian History: African-Canadian Fiction, 1990–2005", in *National Plots: Historical Fiction and Changing Ideas of Canada*, Andrea Cabajsky and Brett Josef Grubisic, eds., Waterloo, Ontario: Wilfrid Laurier University Press, 2010, 113–29.

Currie, Noel Elizabeth. *Constructing Colonial Discourse: Captain Cook at Nootka Sound*, Montreal and Kingston: McGill-Queen's University Press, 2005.

Dandurand, Joseph A. *Please Do Not Touch The Indians*, Candler, NC: Renegade Planets Publishing, 2004.

Darling, Michael. *A.J.M. Smith and His Works*, Toronto: ECW Press, 1990.

Davidson, Arnold E., Priscilla L. Walton and Jennifer Andrews, eds. *Border Crossings: Thomas King's Cultural Inversions*, Toronto: University of Toronto Press, 2003.

Davies, Ioan. "Theory and Creativity in English Canada: Magazines, the State and Cultural Movement", *Journal of Canadian Studies*, 30.1 (Spring 1995): 5–19.

Day, David and Marilyn Bowering, eds. *Many Voices: An Anthology of Contemporary Canadian Poetry*, Vancouver: J.J. Douglas, 1977.

De Gaspé, Philippe-Joseph Aubert. *Canadians of Old*, trans. Jane Brierley, Montreal: Véhicule Press, 1996.

De Gaspé Jr., Philippe-Aubert. *The Influence of a Book*, trans. Claire Rothman, Montreal and Toronto: Robert Davies Publishing, 1993.

De Zepetnek, Steven Tötösy. "Ondaatje's *The English Patient* and Questions of History", in *Comparative Cultural Studies and Michael Ondaatje's Writing*, Steven Tötösy de Zepetnek, ed., West Lafayette, Indiana: Purdue University Press, 2005, 115–31.

Deer, Glenn. "Remapping Vancouver: Composing Urban Spaces in Contemporary Asian Canadian Writing", *Canadian Literature*, 199 (Winter 2008): 118–44.

Delisle, Jean and Gilles Gallichan. "Translating the Two Solitudes", in *History of the Book in Canada, Volume Three: 1918–1980*, Carole Gerson and Jacques Michon, eds., Toronto: University of Toronto Press, 2007, 51–56.

Denham, Paul. *Dorothy Livesay and Her Works*, Toronto: ECW Press, 1983.

Dewart, Edward Hartley, ed., *Selections from Canadian Poets*, Toronto: University of Toronto Press, 1973.

Dickason, Olive Patricia. *Canada's First Nations: A History of Founding Peoples from Earliest Times*, third edition, Ontario: Oxford University Press, 2002.

Dickinson, John and Brian Young. *A Short History of Quebec*, Montreal and Kingston: McGill-Queen's University Press, 2003.

Dickinson, Peter. *Here Is Queer: Nationalisms, Sexualities, and the Literatures of Canada*, Toronto: University of Toronto Press, 1999.

Doyle, James. *Progressive Heritage: The Evolution of a Politically Radical Literary Tradition in Canada*, Waterloo, Ontario: Wilfrid Laurier University Press, 2002.

Dudek, Debra Lynn. *Creative Displacement And Corporeal Defiance: Feminist Canadian Modernism In Margaret Laurence's Manawaka Novels*, Dissertation, University of Saskatchewan, 2000.

Dudek, Louis and Michael Gnarowski, eds. *The Making of Modern Poetry in Canada: Essential Articles on Contemporary Canadian Poetry in English*, Toronto: The Ryerson Press, 1968.

Dull, Monique. "Kinship and Nation in *Amelia* (1848) and *Anne of Green Gables* (1908)", in *The Rhetoric of Canadian Writing*, Conny Steenman-Marcusse, ed., Amsterdam and NY: Rodopi, 2002, 161–78.

Duncan, Sara Jeannette. *The Imperialist*, Toronto: McClelland and Stewart, 1971.

Dunning, Alan and Paul Woodrow. "*Body Degree Zero*: The Mediatized Body in an Interactive Performance", *Canadian Theatre Review*, 127 (Summer 2006): 46–51.

Duquette, Natasha, ed. *Sublimer Aspects: Interfaces between Literature, Aesthetics, and Theology*, Newcastle: Cambridge Scholars, 2007.

Dyer, Klay. "Kirby, William", in *Encyclopedia of Literature in Canada*, W.H. New, ed., Toronto: University of Toronto Press, 2002, 581.

Early, L.R. "'An Old-World Radiance': Roberts' *Orion and Other Poems*", *Canadian Poetry*, 8 (Spring/Summer 1981): 8–32.

Edwards, Brendan Frederick R. "Reading on the 'Rez'", in *History of the Book in Canada, Volume Three: 1918–1980*, Carole Gerson and Jacques Michon, eds., Toronto: University of Toronto Press, 2007, 501–5.

Edwards, Justin D. *Gothic Canada: Reading The Spectre Of A National Literature*, Edmonton: University of Alberta Press, 2005.

Edwards, Mary Jane. "Rosanna Eleanor Leprohon, January 12, 1829–September 20, 1879", *Dictionary of Literary Biography, Volume 99: Canadian Writers Before 1890*, W.H. New, ed., Gale, 1990: 206–8.

Farrell, D.R. "The Canada First Movement and Canadian Political Thought", *Journal of Canadian Studies*, 4.4 (November 1969): 16–26.

Finlay, J.L. and D.N. Sprague. *The Structure of Canadian History*, Scarborough, Ontario: Pearson Prentice-Hall, 2000.

Fischer, Gretl. "Religious Philosophy in the Writings of A.M. Klein", in *The A.M. Klein Symposium*, Seymour Mayne, ed., Ottawa: University of Ottawa Press, 1975, 37–45.

Flint, F.S. "Imagisme", in *Manifesto: A Century of Isms*, Mary Ann Caws, ed., Lincoln and London: University of Nebraska Press, 2001, 352–53.

Foster, Hal. *Compulsive Beauty*, Cambridge, Massachusetts and London, England: The MIT Press, 1993.

Francis, Daniel. *The Imaginary Indian: The Image of the Indian in Canadian Culture*, Vancouver, BC: Arsenal Pulp Press, 1993.

Freiwald, Bina Toledo. "Cartographies of Be/longing: Dionne Brand's *In Another Place: Not Here*, in *Mapping Canadian Cultural Space: Essays on Canadian Literature*", Danielle Schaub, ed., Jerusalem: The Hebrew University Magnes Press, 2000, 37–53.

Fussell, Paul. *The Great War And Modern Memory*, Oxford: Oxford University Press, 1977.

Gagan, David P. "The Relevance of 'Canada First'", *Journal of Canadian Studies*, 5.4 (November 1970): 36–44.

Garner, Hugh. *Storm Below*, Toronto: The Ryerson Press, 1968.

Gerson, Carole. "A Contrapuntal Reading of *A Strange Manuscript Found in a Copper Cylinder*", *Essays on Canadian Writing*, 56 (Fall 1995): 224–35.

——"Anthologies and the Canon of Early Canadian Women Writers", *New Contexts Of Canadian Criticism*, Ajay Heble, Donna Palmateer Pennee and J.R. (Tim) Struthers, eds., Peterborough, Ontario: Broadview, 1997, 146–67.

Gerson, Carole and Cathy Mezei. *The Prose of Life: Sketches from Victorian Canada*, Downsview, Ontario: ECW Press, 1981.

Gibson, William. *Neuromancer*, New York: Ace, 1984.

Gilbert, Helen and Joanne Tompkins. *Post-Colonial Drama: Theory, Practice, Politics*, London and New York: Routledge, 1996.

Gilloch, Graeme. *Walter Benjamin: Critical Constellations*, Cambridge: Polity, 2002.

Godard, Barbara. "Ex-centriques, Eccentric, Avant-Garde: Women and Modernism in the Literatures of Canada", in *Room of One's Own*, 8.4 (1983): 57–75.

Goldman, Marlene. "Mapping the Door of No Return: Deterritorialization and the Work of Dionne Brand", *Canadian Literature*, 182 (Autumn 2004): 13–28.

Golfman, Noreen. *A.M. Klein and His Works*, Toronto: ECW Press, nd.

Gould, Karen. *Writing in the Feminine: Feminism and Experimental Writing in Quebec*, Carbondale and Edwardsville: Southern Illinois University Press, 1990.

Grace, Sherrill. "Theatre and the AutoBiographical Pact: An Introduction", in *Theatre and AutoBiography: Writing and Performing Lives In Theory And Practice*, Sherrill Grace and Jerry Wasserman, eds., Vancouver: Talon, 2006, 13–29.

Grace, Sherrill and Albert-Reiner Glaap, eds. *Performing National Identities: International Perspectives on Contemporary Canadian Theatre*, Vancouver: Talonbooks, 2003.

Gray, Martin. *A Dictionary of Literary Terms*, Harlow, Essex: Longman York Press, 1986.

Griffiths, Linda and Maria Campbell. *The Book of Jessica: A Theatrical Transformation*, Toronto: Coach House Press, 1989.

Gunnars, Kristjana. "Listening: Laurence's Women", in *Margaret Laurence: Critical Reflections*, David Staines, ed., Ottawa: University of Ottawa Press, 2001, 121–27.

Hamilton, Ron. "Telling", *BC Studies*, 89 (Spring 1991): 169.

Harper, J. Russell. *Painting in Canada: A History*, Toronto: University of Toronto Press, 2000.

Harrison, Charles Yale. *Generals Die In Bed*, Ontario: Potlatch, 1974.

Hart, Julia Catherine Beckwith. *St. Ursula's Convent or The Nun of Canada, Containing Scenes from Real Life*, Douglas G. Lochhead, ed., Ottawa: Carleton University Press, 1991.

Heft, Harold. *The Presence of James Joyce in the Poetry and Prose of A.M. Klein*, Dissertation, The University of Western Ontario, 1994.

Hicks, Anne. "Introduction" in *Aleta Dey*, Francis Marion Beynon, New York: Penguin, 1991.

Higginson, Catherine. "The Raced Female Body and the Discourse of *Peuplement* in Rudy Wiebe's *The Temptations of Big Bear* and *The Scorched-Wood People*", *Essays on Canadian Writing*, 72 (Winter 2000): 172–90.

Highway, Tomson. *Kiss of the Fur Queen*, Toronto: Doubleday, 1999 (first published 1998).

Hodgson, Heather, ed. *Seventh Generation: Contemporary Native Writing*, Penticton, BC: Theytus Books, 1989.

Hodkinson, Yvonne. *Female Parts: The Art and Politics of Female Playwrights*, Montreal: Black Rose Books, 1991.

Holmes, Nancy. "'In Flanders Fields' – Canada's Official Poem: Breaking Faith", *Studies in Canadian Literature*, 30.1 (2005): 11–33.

Howells, Coral Ann. "Writing by Women", in *The Cambridge Companion to Canadian Literature*, Eva-Marie Kröller, ed., Cambridge: Cambridge University Press, 2004, 194–215.

Hoy, Helen. "Gabrielle Roy", in *Canadian Writers, 1920–1959, First Series*, William H. New, ed., Detroit: Gale Research, 1988, *Dictionary of Literary Biography*, Vol 68, Literature Resource Center, Web. 2. Dec. 2010, <http://go.galegroup.com.ezproxy.viu.ca/ps/i.do?andid=GALE%7CH1200004352andv=2.1andu=malaspinaandit=randp=LitRCandsw= w>

Hurley, Michael. *The Borders of Nightmare: The Fiction of John Richardson*, Toronto: University of Toronto Press, 1992.

Hutcheon, Linda. *The Canadian Postmodern: A Study of Contemporary English-Canadian Fiction*, Toronto: Oxford University Press, 1988.

Irvine, Dean, ed. *Archive For Our Times: Previously Uncollected And Unpublished Poems of Dorothy Livesay*, Vancouver: Arsenal Pulp Press, 1998.

Ivison, Douglas. "William Gibson (17 March 1948 –)", in *Dictionary of Literary Biography Volume Two Hundred Fifty-One: Canadian Fantasy and Science-Fiction Writers*, Douglas Ivison, ed., Detroit: The Gale Group, 2002.

James, Suzanne. *Gathering Up The Threads: Generic And Discursive Patterns In Catherine Parr Traill's The Backwoods of Canada*, Dissertation, Simon Fraser University, 2003.

Jaspers, Karl. *Philosophy*, volume 2, trans. E.B. Ashton, Chicago and London: University of Chicago Press, 1970.

Johansen, Emily. "'Streets are the dwelling place of the collective': Public Space and Cosmopolitan Citizenship in Dionne Brand's *What We All Long For*", *Canadian Literature*, 196 (Spring 2008): 48–62.

Johnson, E. Pauline (Tekahionwake). *Flint and Feather: The Complete Poems of E. Pauline Johnson (Tekahionwake)*, Toronto: Musson/Hodder and Stoughton, 1967.

Johnston, Denis. "Totem Theatre: AutoBiography of a Company", in *Theatre and AutoBiography: Writing and Performing Lives In Theory And Practice*, Sherrill Grace and Jerry Wasserman, eds., Vancouver: Talon, 2006, 225–48.

Jones, Manina. "*Stolen Life?* Reading through Two I's in Postcolonial Collaborative Autobiography", in *Is Canada Postcolonial? Unsettling Canadian Literature*, Laura Moss, ed., Waterloo: Wilfrid Laurier University Press, 2003, 207–222.

Kamboureli, Smaro. *Scandalous Bodies: Diasporic Literature in English Canada*, Oxford: Oxford University Press, 2000.

——"The Critic, Institutional Culture, and Canadian Literature: Barbara Godard in Conversation with Smaro Kamboureli", in *Canadian Literature at the Crossroads of Language and Culture: Selected Essays by Barbara Godard*, Smaro Kamboureli, ed., Edmonton: NeWest, 2008.

Kamboureli, Smaro and Roy Miki, eds. *Trans.Can.Lit: Resituating the Study of Canadian Literature*, Waterloo, Ontario: Wilfrid Laurier University Press, 2007.

Kearns, Judy. "Rachel and Social Determinism: A Feminist Reading of *A Jest of God*", *Journal of Canadian Fiction*, 27 (1980): 101–23.

Keith, W.J. *Canadian Literature in English*, 2 vols., Ontario: Porcupine's Quill, 2006.

Kerr, Rosalind. *Lesbian Plays: Coming of Age in Canada*, Toronto: Playwrights Canada Press, 2006.

——*Queer Theatre in Canada*, Toronto, Playwrights Canada Press, 2007.

Keshen, Jeffrey A. *Propaganda and Censorship During Canada's Great War*, Edmonton, Alberta: The University of Alberta Press, 1996.

Kidnie, Margaret Jane. "'There's magic in the web of it': Seeing Beyond Tragedy in *Harlem Duet*", in Maureen Moynagh, ed., *African-Canadian Theatre*, Toronto: Playwrights Canada Press, 2005, 40–55.

King, Basil. *The City of Comrades*, New York: Harper, 1919.

King, Thomas. "Godzilla vs. Post-Colonial?", in *New Contexts of Canadian Criticism*, Ajay Heble, Donna Palmateer Pennee and J.R. (Tim) Struthers, eds., Peterborough, Ontario: Broadview, 1997.

Kirby, William. *The Golden Dog [Le Chien D'Or]*, *A Romance of Old Quebec*, Toronto: McClelland and Stewart, 1969.

Klein, A.M. *The Second Scroll*, Toronto: McClelland and Stewart, 1982.

Knowles, Ric. "Translators, Traitors, Mistresses, and Whores: Monique Mojica and the Mothers of the Métis Nations", in *Siting the Other: Re-visions of Marginality in Australian and English-Canadian Drama*, Marc Maufort and Franca Bellarsi, eds., Brussels: Lang, 2001, 247–66.

Knutson, Susan. *Narrative in the Feminine: Daphne Marlatt and Nicole Brossard*, Waterloo: Wilfrid Laurier University Press, 2000.

Kristeva, Julia. *Powers of Horror: An Essay on Abjection*, trans. Leon S. Roudiez, New York: Columbia University Press, 1982.

Kroetsch, Robert. "A Canadian Issue", *Boundary 2*, 3.1 (Autumn 1974): 1–2.

——*A Likely Story: The Writing Life*, Red Deer, Alberta: Red Deer College Press, 1995.

Lamont-Stewart, Linda. "Rescued by Postmodernism: The Escalating Value of James De Mille's *A Strange Manuscript Found in a Copper Cylinder*", *Canadian Literature*, 145 (Summer 1995): 21–36.

Lane, Richard J. "Anti-Panoptical Narrative Structures in Two Novels by Margaret Atwood", *Commonwealth: Essays and Studies*, 16.1 (Autumn 1993): 63–69.

——"British Columbia's War of Two Worlds: The Birth of the Modern Age in Bertrand William Sinclair's Fiction", *Journal of Commonwealth Literature*, 31.1 (1996): 71–81.

——"Pulling Strings: Robert Kroetsch's *The Puppeteer*", *Commonwealth: Essays and Studies*, 19.2 (Spring 1997): 33–41.

——"Fractures: Written Displacements in Canadian/US Literary Relations", in *Postcolonial Literatures: Expanding the Canon*, Deborah Madsen, ed., London: Pluto, 1999a, 45–57.

——"Border Crossings: Forgotten Native Voices in Bertrand William Sinclair's Canadian and American Popular Fiction", *The Hungarian Journal of English and American Studies*, 5.2 (1999b): 81–93.

——*Literature and Loss: Bertrand William Sinclair's British Columbia*, London: The London Network for Modern Fiction Studies, 2000.

——"Performing History: The Reconstruction of Gender and Race in British Columbia Drama", in *Performing National Identities: International Perspectives on Contemporary Canadian Theatre*, Sherrill Grace and Albert-Reiner Glaap, eds., Vancouver: Talonbooks, 2003, 265–77.

——*Reading Walter Benjamin: Writing Through The Catastrophe*, Manchester: Manchester University Press, 2005.

——"Theorizing the Gendered Space of Auto/Biographical Performance via Samuel Beckett and Hans Bellmer", in *Theatre and AutoBiography: Writing and Performing Lives In Theory And Practice*, Sherrill Grace and Jerry Wasserman, eds., Vancouver: Talon, 2006a, 72–88.

——*Fifty Key Literary Theorists*, London and NY: Routledge, 2006b.

——*The Postcolonial Novel*, Cambridge: Polity, 2006c.

——"Kant's 'Safe Place': Security and the Sacred in the Concept of Sublime Experience", in *Sublimer Aspects: Interfaces between Literature, Aesthetics, and Theology*, Natasha Duquette, ed., Newcastle: Cambridge Scholars, 2007, 51–61.

——"Dialectical Images in Canada: Joseph Dandurand, Stan Douglas and The Conjectural Order", in *Image Technologies in Canadian Literature*, Carmen Concilio and Richard J. Lane, eds., Brussels: Lang, 2009, 137–49.

——"Sacred Community, Sacred Culture: Authenticity and Modernity in Contemporary Canadian Native Writings", in *Native Authenticity: Transnational Perspectives on Native American Literary Studies*, Deborah Madsen, ed., Albany: State University of New York, 2010, 151–65.

Lassaigne, Jacques. *El Greco*. London: Thames and Hudson, 1973.

Latham, David. "Sangster, Charles (1822–93)", *The Oxford Companion to Canadian Literature*, Eugene Benson and William Toye, eds., Don Mills, Ontario: Oxford University Press, 1997.

Laurence, Margaret. *This Side Jordan*, London: Macmillan, 1960.

——*Heart of a Stranger*, Toronto: McClelland and Stewart, 1976.

Leacock, Stephen. *Sunshine Sketches of a Little Town*, D.M.R. Bentley, ed., New York and London: Norton, 2006.

Lefebvre, Benjamin. "Stand by Your Man: Adapting L.M. Montgomery's *Anne of Green Gables*", *Essays on Canadian Writing*, 76 (Spring 2002): 149–69.

Leggatt, Judith. "Native Writing, Academic Theory: Post-colonialism across the Cultural Divide", in Laura Moss, ed., *Is Canada Postcolonial? Unsettling Canadian Literature*, Waterloo, Ontario: Wilfrid Laurier University Press, 2003, 111–26.

Lemire, Maurice. "Introduction" to Philippe-Aubert de Gaspé, Jr., *The Influence of a Book*, trans. Claire Rothman, Montreal and Toronto: Robert Davies Publishing, 1993, 9–23.

Leprohon, Rosanna. *Antoinette De Mirecourt, Or, Secret Marrying and Secret Sorrowing, A Canadian Tale,* Toronto: McClelland and Stewart, 2000.

Lewis, Paula Gilbert. "The Incessant Call of the Open Road: Gabrielle Roy's Incorrigible Nomads", *The French Review,* LIII.6 (May 1980): 816–25.

Lochhead, Douglas G. "Editor's Introduction" in Julia Catherine Beckwith Hart, *St. Ursula's Convent or The Nun of Canada, Containing Scenes from Real Life,* Douglas G. Lochhead, ed., Ottawa: Carleton University Press, 1991, xvii–xli.

Loyie, Oskiniko Larry. *Ora Pro Nobis [Pray for Us],* in *Two Plays About Residential School,* Vancouver: Living Traditions, 1998.

Lucas, Alec. "The Function of the Sketches in Susanna Moodie's *Roughing It in the Bush",* in *Re(Dis)covering Our Foremothers: Nineteenth-Century Canadian Women Writers,* Lorraine McMullen, ed., Ottawa: University of Ottawa Press, 1990, 146–54.

Lynch, Gerald. *The One And The Many: English-Canadian Short Story Cycles,* Toronto: University of Toronto Press, 2001.

——"Short Story And Sketch", in *Encyclopedia of Literature in Canada,* W.H. New, ed., Toronto: University of Toronto Press, 2002, 1039–46.

MacCarthy, Bridget. *The Female Pen: Women Writers and Novelists, 1621–1818,* New York: New York University Press, 1994.

MacDonald, Tanis. "Introduction", *Speaking of Power: The Poetry of Di Brandt.* By Diana Brandt. Waterloo, Ontario: Wilfrid Laurier University Press, 2006, ix–xvi.

Maillet, Antonine. *La Sagouine,* trans. Luis de Céspedes, Toronto: Simon and Pierre, 1985.

Manuel, Vera. *Strength of Indian Women,* in *Two Plays About Residential School,* Vancouver: Living Traditions, 1998.

Maracle, Brian. "The First Words", Cynthia Sugars and Laura Moss, eds., *Canadian Literature in English: Texts and Contexts,* Vol 1, Toronto: Pearson Longman, 2009, 1–13.

Maracle, Lee. "Oratory on Oratory", in *Trans.Can.Lit: Resituating the Study of Canadian Literature,* Smaro Kamboureli and Roy Miki, eds., Waterloo, Ontario: Wilfrid Laurier University Press, 2007, 55–70.

Marlatt, Daphne. *Touch to My Tongue,* Edmonton: Longspoon, 1984.

Martin, W.R. and Warren U. Ober, "Alice Munro as Small-Town Historian: 'Spaceships Have Landed'", in *The Rest of the Story: Critical Essays on Alice Munro,* Robert Thacker, ed., Toronto: ECW Press, 1999, 128–146.

Mathias, Chief Joe and Gary R. Yabsley. "Conspiracy of Legislation: The Suppression of Indian Rights in Canada", *BC Studies,* 89 (Spring 1991): 34–45.

McDougall, Colin. *Execution,* New York: St Martin's Press, 1958.

McGillivray, Mary Beatrice. *Colour Out Of Silence: A Study of the Poetry of Bliss Carmen,* Dissertation, Kingston, Ontario: Queen's University, 1985.

McLuhan, Marshall. *The Medium is the Massage: An Inventory of Effects,* Berkeley, California: Gengko Press, 2001.

McMullen, Lorraine. *Frances Brooke and Her Works,* Ontario: ECW Press, 1983.

Megill, Allan. *Prophets of Extremity: Nietzsche, Heidegger, Foucault, Derrida,* Berkeley and Los Angeles: University of California Press, 1985.

Miki, Roy. "Asiancy: Making Space for Asian Canadian Writing" in *Privileging Positions: The Sites of Asian American Studies,* Gary Y. Okihino, Marilyn Alguizola, Dorothy Fujita Rong and K. Scott Wong, eds., Washington: Pullman, 1995, 135–51.

Montogomery, Lucy Maud. *Rilla of Ingleside,* New York: Frederick A. Stokes, 1921.

——*Anne of Green Gables,* Toronto: McClelland and Stewart, 1992.

Morriss, Margaret. "'No Short Cuts': The Evolution of *The Double Hook",* *Canadian Literature,* 173 (Summer 2002): 54–70.

Moses, Daniel David. *Coyote City: A Play in Two Acts*, Stratford, Ontario: Williams-Wallace, 1990.

Moss, John. *A Reader's Guide to the Canadian Novel*, Second Edition, Toronto: McClelland and Stewart, 1987.

Moss, Laura, ed. *Is Canada Postcolonial? Unsettling Canadian Literature*, Waterloo, Ontario: Wilfrid Laurier University Press, 2003.

Mouré, Erin. *Furious*, Toronto: Anansi, 1988.

Moynagh, Maureen. "African-Canadian Theatre: An Introduction", in Maureen Moynagh, ed., *African-Canadian Theatre*, Toronto: Playwrights Canada Press, 2005, vii–xxii.

Munro, Alice. *Lives of Girls and Women*, Harmondsworth, Middlesex: Penguin, 1987.

Neel, David. "Artist's Statement", *BC Studies*, 89 (Spring 1991): 31.

New, W.H., ed. *Encyclopedia of Literature in Canada*, Toronto: University of Toronto Press, 2002.

Nischik, Reingard M., ed. *Margaret Atwood: Works and Impact*, Rochester, NY: Camden House, 2000.

Northey, Margot. *The Haunted Wilderness: The Gothic and Grotesque in Canadian Fiction*, Toronto: University of Toronto Press, 1976.

Novak, Dagmar. *Dubious Glory: The Two World Wars and the Canadian Novel*, New York: Peter Lang, 2000.

O'Neill, Brenda. "The Royal Commission on the Status of Women: Looking Back, Looking Forward", 2003, electronic text, <http://www.uwc-wpg.mb.ca/royal_commission_talk.pdf>.

Odhiambo, David Nandi. *Kipligat's Chance*, New York: St Martin's, 2004.

Ondaatje, Michael. *The English Patient*, London: Picador, 1993.

Ong, Walter J. *Orality and Literacy: The Technologizing of the Word*, London and New York: Methuen, 1982.

Orange, John. *P.K. Page and Her Works*, Toronto: ECW Press, 1989.

Orr, Jeffrey. "Light Writing, Light Reading: Photography and Intersemiotic Translation in Michael Ondaatje", *Image Technologies in Canadian Literature: Narrative, Film, and Photography*, Carmen Concilio and Richard J. Lane, eds., Brussels: Lang, 2009, 47–63.

Palumbo, Alice M. "On the Border: Margaret Atwood's Novels", in *Margaret Atwood: Works and Impact*, Reingard M. Nischik, ed., Rochester, NY: Camden House, 2000, 73–85.

Papoutsis, Natalie. "Intimate Acts with Obsolete Bodies: Theatre Gargantua's *e-DENTITY* and Mediatized Theatre", *Canadian Theatre Review*, 127 (Summer 2006): 18–23.

Parker, George L. "Courting Local and International Markets", in *History of The Book in Canada: Volume One, Beginnings To 1840*, Patricia Lockhart Fleming, Gilles Gallichan and Yvan Lamonde, eds., Toronto: University of Toronto Press, 2004, 339–60.

Parris, Leslie, ed. *The Pre-Raphaelites*, London: Tate Gallery, 1994.

Pell, Barbara. "Postcolonial Place/Sacred Space in Hugh Hood's Christian Allegories", in *Mapping the Sacred: Religion, Geography and Postcolonial Literatures*, Jamie S. Scott and Paul Simpson-Housley, eds., Amsterdam: Rodopi, 2001, 53–67.

——"Suffering and The Sacred: Hugh Hood's *The New Age / Le Nouveau Siècle*", in Holly Faith Nelson, Lynn R. Szabo and Jens Zimmerman, eds., *Through A Glass Darkly: Suffering, the Sacred, and the Sublime in Literature and Theory*, Waterloo, Ontario: Wilfrid Laurier University Press, 2010, 257–67.

Perry, Ruth. *Novel Relations: The Transformation of Kinship in English Literature and Culture, 1748–1818*, Cambridge: Cambridge University Press, 2004.

Petrone, Penny. *Native Literature in Canada: From the Oral Tradition to the Present*, Don Mills, Ontario: Oxford University Press, 1990.

Pierce, Lorne. *An Outline of Canadian Literature (French And English)*, Toronto: The Ryerson Press, 1927.

Pollack, Ellen. *Incest and the English Novel, 1684–1814*, Baltimore and London: The Johns Hopkins University Press, 2003.

Pound, Ezra. "A Few Don'ts by an Imagiste", in *Manifesto: A Century of Isms*, Mary Ann Caws, ed., Lincoln and London: University of Nebraska Press, 2001, 356–59.

Quéma, Anne. "Elizabeth Smart and Cecil Buller: Engendering Experimental Modernism", in *The Canadian Modernists Meet*, Dean Irvine, ed., Ottawa: University of Ottawa Press, 2005, 275–303.

——"The Passionate and Sublime Modernism of Elizabeth Smart", in *Wider Boundaries of Daring: The Modernist Impulse in Canadian Women's Poetry*, Di Brandt and Barbara Godard, eds., Waterloo, Ontario: Wilfrid Laurier University Press, 2009, 297–324.

Rae, Ian. *From Cohen to Carson: The Poet's Novel in Canada*, Montreal and Kingston: McGill-Queen's University Press, 2008.

Raimond, Jean and J.R. Watson. *A Handbook to English Romanticism*, London: Macmillan, 1992.

Reid, Bill and Robert Bringhurst. *The Raven Steals The Light*, Vancouver and Toronto: Douglas and McIntyre, 1988.

Richardson, John. *Wacousta; Or, The Prophecy: A Tale of the Canadas*, Toronto: McClelland and Stewart, 1991.

Ricou, Laurie. *The Arbutus/Madrone Files: Reading The Pacific Northwest*, Edmonton: NeWest, 2002.

Rifkind, Candida. "'A Collection of Solitary Fragments': Miriam Waddington as Critic", in *Wider Boundaries of Daring: The Modernist Impulse in Canadian Women's Poetry*, Di Brandt and Barbara Godard, eds., Waterloo, Ontario: Wilfrid Laurier University Press, 2009, 253–73.

Rigney, Barbara Hill. "Alias Atwood: Narrative Games and Gender Politics", in *Margaret Atwood: Works and Impact*, Reingard M. Nischik, ed., NY: Camden House, 2000, 157–65.

Roberts, Charles G.D. *A History of Canada*, Toronto: Morang, 1904.

Rogers, Katherine M. "Sensibility and Feminism: The Novels of Frances Brooke", *Genre*, 2 (Summer 1978): 159–71.

Rosenzweig, Franz. *The Star of Redemption*, trans. William W. Hallo, Notre Dame and London: The University of Notre Dame Press, 1985.

Ross, Malcolm, ed. *Poets of the Confederation: Carman/Lampma/Roberts/Scott*, Toronto: McClelland and Stewart, 1991.

Ross, Sinclair. *As For Me and My House*, Toronto: McClelland and Stewart, 1970.

Roy, Gabrielle. *The Road Past Altamont*, trans. Joyce Marshall, Toronto: McCLelland and Stewart, 1976.

Roy, Susan. "Performing Musqueam Culture and History at British Columbia's 1966 Centennial Celebrations", *BC Studies*, 135 (Autumn 2002): 55–90.

Rudzik, Orest. "Myth in 'Malcolm's Katie'", *The Isabella Valancy Crawford Symposium*, Frank M. Tierney, ed., Ottawa: University of Ottawa Press, 1979, 49–60.

Rymhs, Deena. *From The Iron House: Imprisonment in First Nations Writing*, Waterloo, Ontario: Wilfrid Laurier University Press, 2008.

Scholl, Dorothee. "French-Canadian Colonial Literature under the Union Jack", in *History of Literature in Canada, English-Canadian and French-Canadian*, Reingard M. Nischik, ed., Rochester, New York: Camden House, 2008, 88–109.

Schorcht, Blanca. "Intersections between Native Oral Traditions and Print Culture", in *History of the Book in Canada, Volume Three: 1918–1980*, Carole Gerson and Jacques Michon, eds., Toronto: University of Toronto Press, 2007, 29–34.

Scott, Shelley. *The Violent Woman As A New Theatrical Character Type: Cases From Canadian Drama*, Lewiston, NY: Edwin Mellen, 2007.

Sellwood, Jane. "'A Little Acid Is Absolutely Necessary': Narrative as Coquette in Frances Brooke's 'The History of Emily Montague'", *Canadian Literature*, 136 (Spring 1993): 60–79.

Shields, Carol. *The Stone Diaries*, Toronto: Vintage Canada, 2002.

Siemerling, Winfried. *Discoveries of the Other: Alterity in the Work of Leonard Cohen, Hubert Aquin, Michael Ondaatje, and Nicole Brossard*, Toronto: University of Toronto Press, 1994.

——"Trans-Can: Globalization, Literary Hemispheric Studies, Citizenship as Project", in Smaro Kamboureli and Roy Miki, eds., *Trans.Can.Lit: Resituating the Study of Canadian Literature*, Waterloo, Ontario: Wilfrid Laurier University Press, 2007, 129–40.

Simms, Brendan. *Three Victories and a Defeat: The Rise and Fall of the First British Empire*, London: Penguin, 2008.

Sinclair, Bertrand William. *Burned Bridges*, New York: Grosset and Dunlap, 1919.

——*The Inverted Pyramid*, Toronto: Frederick D. Goodchild, 1924.

Slemon, Stephen. "Monuments of Empire: Allegory/Counter-Discourse/Post-Colonial Writing", *Kunapipi*, 9.3 (1987): 1–16.

Smart, Elizabeth. *By Grand Central Station I Sat Down And Wept*, Ottawa: Deneau, 1982.

Sprout, Frances. "Ghosts, Leaves, Photographs, and Memory: Seeing and Remembering Photographically in Daphne Marlatt's *Taken*", in *Image Technologies in Canadian Literature: Narrative, Film, and Photography*, Carmen Concilio and Richard J. Lane, eds., Brussels: Peter Lang, 2009, 81–98.

Stacey, Robert David. "Romance, Pastoral Romance, and the Nation in History: William Kirby's *The Golden Dog* and Philippe-Joseph Aubert de Gaspé's *Les Anciens Canadiens*", in *ReCalling Early Canada: Reading the Political in Literary and Cultural Production*, Jennifer Blair, Daniel Coleman, Kate Higginson and Lorraine York, eds., Edmonton: The University of Alberta Press, 2005, 91–116.

Staines, David. "Poetry", in *The Cambridge Companion to Canadian Literature*, Eva-Marie Kröller, ed., Cambridge: Cambridge University Press, 2004, 135–154.

Steenman-Marcusse, Conny. "The Rhetoric of Autobiography in Susan Swan's *The Biggest Modern Woman of the World*", in *The Rhetoric of Canadian Writing*, Conny Steenman-Marcusse, ed., Amsterdam and NY: Rodopi, 2002, 179–88.

Sterling, Shirley. *My Name Is Seepeetza*, Toronto: Douglas and McIntyre, 1998 (first published 1992).

Stevens, Peter. *The Development of Canadian Poetry Between the Wars and Its Reflection of Social Awareness*, Dissertation, University of Saskatchewan, 1968.

Stevenson, Lionel. *The English Novel: A Panorama*, London: Constable, 1960.

Stokes, Mark. "Canada and the Direct Broadcast Satellite: Issues in the Global Communications Flow", *Journal of Canadian Studies*, 27.2 (Summer 1992): 82–96.

Stovel, Nora Foster. *Divining Margaret Laurence: A Study of Her Complete Writings*, Montreal and Kingston: McGill-Queen's University Press, 2008.

Strong-Boag, Veronica and Carole Gerson. *Paddling Her Own Canoe: The Times And Texts Of E. Pauline Johnson (Tekahionwake)*, Toronto: University of Toronto Press, 2000.

Sugars, Cynthia and Laura Moss, eds. *Canadian Literature In English: Texts and Contexts*, Vol 1, Toronto: Pearson Longman, 2009.

Taylor, Drew Haydon. *Funny, You Don't Look Like One*, Penticton, BC: Theytus, 1998.

Tector, Amy. "A Righteous War? L.M. Montgomery's Depiction of the First World War in *Rilla of Ingleside*", *Canadian Literature*, 179 (Winter 2003): 72–86.

Thieme, John. "A Different 'Othello Music': Djanet Sears's *Harlem Duet*", in *Performing National Identities: International Perspectives on Contemporary Canadian Theatre*, Sherrill Grace and Albert-Reiner Glaap, eds., Vancouver: Talonbooks, 2003, 81–91.

Thompson, Dawn. *Writing A Politics of Perception: Memory, Holography, and Women Writers in Canada*, Toronto: University of Toronto Press, 2000.

Tierney, Frank M., ed. *The Isabella Valancy Crawford Symposium*, Ottawa: University of Ottawa Press, 1979.

Toorn, Penny van. "Aboriginal Writing", in *The Cambridge Companion to Canadian Literature*, Eva-Marie Kröller, ed., Cambridge: Cambridge University Press, 2004, 22–48.

Tostevin, Lola Lemire, *'Sophie*, Toronto: Coach House, 1988.

Traill, Catherine Parr. *The Backwoods of Canada: Being Letters From The Wife Of An Emigrant Officer, Illustrative Of The Domestic Economy Of British America*, Ottawa: Carleton University Press, 1997.

Trehearne, Brian. *The Montreal Forties: Modernist Poetry in Transition*, Toronto: University of Toronto Press, 1999.

Ueki, Teruyo. "*Obasan*: Revelations in a Paradoxical Silence", *MELUS*, 18.4 (Winter 1993): 5–20.

Vautier, Marie. "Religion, Postcolonial Side-by-sidedness, and *la transculture*", in Laura Moss, ed., *Is Canada Postcolonial? Unsettling Canadian Literature*, Waterloo, Ontario: Wilfrid Laurier University Press, 2003, 268–81.

Vizenor, Gerald. "*Trickster Discourse*: Comic Holotropes and Language Games", in *Narrative Chance: Postmodern Discourse On Native American Indian Literatures*, Gerald Vizenor, ed., Norman: University of Oklahoma Press, 1993, 187–211.

Ware, Tracy. *A Generic Approach To Confederation Romanticism*, Dissertation, London, Ontario: The University of Western Ontario, 1984.

Waterston, Elizabeth. *Rapt in Plaid: Canadian Literature and Scottish Tradition*, Toronto: University of Toronto Press, 2001.

Watters, R.E. "Introduction", *A Strange Manuscript Found in a Copper Cylinder*. By James De Mille, Toronto: McClelland and Stewart, 1969, vii–xviii.

Werlock, Abby. *Carol Shields's* The Stone Diaries, London and NY: Continuum, 2001.

White, Gilbert. *The Natural History of Selborne*, London and New York: Frederick Warne, nd.

Williams, Dorothy W. "Print and Black Canadian Culture", in *History of the Book in Canada, Volume Two: 1840–1918*, Yvan Lamonde, Patricia Lockhart Fleming and Fiona A. Black, eds., Toronto: University of Toronto Press, 2005, 40–43.

Williams, James. *Gilles Deleuze's* Difference and Repetition: *A Critical Introduction and Guide*, Edinburgh: Edinburgh University Press, 2003.

Willmott, Glenn. *Unreal Country: Modernity in the Canadian Novel in English*, Montreal and Kingston: McGill-Queen's University Press, 2002.

——"Sheila Watson, Aboriginal Discourse, and Cosmopolitan Modernism", in *The Canadian Modernists Meet*, Dean Irvine, ed., Ottawa: University of Ottawa Press, 2005, 101–16.

Winks, Robin W. *The Blacks In Canada: A History*, Second Edition, Montreal and Kingston: McGill-Queen's University Press, 1997.

Wyile, Herb. *Speculative Fictions: Contemporary Canadian Novelists and the Writing of History*, Montreal and Kingston: McGill-Queen's University Press, 2002.

York, Lorraine. *Rethinking Women's Collaborative Writing*, Toronto: University of Toronto Press, 2002.

Zimmerman, Cynthia. *Playwriting Women: Female Voices in English Canada*, Toronto: Simon and Pierre, 1994.

Index

Taylor & Francis

eBooks

ORDER YOUR FREE 30 DAY INSTITUTIONAL TRIAL TODAY!

FOR LIBRARIES

Over 23,000 eBook titles in the Humanities, Social Sciences, STM and Law from some of the world's leading imprints.

Choose from a range of subject packages or create your own!

Benefits for you

▶ Free MARC records
▶ COUNTER-compliant usage statistics
▶ Flexible purchase and pricing options

Benefits for your user

▶ Off-site, anytime access via Athens or referring URL
▶ Print or copy pages or chapters
▶ Full content search
▶ Bookmark, highlight and annotate text
▶ Access to thousands of pages of quality research at the click of a button

For more information, pricing enquiries or to order a free trial, contact your local online sales team.

UK and Rest of World: **online.sales@tandf.co.uk**

US, Canada and Latin America:
e-reference@taylorandfrancis.com

www.ebooksubscriptions.com

 ALPSP Award for BEST eBOOK PUBLISHER 2009 Finalist

 Taylor & Francis eBooks
Taylor & Francis Group

A flexible and dynamic resource for teaching, learning and research.